Table of Conte

Counting and Cardinality

▶ **Know number names and the count sequence.**

▶ **Count to tell the number of objects.**

▶ **Compare numbers.**

Operations and Algebraic Thinking

▶ **Understand addition as putting together and adding to, and understand subtraction as taking apart and taking from.**

Number and Operations in Base Ten

Measurement and Data

Geometry

▶ **Identify and describe shapes (squares, circles, triangles, rectangles, hexagons, cubes, cones, cylinders, and spheres).**

▶ **Analyze, compare, create, and compose shapes.**

Introduction

Core Standards for Math offers two-page lessons for every content standard in the *Common Core State Standards for Mathematics.* The first page of each lesson introduces the concept or skill being taught by providing step-by-step instruction and modeling and checks students' understanding through open-ended practice items. The second page includes multiple-choice practice items as well as problem-solving items.

Common Core State Standards for Mathematics: Content Standards

Content Standards define what students should understand and be able to do. These standards are organized into clusters of related standards to emphasize mathematical connections. Finally, domains represent larger groups of related standards. At the elementary (K–6) level, there are ten content domains. Each grade addresses four or five domains. The table below shows how the domains are placed across Grades K–6.

	Grade Levels						
Domains	**K**	**1**	**2**	**3**	**4**	**5**	**6**
Counting and Cardinality (CC)	•						
Operations and Algebraic Thinking (OA)	•	•	•	•	•	•	
Numbers and Operations in Base Ten (NBT)	•	•	•	•	•	•	
Measurement and Data (MD)	•	•	•	•	•	•	
Geometry (G)	•	•	•	•	•	•	•
Numbers and Operations—Fractions (NF)				•	•	•	
Ratios and Proportional Relationships (RP)							•
The Number System (NS)							•
Expressions and Equations (EE)							•
Statistics and Probability (SP)							•

The lessons in ***Core Standards for Math*** are organized by content standard. The content standard is listed at the top right-hand corner of each page. The entire text of the standards is provided on pages 256–260. The lesson objective listed below the content standard number indicates what part of the standard is emphasized in the lesson. You may choose to have students complete all the lessons for a particular standard or select lessons based on the more focused objectives.

Name ____________________

Lesson 1

COMMON CORE STANDARD CC.K.CC.1

Lesson Objective: Know the count sequence when counting to 50 by ones.

Count to 50 by Ones

1	2	3	4	5	6	7	8	9	10
11	12	13	14	15	16	17	18	19	20
21	22	23	24	25	26	27	28	29	30
31	32	33	34	35	36	37	38	39	40
41	42	43	44	45	46	47	48	49	50

DIRECTIONS 1. Count forward from 1. Draw a dot on each number as you count. Begin with 47 and count forward to 50. Color those numbers yellow.

Name ______________________________

Lesson 1
CC.K.CC.1

11	12	13	14	15	16	17	18	19	20
21	22	23	24	25	26	27	28	29	30
	32	33	34	35	36	37	38	39	40
41	42	43	44	45	46	47	48	49	50

20 ○ 30 ○

21 ○ 31 ○

11	12	13	14	15	16	17	18	19	20
21	22	23	24	25	26	27	28	29	30
31	32	33	34	35	36	37	38	39	40
41	42	43	44	45	46	47		49	50

46 ○ 49 ○

48 ○ 51 ○

11	12	13	14	15	16	17	18	19	20
21	22	23	24	25	26	27	28	29	30
31	32	33	34	35	36	37	38	39	40
41	42	43	44	45	46	47	48	49	50

DIRECTIONS 1. Begin with 11 and count forward to 50. Mark under the missing number. **2.** Begin with 11 and count forward to 50. Mark under the missing number. **3.** I am greater than 39 and less than 41. What number am I? Draw an X over that number.

Name ____________________

Lesson 2

COMMON CORE STANDARD CC.K.CC.1

Lesson Objective: Know the count sequence when counting to 100 by ones.

Count to 100 by Ones

1	2	3	4	5	6	7	8	9	10
11	12	13	14	15	16	17	18	19	20
21	22	23	24	25	26	27	28	29	30
31	32	33	34	35	36	37	38	39	40
41	42	43	44	45	46	47	48	49	50
51	52	53	54	55	56	57	58	59	60
61	62	63	64	65	66	67	68	69	70
71	72	73	74	75	76	77	78	79	80
81	82	83	84	85	86	87	88	89	90
91	92	93	94	95	96	97	98	99	100

DIRECTIONS 1. Count forward from 1. Draw a dot on each number as you count. Begin with 97 and count forward to 100. Color those numbers yellow.

Name ______________________

61	62	63	64	65	66	67	68	69	70
71	72	73	74	75	76	77	78	79	80
81	82	83	84	85	86	87	88	89	90
91	92	93		95	96	97	98	99	100

81 ○ 94 ○

90 ○ 100 ○

61	62		64	65	66	67	68	69	70
71	72	73	74	75	76	77	78	79	80
81	82	83	84	85	86	87	88	89	90
91	92	93	94	95	96	97	98	99	100

60 ○ 63 ○

62 ○ 65 ○

31	32	33	34	35	36	37	38	39	40
41	42	43	44	45	46	47	48	49	50
51	52	53	54	55	56	57	58	59	60

DIRECTIONS **1–2.** Begin with 61 and count to 100. Mark under the missing number. **3.** Mark an X on the number that is one greater than 35. Draw a circle around the number that is one less than 58.

Name ______________________________

Lesson 3

COMMON CORE STANDARD CC.K.CC.1

Lesson Objective: Know the count sequence when counting to 100 by tens.

Count to 100 by Tens

1	2	3	4	5	6	7	8	9	10
11	12	13	14	15	16	17	18	19	20
21	22	23	24	25	26	27	28	29	30
31	32	33	34	35	36	37	38	39	40
41	42	43	44	45	46	47	48	49	50
51	52	53	54	55	56	57	58	59	60
61	62	63	64	65	66	67	68	69	70
71	72	73	74	75	76	77	78	79	80
81	82	83	84	85	86	87	88	89	90
91	92	93	94	95	96	97	98	99	100

DIRECTIONS 1. Color the boxes of all the numbers that end with a zero. Count by tens as you point to the numbers in the boxes you colored.

Name ______________________________

Lesson 3
CC.K.CC.1

1	2	3	4	5	6	7	8	9	10
11	12	13	14	15	16	17	18	19	20
21	22	23	24	25	26	27	28	29	30
31	32	33	34	35	36	37	38	39	40

10 ○ 30 ○

20 ○ 40 ○

41	42	43	44	45	46	47	48	49	50
51	52	53	54	55	56	57	58	59	60
61	62	63	64	65	66	67	68	69	70
71	72	73	74	75	76	77	78	79	80

70 ○ 80 ○

79 ○ 81 ○

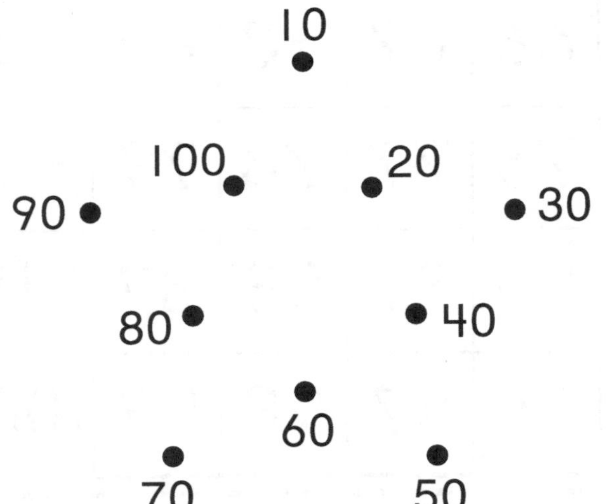

____

DIRECTIONS **1.** Evan counts by tens and colors those numbers on the chart. Mark under the number he should color next. **2.** Elena counts by tens and colors those numbers on the chart. Mark under the number she should color next. **3.** Count by tens as you draw lines to connect the dots and complete the shape. Write your favorite number from the shape.

Name ____________________

Lesson 4

COMMON CORE STANDARD CC.K.CC.1

Count by Tens

Lesson Objective: Use sets of tens to count to 100.

1

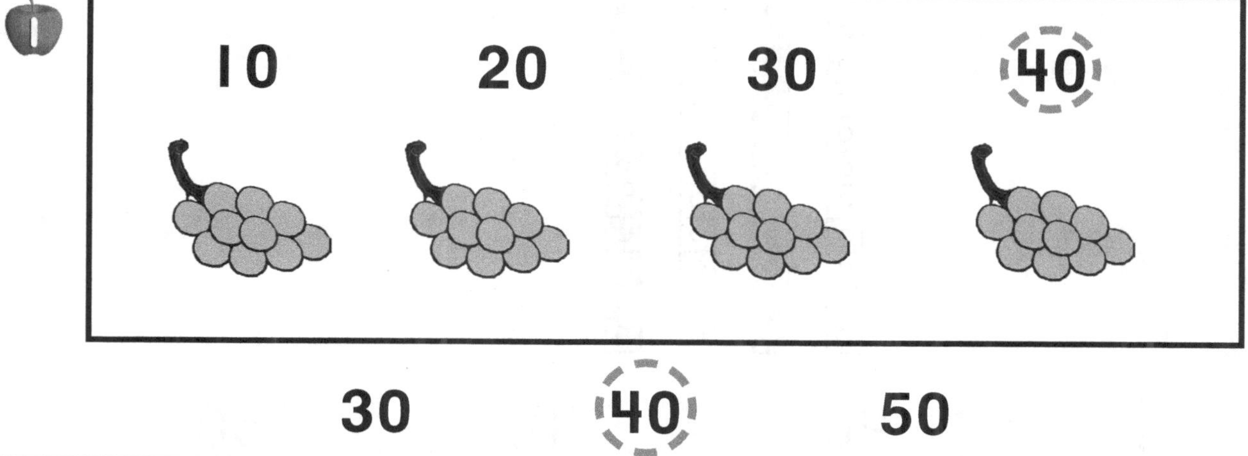

30 40 50

2

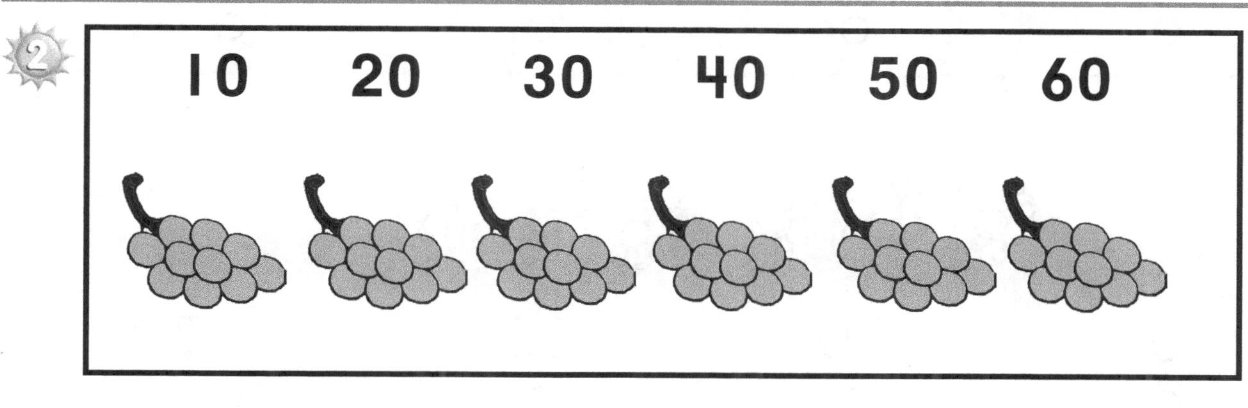

40 50 60

3

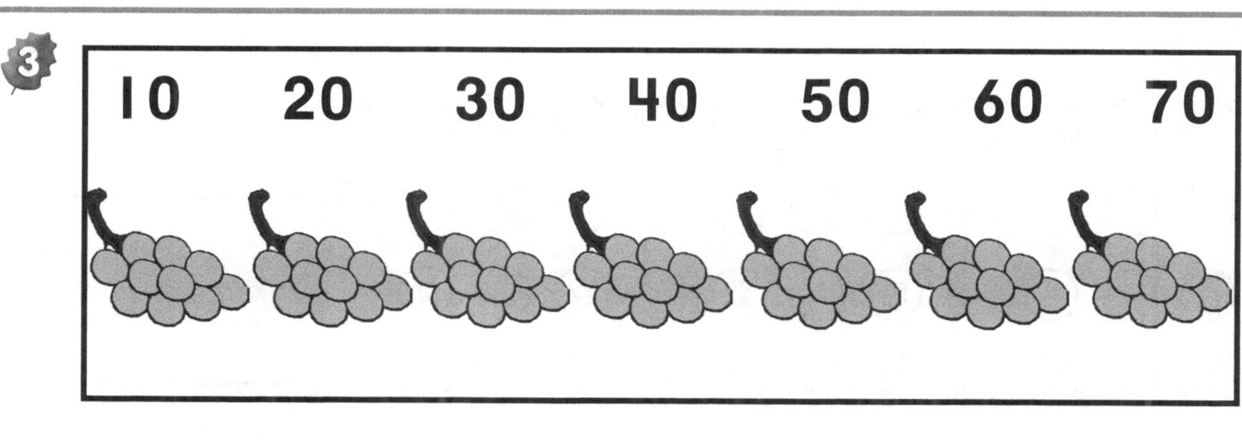

70 80 90

DIRECTIONS 1–3. Point to each number above the sets of 10 as you count by tens. Circle the last number you count. Circle the number below that shows how many.

Name ______________________________

Lesson 4
CC.K.CC.1

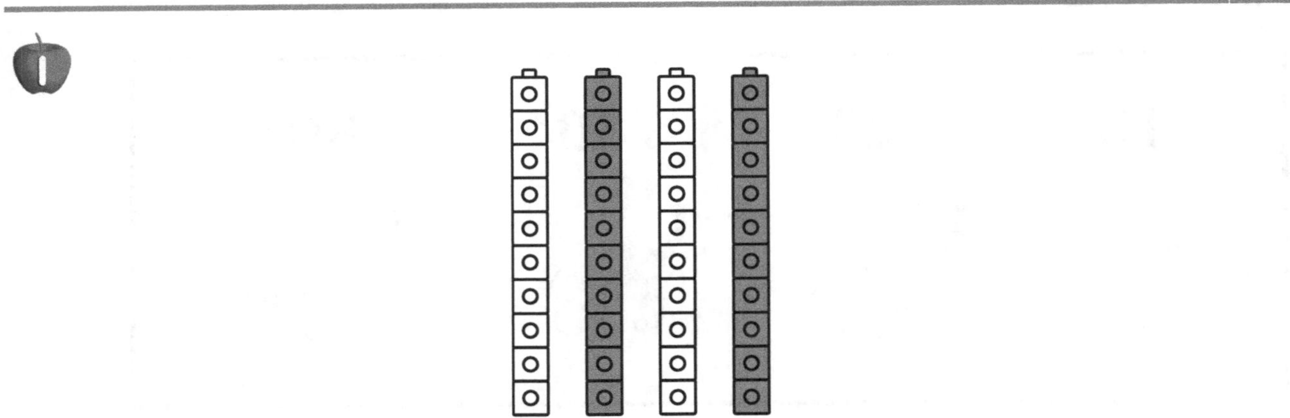

14 ○ 40 ○ 44 ○ 50 ○

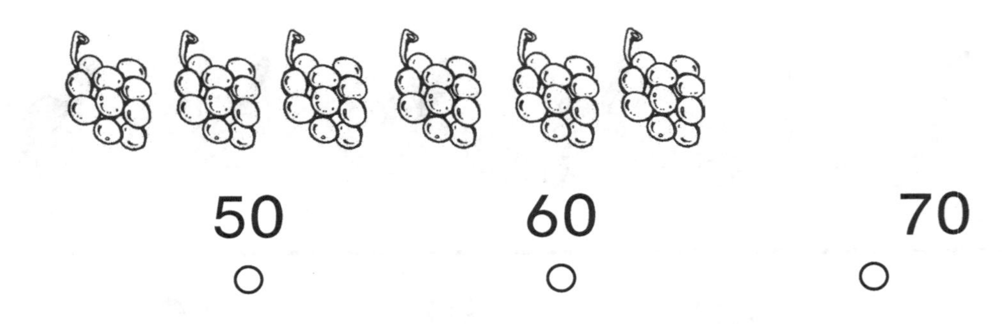

6 ○ 50 ○ 60 ○ 70 ○

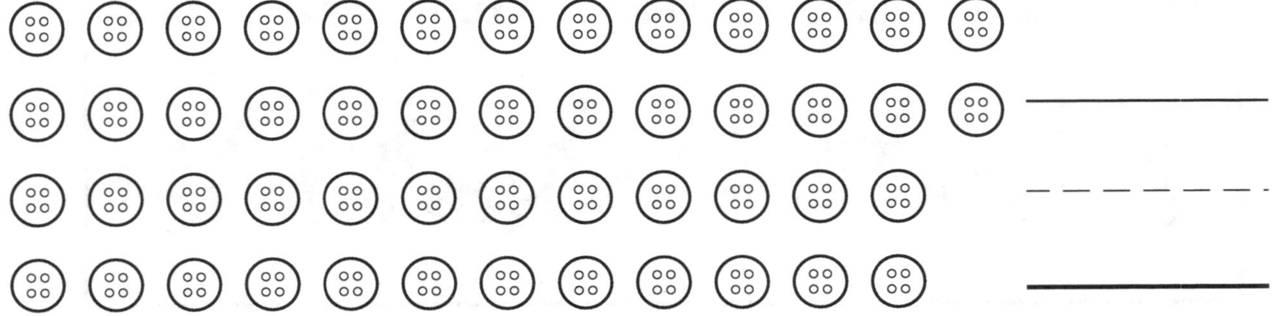

DIRECTIONS 1. Count the cube towers by tens. Mark under the number that tells how many cubes. **2.** Count the grapes by tens. Mark under the number that tells how many grapes. **3.** Circle sets of 10 buttons. Count the buttons by tens. Write how many you circled in all.

Name ____________________

Lesson 5

COMMON CORE STANDARD CC.K.CC.2

Lesson Objective: Count forward to 10 from a given number.

Count and Order to 10

DIRECTIONS 1. Trace the numbers. Make a cube train to show each number. Draw each cube train. 2. Write the numbers in order as you count forward from 6.

Name ______________________________

Lesson 5
CC.K.CC.2

1

7 8 ___ 10

4 ○ 8 ○ 9 ○ 10 ○

2

5 ___ 7 8

4 ○ 6 ○ 8 ○ 10 ○

3

5 6 ___ 8

3 ○ 5 ○ 6 ○ 7 ○

4

6 7 ___ 9

4 ○ 6 ○ 8 ○ 9 ○

5

4 5 6 ___ 8

DIRECTIONS 1–4. Count forward. Mark under the number that is missing. **5.** Count forward. Write the number that is missing.

Name ________________________________

Lesson 6

COMMON CORE STANDARD CC.K.CC.2

Lesson Objective: Count forward to 20 from a given number.

Count and Order to 20

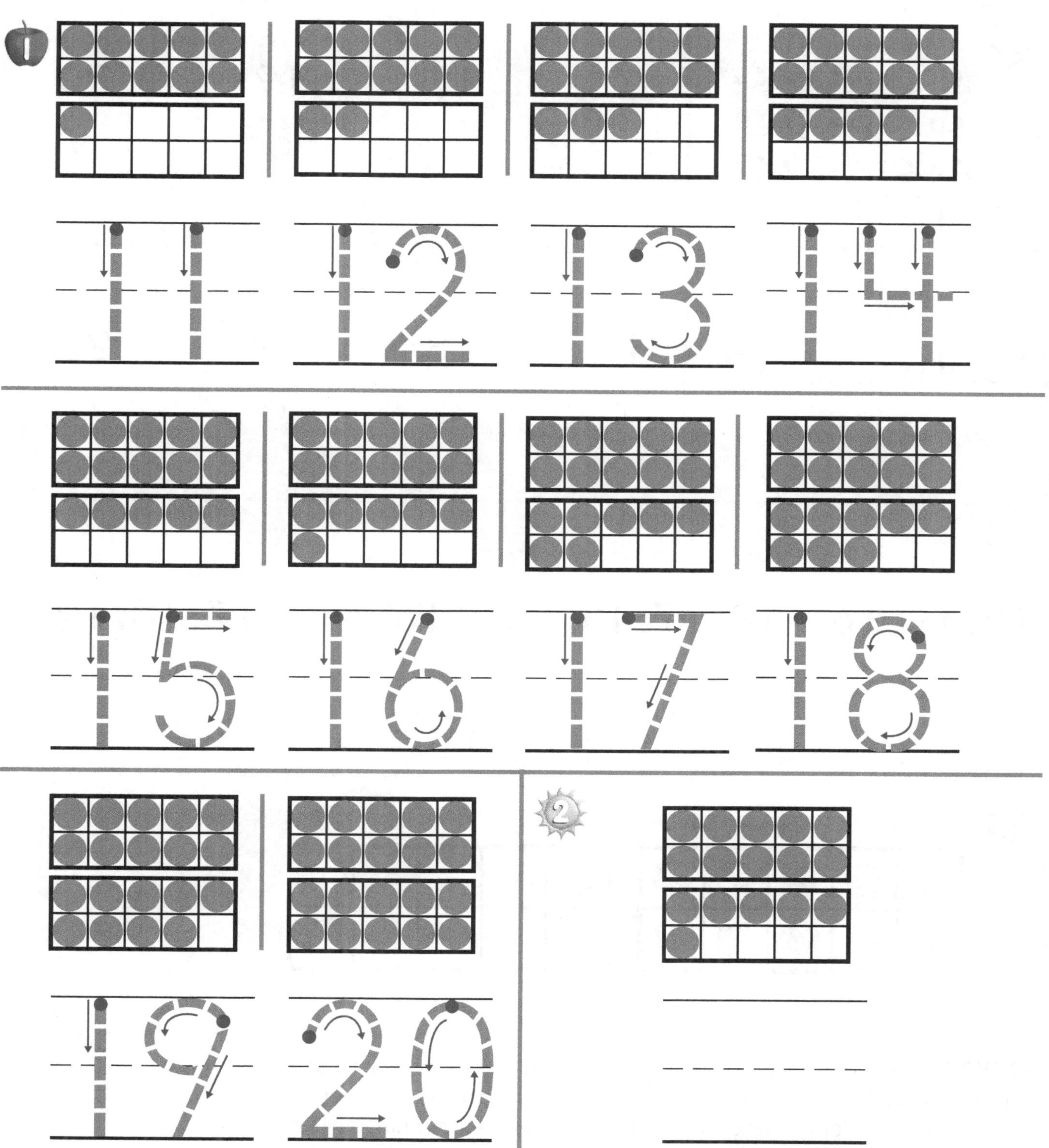

DIRECTIONS 1. Count the dots in each set of ten frames. Trace the numbers. Then point to each number as you count in order from 10. 2. Write the number that comes after 15.

Name ____________________

Lesson 6
CC.K.CC.2

17	18	19	20
○	○	○	○

15, 16, ___, 18

17	18	19	20
○	○	○	○

15, 14, 16	18, 17, 19	15, 16, 14	17, 18, 19
○	○	○	○

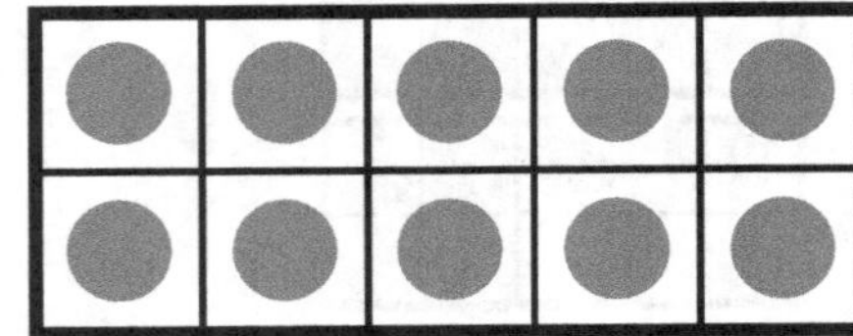 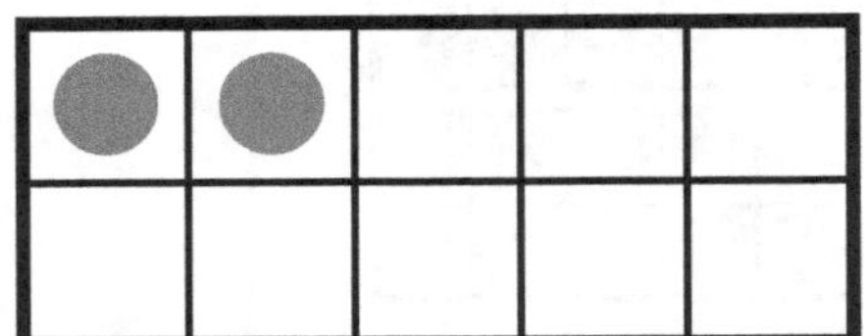

______

DIRECTIONS 1. Count how many hats. Mark under the number that is one **greater than** the number of hats. 2. Use the numbers to count forward. Mark under the missing number. 3. Which set of numbers is in order? Mark under your answer. 4. Draw counters to make the picture show 18. Write how many counters in all.

Name ______________________________

Lesson 7

COMMON CORE STANDARD CC.K.CC.3

Lesson Objective: Represent 1 and 2 objects with number names and written numerals.

Count and Write 1 and 2

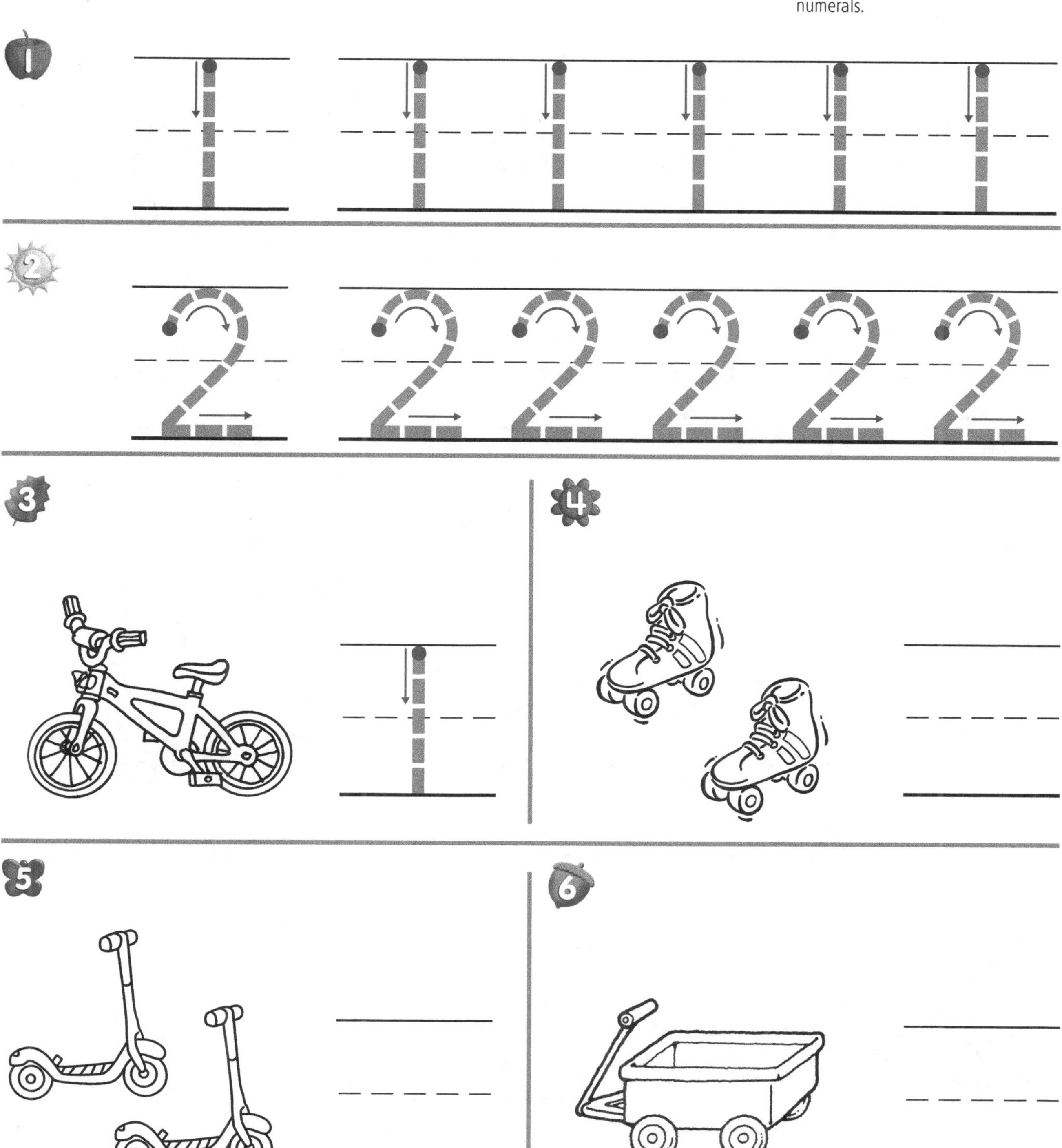

DIRECTIONS **1–2.** Say the number. Trace the numbers. **3.** Draw a dot on each object as you count. Tell how many. Trace the number. **4–6.** Draw a dot on each object as you count. Write the number.

Name ______________________________

1

○ ○ ○ ○

2

one ○ two ○ three ○ four ○

2

  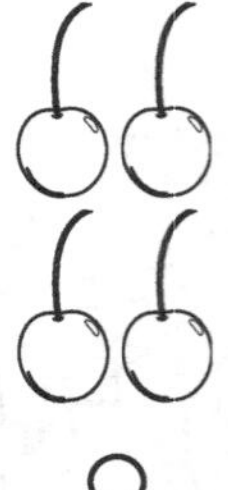

○ ○ ○ ○

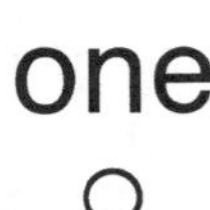

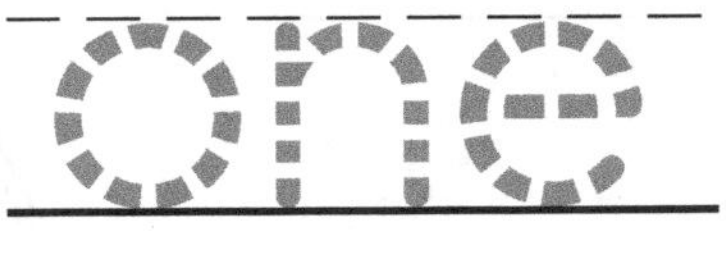

DIRECTIONS 1. Mark under the set of bananas that shows the number at the beginning of the row. **2.** Mark under the word that matches the number at the beginning of the row. **3.** Mark under the set of cherries that shows the number at the beginning of the row. **4.** Trace the word that shows how many birds.

Name ________________________________

Lesson 8

COMMON CORE STANDARD CC.K.CC.3

Lesson Objective: Represent 3 and 4 objects with number names and written numerals.

Count and Write 3 and 4

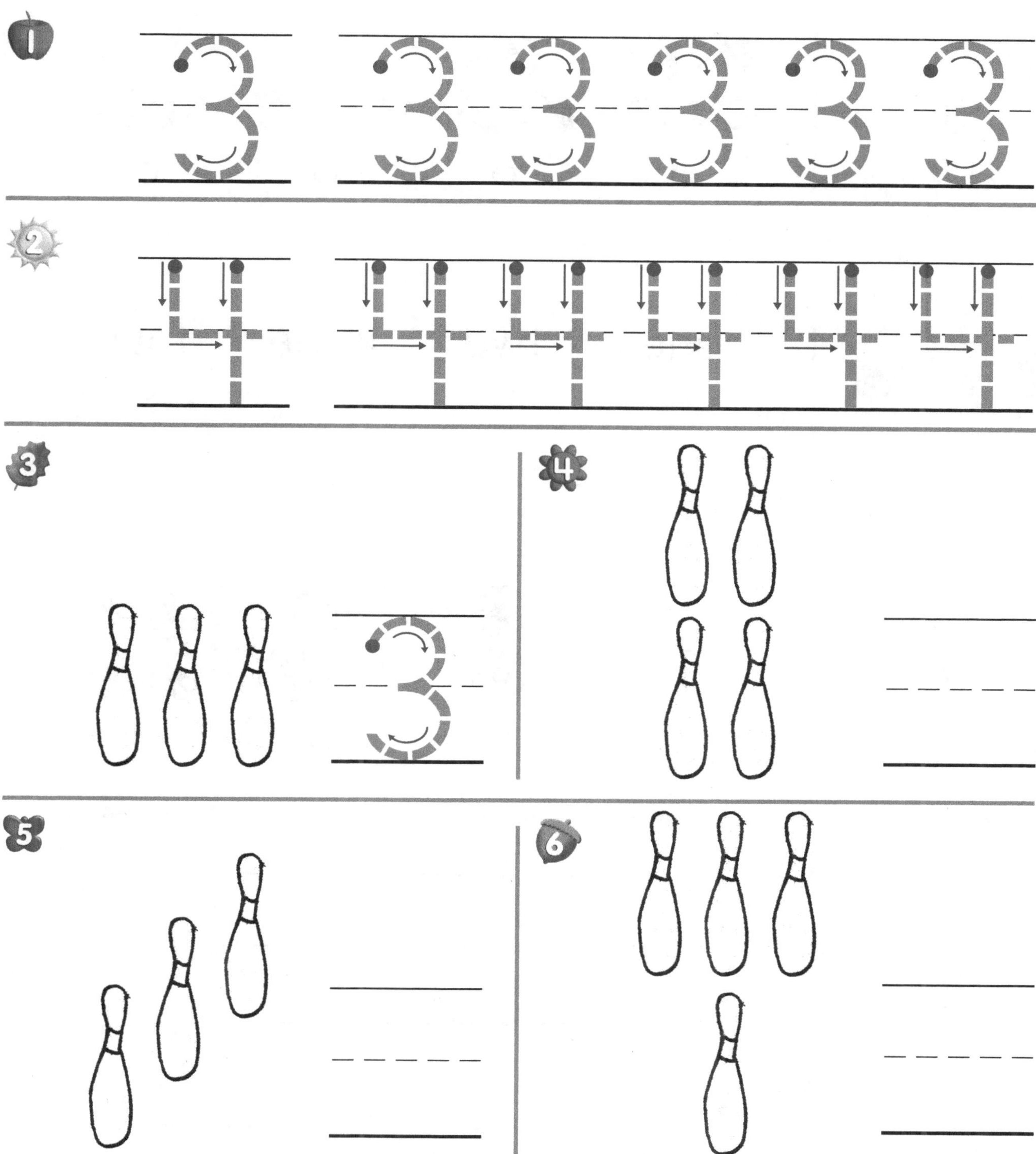

DIRECTIONS 1–2. Say the number. Trace the numbers. **3.** Draw a dot on each object as you count. Tell how many. Trace the number. **4–6.** Draw a dot on each object as you count. Write the number.

Name ____________________

Lesson 8
CC.K.CC.3

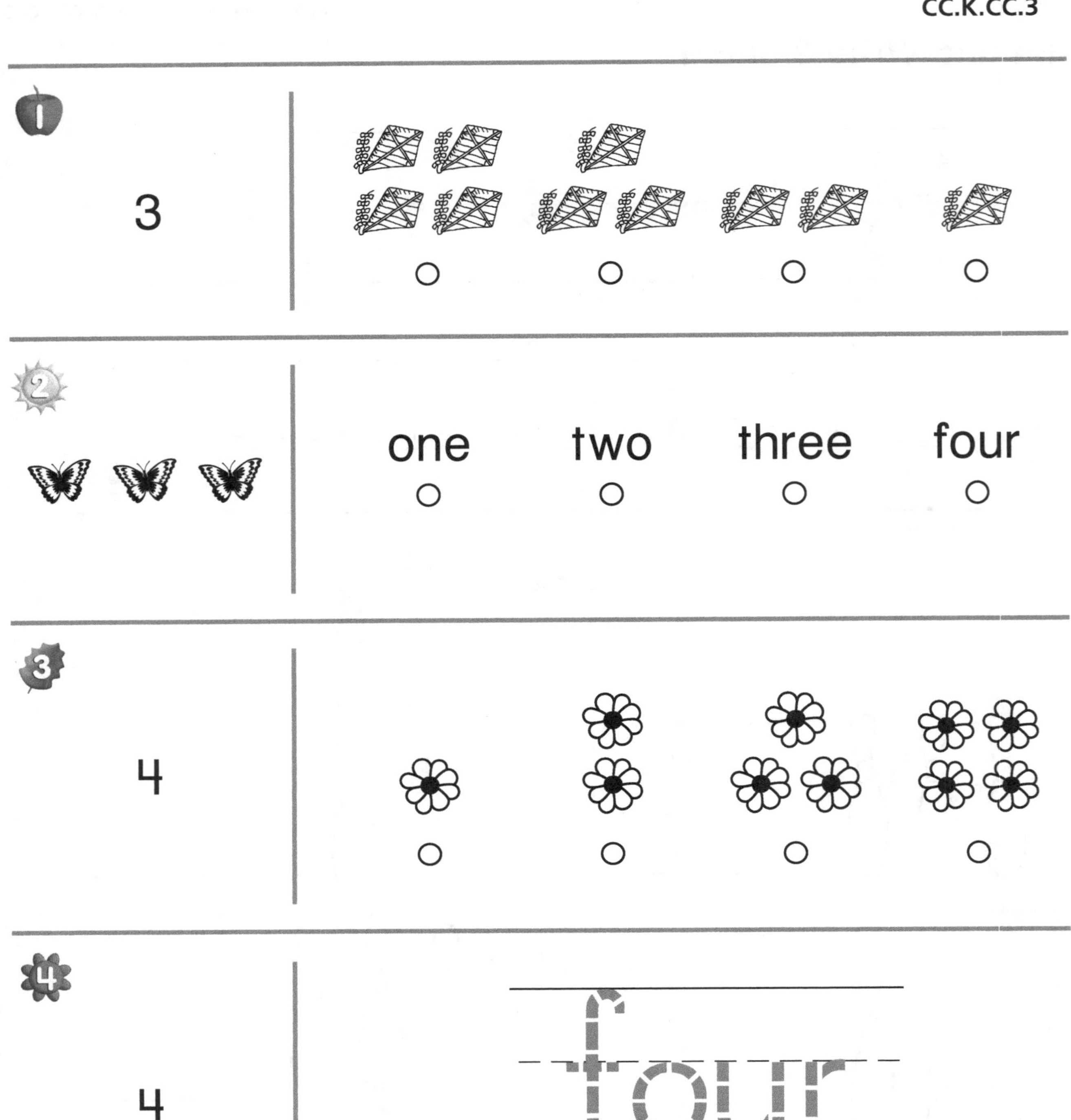

DIRECTIONS 1. Mark under the set of kites that shows the number at the beginning of the row. **2.** Mark under the word that shows how many butterflies at the beginning of the row. **3.** Mark under the set of flowers that shows the number at the beginning of the row. **4.** Trace the word that matches the number at the beginning of the row.

Name ______________________________

Lesson 9

COMMON CORE STANDARD CC.K.CC.3

Lesson Objective: Solve problems by using the strategy *make a model.*

Problem Solving • Understand 0

1

0

2

3

DIRECTIONS 1. Place a cube on the dinner table. Take the cube off the dinner table. How many cubes are on the dinner table now? Trace the number. **2.** Place a cube on each plate. Take the cubes off the plates. How many cubes are on the plates now? Write the number. **3.** Place a cube on each bowl. Take the cubes off the bowls. How many cubes are on the bowls now? Write the number.

Name ______________________________

Lesson 9
CC.K.CC.3

1

0	1	2	3
○	○	○	○

2

3	2	1	0
○	○	○	○

3

0	1	2	3
○	○	○	○

4

______

DIRECTIONS **1.** The counters show how many pencils Dan has. Dan gives away all his pencils. Mark under the number that shows how many pencils Dan has now. **2.** The counters show how many markers Sophie has. Sophie gives all her markers to the teacher. Mark under the number that shows how many markers Sophie has now. **3.** The counter shows how many paint brushes Luis has. Emma has one fewer paint brush than Luis. Mark under the number that shows how many paint brushes Emma has. **4.** The counters show how many glue sticks Jan has. She gives 1 glue stick to her friend and 2 glue sticks to the teacher. Write the number that shows how many glue sticks Jan has now.

Name ______________________

Lesson 10

COMMON CORE STANDARD CC.K.CC.3

Lesson Objective: Represent 0 objects with a number name and a written numeral.

Identify and Write 0

DIRECTIONS **1.** Touch each piece of fruit on the plate. How many did you touch? Trace the number. Circle the plate if it has 0 pieces of fruit. **2–4.** Which plates have 0 pieces of fruit? Circle the plates. Write how many pieces of fruit.

Name ______________________

Lesson 10
CC.K.CC.3

○  ○ 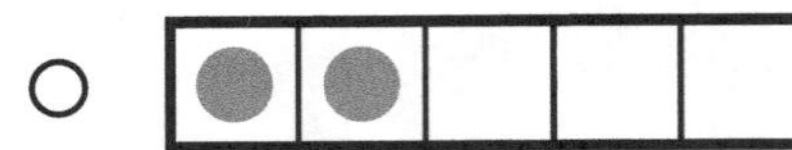

○  ○ 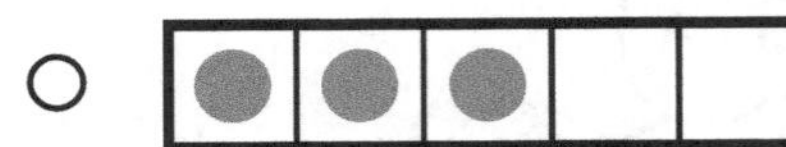

0	1	2	3
○	○	○	○

○ ○ ○ ○

______

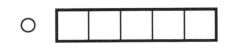

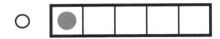

DIRECTIONS 1. Mark next to the five frame that shows zero counters.
2. Mark under the number that shows how many fish are in the bowl.
3. Mark under the picture that shows zero flowers in a vase. 4. Write the number that shows how many apples are in the bowl.

Name ______________________

Lesson 11

COMMON CORE STANDARD CC.K.CC.3

Lesson Objective: Represent 6 objects with a number name and a written numeral.

Count and Write 6

1

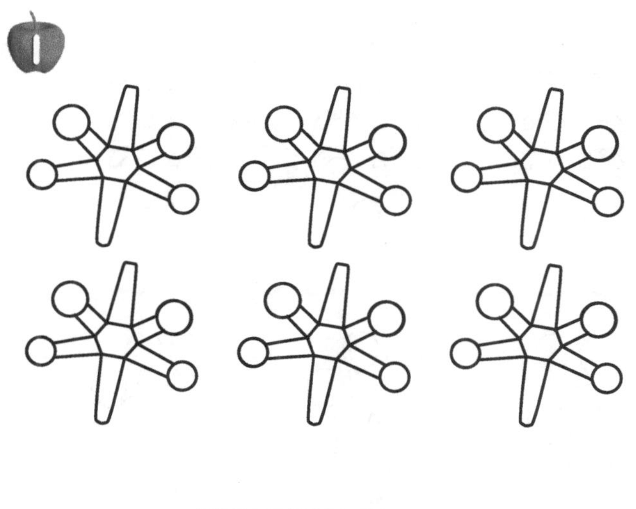

2

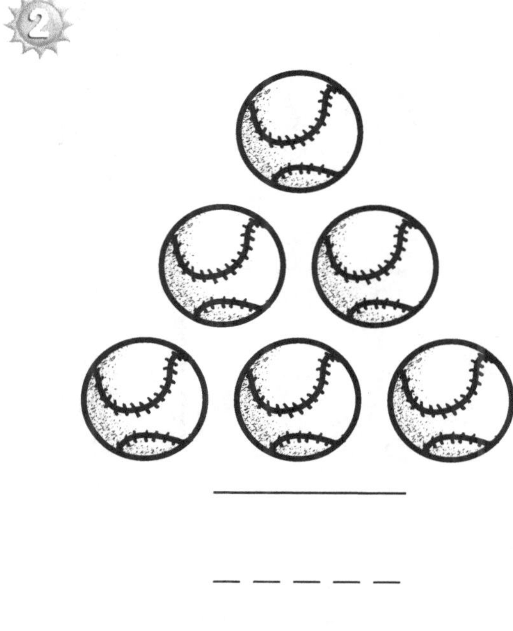

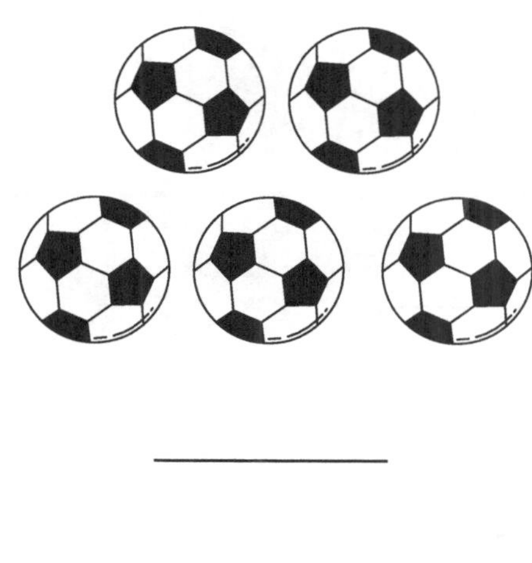

DIRECTIONS 1–4. Draw a dot on each toy as you count. Write the number.

Name ______________________

Lesson 11
CC.K.CC.3

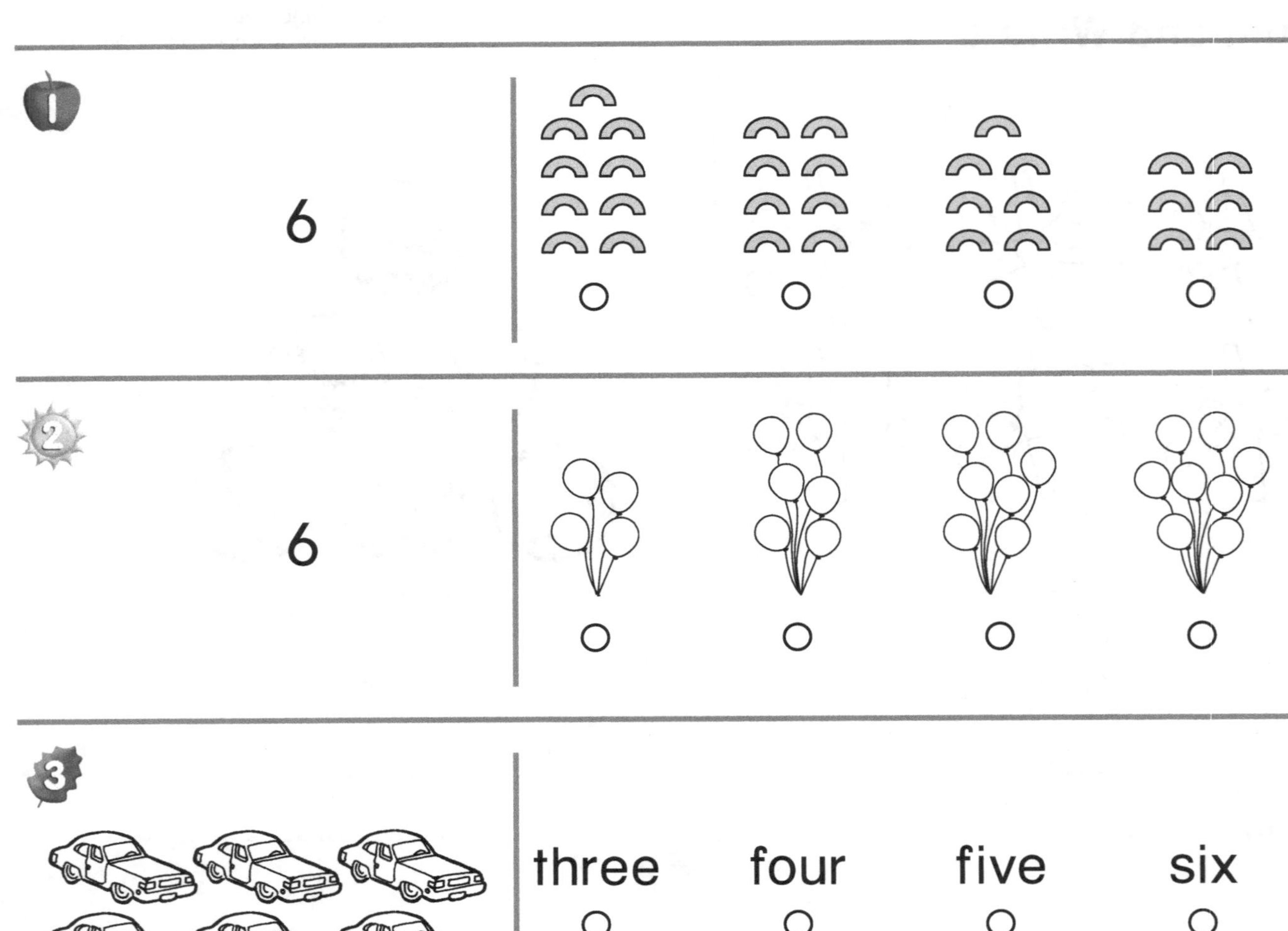

DIRECTIONS 1–2. Mark under the set that models the number at the beginning of the row. 3. Mark under the word that matches the number of cars at the beginning of the row. 4. Count the cubes. Write the number.

Name ______________________

Lesson 12

COMMON CORE STANDARD CC.K.CC.3

Lesson Objective: Represent 7 objects with a number name and a written numeral.

Count and Write 7

1

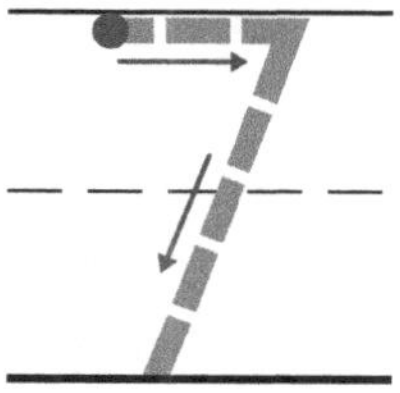

7

2

3

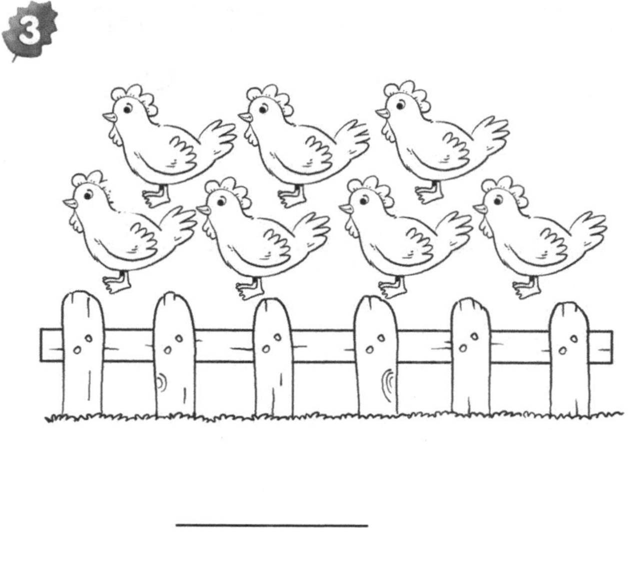

4

DIRECTIONS 1–4. Draw a dot on each animal as you count. Write the number. Circle the sets of 7 animals.

Name ______________________________

Lesson 12
CC.K.CC.3

4	5	6	7
○	○	○	○

six	seven	eight	nine
○	○	○	○

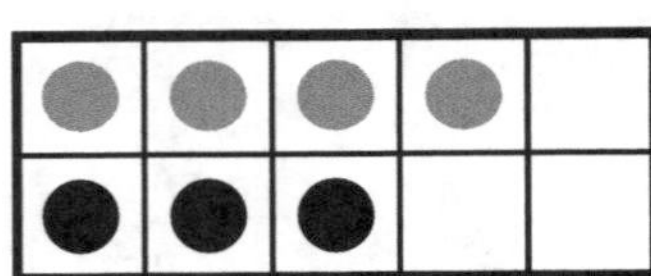

four	five	six	seven
○	○	○	○

______

DIRECTIONS **1.** Mark under the number that matches the number of cubes at the beginning of the row. **2–3.** Mark under the word that matches the set at the beginning of the row. **4.** Write the number that matches the number of hats at the beginning of the row.

Name ______________________

Lesson 13

COMMON CORE STANDARD CC.K.CC.3

Lesson Objective: Represent 8 objects with a number name and a written numeral.

Count and Write 8

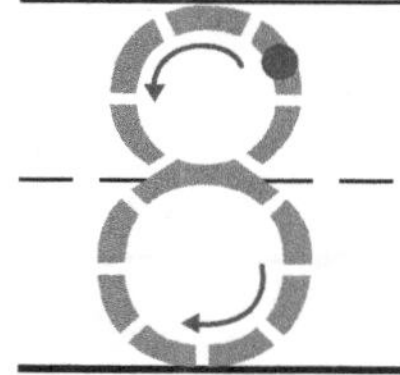

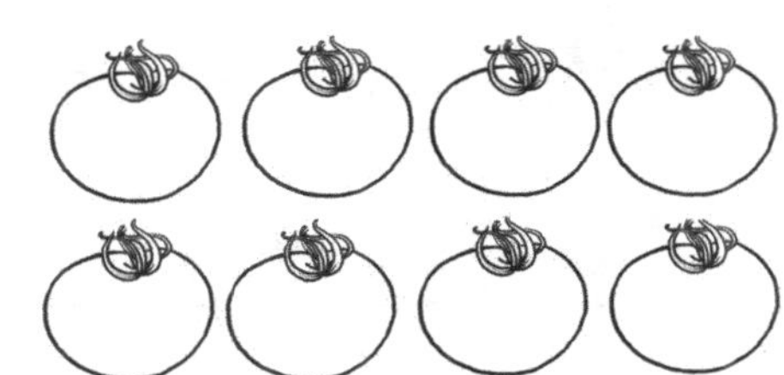

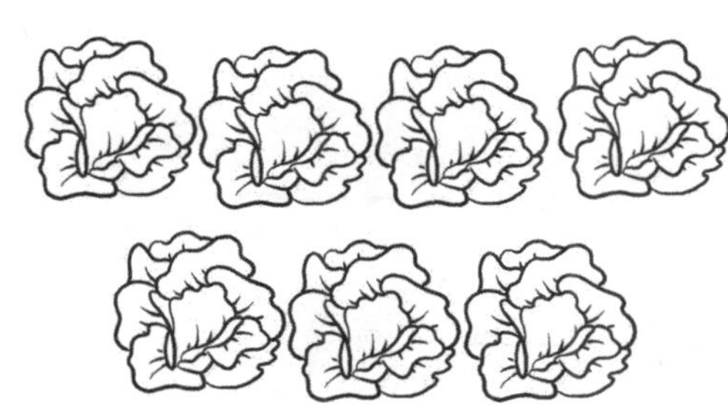

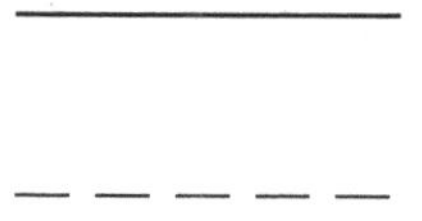

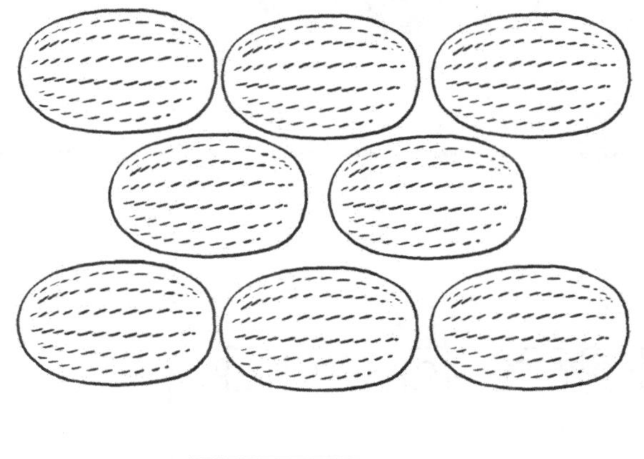

DIRECTIONS **1–4.** Draw a dot on each object as you count. Write the number. Circle the sets of 8 objects.

Name ______________________

Lesson 13
CC.K.CC.3

8

five	six	seven	eight
○	○	○	○

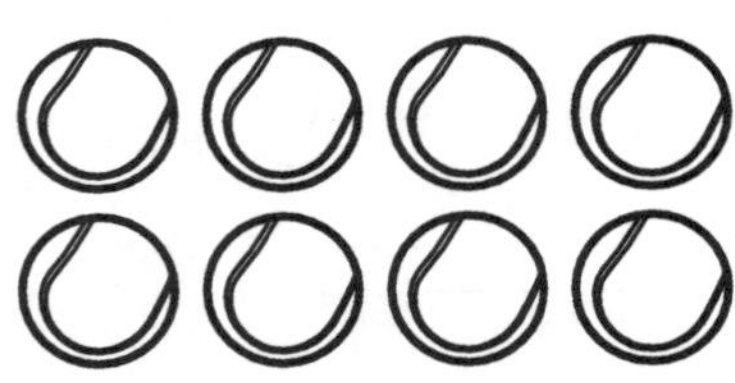

6	7	8	9
○	○	○	○

six	seven	eight	nine
○	○	○	○

______

DIRECTIONS **1.** Mark under the word that matches the number at the beginning of the row. **2.** Mark under the number that matches the model at the beginning of the row. **3.** Mark under the word that matches the model at the beginning of the row. **4.** Write the number that matches the model at the beginning of the row.

Name ______________________

Lesson 14

COMMON CORE STANDARD CC.K.CC.3

Lesson Objective: Represent 9 objects with a number name and a written numeral.

Count and Write 9

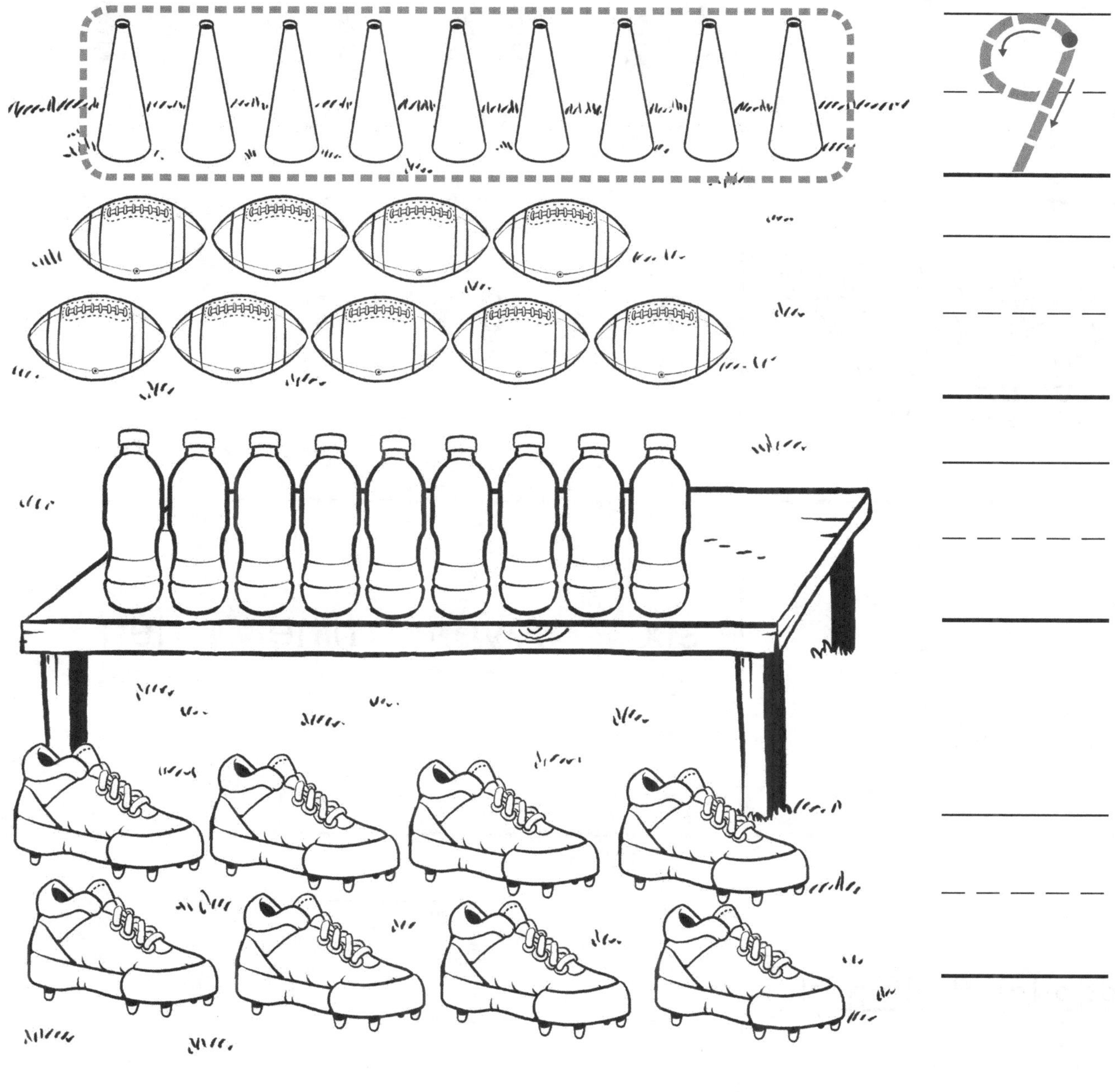

9

DIRECTIONS 1. Draw a dot on each object as you count. Write the number. Circle the sets of 9 objects.

Name ____________________

9

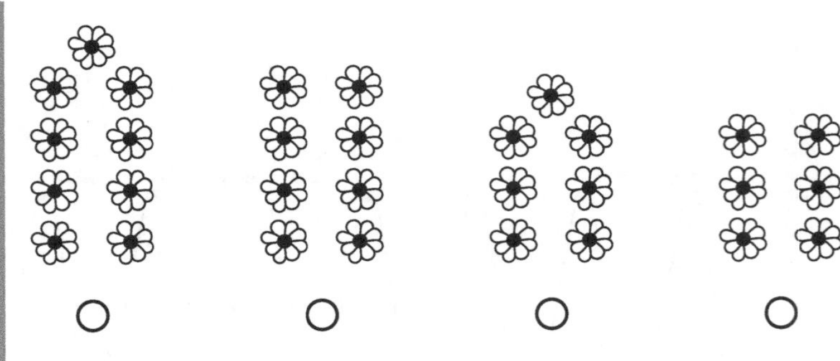

○ ○ ○ ○

9 ○ 8 ○ 7 ○ 6 ○

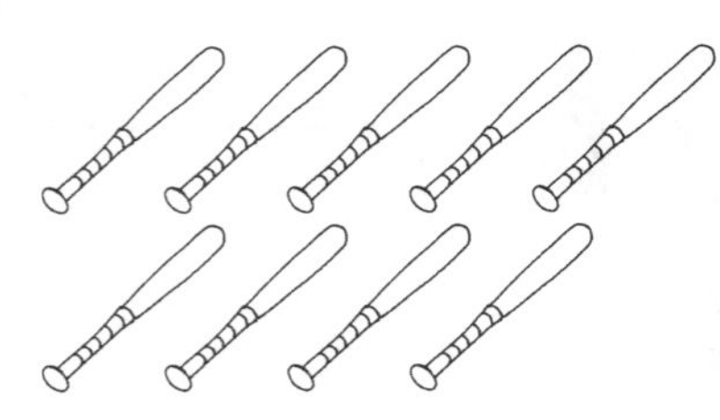

six ○ seven ○ nine ○ ten ○

4

____

DIRECTIONS 1. Mark under the set that models the number at the beginning of the row. **2.** Mark under the number that matches the model at the beginning of the row. **3.** Mark under the word that matches the model at the beginning of the row. **4.** Write the number that matches the model at the beginning of the row.

Name ________________________________

Lesson 15

COMMON CORE STANDARD CC.K.CC.3

Lesson Objective: Represent 10 objects with a number name and a written numeral.

Count and Write 10

10

ten

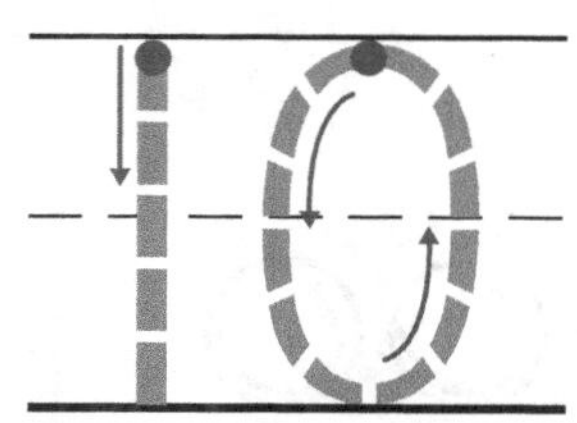

DIRECTIONS 1. Draw a dot on each acorn as you count. Tell how many. Trace the number. **2–5.** Draw a dot on each acorn as you count. Tell how many. Write the number.

Name ______________________

Lesson 15
CC.K.CC.3

10 ○ 9 ○ 7 ○ 5 ○

6 ○ 7 ○ 8 ○ 9 ○

seven ○ eight ○ nine ○ ten ○

6 ○ 7 ○ 8 ○ 9 ○

5

______

DIRECTIONS **1–2.** Mark under the number that shows how many. **3.** Mark under the word that shows how many. **4.** Mark under the number that shows how many. **5.** Write the number that shows how many fish.

Name ___________________________

Lesson 16

COMMON CORE STANDARD CC.K.CC.3

Lesson Objective: Represent 11 and 12 objects with number names and written numerals.

Count and Write 11 and 12

1

11

eleven

2

3

4

___ + ___ = ___

DIRECTIONS 1. Count and tell how many. Draw a dot on each object as you count. Trace the number. 2. Look at the objects in the ten frame in Exercise 1. Count and write the number. 3. Look at the object below the ten frame in Exercise 1. Count and write the number. 4. Look at the ten ones and some more ones in Exercise 1. Complete the addition sentence to match.

Name ____________________

Lesson 16
CC.K.CC.3

10 ○ 11 ○ 12 ○ 13 ○

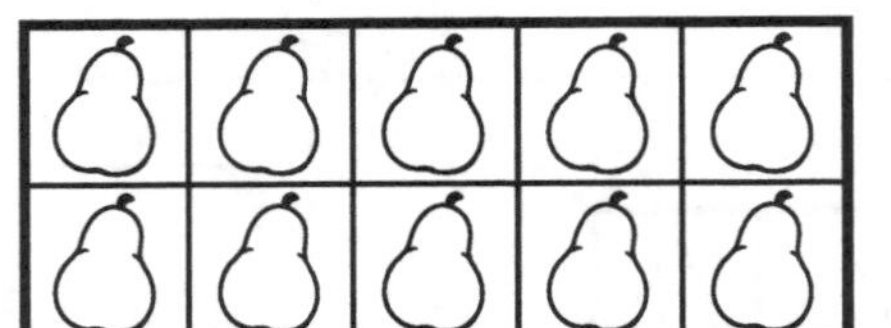

10 ○ 11 ○ 12 ○ 13 ○

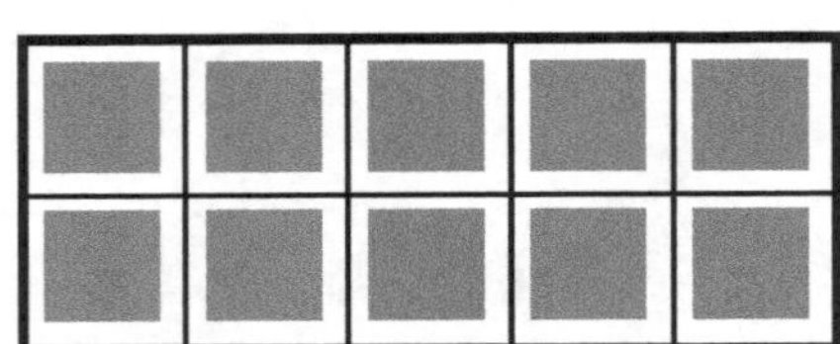

○ $10 + 0 = 10$ ○ $10 + 1 = 11$

○ $10 + 2 = 12$ ○ $10 + 3 = 13$

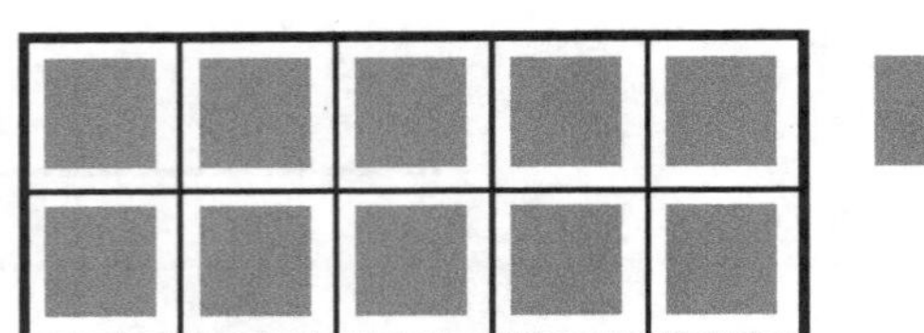

DIRECTIONS 1–2. Count. Mark under the number that tells how many. **3.** Look at the ten ones and some more ones. Mark next to the addition sentence that matches. **4.** Count and tell how many. Write the number.

Name ______________________

Lesson 17

COMMON CORE STANDARD CC.K.CC.3

Lesson Objective: Represent 13 and 14 objects with number names and written numerals.

Count and Write 13 and 14

1

13

thirteen

2

3

4

+

=

DIRECTIONS 1. Count and tell how many. Draw a dot on each object as you count. Trace the number. 2. Look at the objects in the ten frame in Exercise 1. Count and write the number. 3. Look at the objects below the ten frame in Exercise 1. Count and write the number. 4. Look at the ten ones and some more ones in Exercise 1. Complete the addition sentence to match.

Name ______________________

Lesson 17
CC.K.CC.3

14 ○ 13 ○ 12 ○ 11 ○

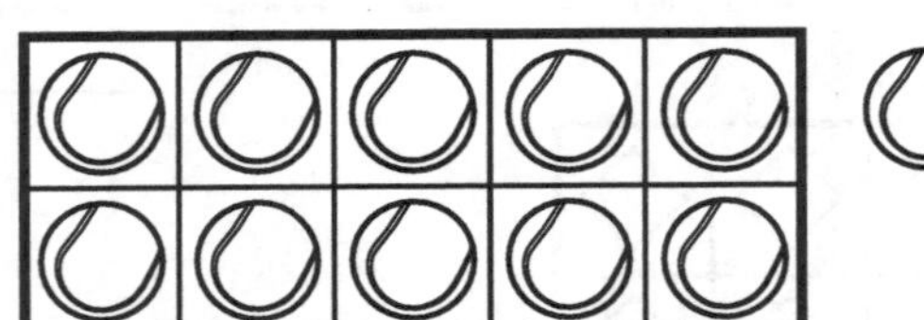

10 ○ 11 ○ 12 ○ 13 ○

3

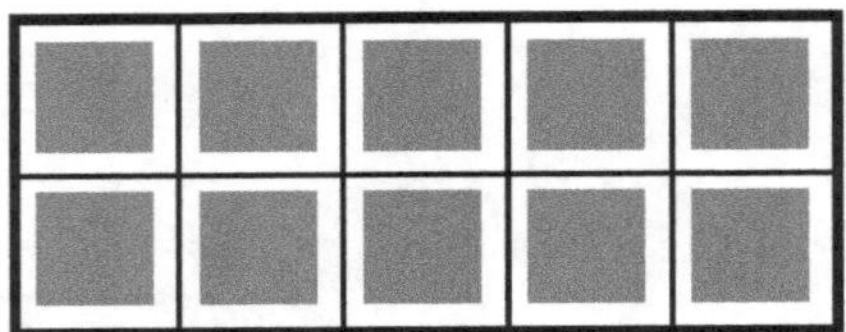

○ $10 + 1 = 11$ ○ $10 + 2 = 12$

○ $10 + 3 = 13$ ○ $10 + 4 = 14$

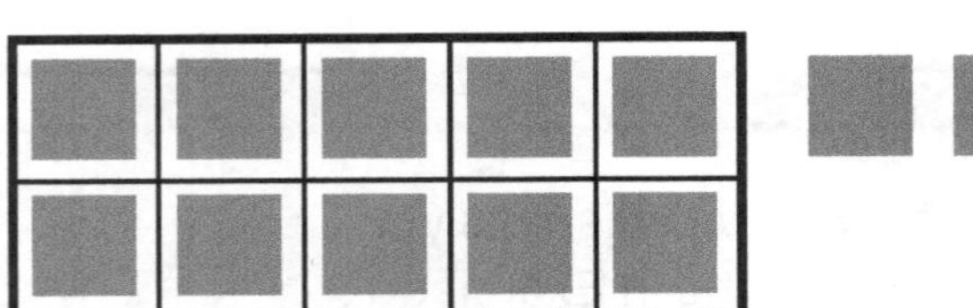

______

DIRECTIONS **1–2.** Count. Mark under the number that tells how many. **3.** Look at the ten ones and some more ones. Mark next to the addition sentence that matches. **4.** Count. Write the number that tells how many.

Name ___________________________

Lesson 18

COMMON CORE STANDARD CC.K.CC.3

Lesson Objective: Solve problems by using the strategy *draw a picture.*

Problem Solving • Use Numbers to 15

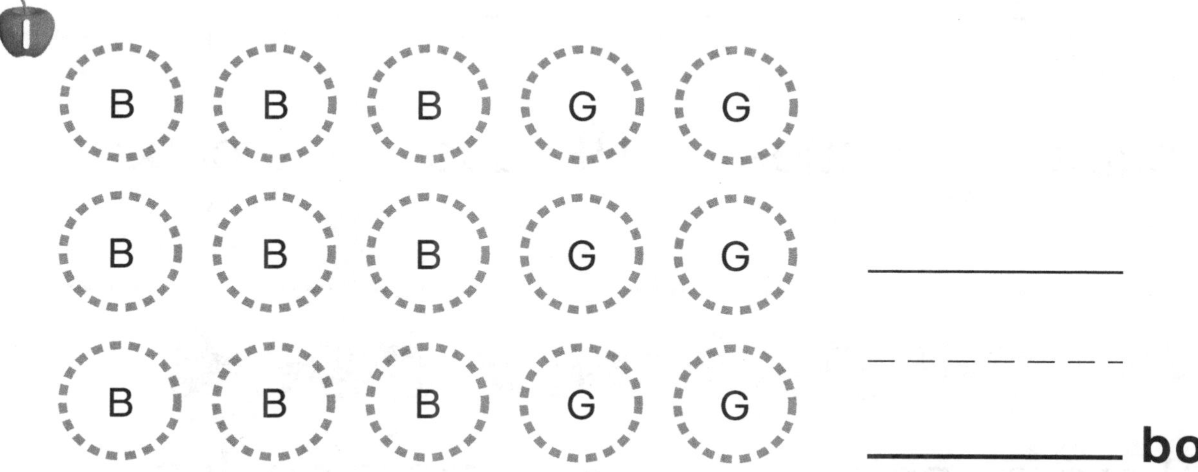

_______ boys

_______ girls

DIRECTIONS **1.** There are 15 children in Mrs. Joiner's class. They sit in rows of 5. There are 3 boys and 2 girls in each row. How many boys are in the class? Trace the 3 rows of 5 circles. *B* is for boy and *G* is for girl. Count the boys. Write the number. **2.** There are 15 children in Mr. Gilbert's class. They sit in rows of 5. There are 4 boys and 1 girl in each row. How many girls are in the class? Draw to solve the problem.

Name ______________________________

Lesson 18
CC.K.CC.3

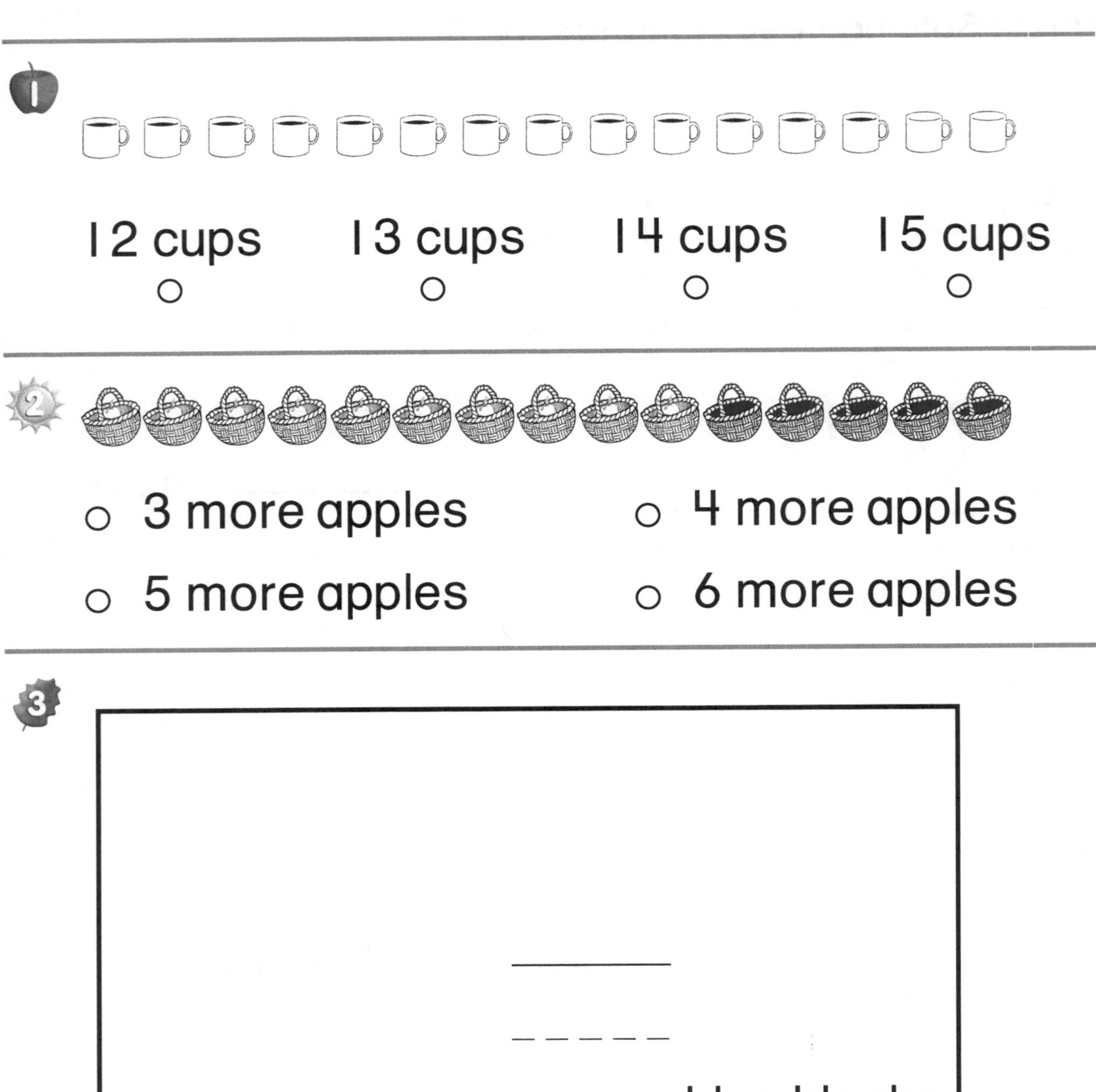

DIRECTIONS 1. There are 13 cups with juice in them. There are 2 cups with no juice. How many cups are there? Mark under the number that shows how many cups there are. 2. Kate has 15 baskets. Ten baskets have 1 apple in them. How many more apples would Kate need to have 1 apple in each basket? Mark next to the number that shows how many more apples. 3. Kevin has 15 blocks. He puts them in rows of 5. There are 4 red blocks and 1 blue block in each row. How many blue blocks does Kevin have? Draw to solve the problem. Write how many blue blocks.

Name ______________________________

Lesson 19

COMMON CORE STANDARD CC.K.CC.3

Lesson Objective: Represent 16 and 17 objects with number names and written numerals.

Count and Write 16 and 17

1

16

sixteen

2

3

4

DIRECTIONS **1.** Count and tell how many. Draw a dot on each object as you count. Trace the number. **2.** Look at the objects in the top ten frame in Exercise 1. Count and write the number. **3.** Look at the objects in the bottom ten frame in Exercise 1. Count and write the number. **4.** Look at the ten frames in Exercise 1. Complete the addition sentence to match.

Name ___________________________

Lesson 19
CC.K.CC.3

6	11	16	17
○	○	○	○

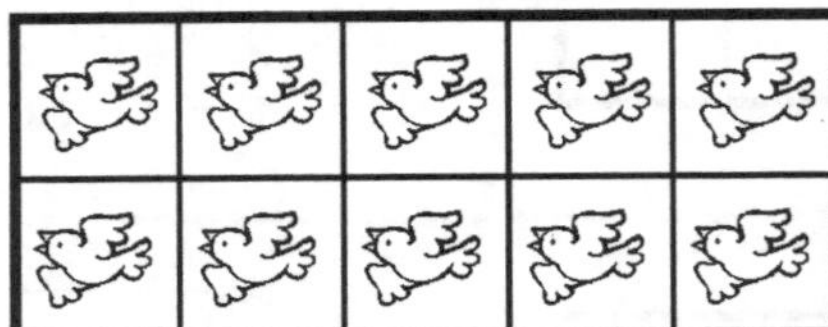
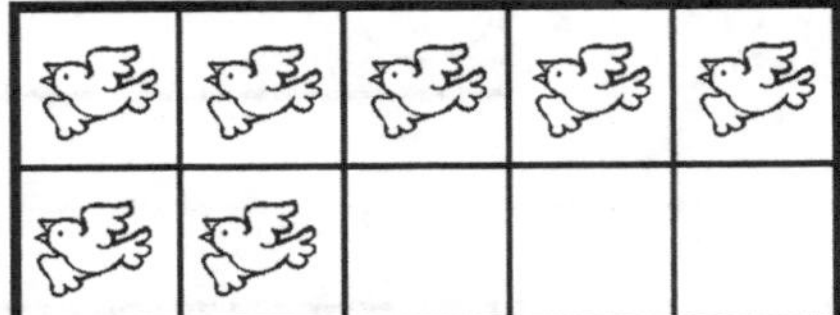

17	16	12	5
○	○	○	○

3

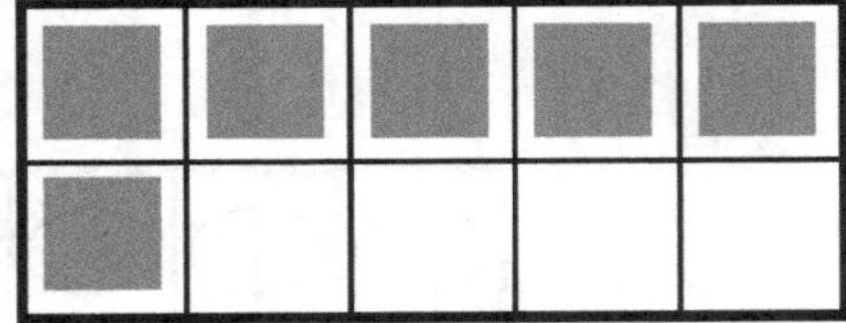

○ $10 + 7 = 17$　　○ $10 + 6 = 16$

○ $10 + 5 = 15$　　○ $10 + 1 = 11$

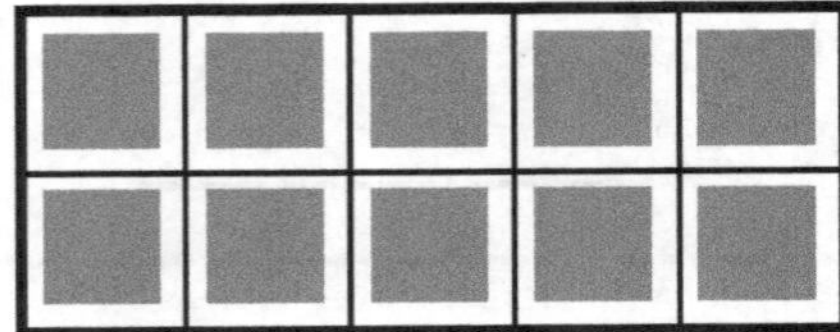
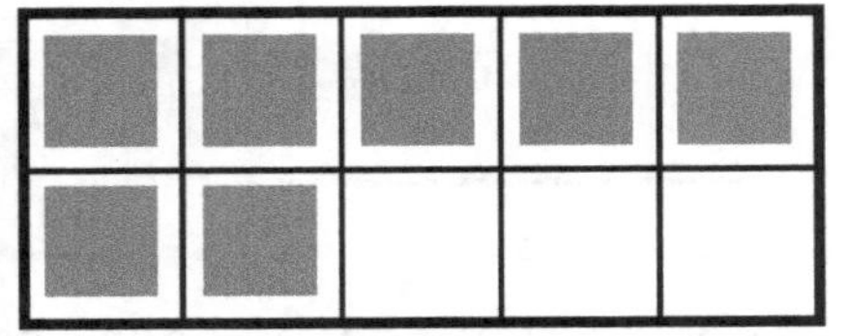

______

DIRECTIONS **1–2.** Mark under the number that tells how many. **3.** Look at the ten frames. Mark next to the addition sentence that matches. **4.** Write the number that tells how many.

Name ______________________________

Lesson 20

COMMON CORE STANDARD CC.K.CC.3

Lesson Objective: Represent 18 and 19 objects with number names and written numerals.

Count and Write 18 and 19

1

18

eighteen

2

3

4

+

=

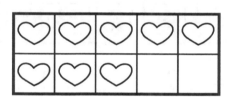

DIRECTIONS 1. Count and tell how many. Draw a dot on each object as you count. Trace the number. 2. Look at the objects in the top ten frame in Exercise 1. Count and write the number. 3. Look at the objects in the bottom ten frame in Exercise 1. Count and write the number. 4. Look at the ten frames in Exercise 1. Complete the addition sentence to match.

Name ______________________________

Lesson 20
CC.K.CC.3

1

9 ○   14 ○   18 ○   19 ○

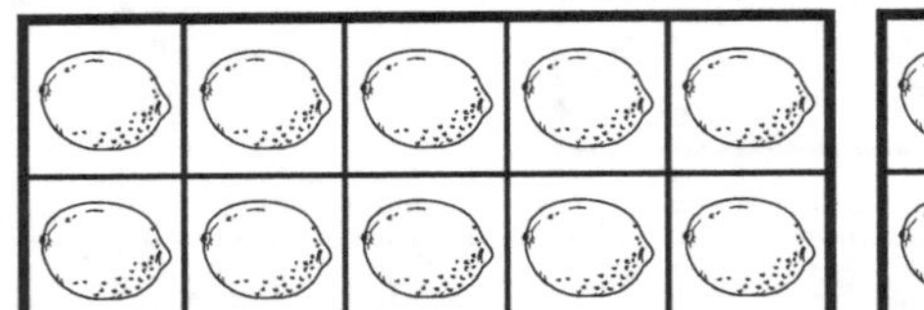 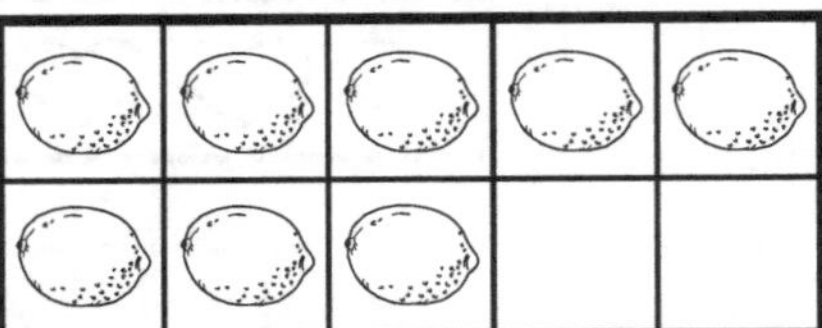

8 ○   13 ○   18 ○   19 ○

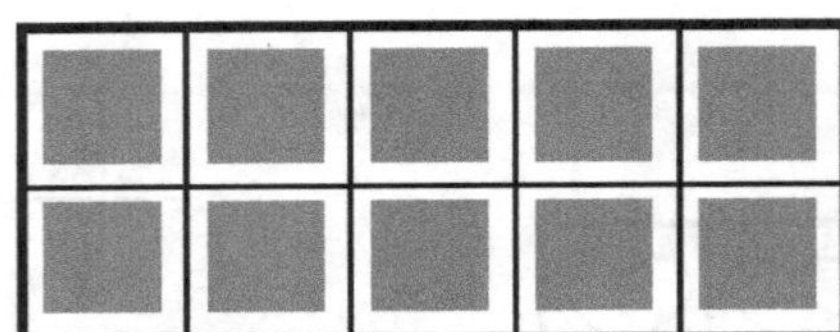 

○ $10 + 9 = 19$ ○ $10 + 8 = 18$

○ $10 + 5 = 15$ ○ $10 + 4 = 14$

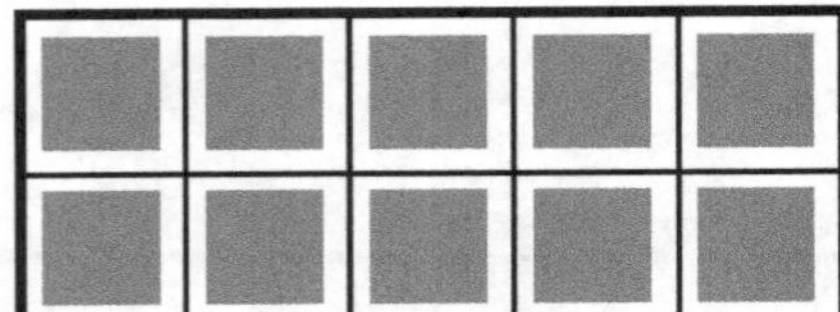 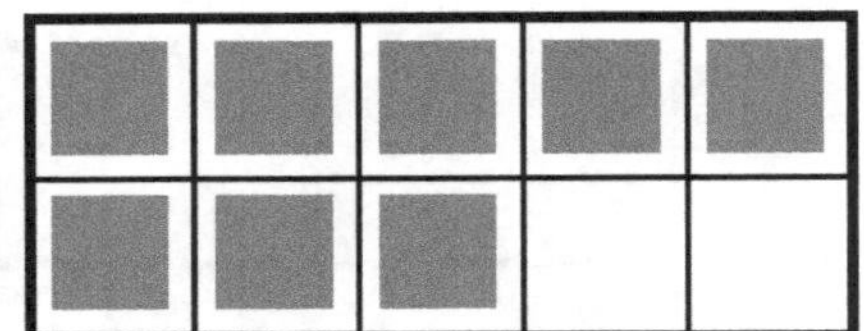

______

DIRECTIONS **1–2.** Mark under the number that tells how many. **3.** Look at the ten frames. Mark next to the addition sentence that matches. **4.** Write the number that tells how many.

Name ______________________________

Lesson 21

COMMON CORE STANDARD CC.K.CC.3

Lesson Objective: Represent 20 objects with a number name and a written numeral.

Count and Write 20

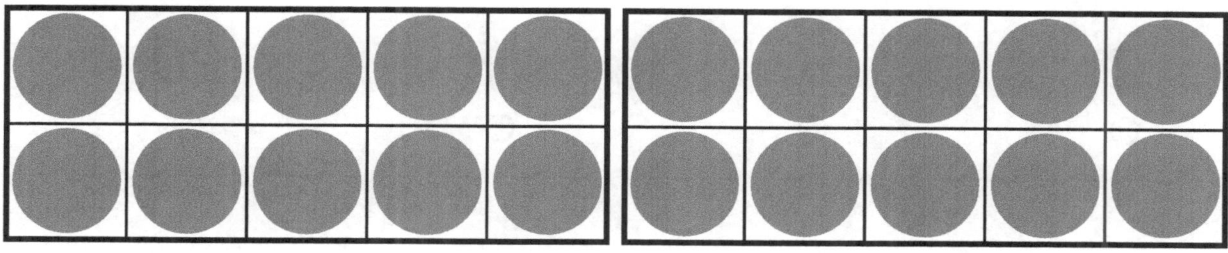

20
twenty

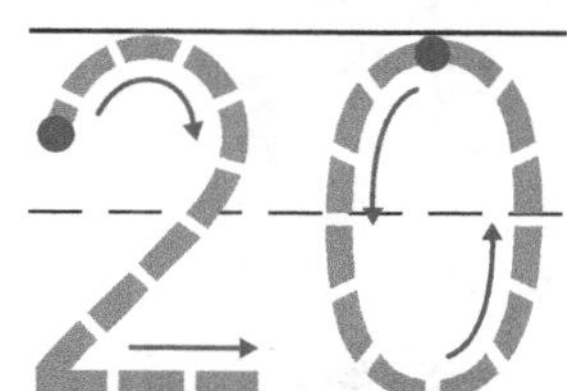
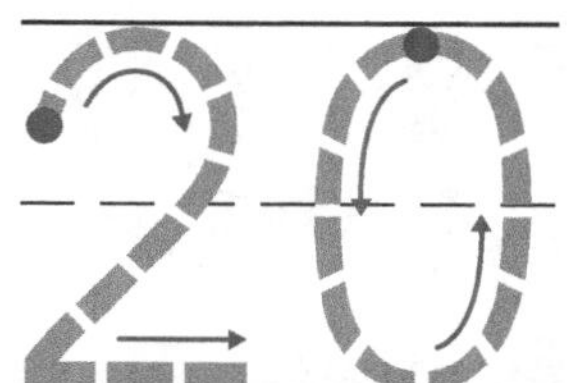
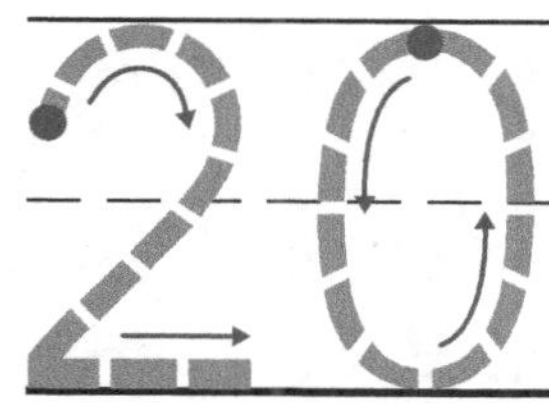

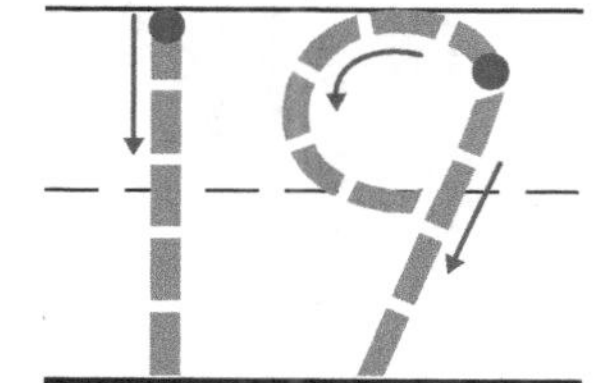

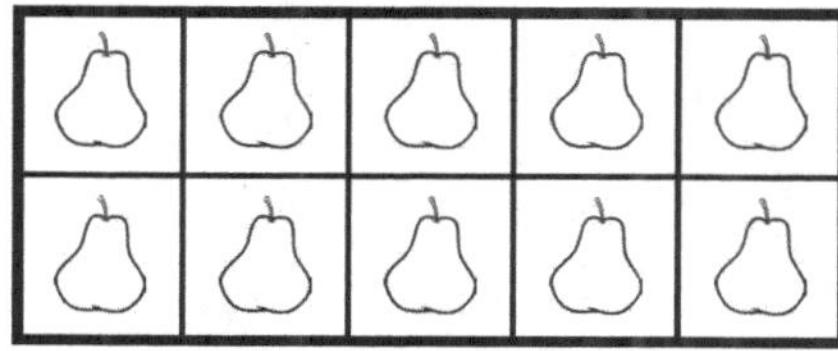
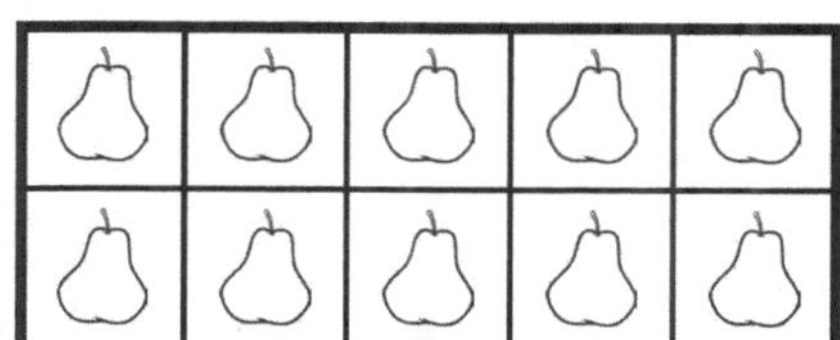
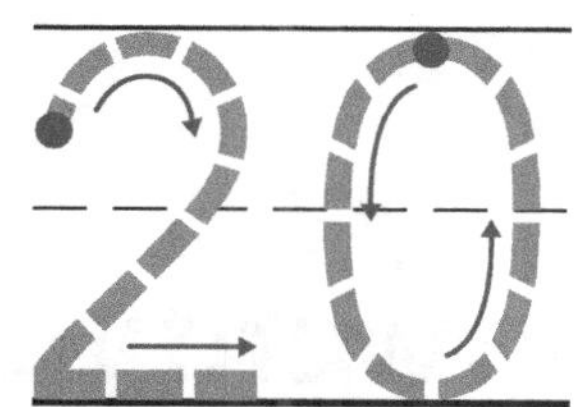

DIRECTIONS **1.** Count and tell how many counters. Draw a dot on each counter as you count them. Trace the numbers as you say them. **2–3.** Count and tell how many pieces of fruit. Touch each fruit as you count. Trace the number.

Name ______________________________

Lesson 21
CC.K.CC.3

2 ○ 10 ○ 18 ○ 20 ○

2

○

○

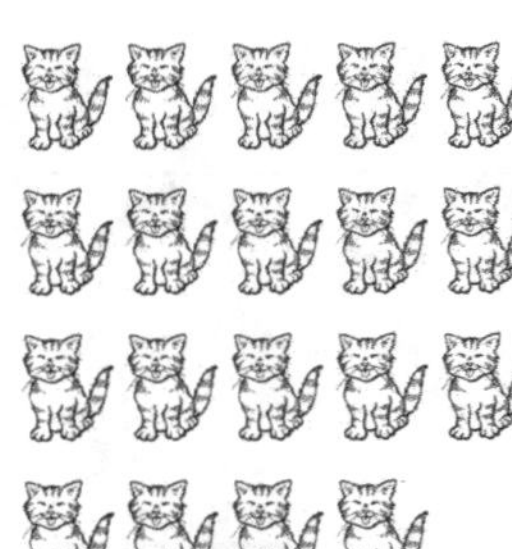
○

○

○

○

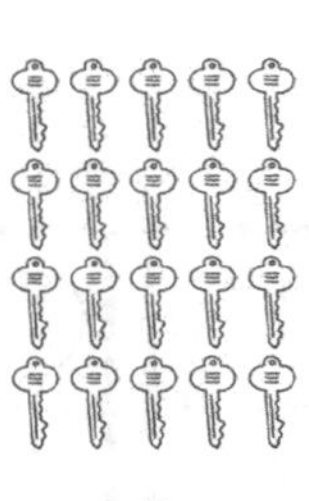
○

○

____

_ _ _ _ _ _ _ _ _ _

twenty ______________

DIRECTIONS **1.** Count the shoes. Mark under the number that tells how many. **2.** Which set shows 20 cats? Mark under that set. **3.** Which set has one less key than 20? Mark under that set. **4.** Write the number 20. Then draw 20 Ts.

Name ____________________

Lesson 22

COMMON CORE STANDARD CC.K.CC.4a

Lesson Objective: Model and count 1 and 2 with objects.

Model and Count 1 and 2

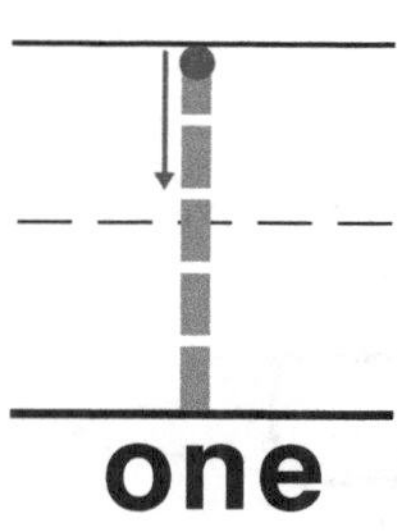

one

two

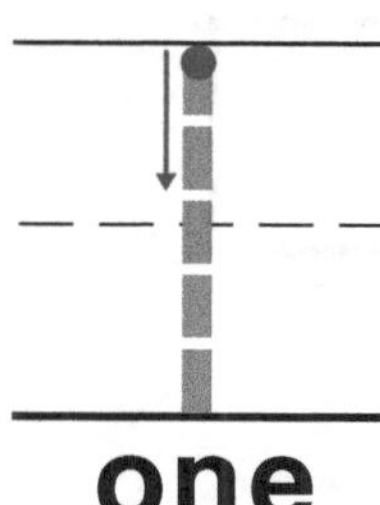

one

DIRECTIONS Draw a dot on each toy as you count. Use cubes to show the number of objects. **1.** Say the number. Trace the number and the cube. **2–3.** Say the number. Trace the number. Draw the cubes.

Name ____________________

Lesson 22
CC.K.CC.4a

1 ○ 2 ○ 3 ○ 4 ○

○ ○ 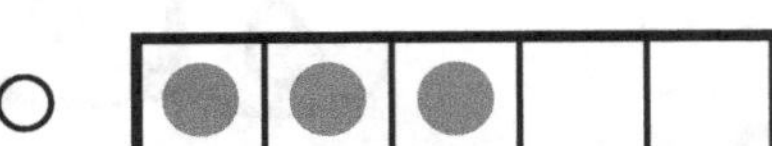

○ ○ 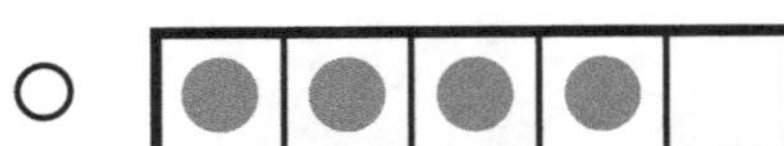

1 ○ 2 ○ 3 ○ 4 ○

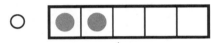

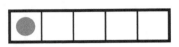

two

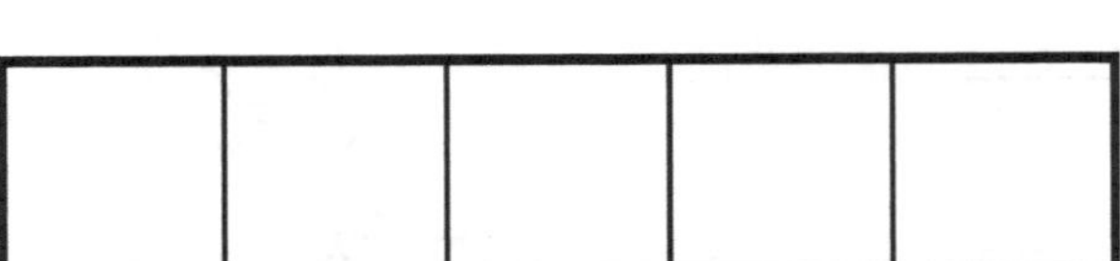

DIRECTIONS **1.** Mark under the number that shows how many counters are in the five frame. **2.** Mark next to the five frame that shows two counters. **3.** Mark under the number that shows how many apples. **4.** Say the number. Draw that many counters in the five frame.

Name ________________________________

Lesson 23

COMMON CORE STANDARD CC.K.CC.4a

Lesson Objective: Model and count 3 and 4 with objects.

Model and Count 3 and 4

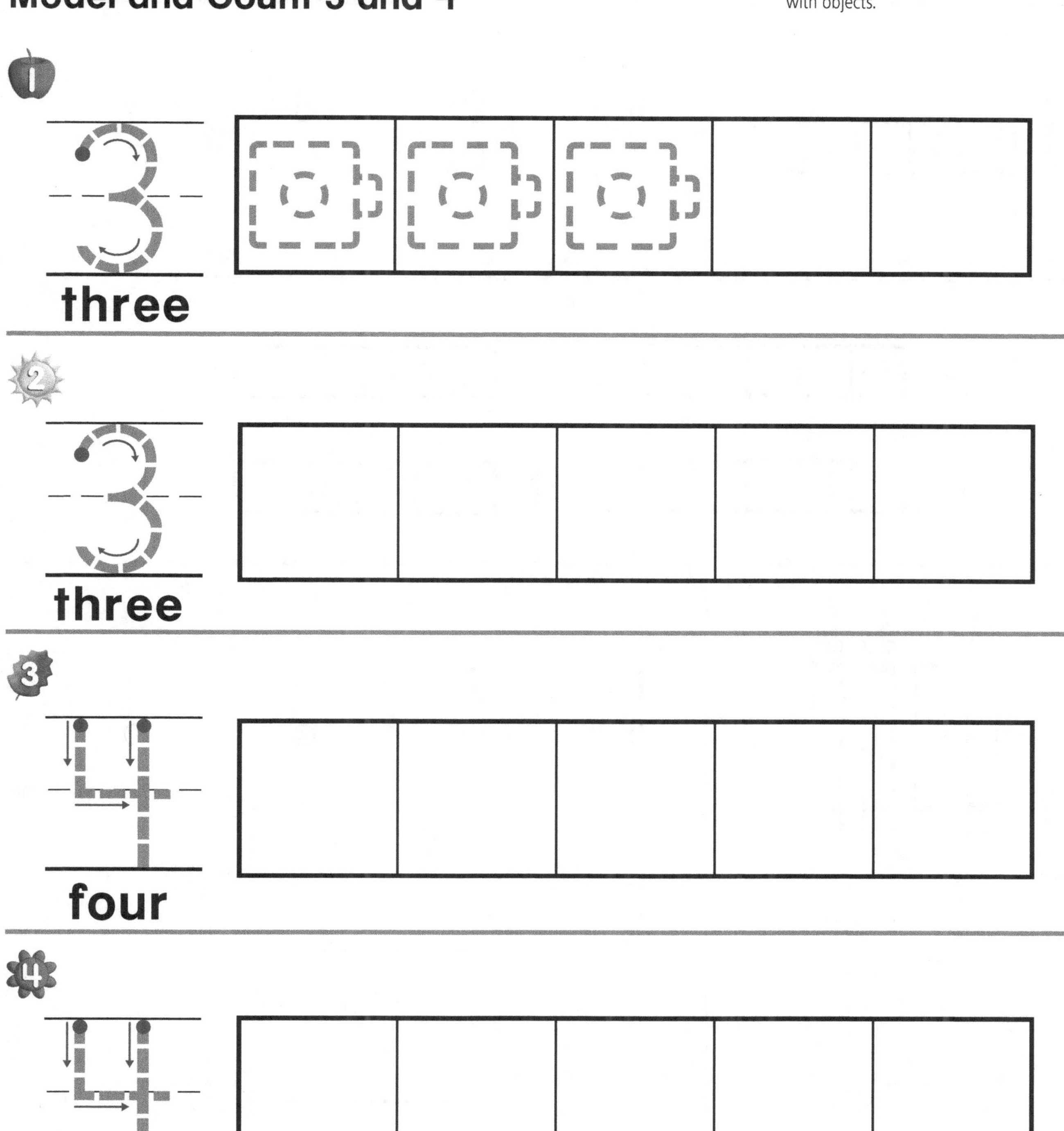

DIRECTIONS **1.** Say the number as you trace it. Count out that many cubes in the five frame. Trace the cubes. **2–4.** Say the number as you trace it. Count that many cubes in the five frame. Draw the cubes.

Name ____________________

Lesson 23
CC.K.CC.4a

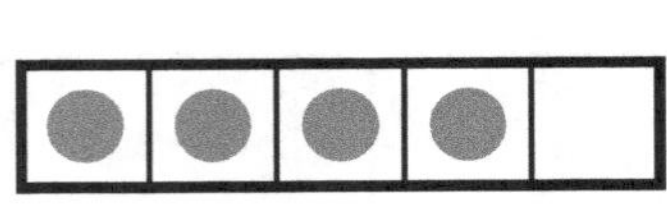

1	2	3	4
○	○	○	○

○ ○ 

○ 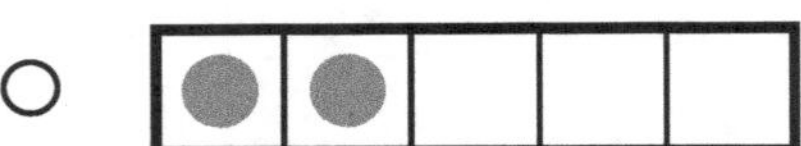 ○ 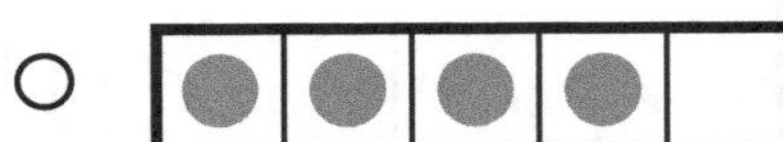

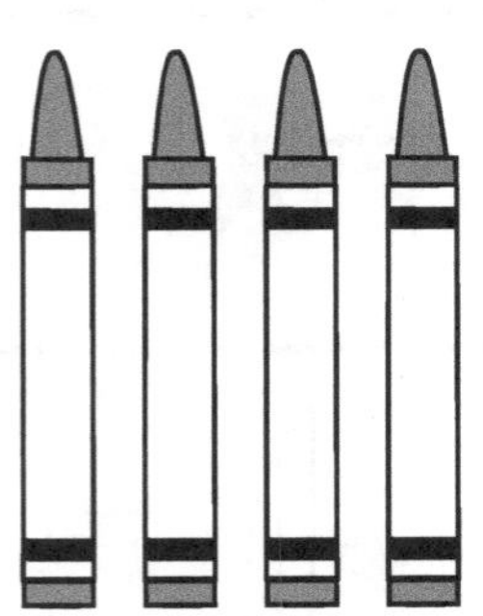

1	2	3	4
○	○	○	○

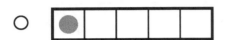

4

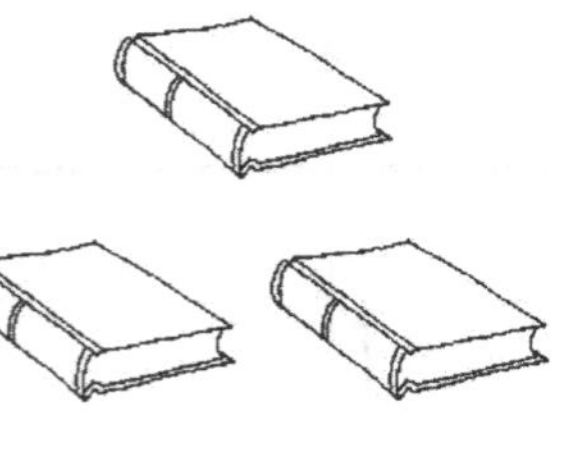

____

DIRECTIONS 1. Mark under the number that shows how many counters are in the five frame. **2.** Mark next to the five frame that shows three counters. **3.** Mark under the number that shows how many crayons. **4.** Write the number that shows how many books.

Name ______________________________

Lesson 24

COMMON CORE STANDARD CC.K.CC.4a

Lesson Objective: Model and count 5 with objects.

Model and Count 5

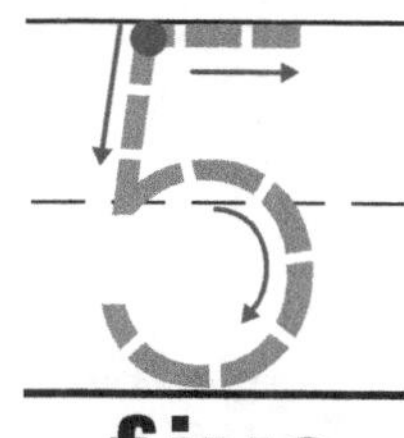

five

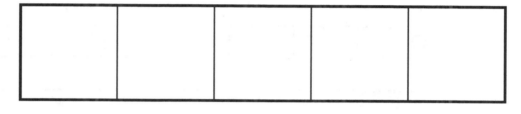

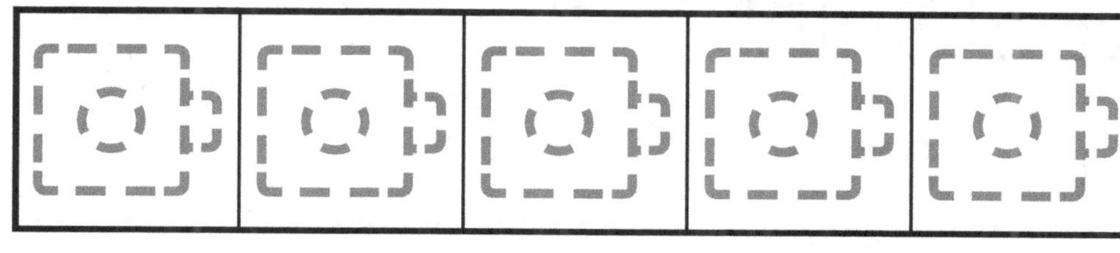

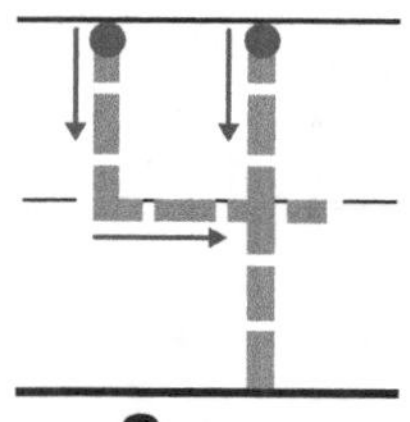

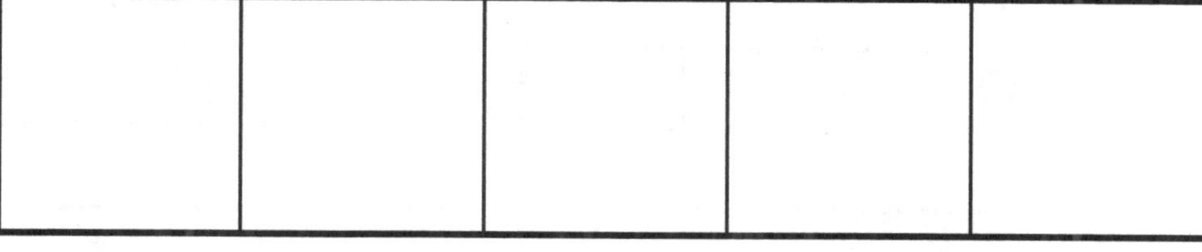

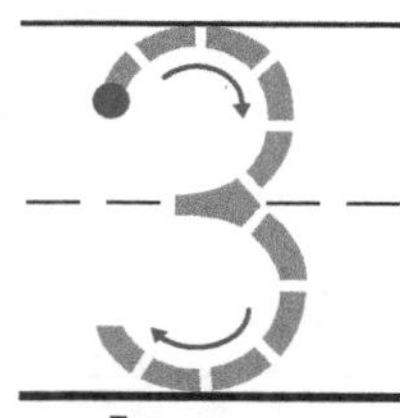

three

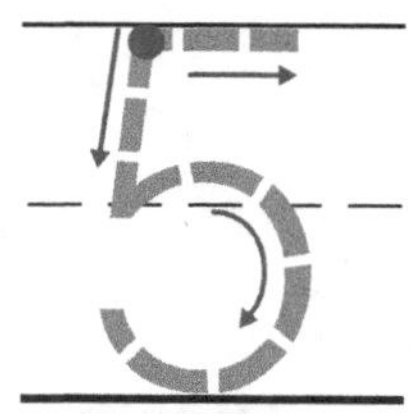

five

DIRECTIONS **1.** Say the number as you trace it. Place cubes to show the number. Trace the cubes. **2–4.** Say the number as you trace it. Place cubes to show the number. Draw the cubes.

Name ______________________

Lesson 24
CC.K.CC.4a

2 3 4 5

○ ○ ○ ○

○ 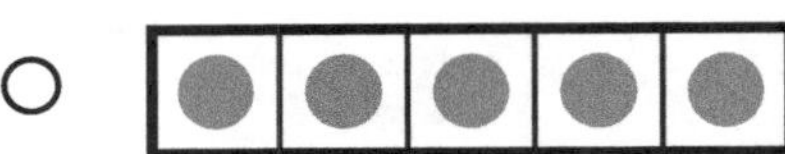

○ 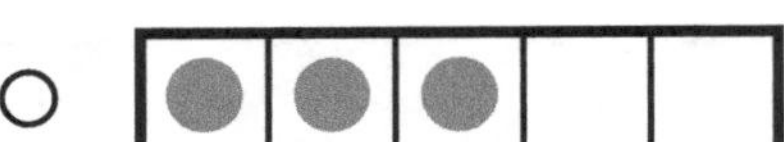

○ 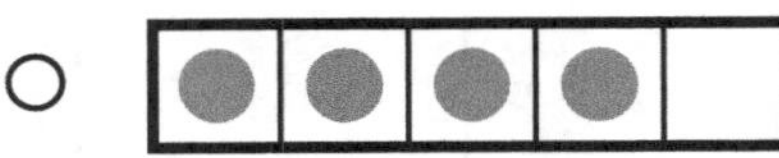

○ 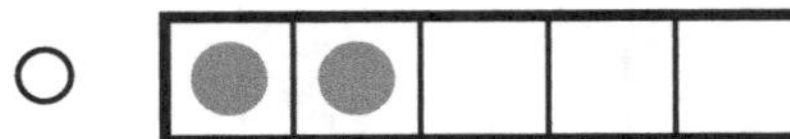

2 3 4 5

○ ○ ○ ○

4

______

DIRECTIONS 1. Mark under the number that shows how many counters are in the five frame. **2.** Mark next to the five frame that shows five counters. **3.** Mark under the number that shows how many baseballs. **4.** Write the number that shows how many soccer balls.

Name ________________________________

Lesson 25

COMMON CORE STANDARD CC.K.CC.4b

Lesson Objective: Represent 5 objects with a number name and a written numeral.

Count and Write 5

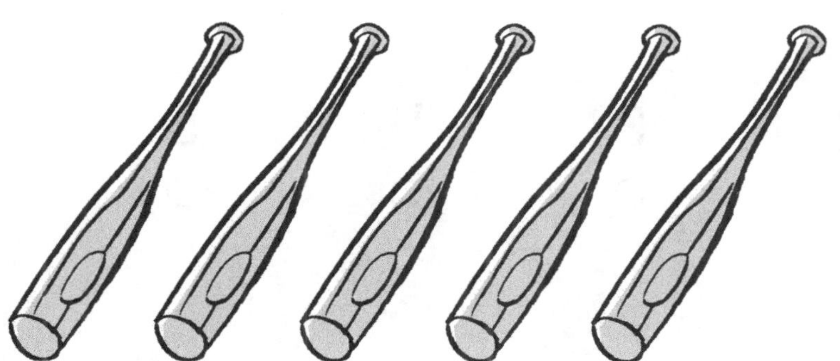

five

DIRECTIONS 1. Draw a dot on each baseball bat as you count. Tell how many. Trace the number. Draw one baseball above each bat to show a set of 5 baseballs. **2.** Circle the sets of 5 objects.

Name ____________________

Lesson 25
CC.K.CC.4b

5

 ○  ○  ○ 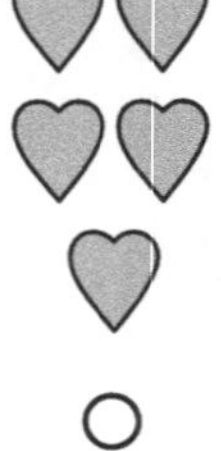 ○

five

2 ○ 3 ○ 4 ○ 5 ○

5 ○ 4 ○ 3 ○ 2 ○

DIRECTIONS 1. Mark under the set of hearts that shows the number at the beginning of the row. **2.** Mark under the number that matches the word at the beginning of the row. **3.** Mark under the number that shows how many shells. **4.** Trace the word for the number that shows how many stars.

Name ______________________________

Lesson 26

COMMON CORE STANDARD CC.K.CC.4c

Lesson Objective: Know that each successive number refers to a quantity that is one larger.

Count and Order to 5

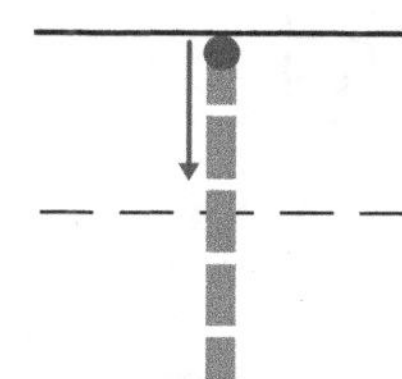

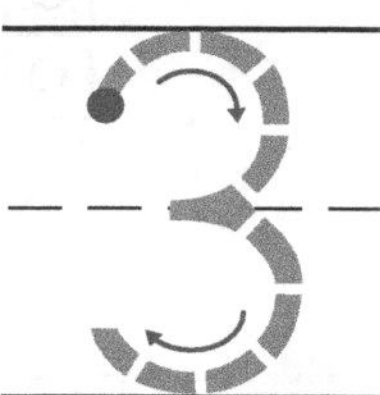
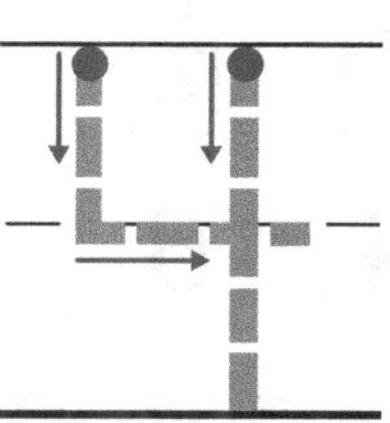
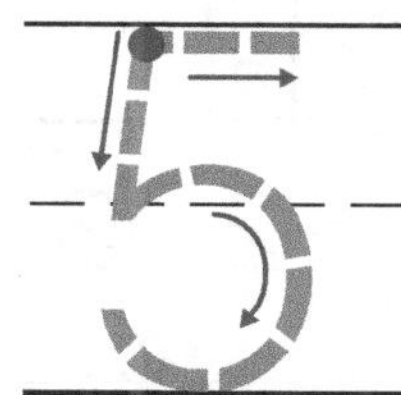

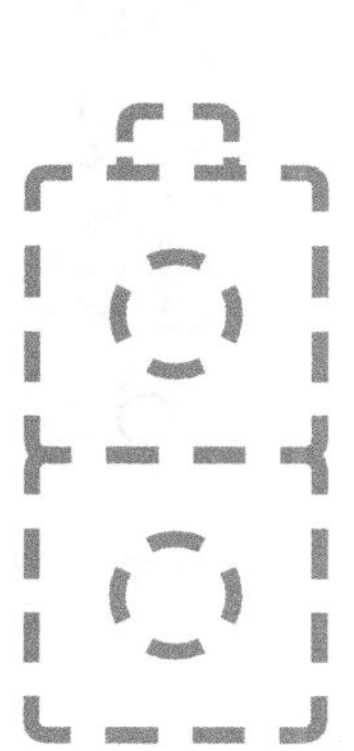
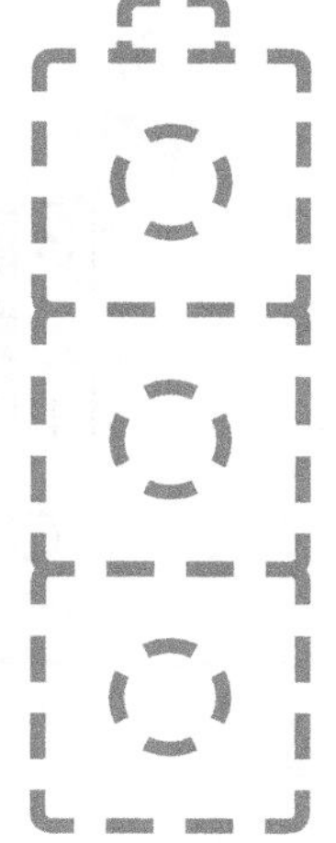
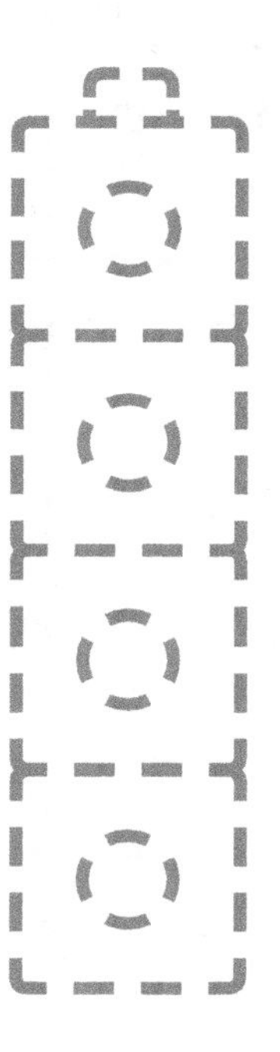
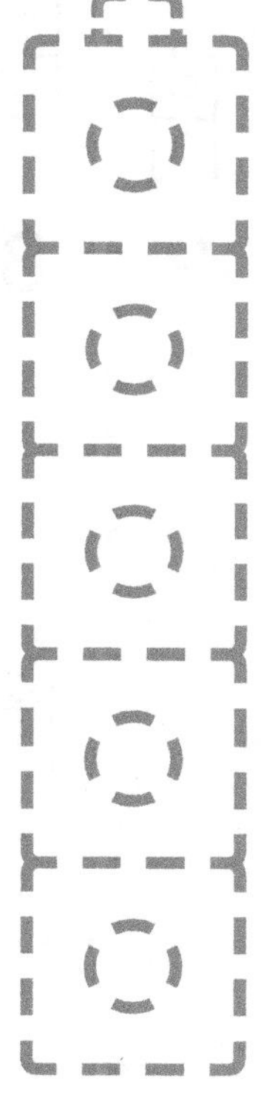

DIRECTIONS **1.** Trace the numbers. Make a cube tower to show each number. **2.** Place the cube towers in order. Trace the cube towers. Write the number of cubes for each tower.

Name ______________________________

Lesson 26
CC.K.CC.4c

1

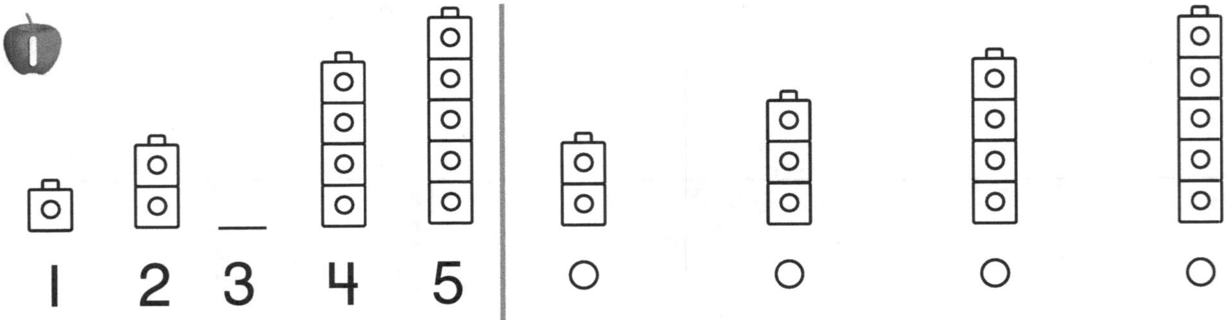

1 2 3 4 5

○ ○ ○ ○

2

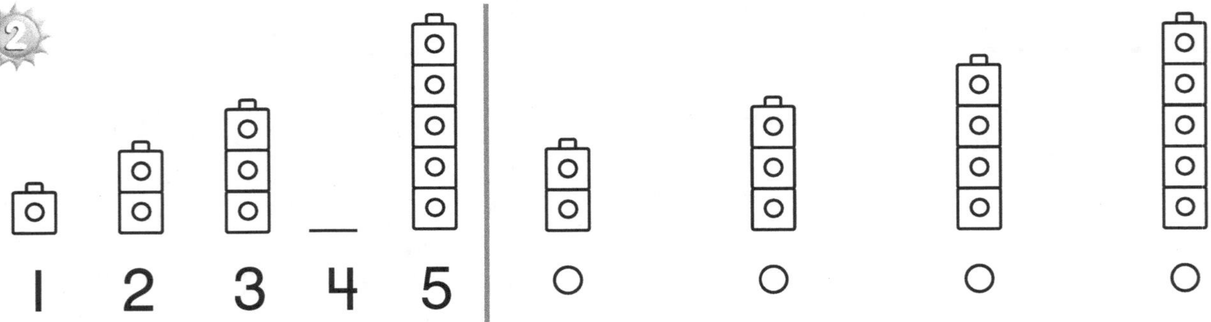

1 2 3 4 5

○ ○ ○ ○

3

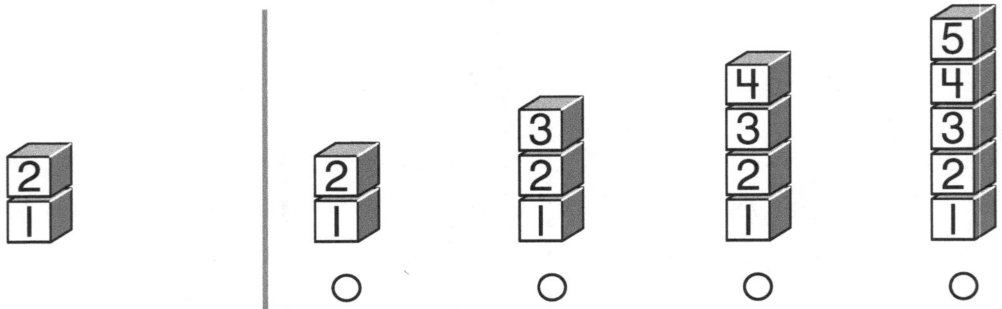

○ ○ ○ ○

4

DIRECTIONS 1–2. The cube towers are in order from 1 to 5. Mark under the missing cube tower. 3. Mark under the set of blocks that is one larger than the set of 2 blocks at the beginning of the row. 4. Draw the set of blocks that is one larger than the set of 3 blocks at the beginning of the row.

Name ______________________

Lesson 27

COMMON CORE STANDARD CC.K.CC.5

Lesson Objective: Model and count 6 with objects.

Model and Count 6

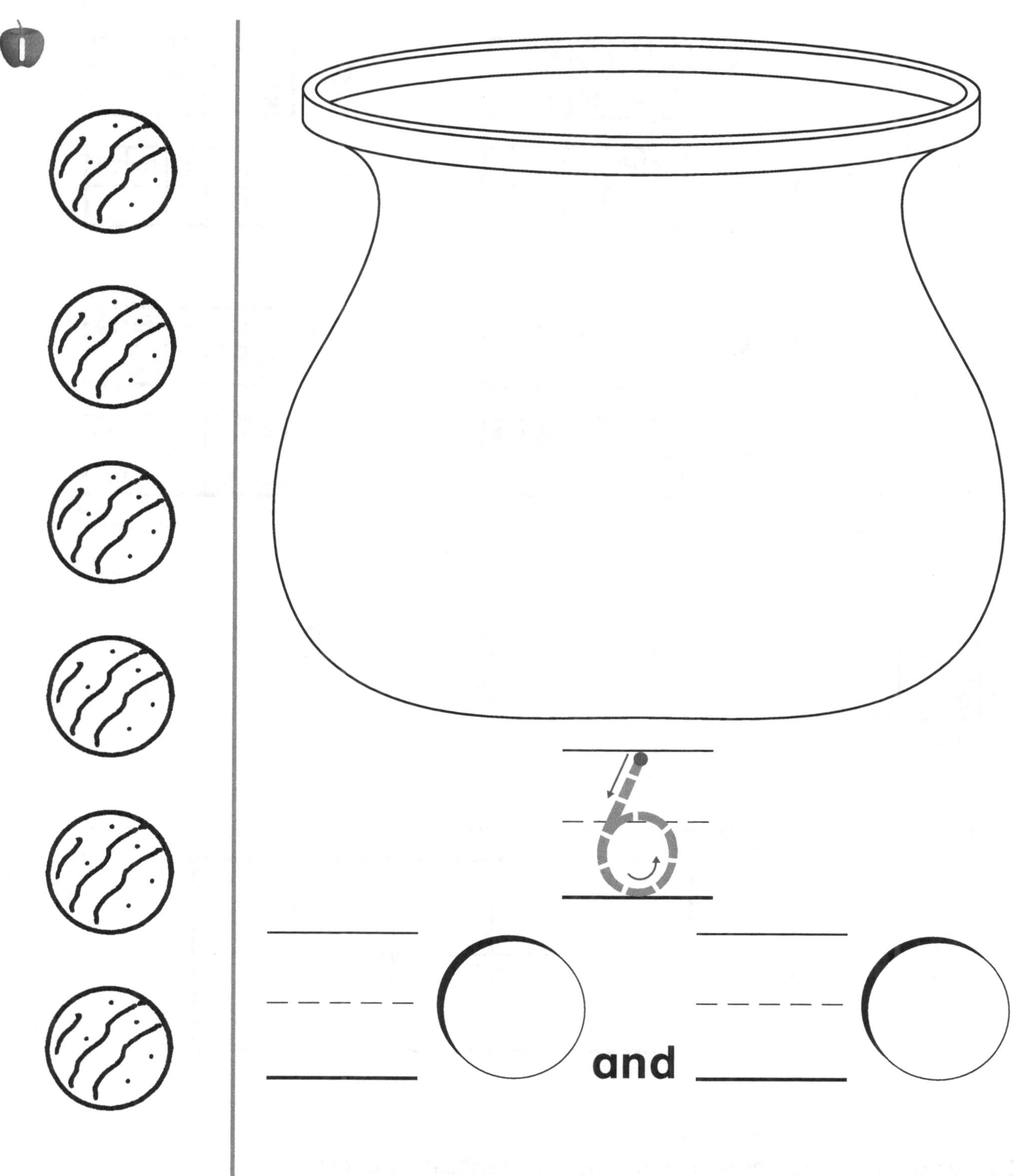

DIRECTIONS 1. Place a red counter on each marble. Move the counters to the basket. Trace the number. Turn some of the counters over. Color to show the counters below. Write to show a pair of numbers that makes 6.

Name ________________________________

Lesson 27
CC.K.CC.5

1

6

○ ○
○ ○

2

6

○ ○
○ ○

3

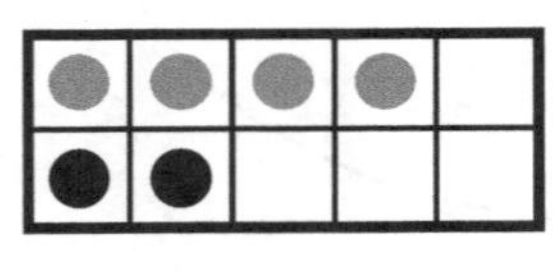

6	7	8	9
○	○	○	○

4

6

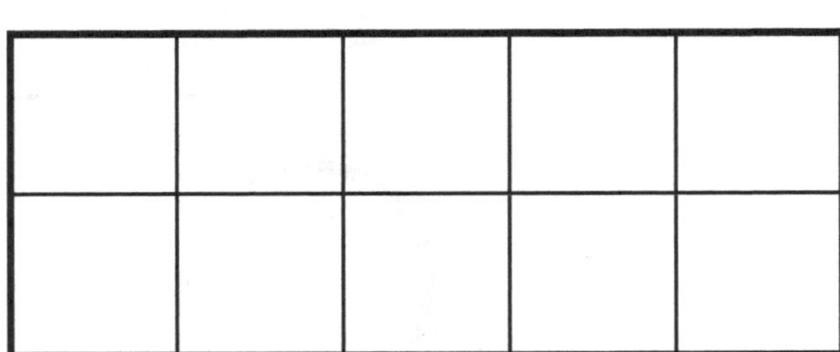

DIRECTIONS **1–2.** Mark next to the set that models the number at the beginning of the row. **3.** Mark under the number that matches the model at the beginning of the row. **4.** Use two different-color crayons to draw counters to model a way to make the number at the beginning of the row.

Name ____________________

Model and Count 7

Lesson 28

COMMON CORE STANDARD CC.K.CC.5

Lesson Objective: Model and count 7 with objects.

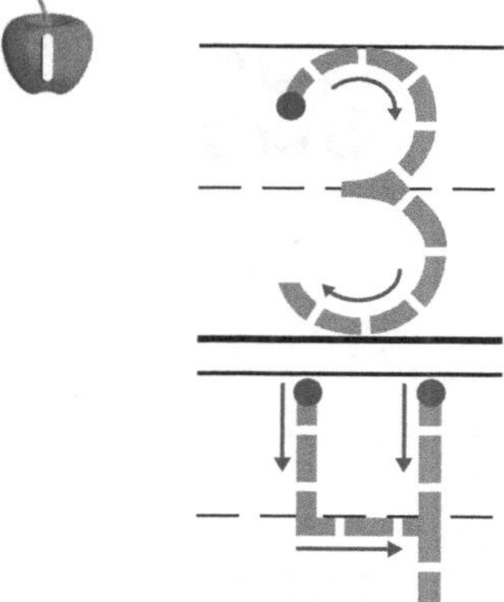

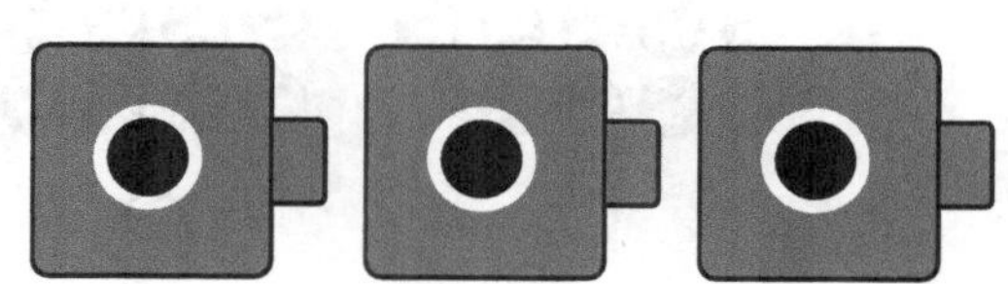

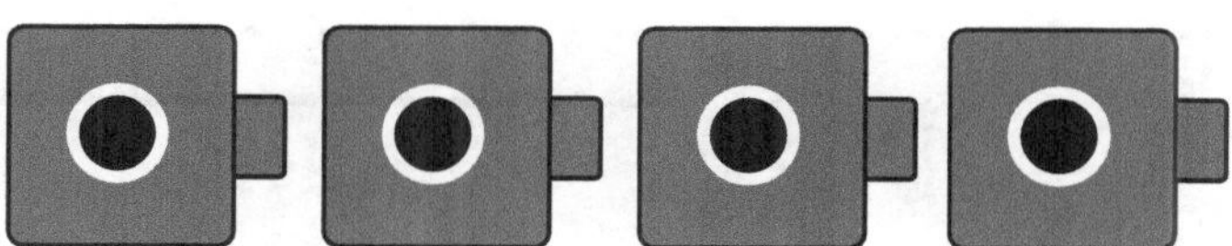

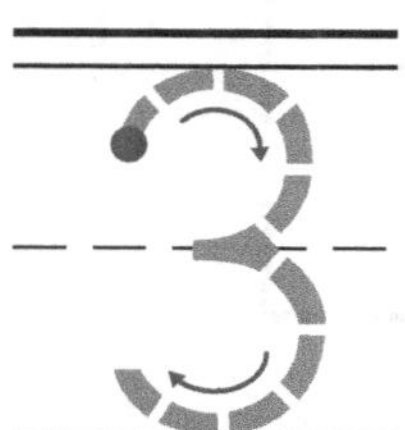

DIRECTIONS **1.** Draw a dot on each cube as you count. Trace the number. Place more cubes below to make 7. Trace the cubes. Trace the number. **2–3.** Draw a dot on each cube as you count. Write the number. Place more cubes below to make 7. Draw the cubes. Trace the number.

Name ______________________________

Lesson 28
CC.K.CC.5

1

7

○ ○ ○ ○

2

7

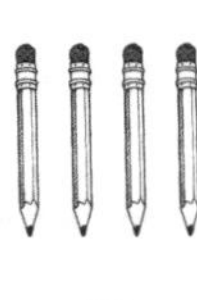

○ ○ ○ ○

3

7

○ 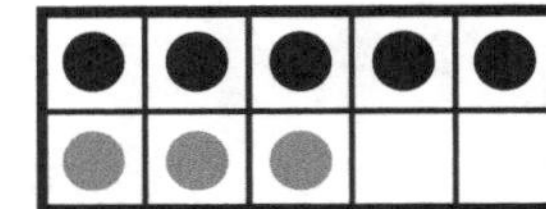 ○ 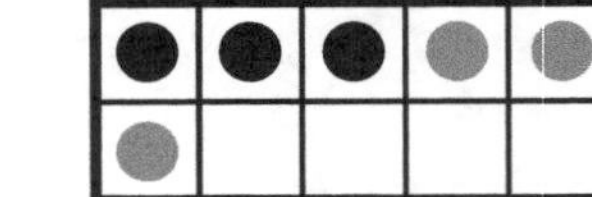

○ 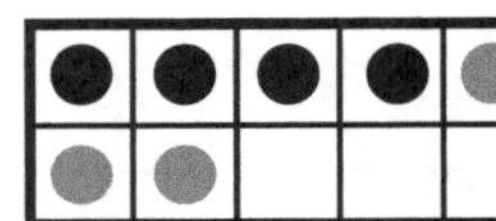 ○ 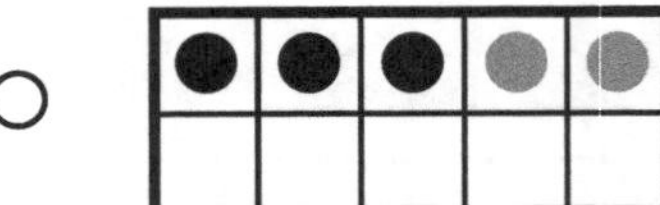

4

7

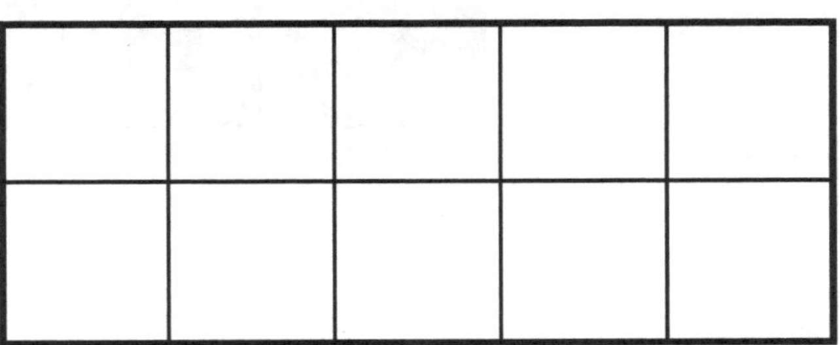

DIRECTIONS **1–2.** Mark under the set that models the number at the beginning of the row. **3.** Mark next to the set that models the number at the beginning of the row. **4.** Use two different-color crayons to draw counters to model a way to make the number at the beginning of the row.

Name ______________________

Lesson 29

COMMON CORE STANDARD CC.K.CC.5

Lesson Objective: Model and count 8 with objects.

Model and Count 8

1

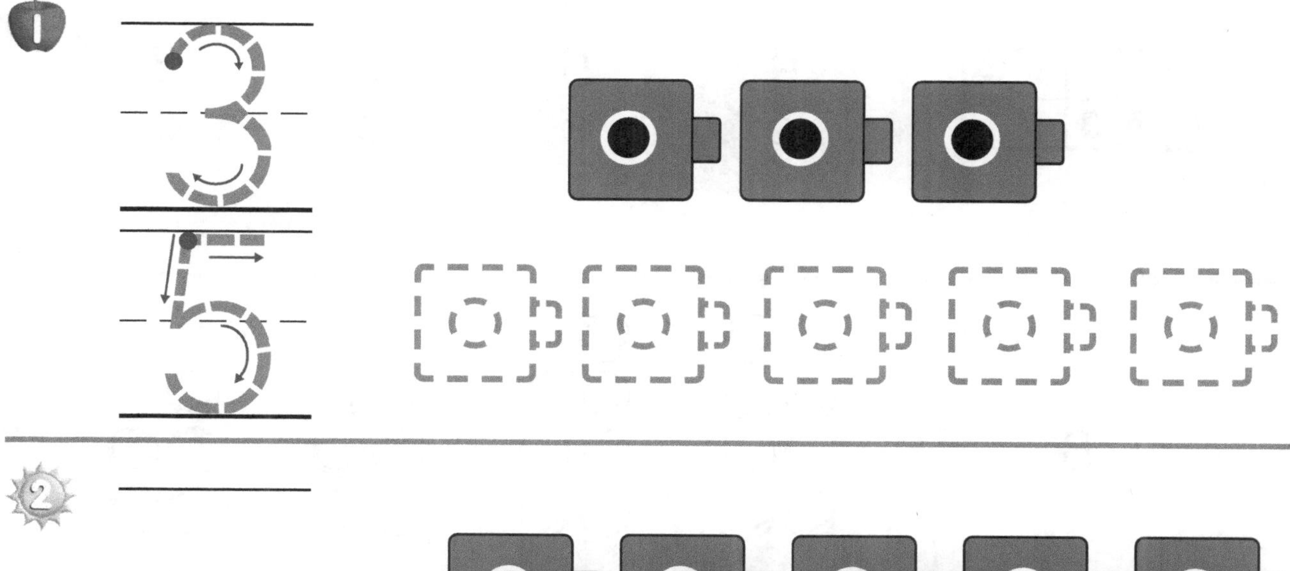

2

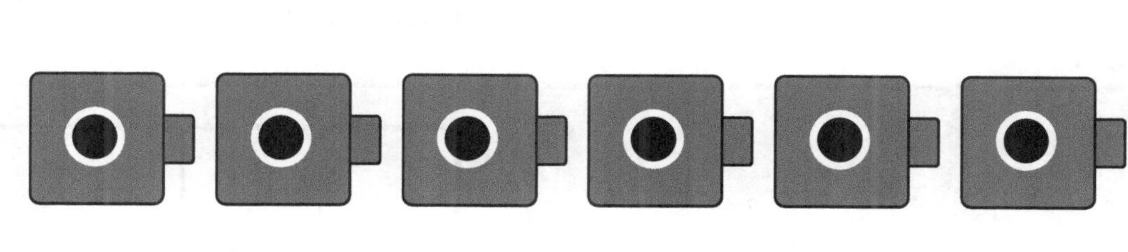

3

DIRECTIONS 1. Draw a dot on each cube as you count. Trace the number. Place more cubes below to make 8. Trace the cubes. Trace the number. **2–3.** Draw a dot on each cube as you count. Write the number. Place more cubes below to make 8. Draw the cubes. Trace the number.

Name ______________________________

Lesson 29
CC.K.CC.5

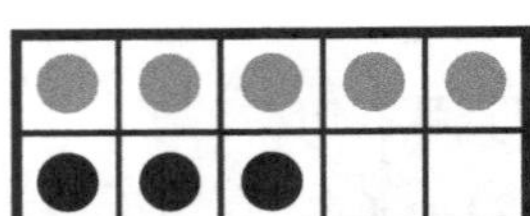

4 ○ 5 ○ 7 ○ 8 ○

2

8

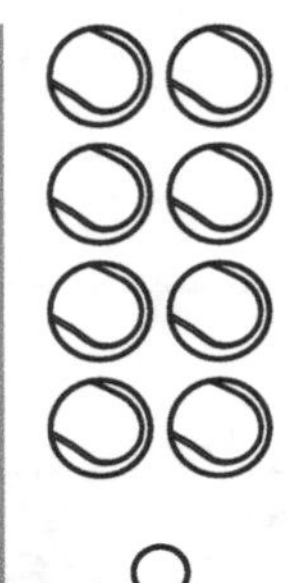

○ ○ ○ ○

8

○ 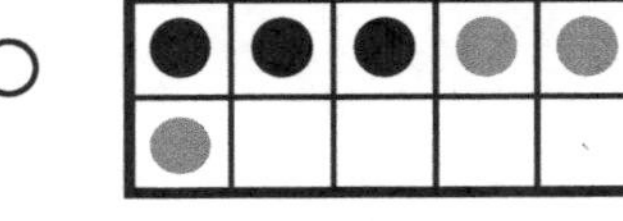 ○ 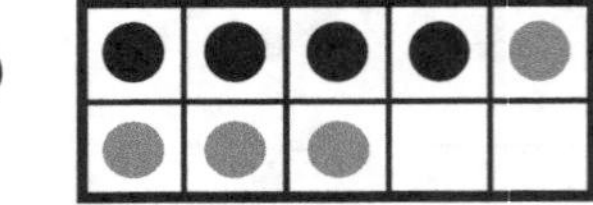

○ 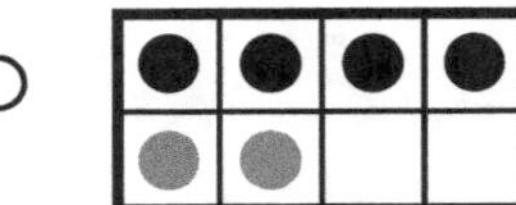 ○ 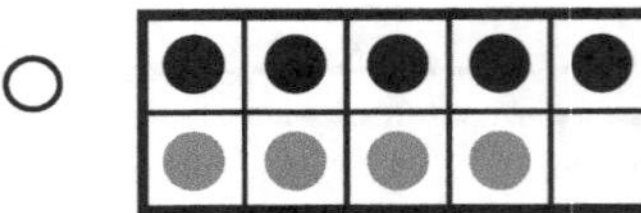

4

8

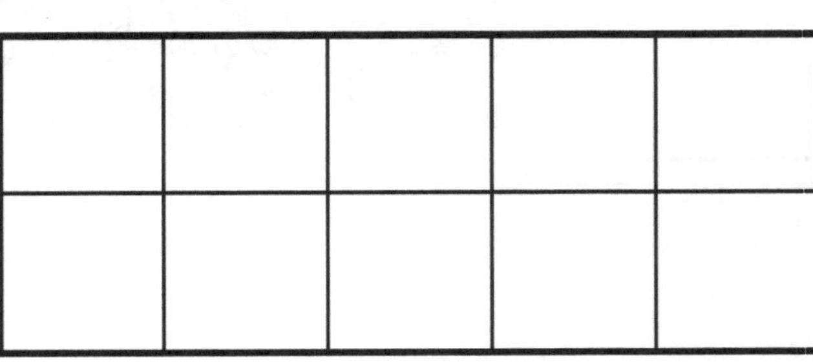

DIRECTIONS 1. Mark under the number that matches the model at the beginning of the row. 2. Mark under the set that models the number at the beginning of the row. 3. Mark next to the set that models the number at the beginning of the row. 4. Use two different-color crayons to draw counters to model a way to make the number at the beginning of the row.

Name ___________________________

Lesson 30

COMMON CORE STANDARD CC.K.CC.5

Lesson Objective: Model and count 9 with objects.

Model and Count 9

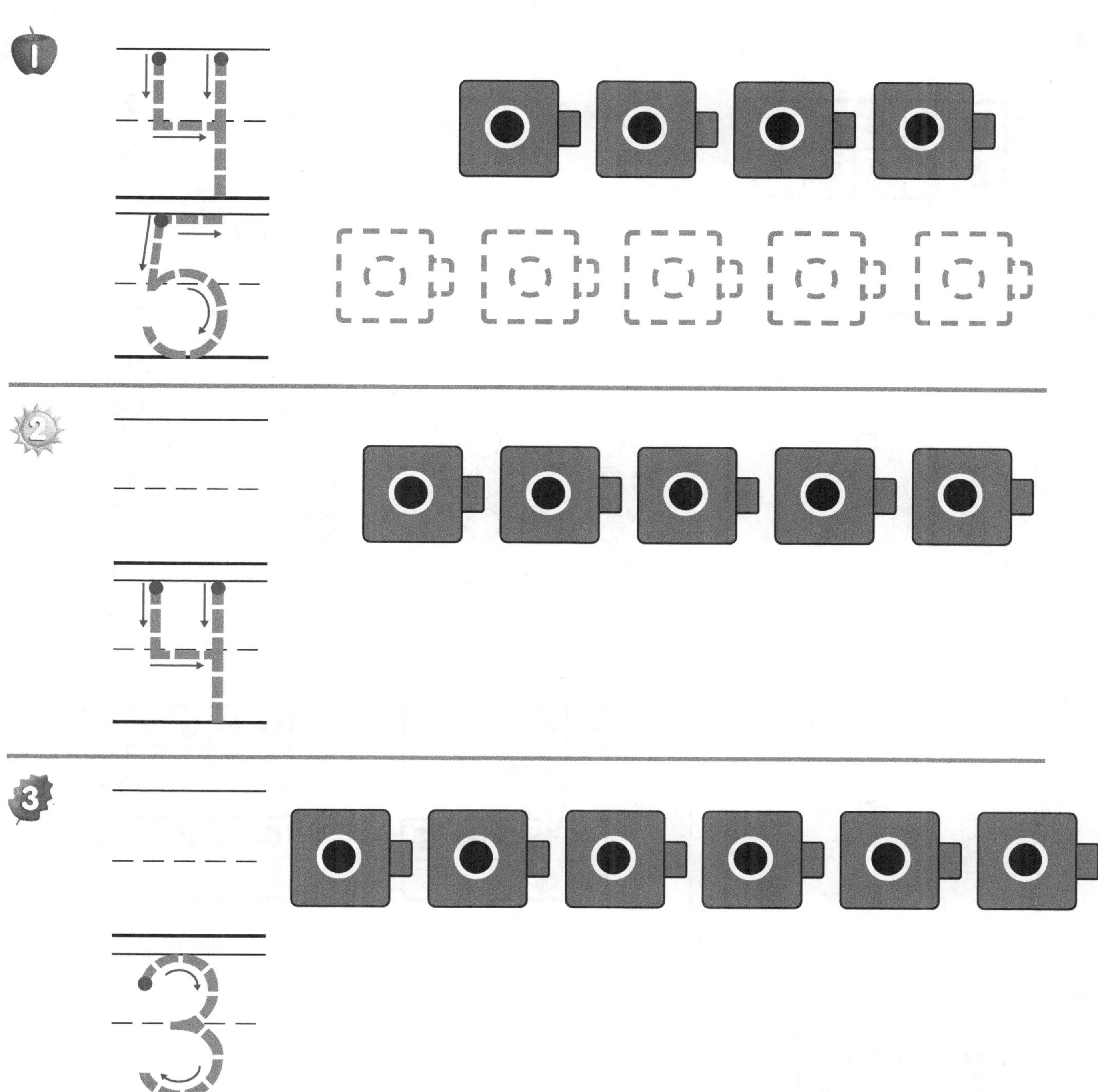

DIRECTIONS **1.** Draw a dot on each cube as you count. Trace the number. Place more cubes below to make 9. Trace the cubes. Trace the number. **2–3.** Draw a dot on each cube as you count. Write the number. Place more cubes below to make 9. Draw the cubes. Trace the number.

Name ______________________

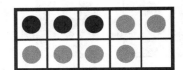

6 ○ 7 ○ 8 ○ 9 ○

2

9

○ ○ ○ ○

3

9

○ 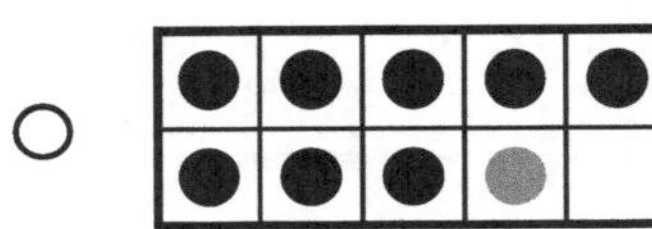 ○ 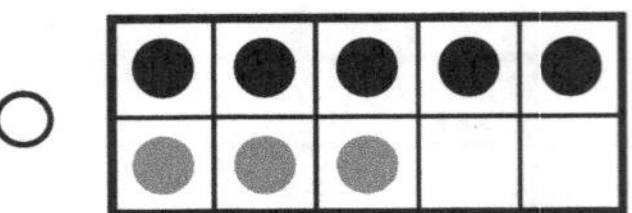

○ 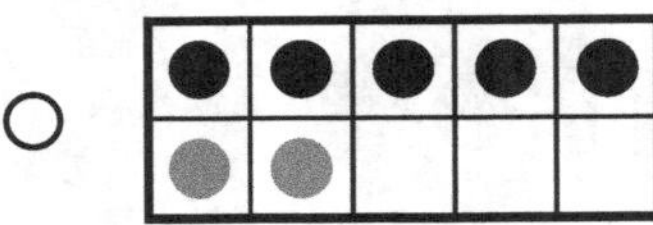 ○ 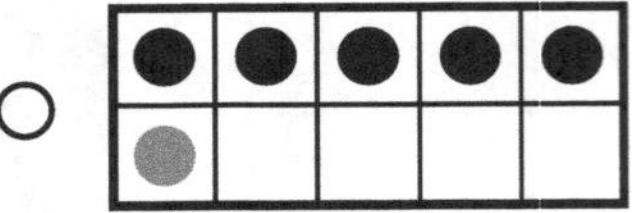

4

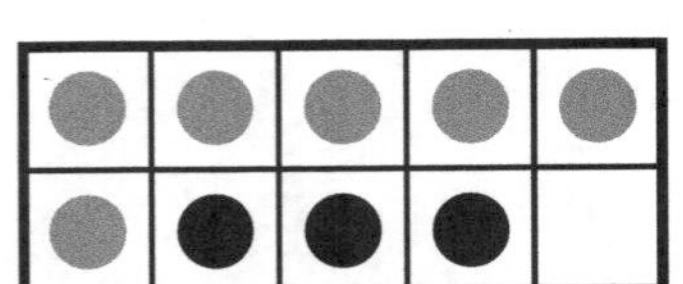

______

DIRECTIONS 1. Mark under the number that matches the model at the beginning of the row. 2. Mark under the set that models the number at the beginning of the row. 3. Mark next to the set that models the number at the beginning of the row. 4. Write the number that matches the model at the beginning of the row.

Name ______________________________

Lesson 31

COMMON CORE STANDARD CC.K.CC.5

Lesson Objective: Model and count 10 with objects.

Model and Count 10

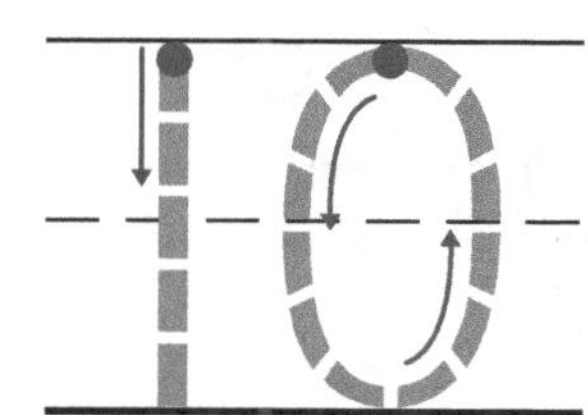

DIRECTIONS **1.** Place a cube on each plant. Trace the cubes. **2.** Move the cubes to the ten frame. Draw the cubes. Point to each cube as you count. Trace the number.

Name ______________________________

Lesson 31
CC.K.CC.5

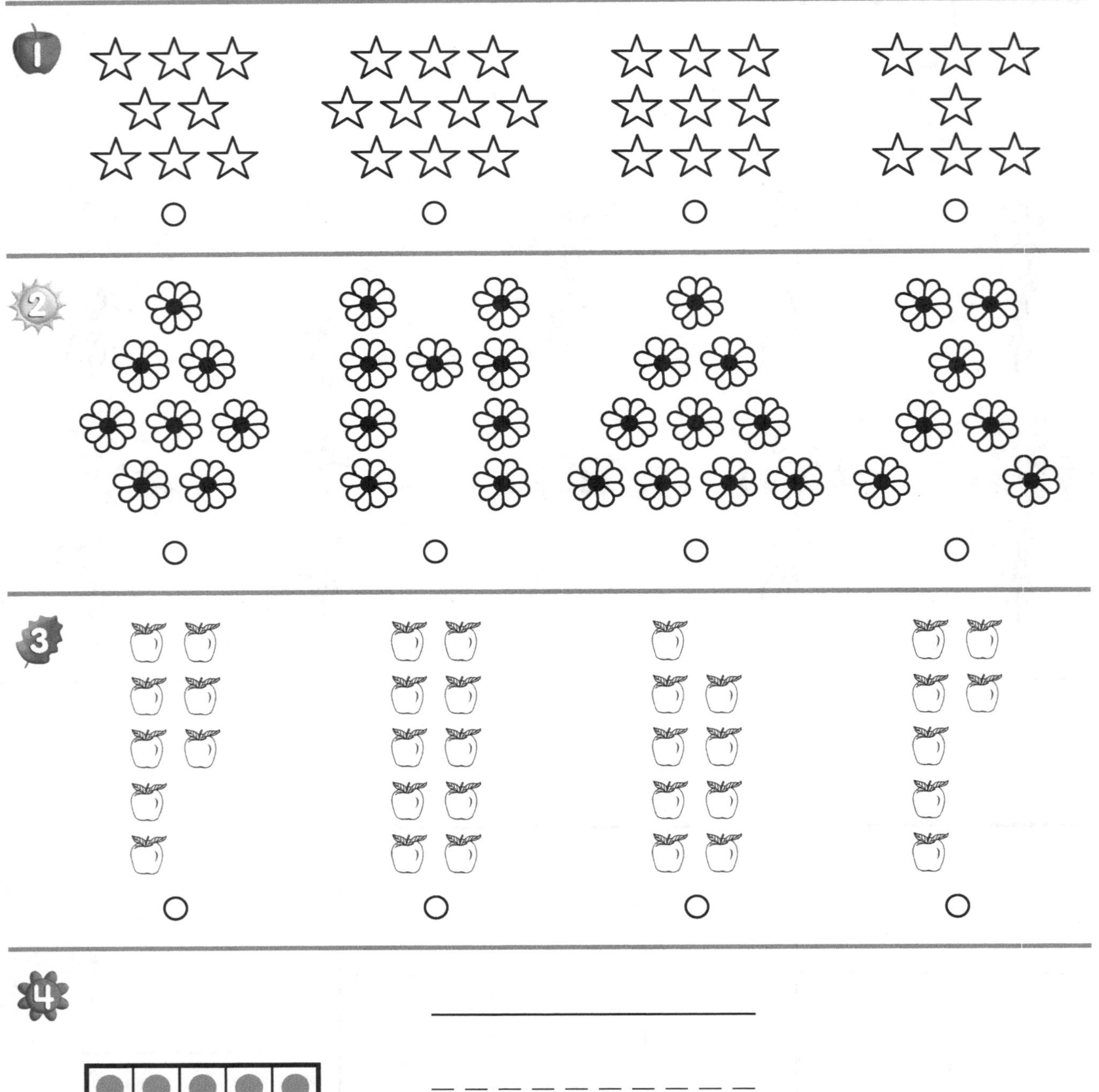

DIRECTIONS 1. Count how many stars are in each set. Mark under the set that shows ten stars. 2. Count how many flowers are in each set. Mark under the set that shows ten flowers. 3. Count how many apples are in each set. Mark under the set that shows ten apples. 4. Count how many counters are in the ten frame. Write the number.

Name ______________________________

Lesson 32

COMMON CORE STANDARD CC.K.CC.5

Lesson Objective: Model and count 20 with objects.

Model and Count 20

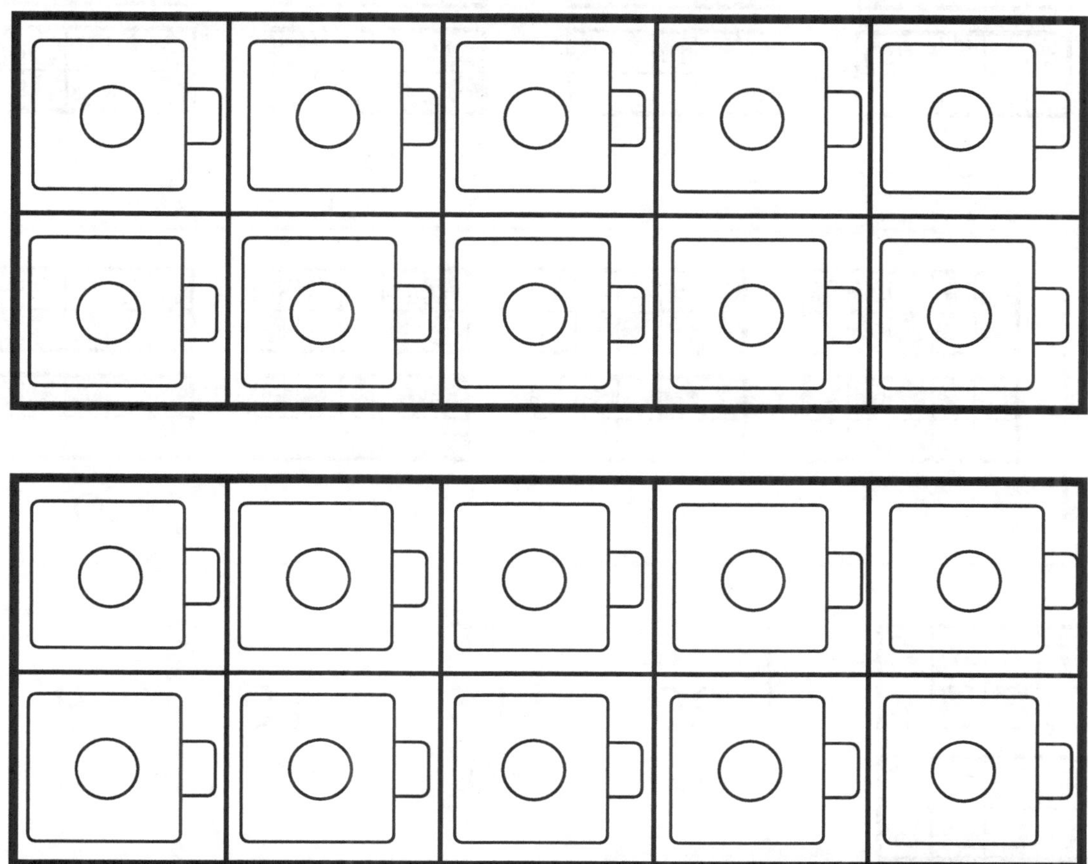

20

twenty

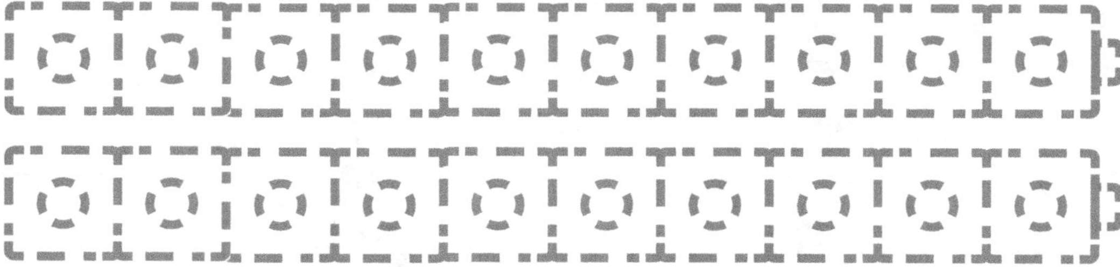

DIRECTIONS 1. Place a cube on each cube shown. Count and tell how many cubes. Touch each cube as you count. **2.** Use the cubes from Exercise 1 to model ten-cube trains. Trace the cube trains shown. Count and tell how many cubes. Touch each cube as you count.

Name ______________________

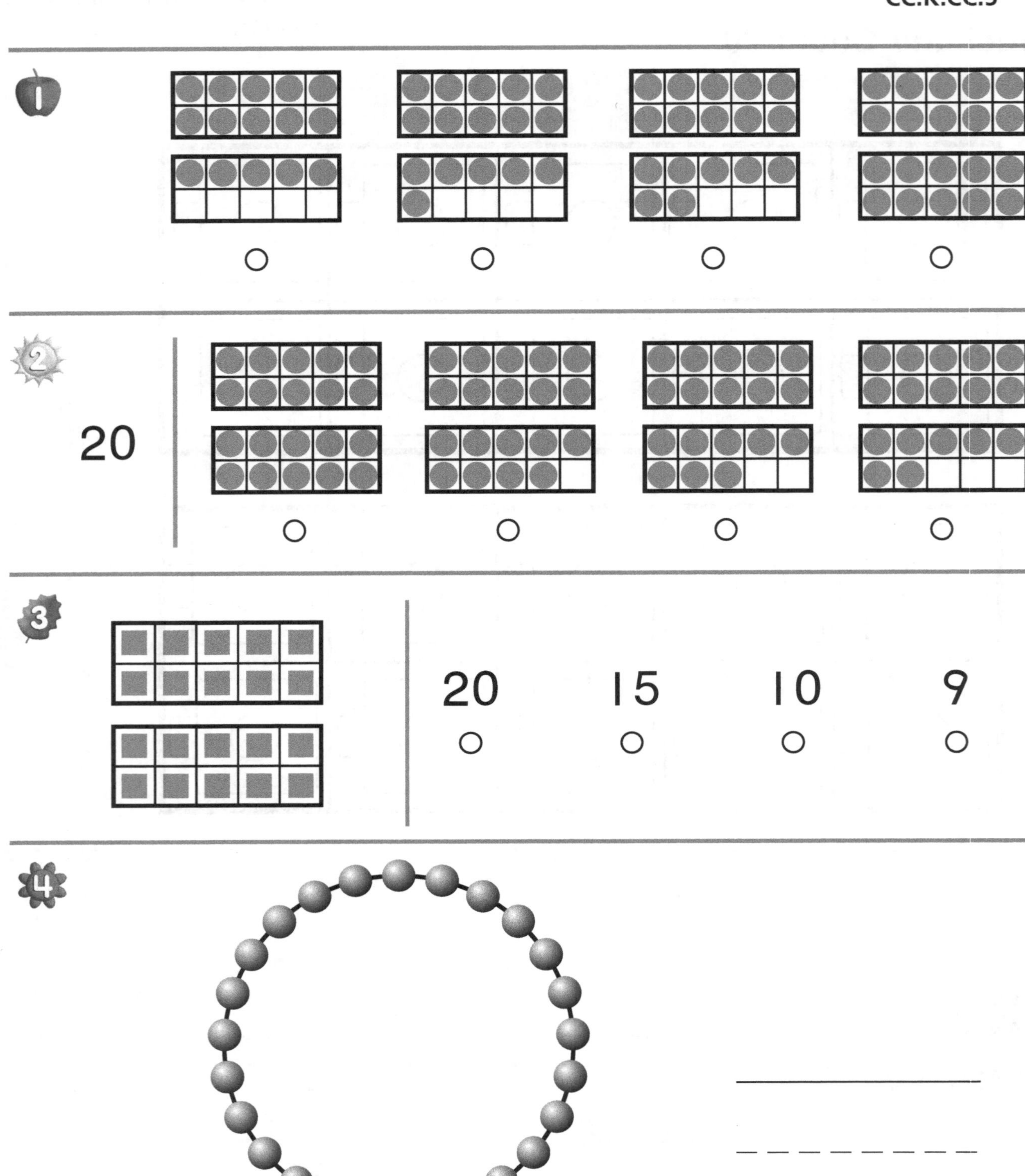

DIRECTIONS 1. Mark under the set that shows 20. 2. Which set of counters shows the number? Mark under that set. 3. Mark under the number that shows how many. 4. Draw Xs on 20 beads. Then write the number 20.

Name ___________________________

Lesson 33

COMMON CORE STANDARD CC.K.CC.6

Lesson Objective: Use matching and counting strategies to compare sets with the same number of objects.

Same Number

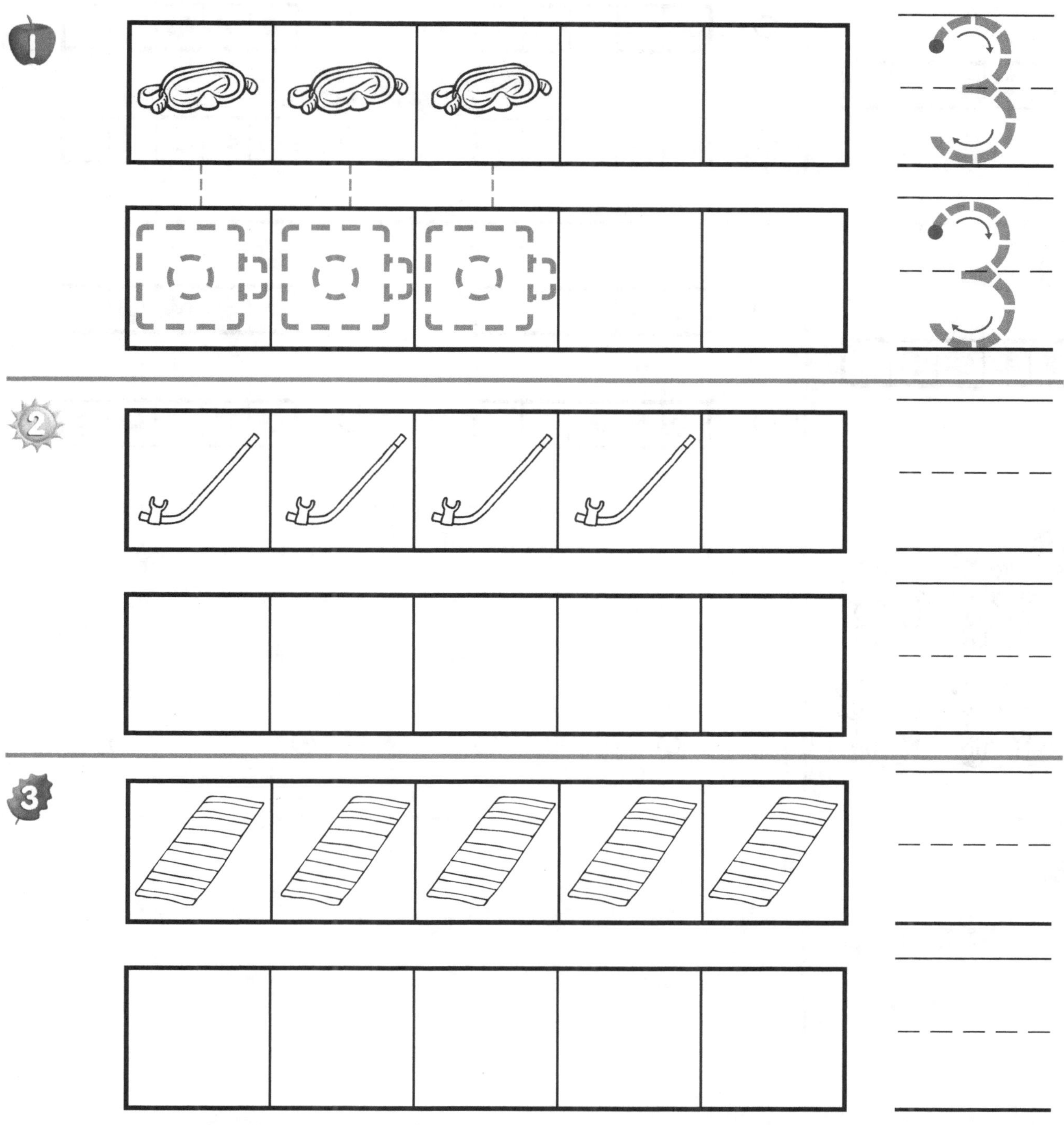

DIRECTIONS **1–3.** Place a cube below each object to show the same number of objects. Trace or draw those cubes. Trace or draw a line to match an object to a cube in each set. Count and tell how many in each set. Trace or write the numbers.

Name ______________________

Lesson **33**
CC.K.CC.6

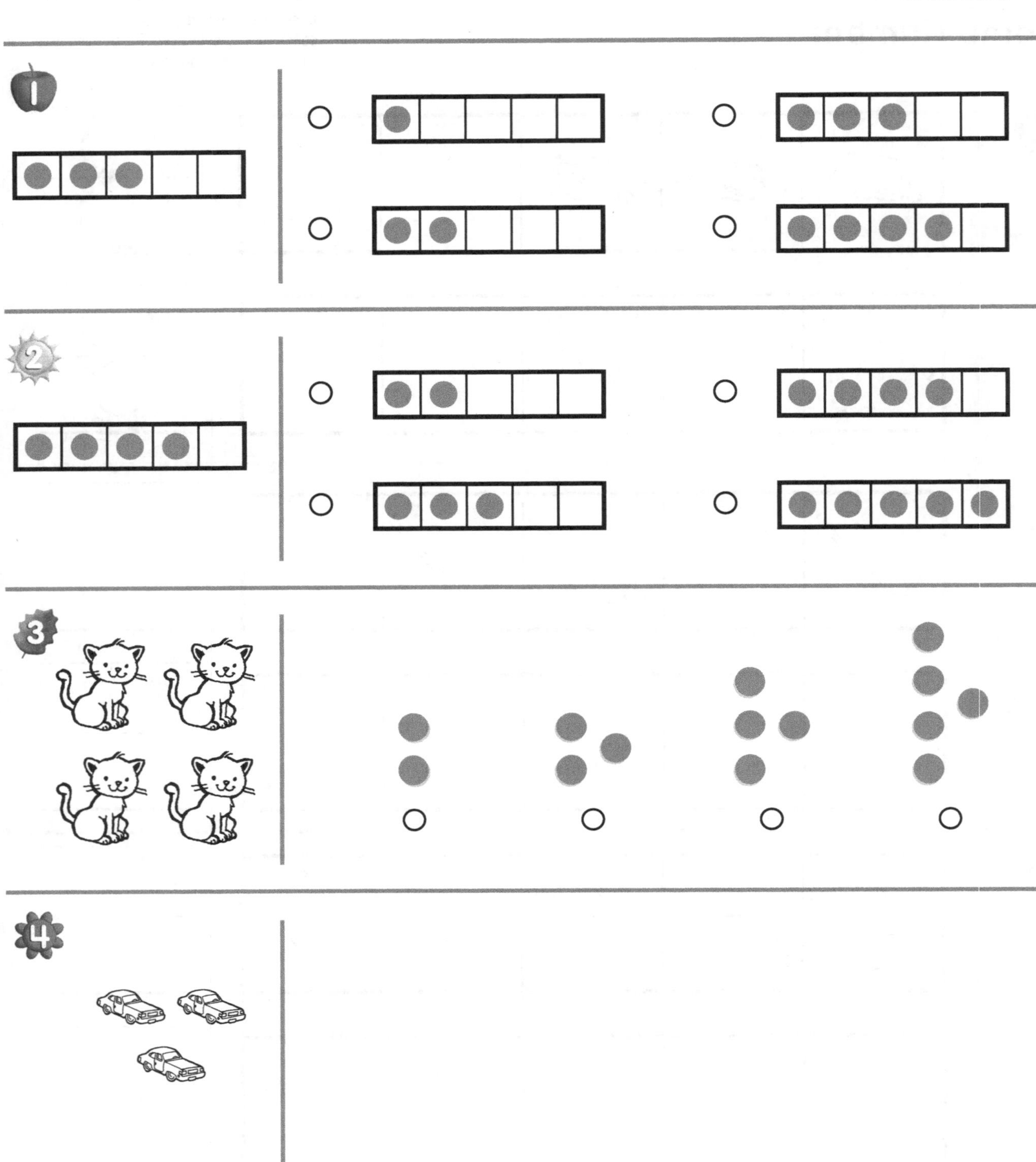

DIRECTIONS **1–2.** Mark beside the set that has the same number of counters as the set at the beginning of the row. **3.** Mark under the set that has the same number of counters as the number of cats at the beginning of the row. **4.** Draw a set that has the same number of counters as the number of cars at the beginning of the row.

Name ________________________________

Greater Than

Lesson 34

COMMON CORE STANDARD CC.K.CC.6

Lesson Objective: Use matching and counting strategies to compare sets when the number of objects in one set is greater than the number of objects in the other set.

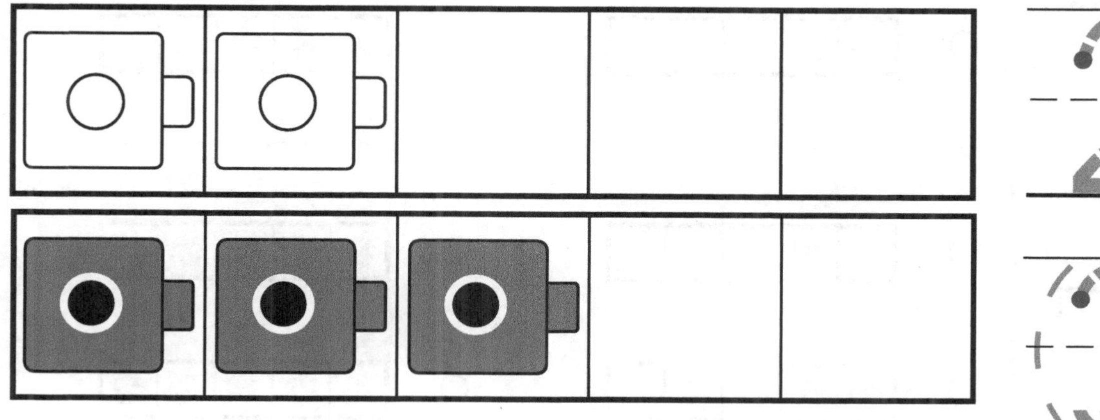

2

3

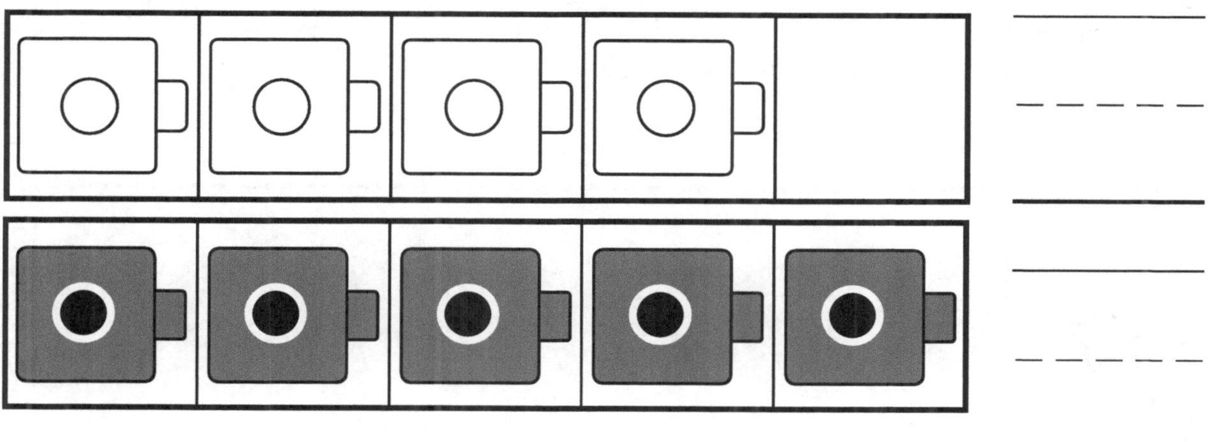

DIRECTIONS **1.** Place cubes as shown. Count and tell how many in each set. Trace the numbers. Trace the circle to show the number that is greater. **2.** Place cubes as shown. Count and tell how many in each set. Write the numbers. Circle the number that is greater.

Name ______________________

Lesson 34
CC.K.CC.6

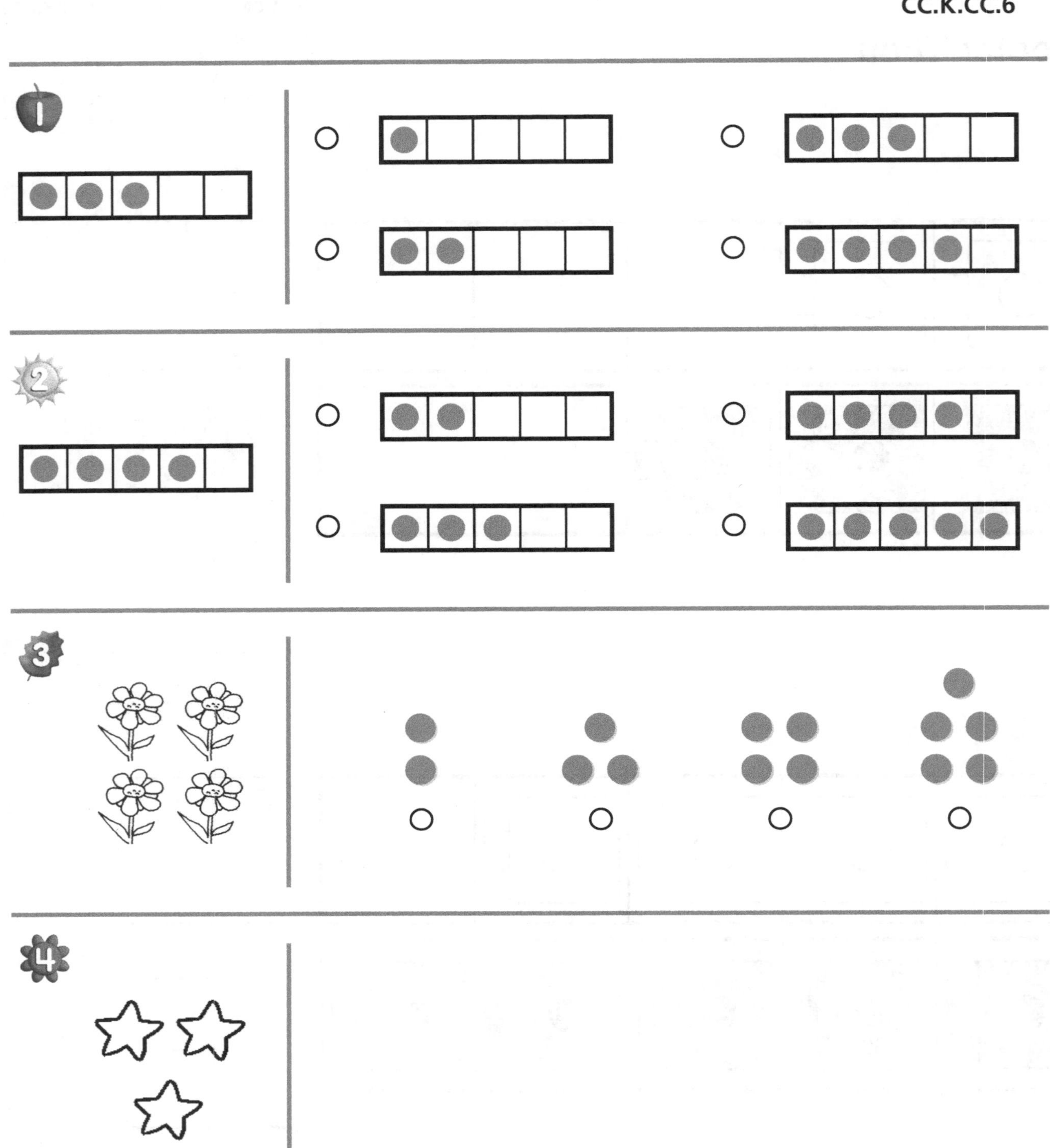

DIRECTIONS 1–2. Mark beside the set that has a number of counters that is greater than the number of counters in the set at the beginning of the row. **3.** Mark under the set that has a number of counters that is greater than the number of flowers at the beginning of the row. **4.** Draw a set that has a number of counters that is greater than the number of stars at the beginning of the row.

Name ______________________________

Lesson 35

COMMON CORE STANDARD CC.K.CC.6

Lesson Objective: Use matching and counting strategies to compare sets when the number of objects in one set is less than the number of objects in the other set.

Less Than

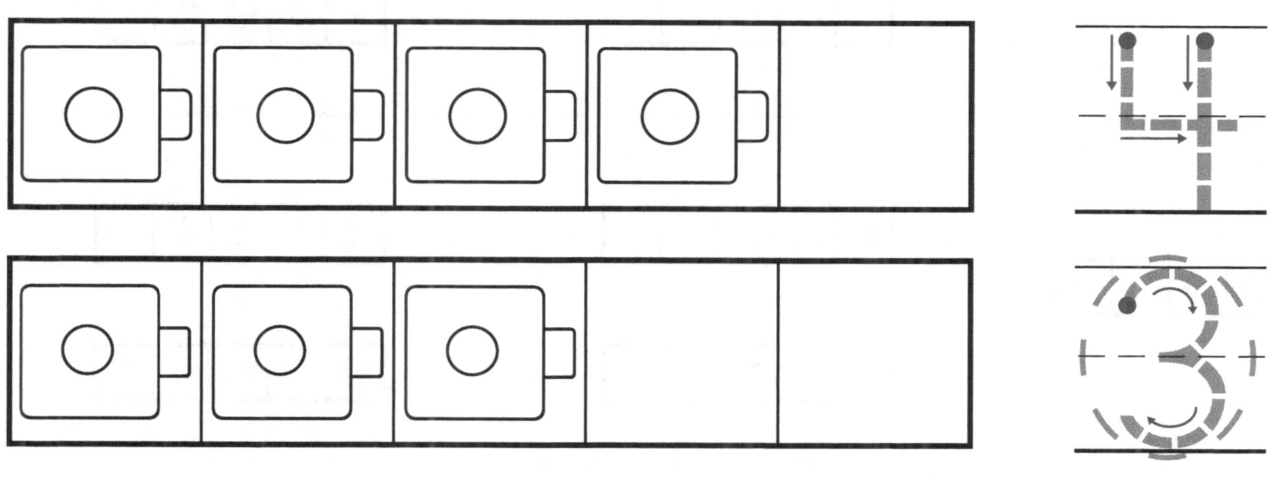

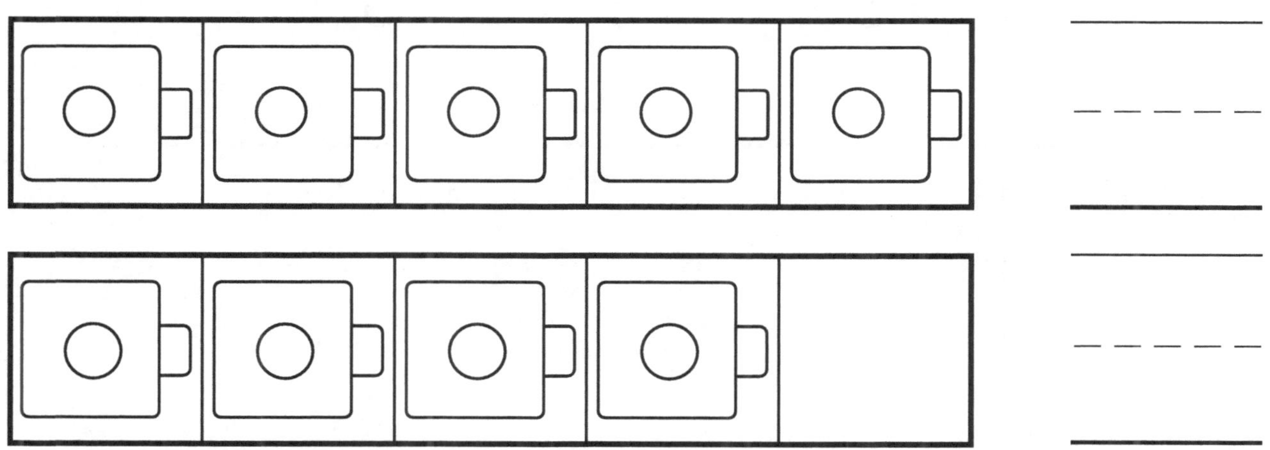

DIRECTIONS **1–2.** Place cubes on the five frames as shown. Count and tell how many in each set. Write the numbers. Compare the sets by matching. Circle the number that is less.

Name ______________________________

Lesson 35
CC.K.CC.6

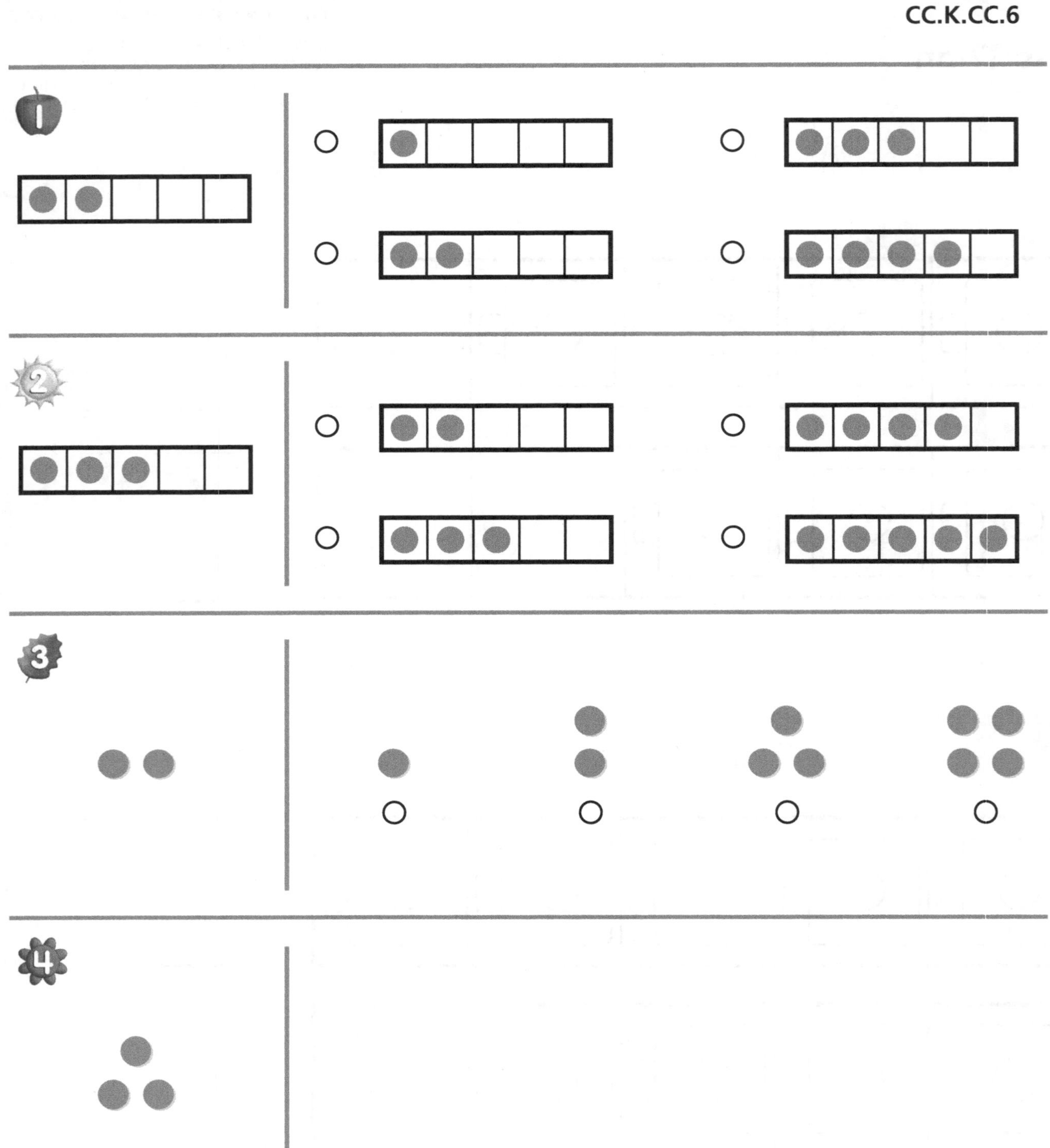

DIRECTIONS **1–2.** Mark beside the set that has a number of counters that is less than the number of counters in the set at the beginning of the row. **3.** Count the counters at the beginning of the row. Mark under the set that has a number of counters that is less than the number of counters at the beginning of the row. **4.** Draw a set that has a number of counters that is less than the number of counters at the beginning of the row.

Name ______________________________

Lesson 36

COMMON CORE STANDARD CC.K.CC.6

Lesson Objective: Make a model to solve problems using a matching strategy.

Problem Solving • Compare by Matching Sets to 5

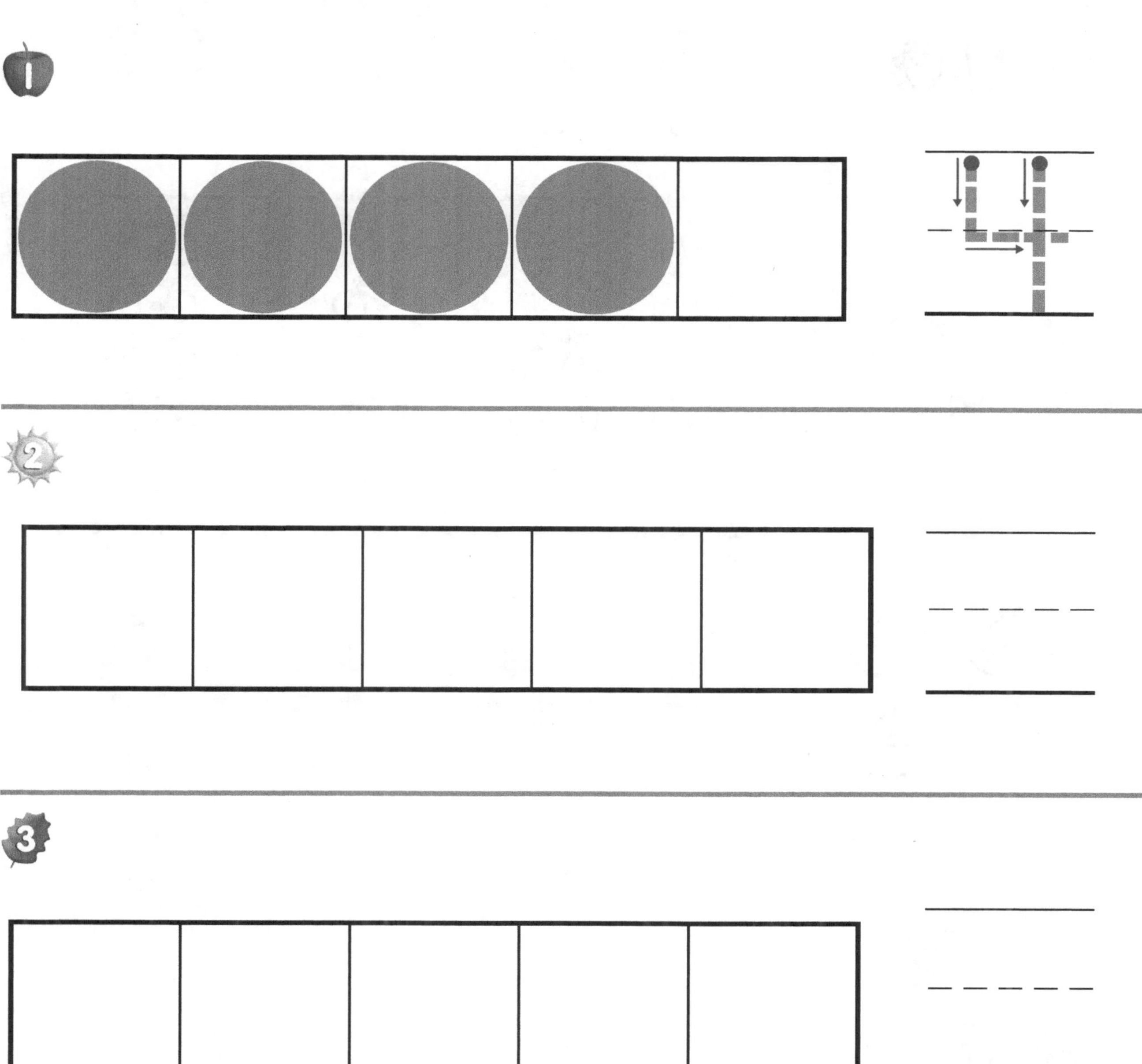

DIRECTIONS 1. How many counters are there? Trace the number. 2. Place counters to model a set that has a number of counters greater than 4. Draw the counters. Write how many. 3. Place counters to model a set that has a number of counters less than 4. Draw the counters. Write how many.

Name ______________________

Lesson 36
CC.K.CC.6

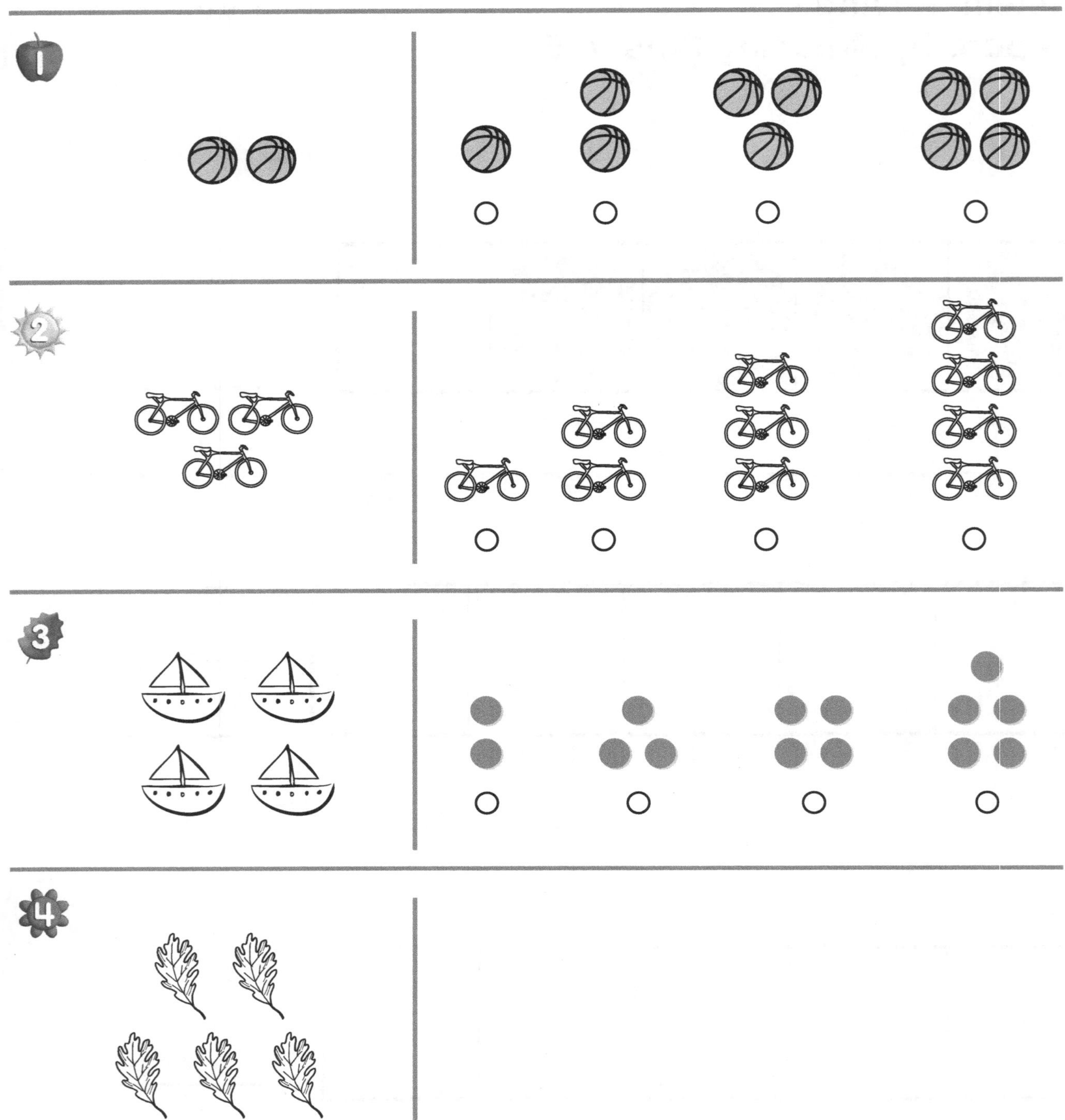

DIRECTIONS 1. Sam has two basketballs. Mark under the set that has a number of basketballs that is less than the number of basketballs Sam has. 2. Jill has three bikes. Mark under the set that has a number of bikes that is greater than the number of bikes Jill has. 3. Mark under the set that has a number of counters that is greater than the number of boats at the beginning of the row. 4. Draw a set that has the same number of counters as the number of leaves at the beginning of the row.

Name ____________________

Lesson 37

COMMON CORE STANDARD CC.K.CC.6

Lesson Objective: Use a counting strategy to compare sets of objects.

Compare by Counting Sets to 5

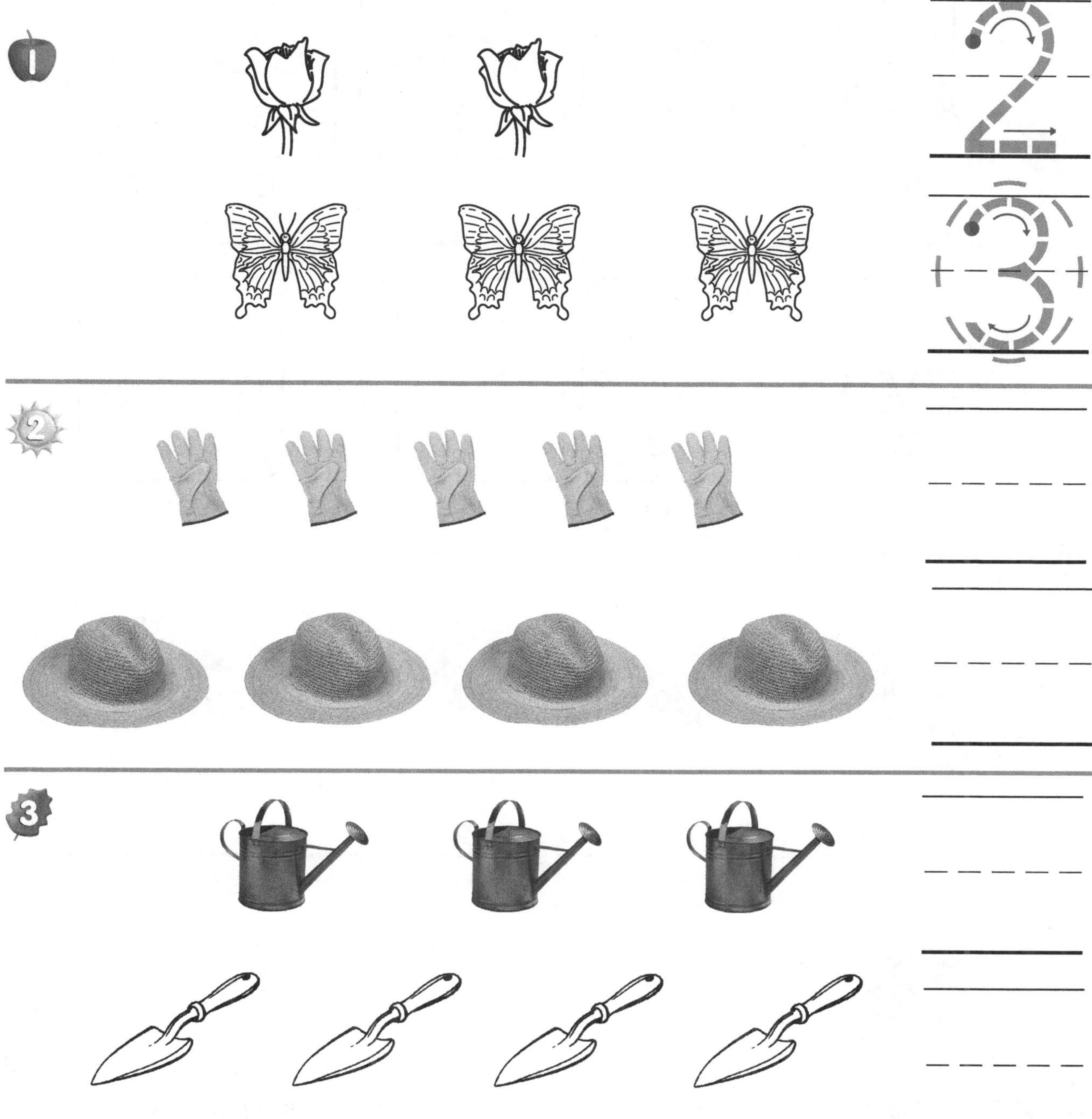

DIRECTIONS 1–2. Draw a dot on each object in the sets as you count. Trace or write the numbers. Compare the numbers. Circle the number that is greater. **3.** Draw a dot on each object in the sets as you count. Write the numbers. Compare the numbers. Circle the number that is less.

Name ______________________________

Lesson 37
CC.K.CC.6

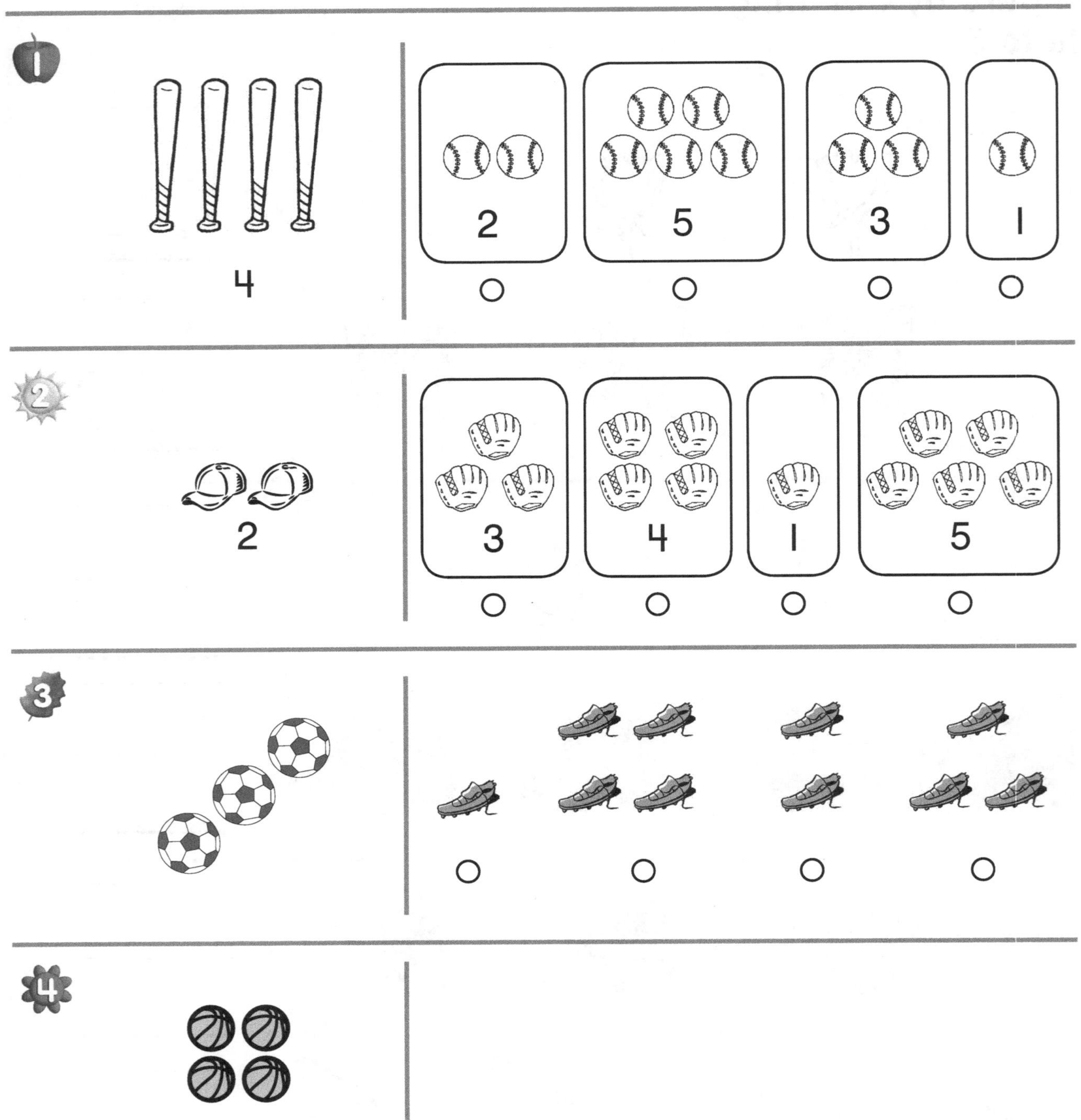

DIRECTIONS **1.** Mark under the set that has a number of baseballs that is greater than the number of bats at the beginning of the row. **2.** Mark under the set that has a number of mitts that is less than the number of hats at the beginning of the row. **3.** Mark under the set that has a number of shoes that is greater than the number of soccer balls at the beginning of the row. **4.** Draw a set that has the same number of counters as the number of basketballs at the beginning of the row.

Name ____________________

Lesson 38

COMMON CORE STANDARD CC.K.CC.6

Lesson Objective: Solve problems by using the strategy *draw a picture.*

Problem Solving • Numbers to 9

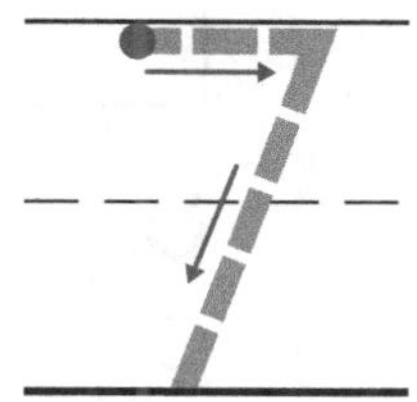

DIRECTIONS Draw to solve these problems. **1.** Ben found 5 acorns. The number of acorns Miriam found is two greater than 5. How many acorns did Miriam find? Draw the acorns. Write how many. **2.** Carly found eight leaves. The number of leaves Tim found is one greater than 8. How many leaves did Tim find? Draw the leaves. Write how many.

Name ______________________

Lesson **38**
CC.K.CC.6

1

6 ○ 7 ○ 8 ○ 9 ○

2

8 ○ 7 ○ 6 ○ 5 ○

3

3 ○ 4 ○ 5 ○ 6 ○

4

____

DIRECTIONS 1. Ryan buys 6 stickers. Mia buys a number of stickers that is two more than 6. Draw the stickers. How many stickers does Mia have? Mark under your answer. **2.** Don has 8 toy cars. Sandy has a number of toy cars that is one less than 8. Draw the toy cars. How many toy cars does Sandy have? Mark under your answer. **3.** Jan has 7 books. Four of the books are old. The rest are new. Draw the books. How many books are new? Mark under your answer. **4.** Kendra has 5 tulips and 4 daisies. Draw the flowers. How many flowers does Kendra have? Write the number.

Name ______________________________

Lesson 39

COMMON CORE STANDARD CC.K.CC.6

Lesson Objective: Solve problems by using the strategy *make a model.*

Problem Solving • Compare by Matching Sets to 10

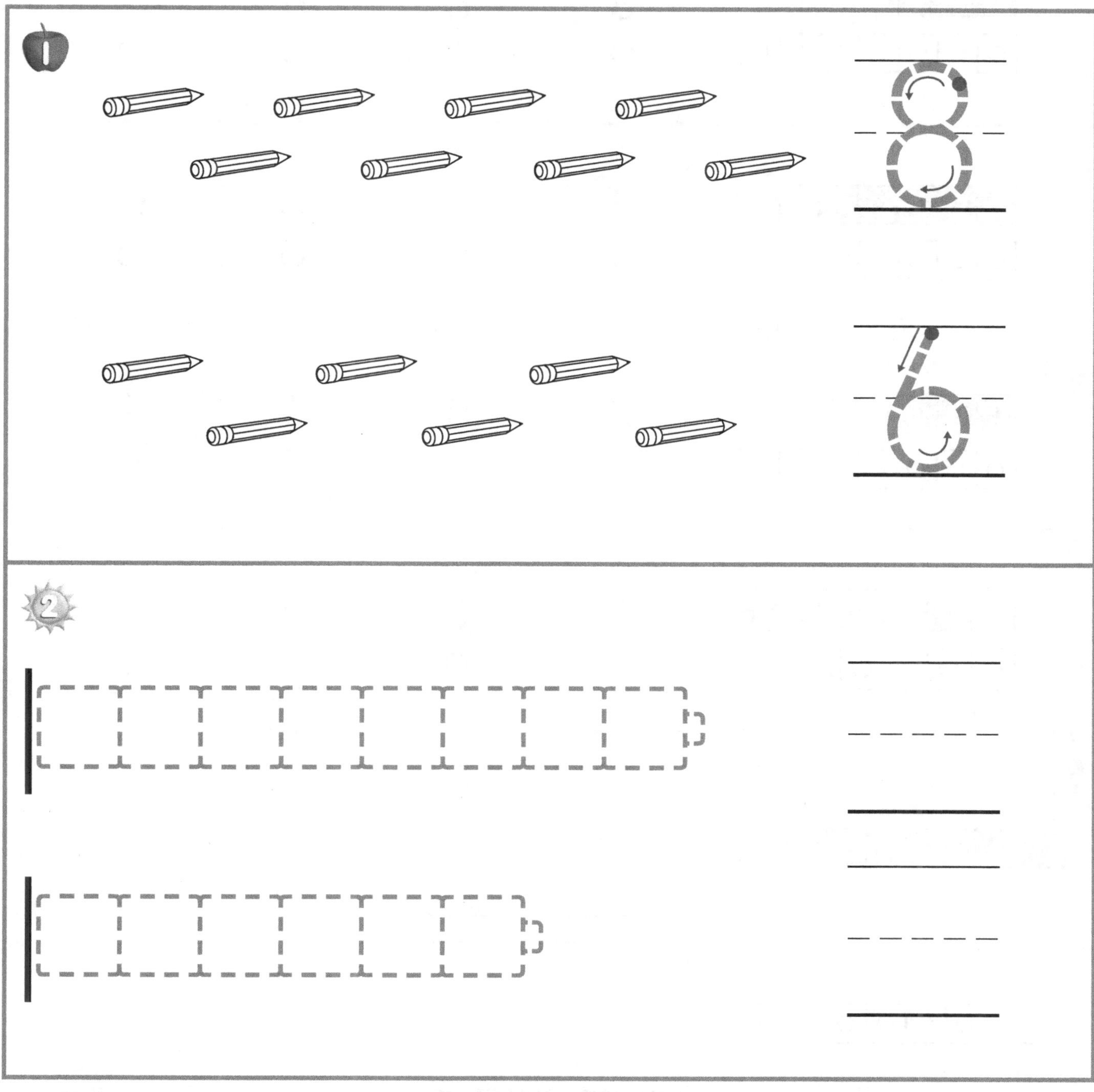

DIRECTIONS Joe has 8 red pencils. Ali has 6 blue pencils. Who has fewer pencils? **1.** Count the pencils in each set. Trace the number. **2.** Use cube trains to model the set of pencils. Compare the cube trains by matching. Trace and color the cube trains shown. Write how many. Circle the number that is less.

Name ___________________________

1

3 ○ 5 ○ 6 ○ 7 ○

2

4 ○ 5 ○ 6 ○ 10 ○

3

3 ○ 4 ○ 6 ○ 7 ○

4

2 ○ 3 ○ 4 ○ 7 ○

5

DIRECTIONS **1–2.** Which set has more cubes? Mark under the number that matches that set. **3–4.** Which set has fewer cubes? Mark under the number that matches that set. **5.** Compare the cube trains by matching. Write how many in each set. Which number is greater? Circle that number.

Name ______________________

Lesson 40

COMMON CORE STANDARD CC.K.CC.6

Lesson Objective: Use counting strategies to compare sets of objects.

Compare by Counting Sets to 10

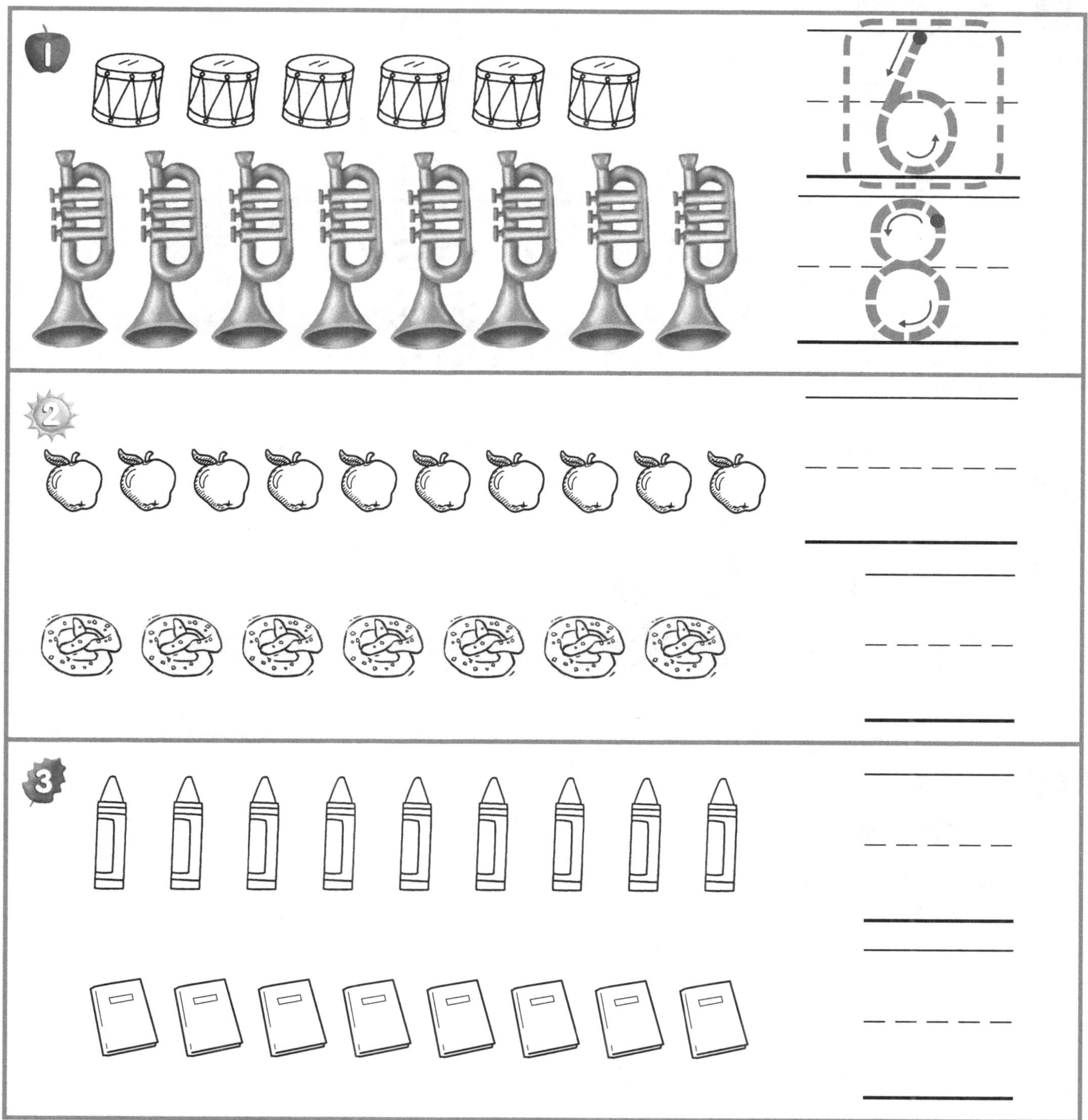

DIRECTIONS **1–2.** Draw a dot on each object in the first set as you count. Trace or write the number. Draw a dot on each object in the second set as you count. Trace or write the number. Circle the number that is less. **3.** Draw a dot on each object in the first set as you count. Write the number. Draw a dot on each object in the second set as you count. Write the number. Circle the greater number.

Name ______________________________

Lesson 40
CC.K.CC.6

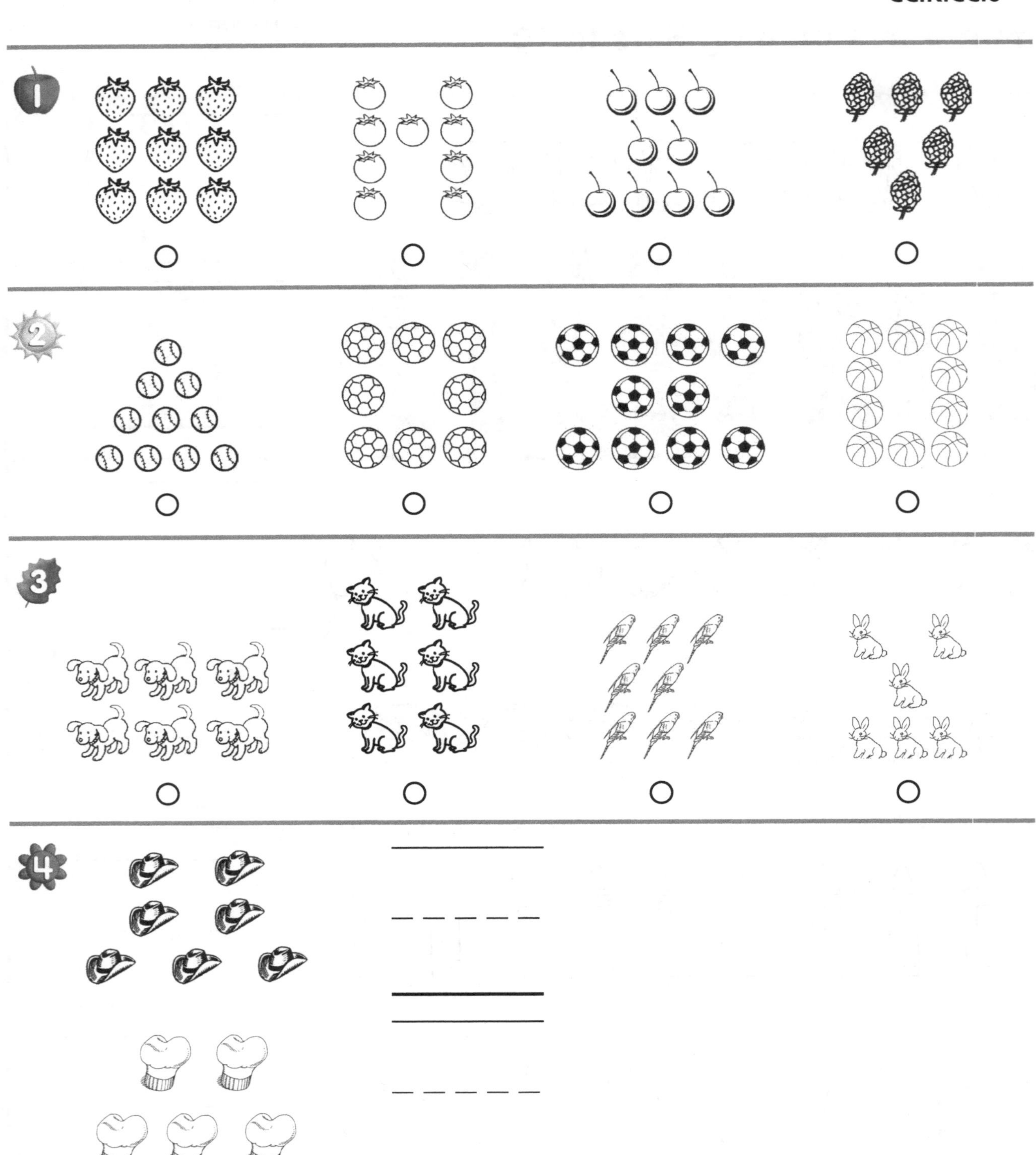

DIRECTIONS **1–2.** Compare the sets by counting. Mark under the set of objects that has less than all the others. **3.** Compare the sets by counting. Mark under the set of objects that has more than all the others. **4.** Count how many in each set. Write the number of objects in each set. Compare the numbers. Circle the number that is less.

Name ____________________

Lesson 41

COMMON CORE STANDARD CC.K.CC.6

Lesson Objective: Solve problems by using the strategy *make a model.*

Problem Solving • Compare Numbers to 20

1

2

DIRECTIONS Use cubes to model the sets. **1.** Dana has 19 cubes. Trace the cubes. Write the number. **2.** Dana has a number of cubes two greater than Ethan. Trace the cubes. Write the number. Compare the sets of cubes in Exercises 1 and 2. Circle the greater number.

Name ________________________________

Lesson 41
CC.K.CC.6

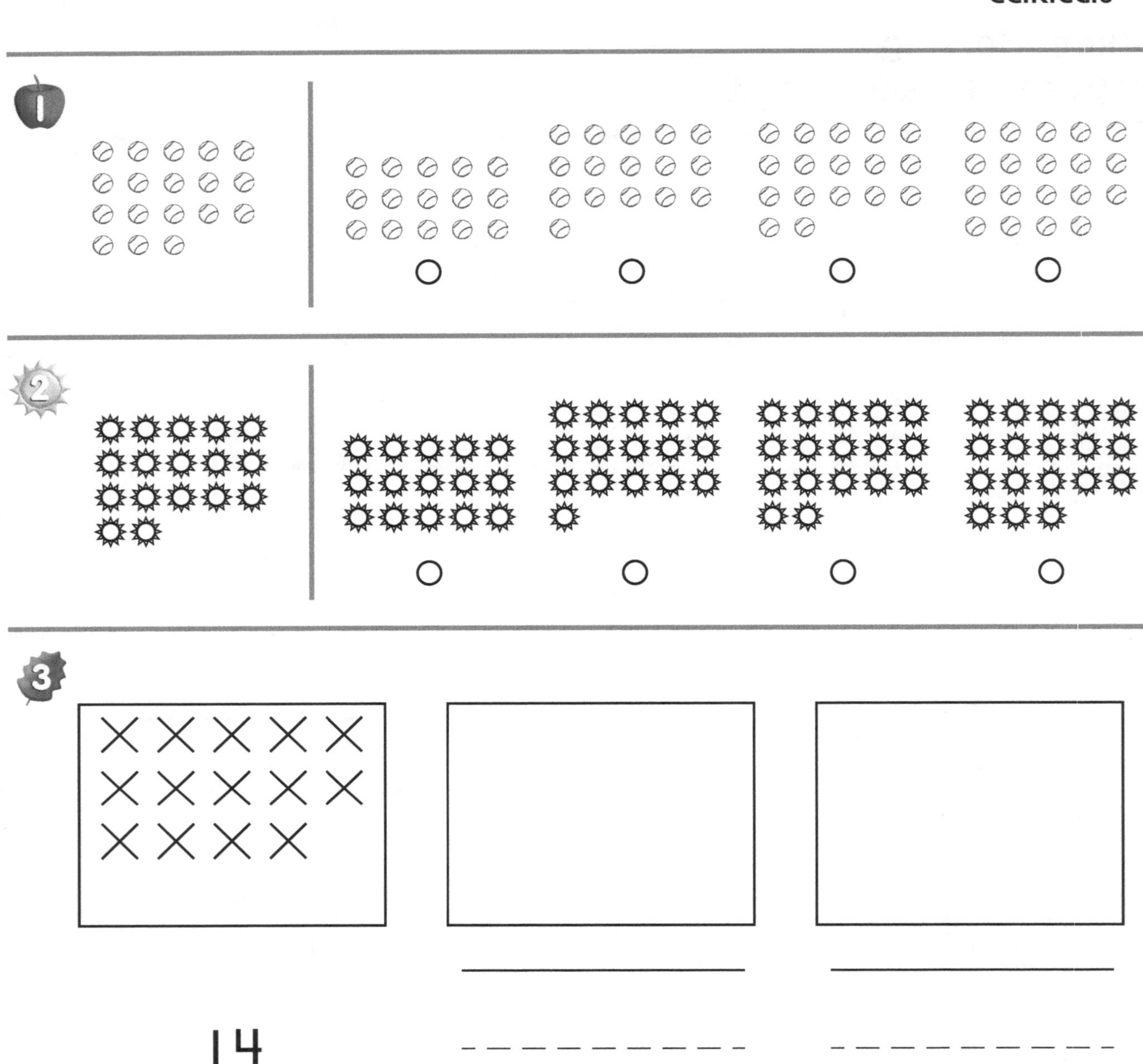

DIRECTIONS **1.** Sue has 18 baseballs. Mark under the set that shows a number of baseballs one greater than 18. **2.** Jared has 17 sun stickers. Mark under the set that shows a number of stickers one less than 17. **3.** There are 14 Xs in the first box. In the next box, draw a number of Xs that is two more than 14. Write the number. In the last box, draw a number of Xs that is one less than 14. Write the number.

Name ___________________________________

Lesson 42

COMMON CORE STANDARD CC.K.CC.7

Lesson Objective: Compare two numbers between 1 and 10.

Compare Two Numbers

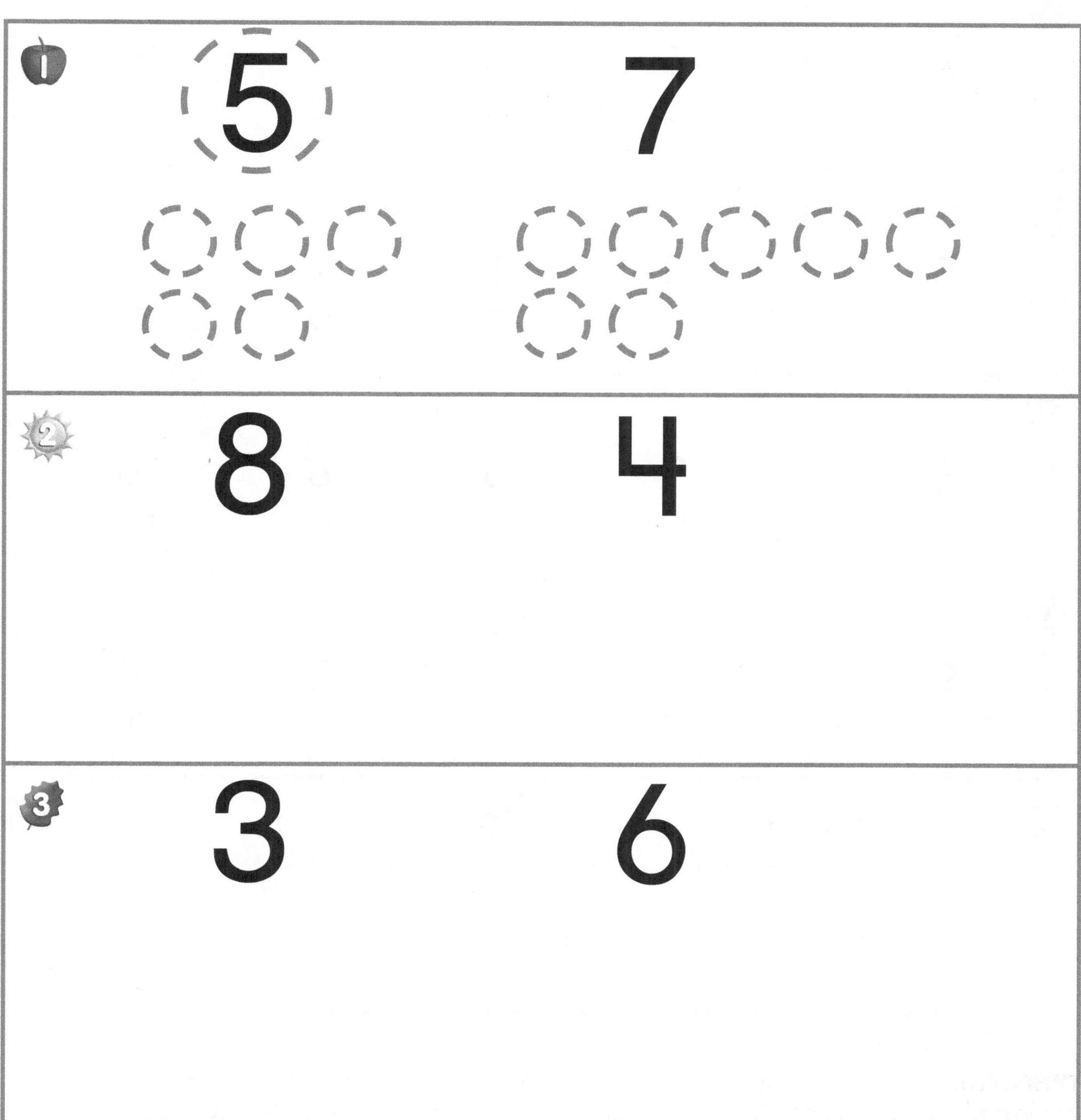

DIRECTIONS **1–2.** Look at the numbers. Trace or draw counters to model the numbers. Compare the sets. Draw a circle around the number that is less. **3.** Look at the numbers. Draw counters to model the numbers. Compare the sets. Draw a circle around the number that is greater.

Name ______________________

Lesson 42
CC.K.CC.7

1	6	5 ○	7 ○	8 ○	9 ○
2	5	3 ○	1 ○	7 ○	5 ○
3	8	9 ○	6 ○	8 ○	10 ○
4	9	4 ○	6 ○	8 ○	10 ○

5

Beth	**Tom**
______	______

DIRECTIONS 1. Mark under the number that is less than the number at the beginning of the row. 2. Mark under the number that is greater than the number at the beginning of the row. 3. Mark under the number that is less than the number at the beginning of the row. 4. Mark under the number that is greater than the number at the beginning of the row. 5. Beth has a number of markers that is three greater than 5. Tom has a number of markers that is greater than 4 and less than 6. Write how many markers each child has. Compare the numbers. Circle the number that is greater.

Name ______________________

Lesson 43

COMMON CORE STANDARD CC.K.OA.1

Lesson Objective: Use expressions to represent addition within 5.

Addition: Add To

1

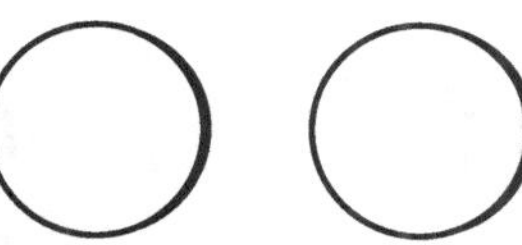

and

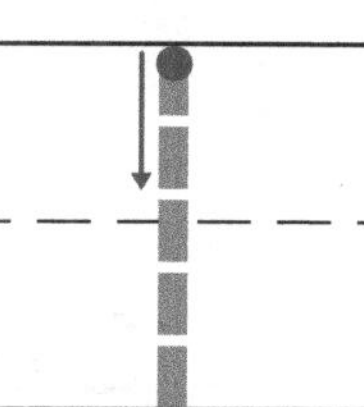

DIRECTIONS **1.** Joy has a cup with two white counters. Then she adds one gray counter. Trace the number that shows how many white counters Joy has. Trace the number that shows the counter being added. **2.** Trace the counters in Joy's cup now. **3.** Write how many counters are in Joy's cup now.

Name ______________________

Lesson 43
CC.K.OA.1

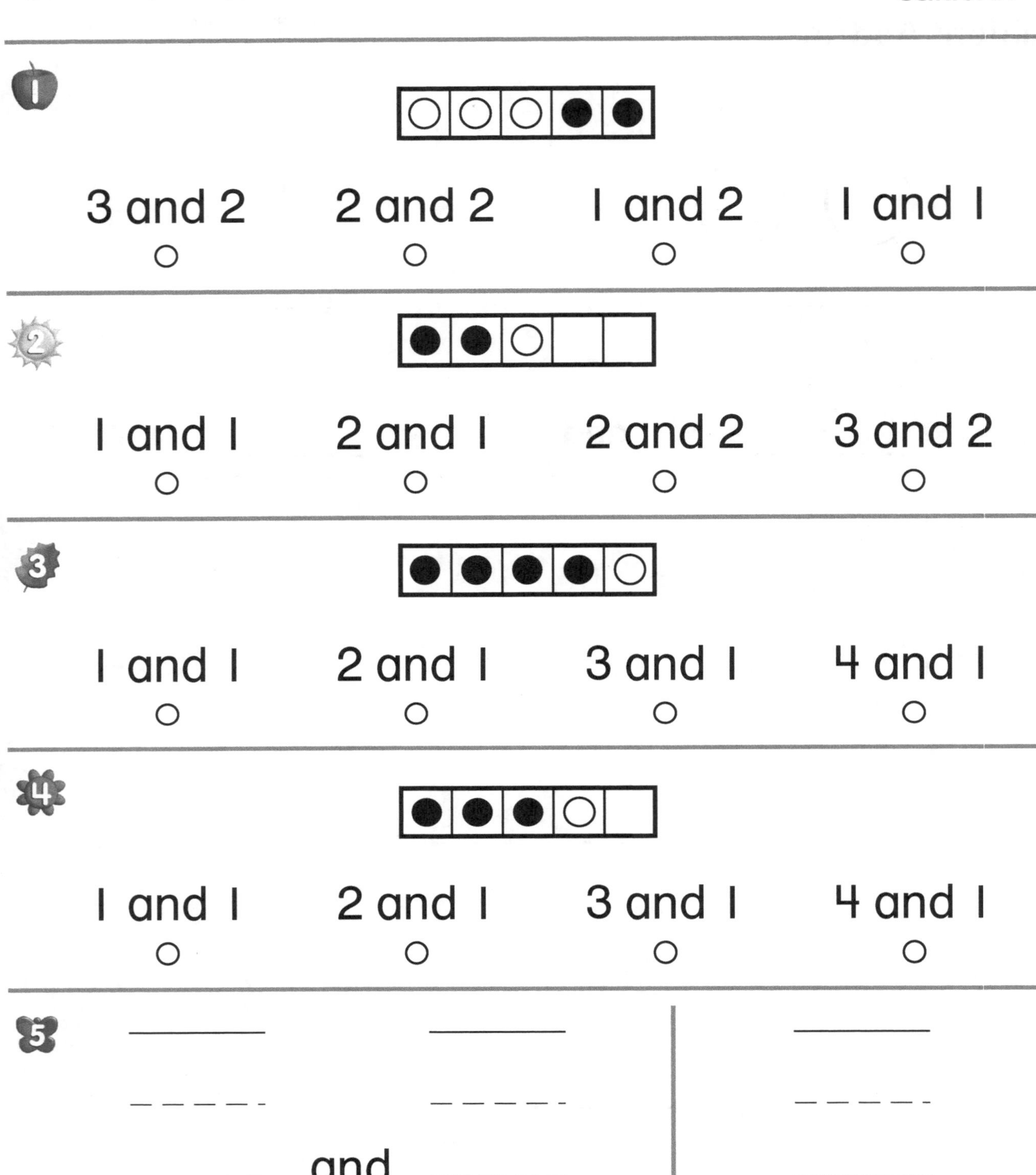

DIRECTIONS 1. Which shows the black counters being added to the five frame? Mark under your answer. **2–4.** Which shows the white counter being added to the five frame? Mark under your answer. **5.** One frog is in the pond. Three frogs are added to the pond. Write the numbers that show the frogs being added. Write how many frogs are in the pond now.

Name ______________________

Lesson 44

COMMON CORE STANDARD CC.K.OA.1

Lesson Objective: Use expressions to represent addition.

Addition: Put Together

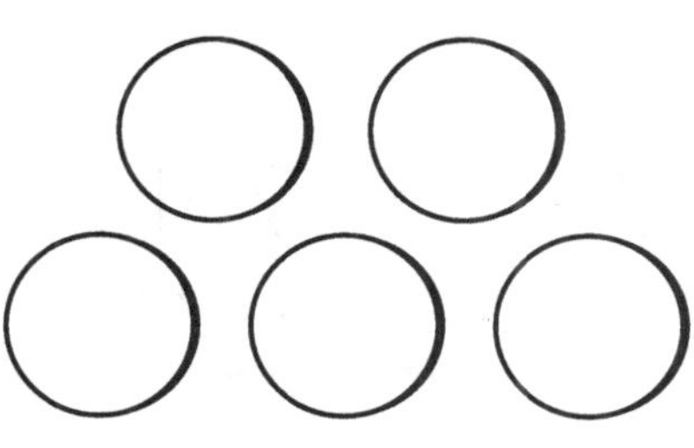

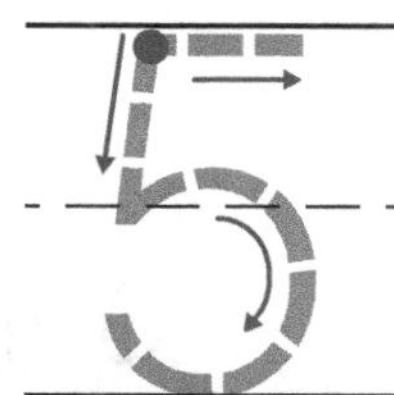

and

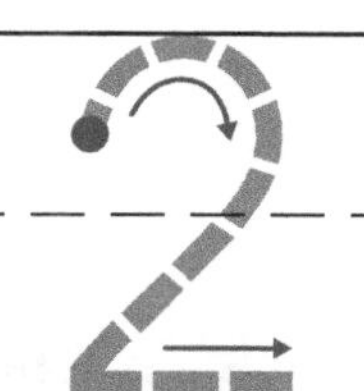

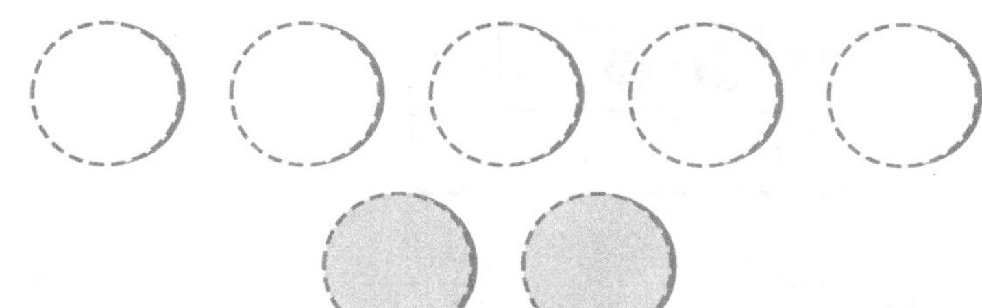

DIRECTIONS **1–3.** Kim has 5 white counters and 2 gray counters. How many counters does she have in all? **1.** Count the white counters. Trace the number. Count the gray counters. Trace the number. **2.** Trace the counters to model the sets that are put together. Write the numbers and trace the symbol. **3.** Write how many counters Kim has in all.

Name ______________________

Lesson 44
CC.K.OA.1

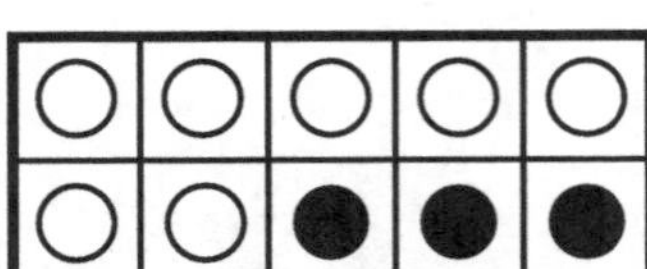

2 + 3 ○ 5 + 2 ○ 5 + 3 ○ 7 + 3 ○

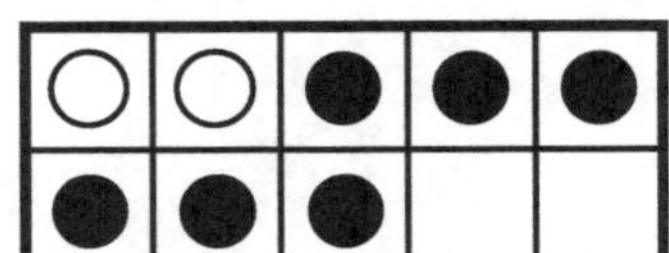

2 + 3 ○ 2 + 6 ○ 3 + 6 ○ 3 + 7 ○

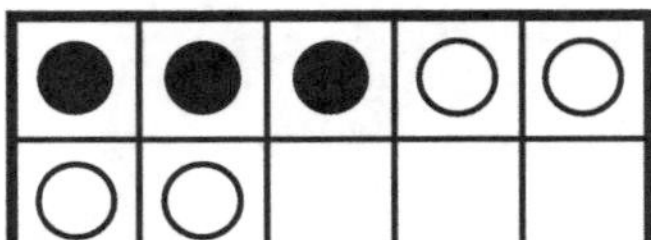

3 + 4 ○ 3 + 5 ○ 3 + 6 ○ 3 + 7 ○

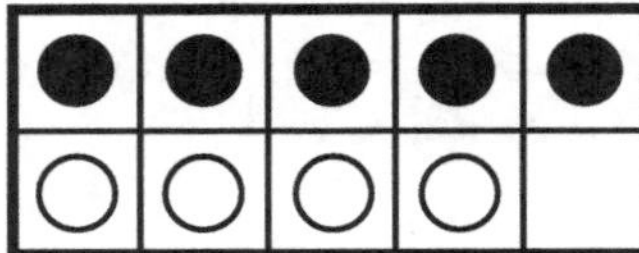

4 + 1 ○ 4 + 4 ○ 5 + 1 ○ 5 + 4 ○

5

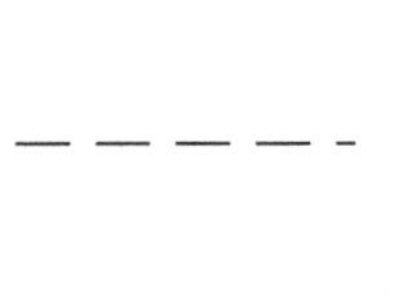

DIRECTIONS 1–4. Which numbers show the sets that are put together? Mark under your answer. **5.** Three red crayons and five blue crayons are on the desk. Write the numbers and trace the symbol to show the crayons being put together. Write the number to show how many crayons in all.

Name ______________________________

Lesson 45

COMMON CORE STANDARD CC.K.OA.1

Lesson Objective: Solve problems by using the strategy *act it out.*

Problem Solving • Act Out Addition Problems

DIRECTIONS Act out the addition word problem. **1.** There were two books on the table. A girl brings two more books. How many books are on the table now? Trace the numbers and the symbol. **2.** Place a cube on each book on the table in Exercise 1. Write the number. Place a cube on each book the girl has. Write the number. Count how many cubes. Write the number to show how many books there are in all. Trace the symbols.

Name ____________________

Lesson 45
CC.K.OA.1

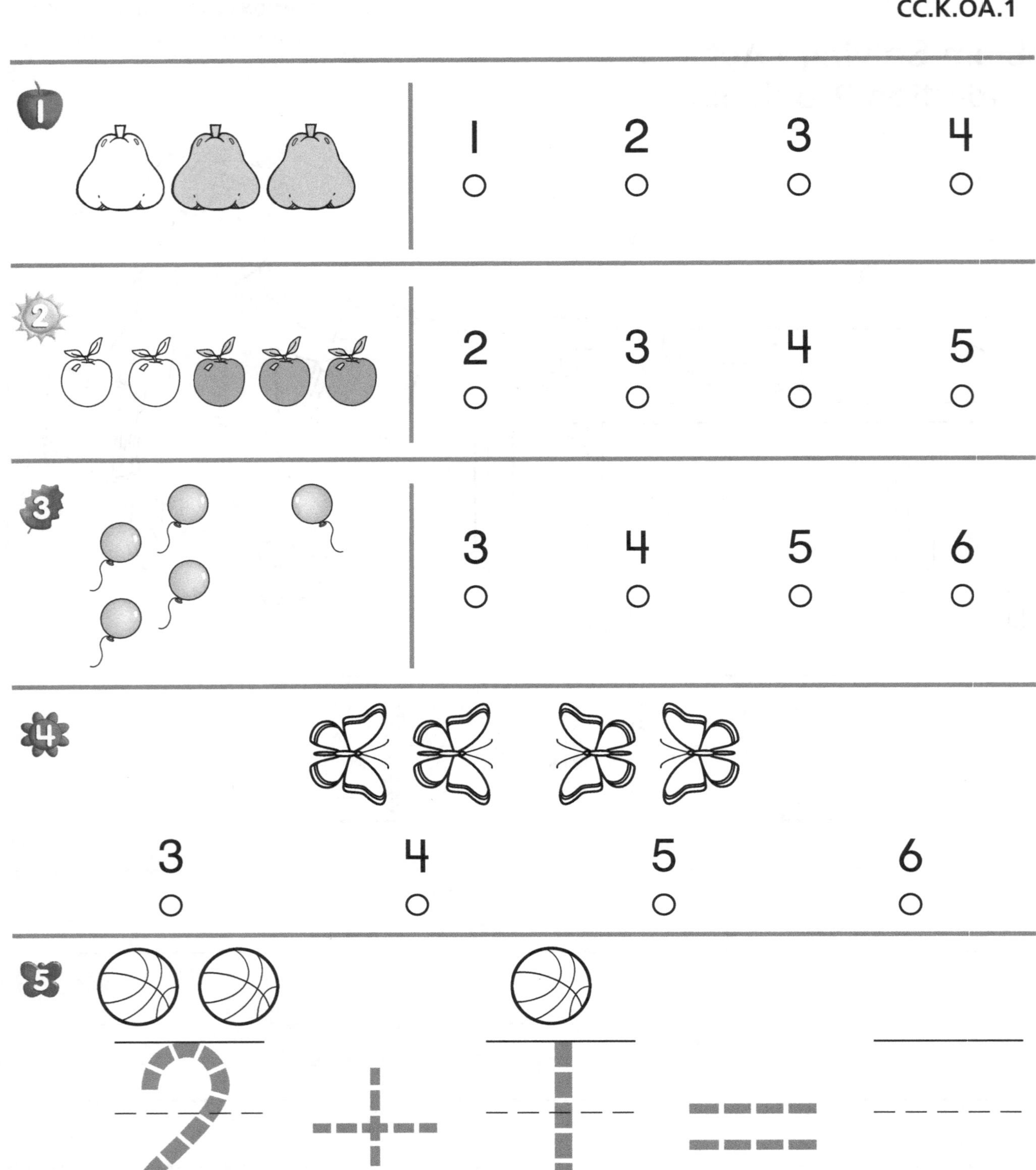

DIRECTIONS 1. Mark under the number that shows how many pears in all. 2. Mark under the number that shows how many apples in all. 3. Mark under the number that shows how many balloons in all. 4. Mark under the number that shows how many butterflies in all. 5. Tell an addition word problem about the basketballs. Trace the numbers and the symbols. Write the number that shows how many basketballs there are now.

Name ______________________________

Lesson 46

COMMON CORE STANDARD CC.K.OA.1

Lesson Objective: Use expressions to represent subtraction within 5.

Subtraction: Take From

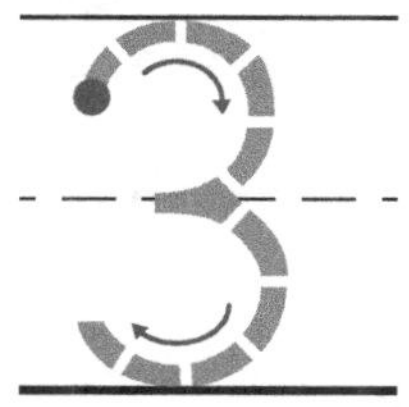

take away

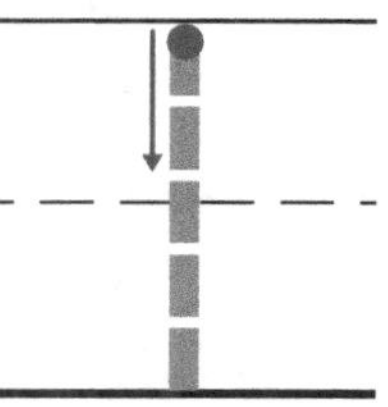

DIRECTIONS 1. Look at the picture. How many children in all? Draw a dot on each child as you count. Trace the 3. How many children are leaving? Circle the child who is leaving. Trace the 1. How many children are left? Draw a line under the two children sitting. Trace the 2.

Name ______________________

Lesson 46
CC.K.OA.1

3 − 2	3 − 1	4 − 2	4 − 1
○	○	○	○

5 − 2	4 − 3	4 − 2	3 − 2
○	○	○	○

5 − 4	5 − 3	5 − 2	5 − 1
○	○	○	○

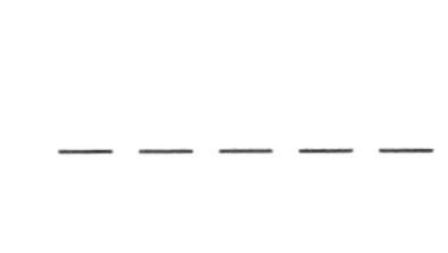  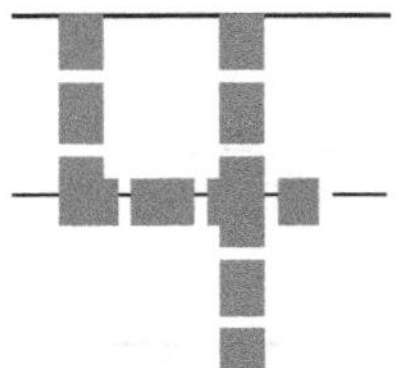 | ______

DIRECTIONS **1–3.** Mark under the subtraction that matches the picture. **4.** Write the number that shows how many children in all. Trace the number and symbol that shows four children are leaving. Write the number that shows how many children are left.

Name ______________________________

Lesson 47

COMMON CORE STANDARD CC.K.OA.1

Lesson Objective: Use expressions to represent subtraction.

Subtraction: Take Apart

1

7 minus 2

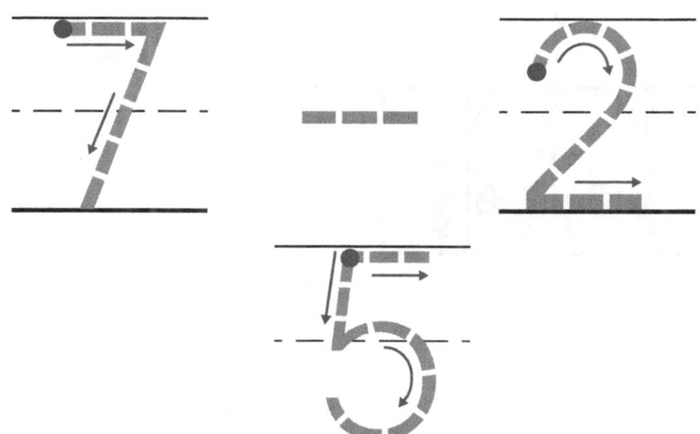

DIRECTIONS 1. Henry has seven counters. Place seven red counters in the workspace. Trace the number 7 to show how many in all. Two of Henry's counters are yellow. Turn two of the counters to the yellow side. Trace the number 2. How many of Henry's counters are red? Count the red counters. Trace the number 5. Trace and color the counters you placed.

Name ______________________

Lesson 47
CC.K.OA.1

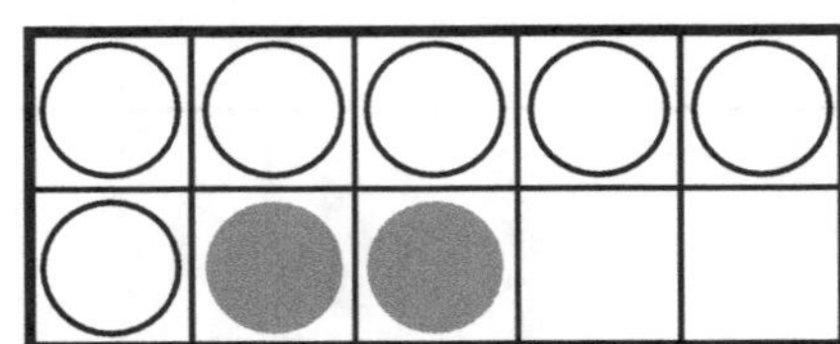

8 − 2 ○ 7 − 3 ○ 6 − 2 ○ 5 − 3 ○

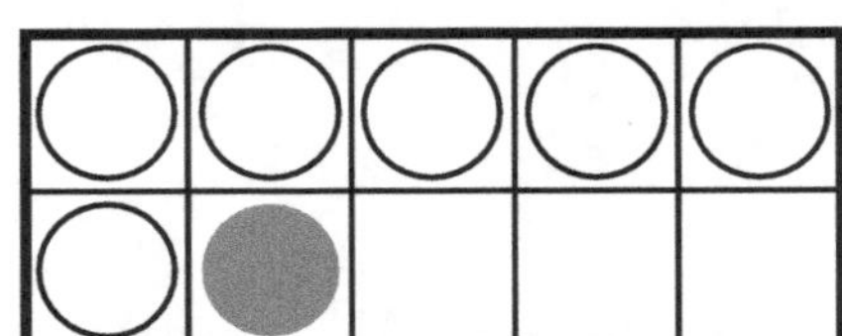

6 − 2 ○ 6 − 1 ○ 7 − 2 ○ 7 − 1 ○

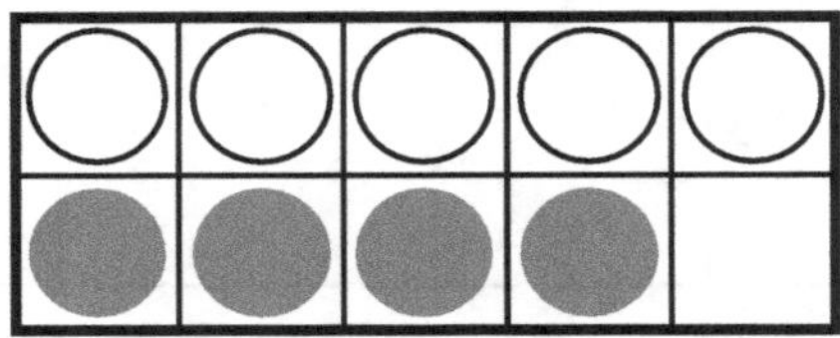

5 − 4 ○ 9 − 4 ○ 9 − 5 ○ 10 − 4 ○

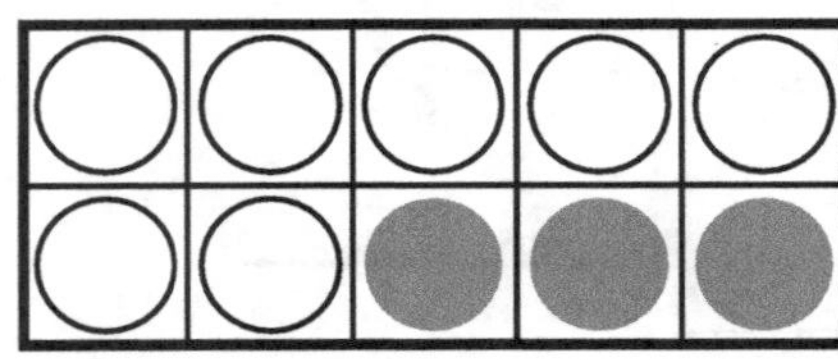

______ ▬ ______ | ______

DIRECTIONS **1–3.** Mark under the subtraction that matches the counters. **4.** Write the number that shows how many counters in all. Write the number that shows how many counters are gray. Write the number that shows how many counters are white.

Name ___________________________

Lesson 48

COMMON CORE STANDARD CC.K.OA.1

Lesson Objective: Solve problems by using the strategy *act it out.*

Problem Solving • Act Out Subtraction Problems

4 – 1 = 3

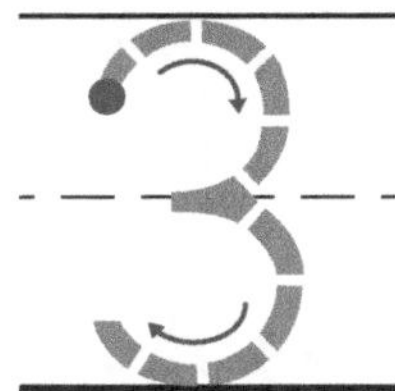

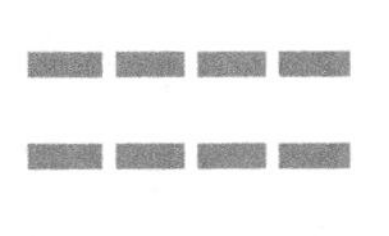

3 – 2 = ___

DIRECTIONS Listen to and act out the subtraction word problems. **1.** There are four children sitting on the floor. Trace the number 4. Then one child leaves. Trace the number 1. How many children are sitting on the floor now? Trace the number 3 to show how many children are left. **2.** There are three children at the table. Then two children walk away. Write the number that shows how many children are left. Trace to complete the subtraction sentence.

Name ______________________

Lesson 48
CC.K.OA.1

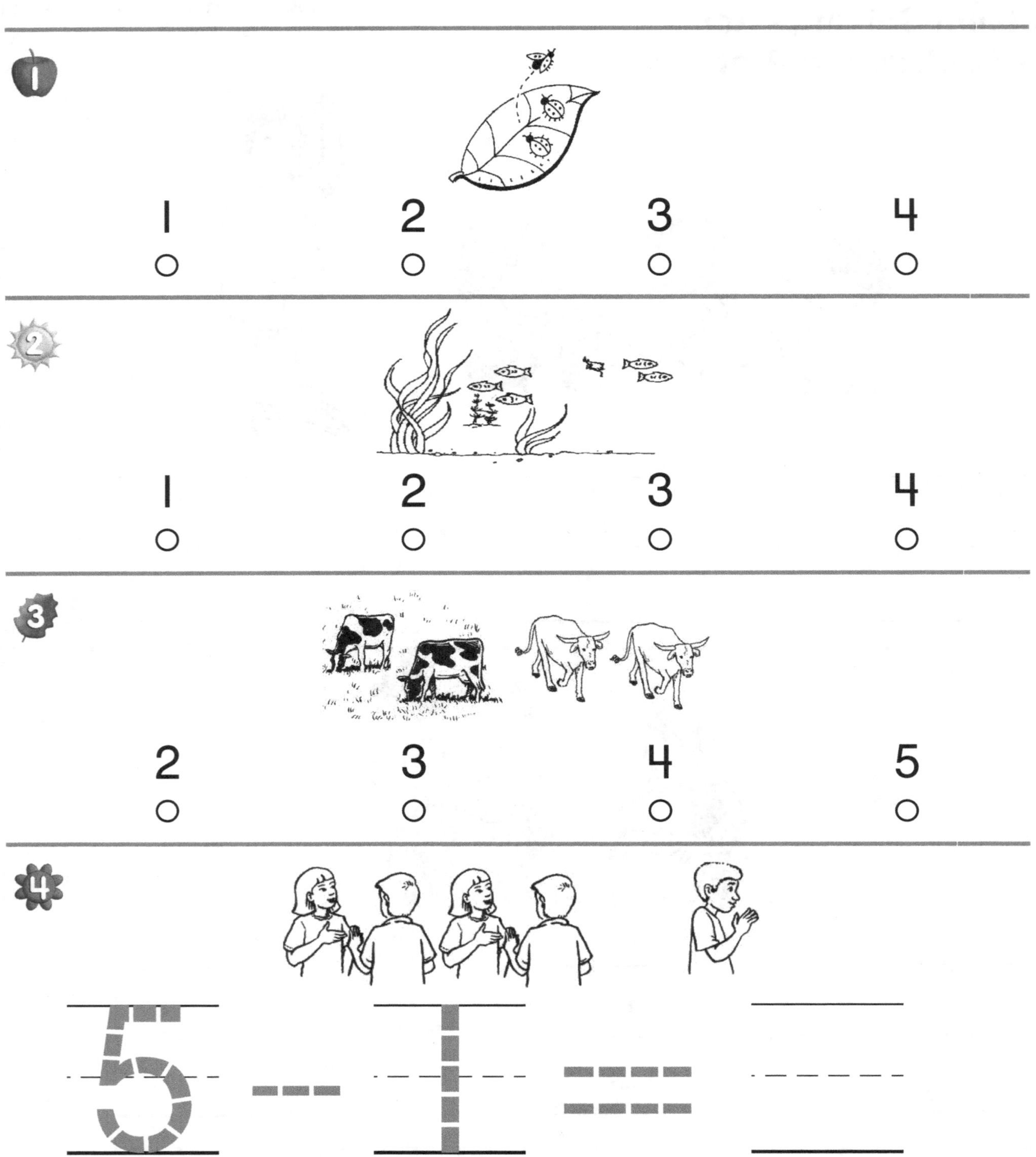

DIRECTIONS 1. Mark under the number that shows how many ladybugs are left on the leaf. 2. Mark under the number that shows how many fish are left near the seaweed. 3. Mark under the number that shows how many cows are left eating grass. 4. Trace the numbers and the symbols. Write the number that shows how many children are left.

Name ________________________________

Lesson 49

COMMON CORE STANDARD CC.K.OA.2

Lesson Objective: Solve addition word problems within 10 and record the equation.

Algebra • Write More Addition Sentences

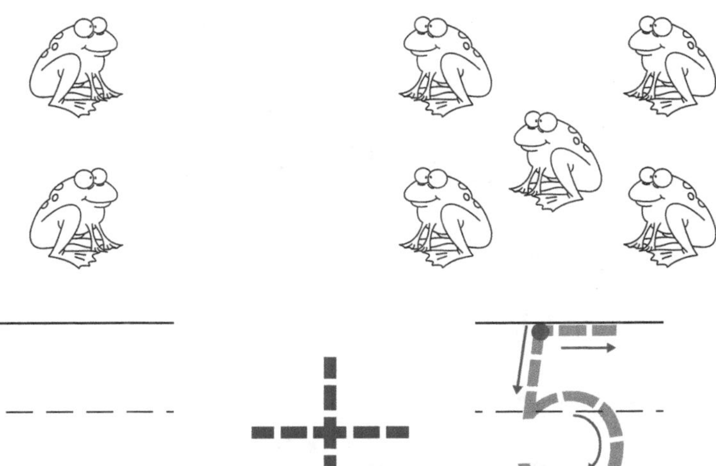

___ + 5

___

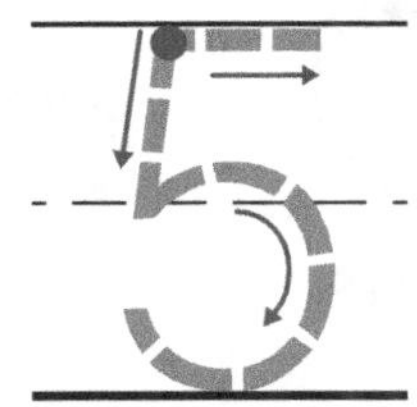

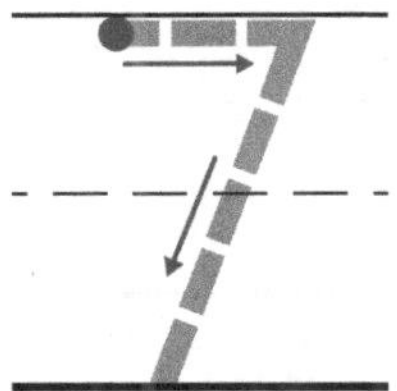

2 + 5 = 7

DIRECTIONS There were some frogs. Five more frogs come. Then there were seven frogs. How many frogs were there before? **1.** Circle the frogs being added. Trace the number. How many frogs are in the set to start with? Write the number. **2.** How many frogs are there now? Write the number. **3.** Trace the numbers and symbols to show this as an addition sentence.

Name ____________________

Lesson 49
CC.K.OA.2

$\_\_\_ + 4 = 9$

4	5	6	7
○	○	○	○

$\_\_\_ + 5 = 7$

2	3	4	6
○	○	○	○

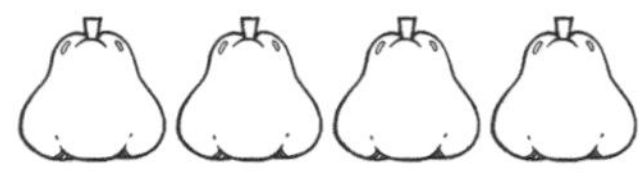 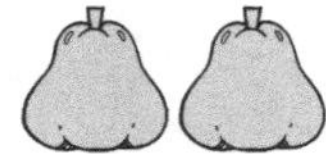

 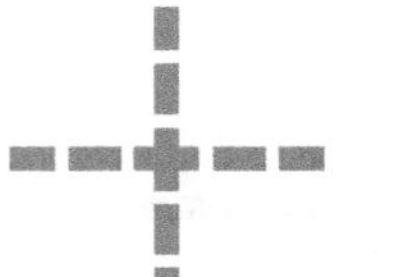  

DIRECTIONS **1–2.** Mark under the number that would complete the addition sentence. **3.** Kelly had some pears. Then she got 2 more pears. Now she has 6 pears. How many pears did Kelly have to start? Complete the addition sentence.

Name ______________________

Lesson 50

COMMON CORE STANDARD CC.K.OA.2

Lesson Objective: Solve subtraction word problems within 10 and record the equation.

Algebra • Write More Subtraction Sentences

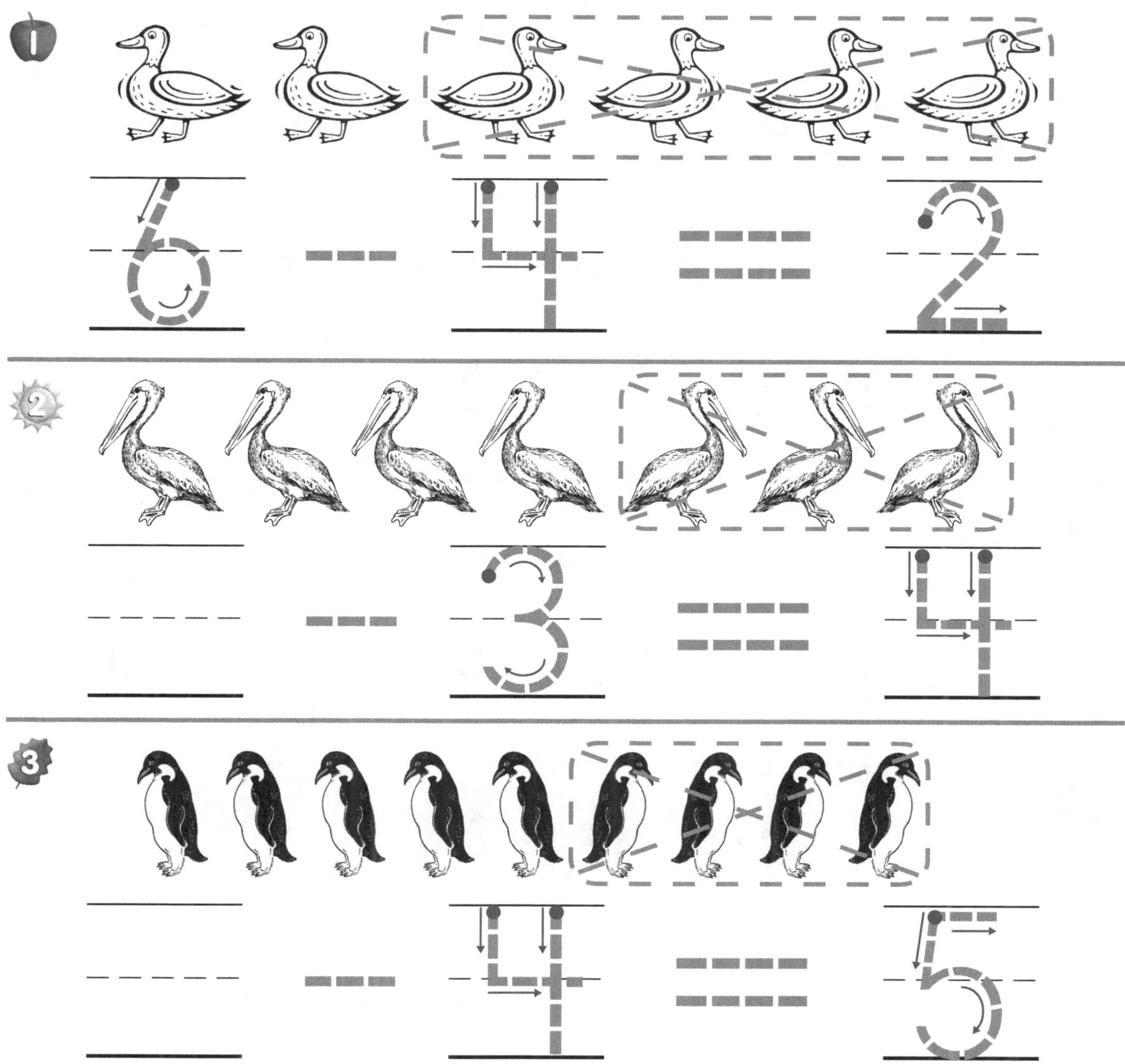

DIRECTIONS **1.** Listen to the subtraction word problem. Some ducks are sitting. Four ducks leave. There are two ducks left. How many ducks are there to start with? Count the entire set to find how many ducks there are to start with. Trace the number. Then trace the circle and X to show how many are being taken from the set. Trace to complete the subtraction sentence. **2–3.** Tell a subtraction word problem about the birds. Count the entire set to find how many there are to start with. Write and trace to complete the subtraction sentence.

Name ______________________

Lesson 50
CC.K.OA.2

___ − 1 = 3

1	2	3	4
○	○	○	○

___ − 2 = 3

5	6	7	8
○	○	○	○

___ − 3 = 4

2	3	7	10
○	○	○	○

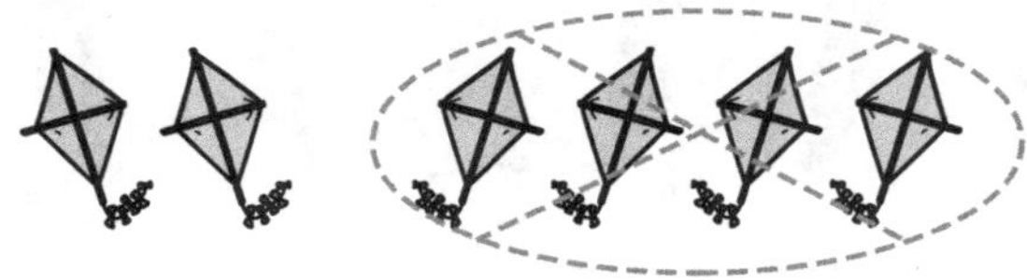

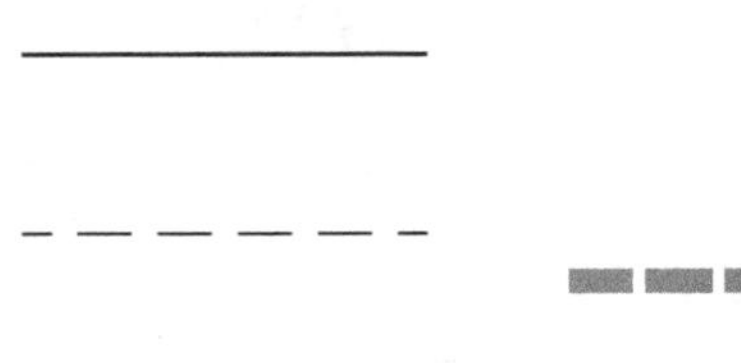

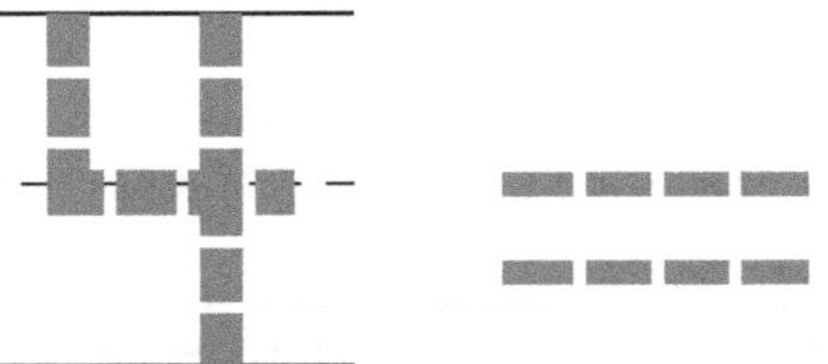

___ − 4 = 2

DIRECTIONS 1. Mark under the number that shows how many clouds you started with. 2. Mark under the number that shows how many planes you started with. 3. Mark under the number that shows how many birds you started with. 4. Count the entire set to find how many kites there are to begin with. Trace the circle and the X to show how many are being taken from the set. Write and trace to complete the subtraction sentence.

Name ______________________

Lesson 51

COMMON CORE STANDARD CC.K.OA.2

Lesson Objective: Understand addition as putting together or adding to and subtraction as taking apart or taking from to solve word problems.

Algebra • Addition and Subtraction

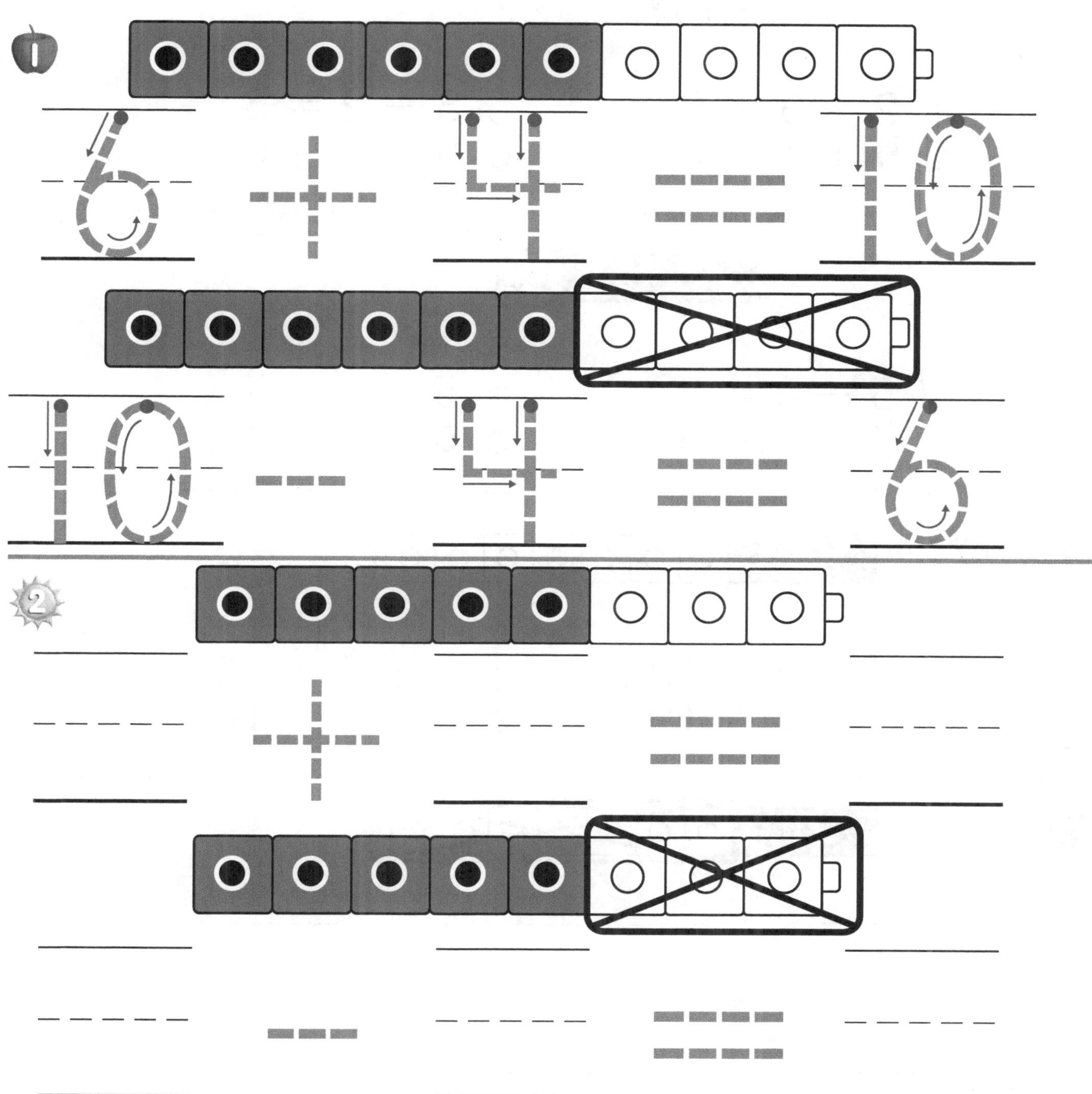

DIRECTIONS 1. Listen to the addition and subtraction word problems. Use cubes to add and to subtract. Complete the number sentences. Max has six blue cubes. Then he finds four yellow cubes. How many cubes does he have in all? Max has ten cubes. Then he gives four cubes to a friend. How many cubes does he have now? 2. Tell addition and subtraction word problems. Use cubes to add and to subtract. Complete the number sentences.

Name ______________________

Lesson 51
CC.K.OA.2

○ 2 + 3 = 5 ○ 3 + 2 = 5
○ 4 + 1 = 5 ○ 5 + 1 = 6

○ 5 − 3 = 2 ○ 5 − 1 = 4
○ 4 − 1 = 3 ○ 6 − 5 = 1

○ 4 + 6 = 10 ○ 2 + 8 = 10
○ 1 + 9 = 10 ○ 3 + 7 = 10

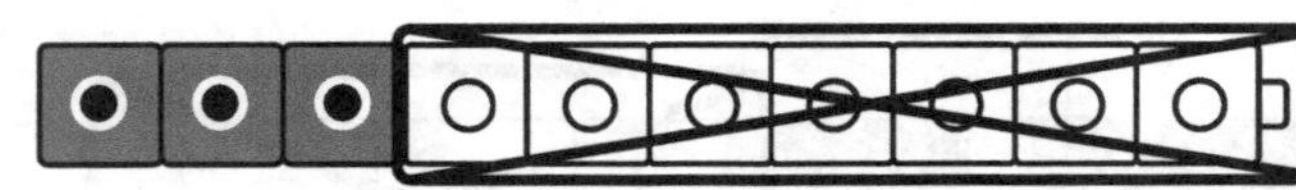

____ − ____ = ____

DIRECTIONS 1. Mark next to the addition sentence that matches the picture. **2.** Mark next to the subtraction sentence that matches the picture. **3.** Mark next to the addition sentence that matches the picture. **4.** Use cubes to subtract. Complete the number sentence.

Name ______________________

Lesson 52

COMMON CORE STANDARD CC.K.OA.3

Lesson Objective: Use objects or drawings to decompose 5 into pairs in more than one way.

Algebra • Ways to Make 5

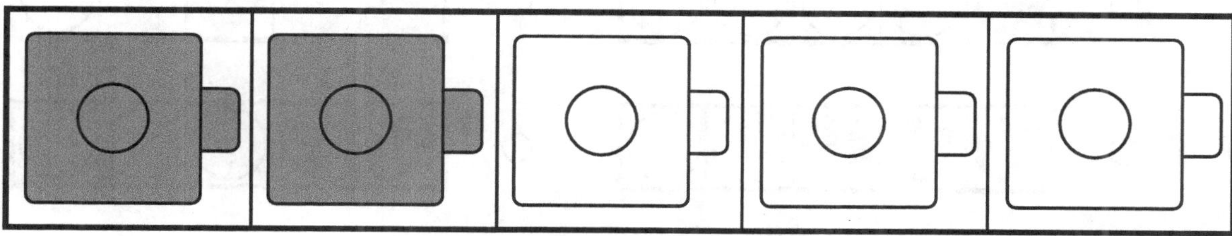

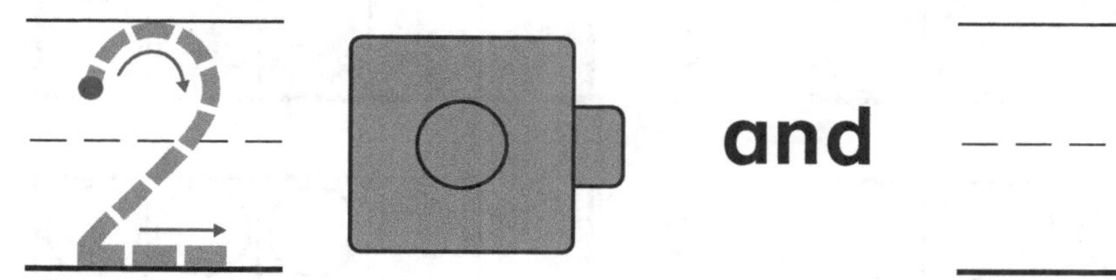

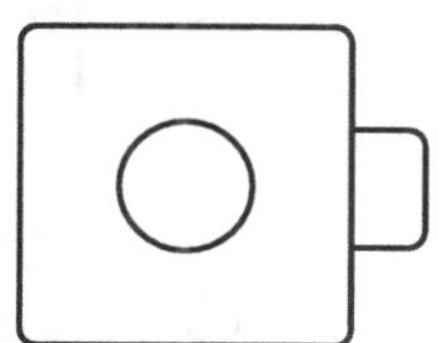

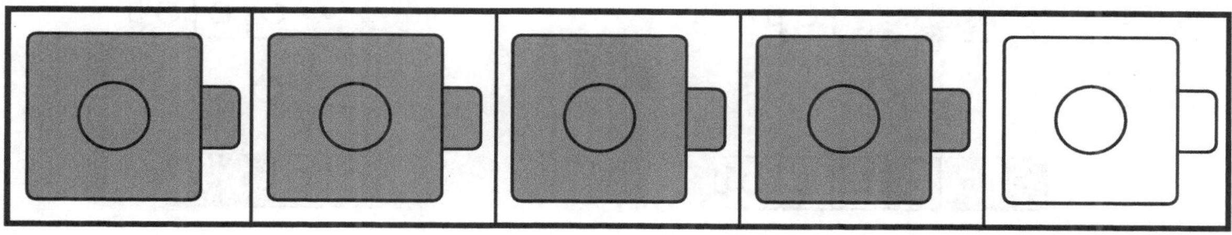

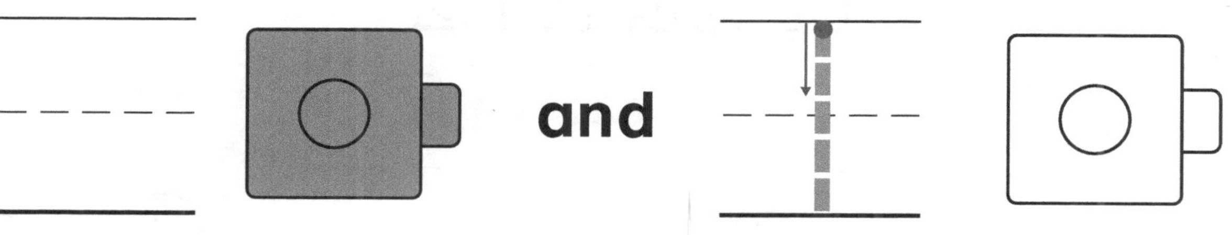

DIRECTIONS **1.** Count the gray cubes in the five frame. Trace the number. Count the white cubes in the five frame. Write the number to show a way to make 5. **2.** Count the gray cubes in the five frame. Write the number. Count the white cubes in the five frame. Trace the number to show a way to make 5.

Name ______________________

Lesson 52
CC.K.OA.3

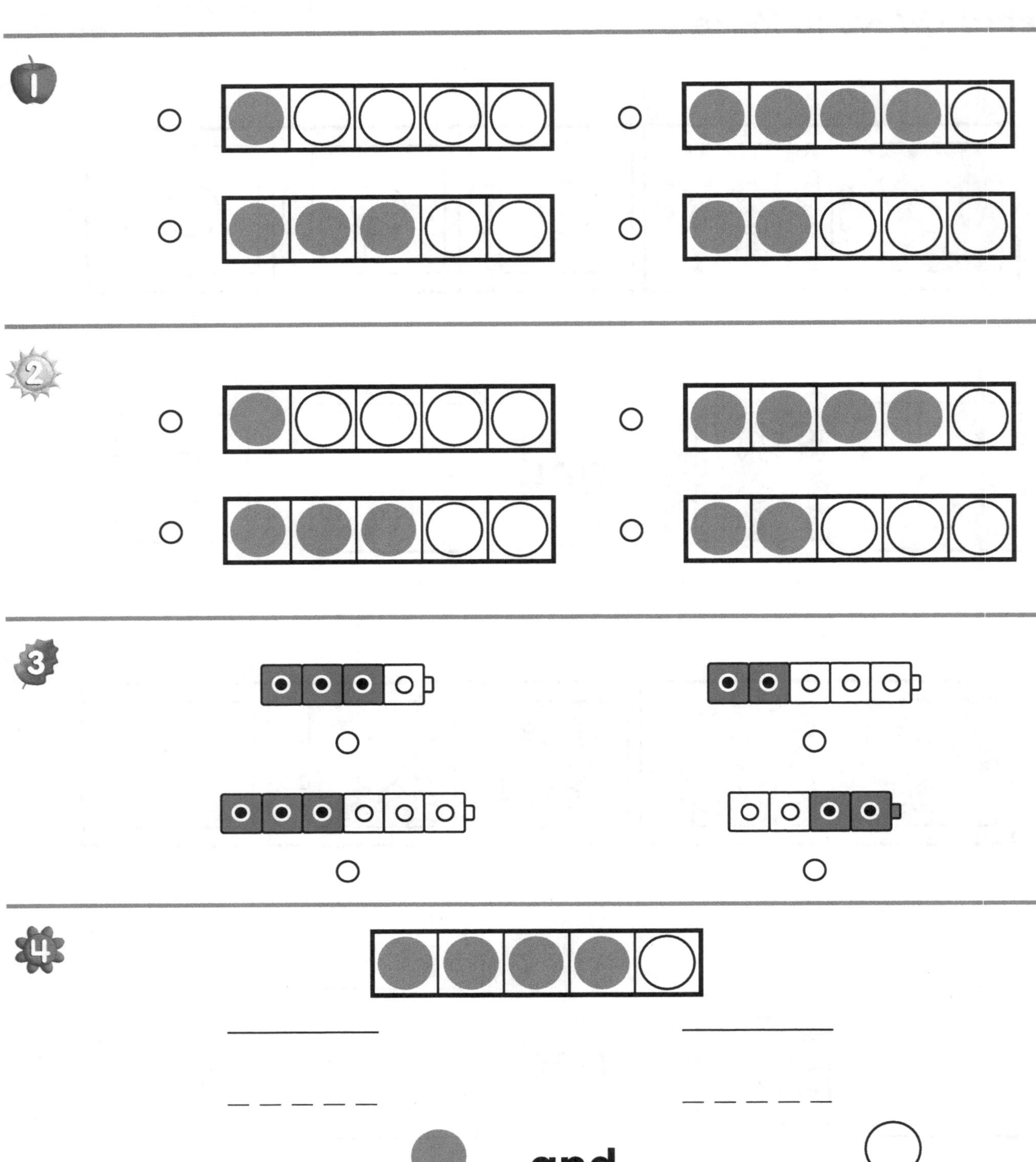

DIRECTIONS 1. Mark next to the five frame that shows three gray counters and two white counters. 2. Mark next to the five frame that shows one gray counter and four white counters. 3. Mark under the cube train that shows a way to make 5. 4. Write the numbers to show the pair that makes 5.

Name ______________________

Lesson 53

COMMON CORE STANDARD CC.K.OA.3

Lesson Objective: Decompose numbers within 5 into pairs in more than one way and record each decomposition with an equation.

Algebra • Number Pairs to 5

5 = 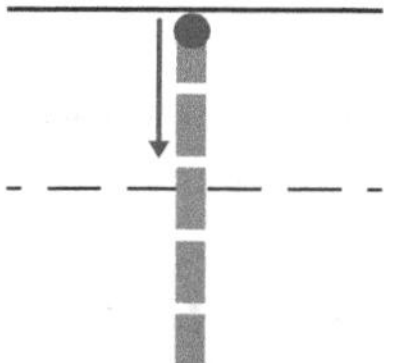  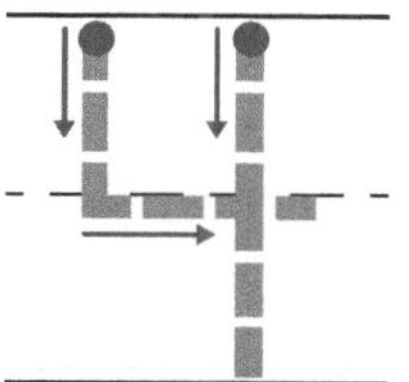

5 =   ____

5 =   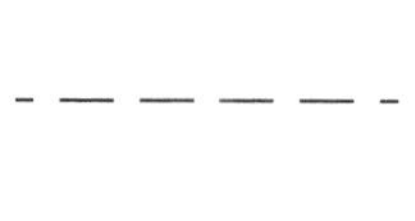

  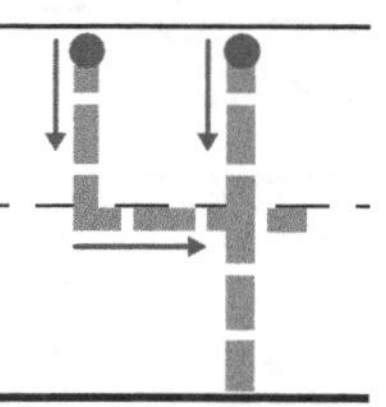  ____

DIRECTIONS Use two-color counters. **1–4.** Place five yellow counters in a row as shown. Look at the gray number. Turn that many counters to red. How many counters are yellow? Trace or write the numbers to show a number pair that makes 5.

Name ______________________

- ○ $3 = 2 + 1$
- ○ $4 = 3 + 1$
- ○ $2 = 1 + 1$
- ○ $4 = 2 + 2$

- ○ $3 = 1 + 2$
- ○ $4 = 2 + 2$
- ○ $4 = 1 + 3$
- ○ $5 = 2 + 3$

- ○ $5 = 1 + 4$
- ○ $5 = 4 + 1$
- ○ $4 = 2 + 2$
- ○ $5 = 3 + 2$

- ○ $5 = 4 + 1$
- ○ $5 = 2 + 3$
- ○ $5 = 3 + 2$
- ○ $4 = 3 + 1$

5

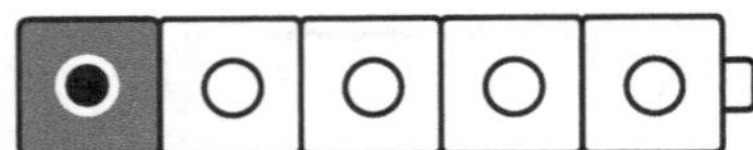

5 =

DIRECTIONS **1–4.** Mark beside the addition sentence that shows the number pair for the cube train. **5.** Complete the addition sentence that shows the number pair for the cube train.

Name ______________________________

Lesson 54

COMMON CORE STANDARD CC.K.OA.3

Lesson Objective: Decompose 6 and 7 into pairs in more than one way and record each decomposition with an equation.

Algebra • Number Pairs for 6 and 7

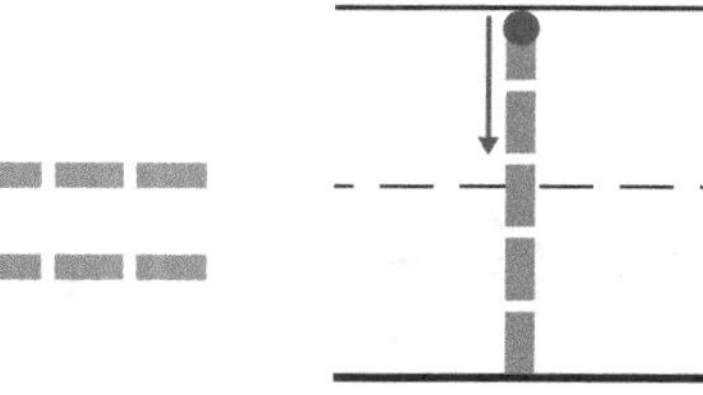

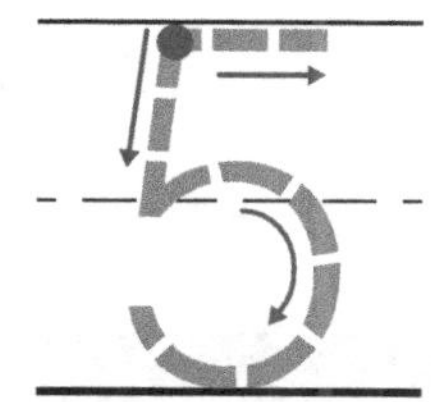

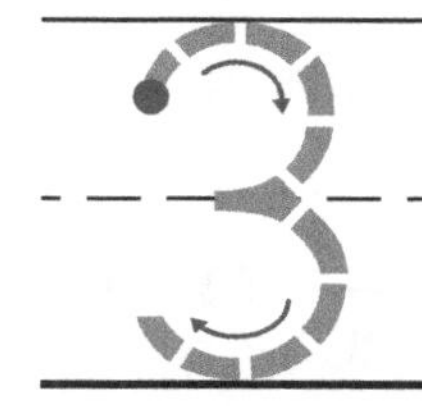

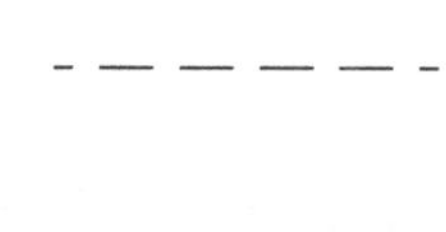

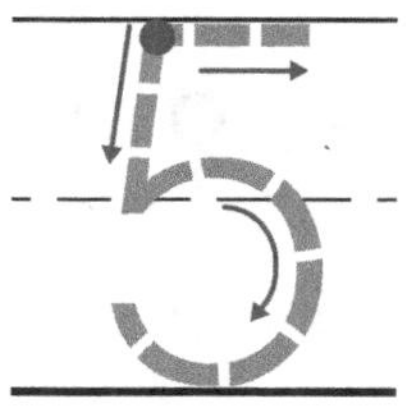

DIRECTIONS Use two-color counters. **1–2.** Place six yellow counters in a row as shown. Look at the gray number. Turn that many counters to red. How many counters are yellow? Trace or write the numbers to show a number pair that makes 6. **3.** Place seven yellow counters in a row as shown. Look at the gray number. Turn that many counters to red. How many counters are yellow? Trace or write the numbers to show a number pair that makes 7.

Name ____________________

Lesson 54
CC.K.OA.3

○ 6 = 2 + 4 ○ 6 = 5 + 1

○ 6 = 4 + 2 ○ 6 = 3 + 3

○ 6 = 5 + 1 ○ 6 = 2 + 4

○ 6 = 4 + 2 ○ 6 = 3 + 3

○ 7 = 6 + 1 ○ 7 = 4 + 3

○ 7 = 5 + 2 ○ 7 = 2 + 5

○ 7 = 3 + 4 ○ 7 = 4 + 3

○ 7 = 2 + 5 ○ 7 = 6 + 1

5

7 = 

DIRECTIONS **1–4.** Mark beside the addition sentence that shows the number pair for the cube train. **5.** Complete the addition sentence that shows the number pair for the cube train.

Name ______________________

Lesson 55

COMMON CORE STANDARD CC.K.OA.3

Lesson Objective: Decompose 8 into pairs in more than one way and record each decomposition with an equation.

Algebra • Number Pairs for 8

  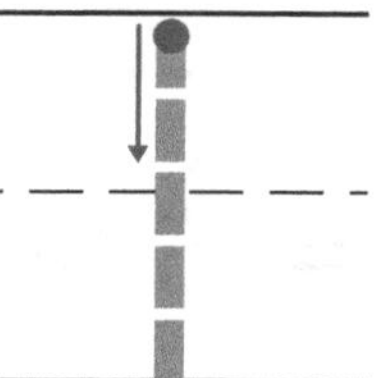  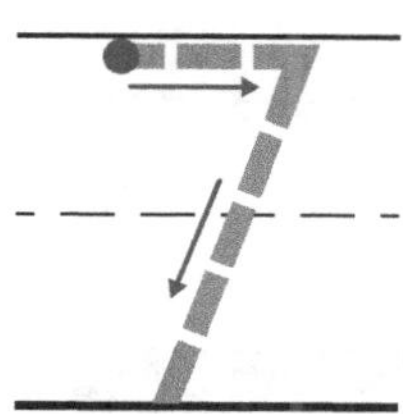

8 = 1 + 7

 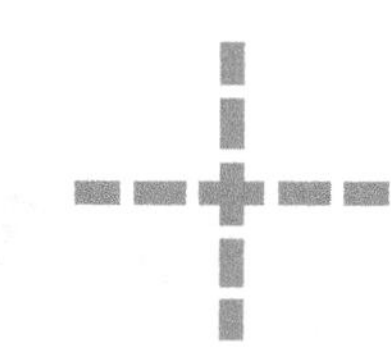

8 = 2 + ___

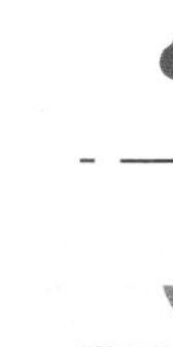  

8 = 3 + ___

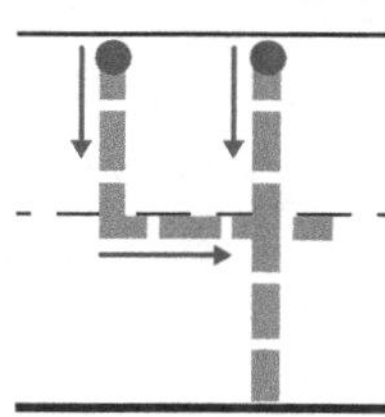 

8 = 4 + ___

DIRECTIONS Use two-color counters. **1–4.** Place eight yellow counters in a row as shown. Look at the gray number. Turn that many counters to red. How many counters are yellow? Trace or write the numbers to show a number pair that makes 8.

Name ______________________

Lesson 55
CC.K.OA.3

○ $8 = 5 + 3$ ○ $8 = 6 + 2$

○ $8 = 4 + 4$ ○ $8 = 1 + 7$

○ $8 = 5 + 3$ ○ $8 = 3 + 5$

○ $8 = 6 + 2$ ○ $8 = 7 + 1$

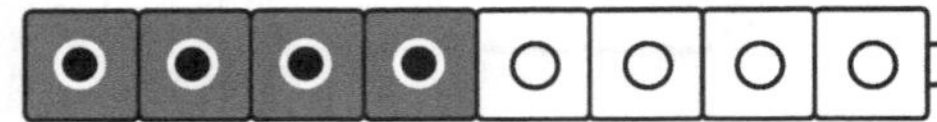

○ $8 = 7 + 1$ ○ $8 = 6 + 2$

○ $8 = 4 + 4$ ○ $8 = 5 + 3$

○ $8 = 4 + 4$ ○ $8 = 7 + 1$

○ $8 = 3 + 5$ ○ $8 = 2 + 6$

5

8 = ____ + ____

DIRECTIONS **1–4.** Mark beside the addition sentence that shows the number pair for the cube train. **5.** There are eight pencils in a packet. Eight of the pencils are orange. How many pencils are not orange? Draw and color to show how you solved. Complete the addition sentence to show the number pair.

Name ____________________

Lesson 56

COMMON CORE STANDARD CC.K.OA.3

Lesson Objective: Decompose 9 into pairs in more than one way and record each decomposition with an equation.

Algebra • Number Pairs for 9

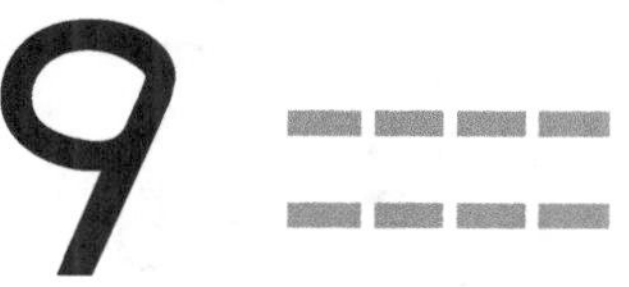

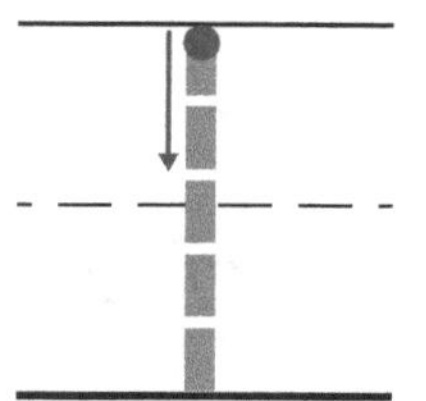

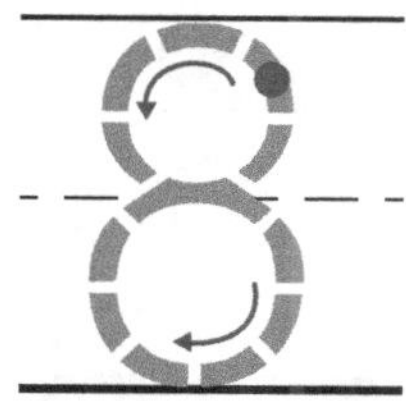

1. 9 = 1 + 8

2. 9 = 2 + ___

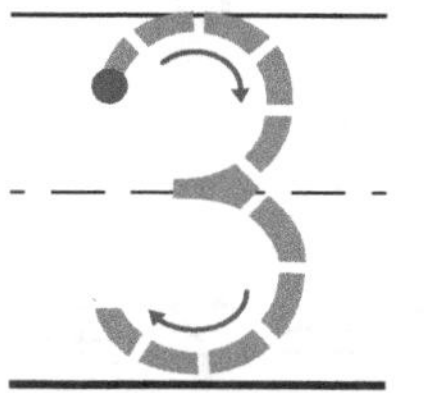

3. 9 = 3 + ___

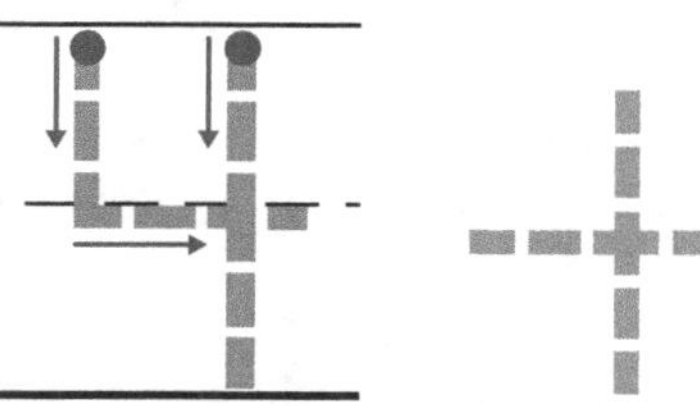

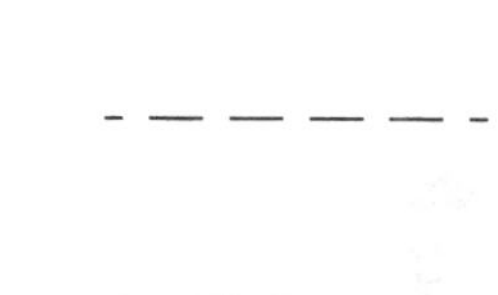

4. 9 = 4 + ___

DIRECTIONS Use two-color counters. **1–4.** Place nine yellow counters in a row as shown. Look at the gray number. Turn that many counters to red. How many counters are yellow? Trace or write the numbers to show a number pair that makes 9.

Name ______________________

Lesson 56
CC.K.OA.3

○ 9 = 8 + 1 ○ 9 = 3 + 6

○ 9 = 2 + 7 ○ 9 = 5 + 4

○ 9 = 7 + 2 ○ 9 = 5 + 4

○ 9 = 4 + 5 ○ 9 = 6 + 3

○ 9 = 2 + 7 ○ 9 = 3 + 6

○ 9 = 6 + 3 ○ 9 = 4 + 5

○ 9 = 7 + 2 ○ 9 = 2 + 7

○ 9 = 1 + 8 ○ 9 = 5 + 4

DIRECTIONS 1–4. Mark beside the addition sentence that shows the number pair for the cube train. **5.** There are nine children in a swimming class. None of them are girls. How many are boys? Complete the addition sentence to show the number pair.

Name ____________________

Lesson 57

COMMON CORE STANDARD CC.K.OA.3

Lesson Objective: Decompose 10 into pairs in more than one way and record each decomposition with an equation.

Algebra • Number Pairs for 10

10 = 1 + 9

10 = 2 + ____

10 = 3 + ____

4

10 = 4 + ____

DIRECTIONS Use two-color counters. **1–4.** Place ten yellow counters in a row as shown. Look at the gray number. Turn that many counters to red. How many counters are yellow? Trace or write the numbers to show a number pair that makes 10.

Name ______________________

Lesson 57
CC.K.OA.3

○ 10 = 4 + 6 ○ 10 = 7 + 3

○ 10 = 5 + 5 ○ 10 = 2 + 8

○ 10 = 7 + 3 ○ 10 = 8 + 2

○ 10 = 9 + 1 ○ 10 = 3 + 7

○ 10 = 5 + 5 ○ 10 = 6 + 4

○ 10 = 3 + 7 ○ 10 = 4 + 6

○ 10 = 6 + 4 ○ 10 = 8 + 2

○ 10 = 7 + 3 ○ 10 = 9 + 1

5

10 = ______ + ______

DIRECTIONS 1–4. Mark beside the addition sentence that shows the number pair for the cube train. **5.** Complete the addition sentence that shows the number pair for the cube train.

Name ______________________

Lesson 58

COMMON CORE STANDARD CC.K.OA.4

Lesson Objective: Use a drawing to make 10 from a given number.

Algebra • Ways to Make 10

1

7 yellow

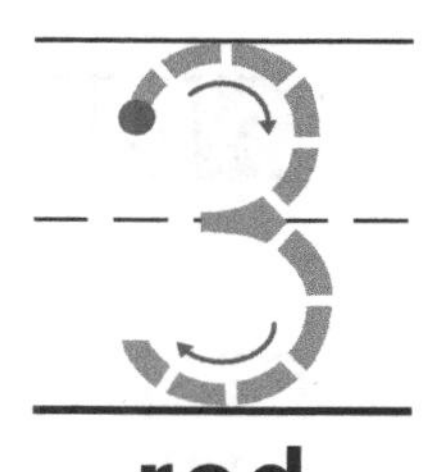

3 red

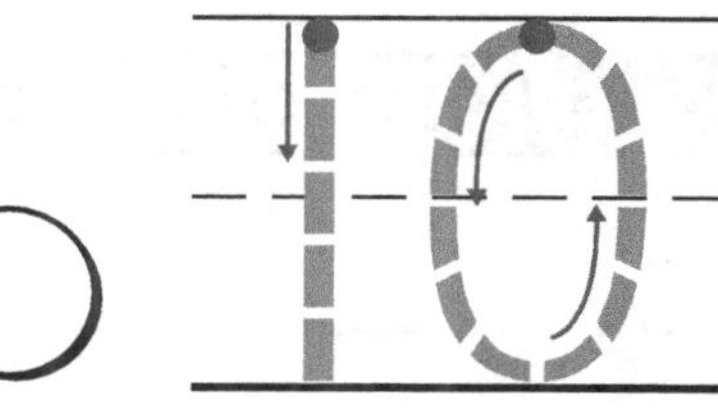

10 counters

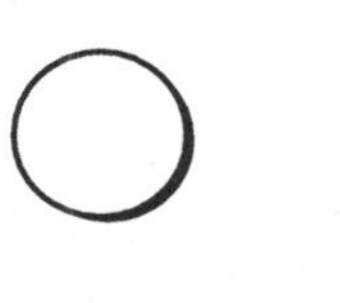

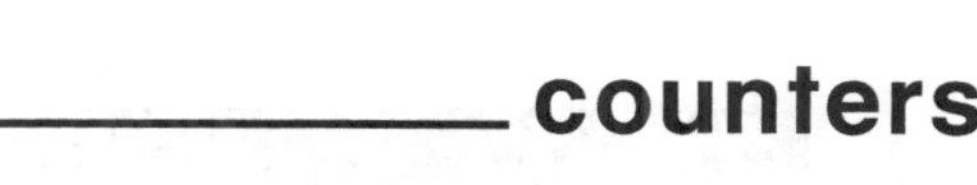

yellow ______ red ______ counters

yellow ______ red ______ counters

DIRECTIONS **1.** Look at the first number. Color that many counters yellow. Color the rest of the counters red. Trace the numbers. **2–3.** Look at the first number. Color that many counters yellow. Color the rest of the counters red. Write how many red counters. Write how many counters in all.

Name ______________________

Lesson 58
CC.K.OA.4

cubes

DIRECTIONS **1–3.** Mark next to the cube train that shows a way to make 10. **4.** Shade 7 cubes. Do not shade the other cubes. Write the number of shaded cubes. Write the number of unshaded cubes. Write how many in all.

Name ____________________

Lesson 59

COMMON CORE STANDARD CC.K.OA.4

Lesson Objective: Use a drawing to find 10 from a given number and record the equation.

Algebra • Write Addition Sentences for 10

1

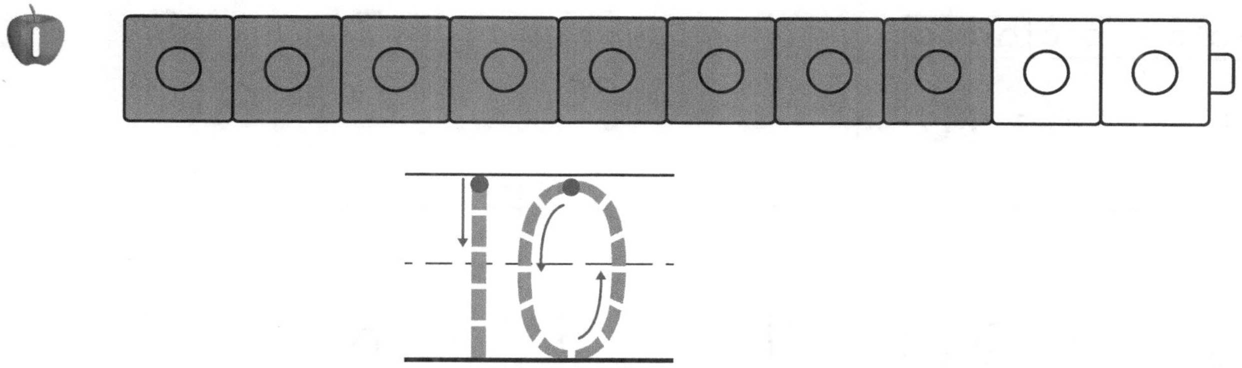

2

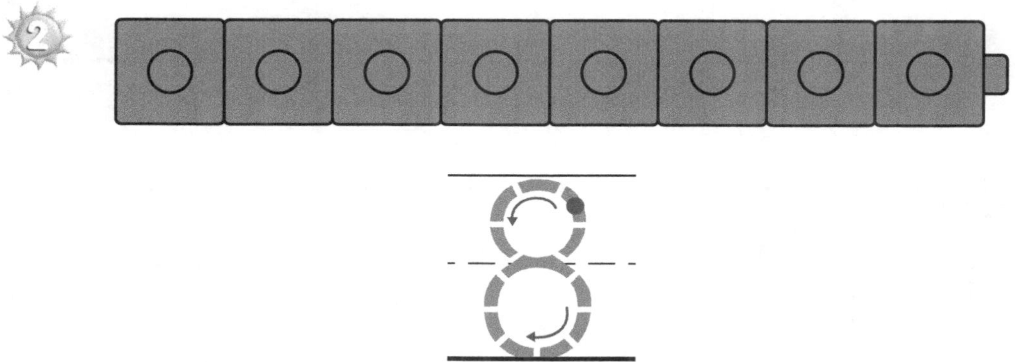

3

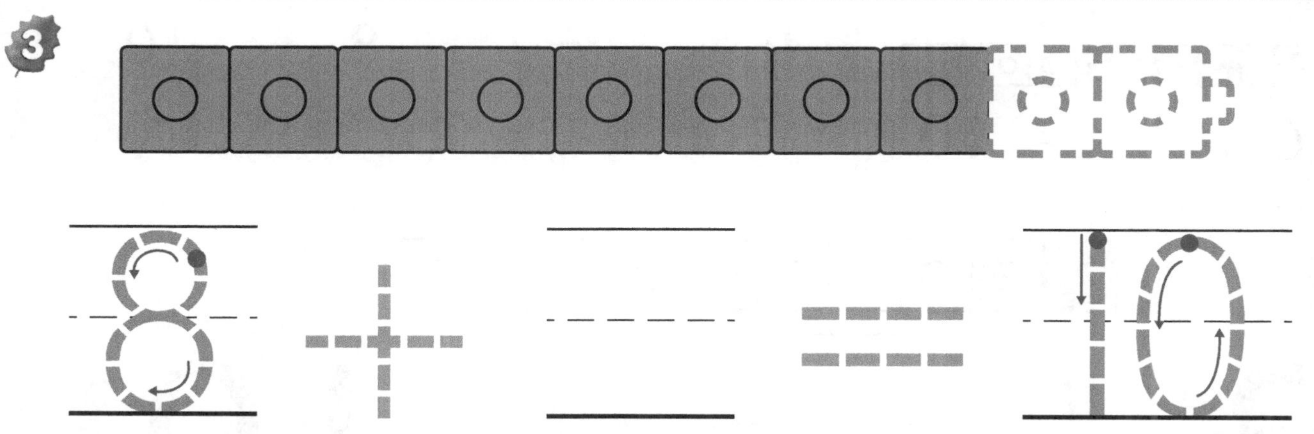

DIRECTIONS 1. Count the number of cubes. How many are there? Trace the number. **2.** How many gray cubes? Draw a dot on each gray cube as you count. Trace the number. **3.** How many white cubes do you need to make 10? Trace each white cube as you count. Write and trace to show this as an addition sentence.

Name ____________________

Lesson 59
CC.K.OA.4

1

1 + ___ = 10

3	5	7	9
○	○	○	○

2

5 + ___ = 10

4	5	6	7
○	○	○	○

3

3 + ___ = 10

6	7	8	9
○	○	○	○

4

6 + ___ = 10

4	6	8	10
○	○	○	○

5

2   10

DIRECTIONS **1–4.** Look at the cube train. Mark under the number that makes 10 when put together with the given number. **5.** Look at the cube train. Trace the symbols. Write the number that makes 10 when put together with the given number.

Name ______________________________

Lesson 60

COMMON CORE STANDARD CC.K.OA.5

Lesson Objective: Use objects and drawings to solve addition word problems within 5.

Algebra • Model and Draw Addition Problems

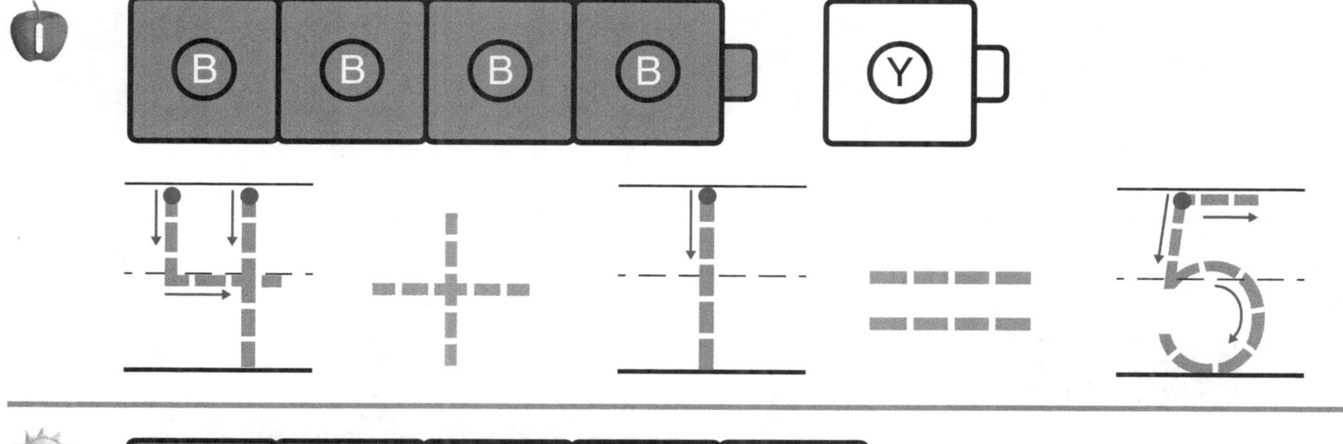

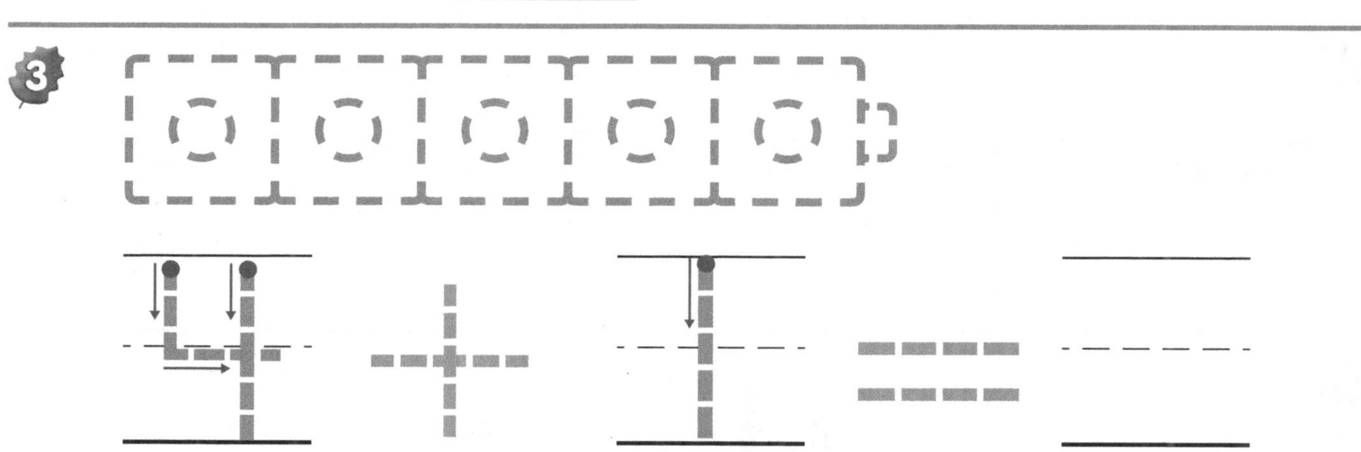

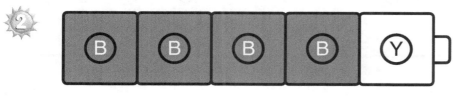

DIRECTIONS Emma has four blue cubes and one yellow cube. How many cubes does she have? **1.** Place cubes as shown to show the sets of cubes. Count how many in each set. Trace the numbers and the symbol. **2.** Place cubes as shown to model the cubes put together. Count the cubes. Write the number. **3.** Trace the cube train. Color to show the cubes put together. Trace and write to complete the addition sentence.

Name ________________________________

Lesson **60**
CC.K.OA.5

1 ○ 2 ○ 3 ○ 4 ○

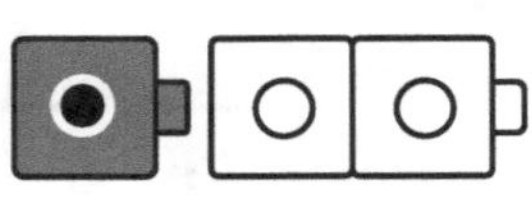

1 ○ 2 ○ 3 ○ 4 ○

2 ○ 3 ○ 4 ○ 5 ○

2 ○ 3 ○ 4 ○ 5 ○

5

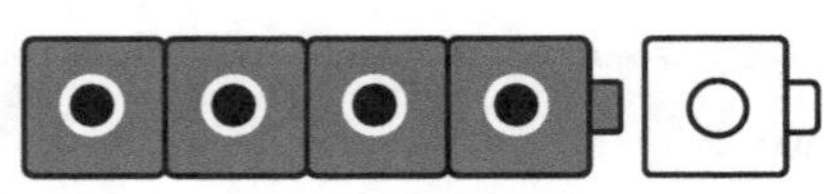

 +  =  

4 + 1 = ____

DIRECTIONS 1–4. Mark under the number that shows how many cubes there are after the cubes have been put together. **5.** Complete the addition sentence to show how many cubes there are after the cubes have been put together.

Name ______________________

Lesson 61

COMMON CORE STANDARD CC.K.OA.5

Lesson Objective: Solve addition word problems within 5 and record the equation.

Algebra • Write Addition Sentences

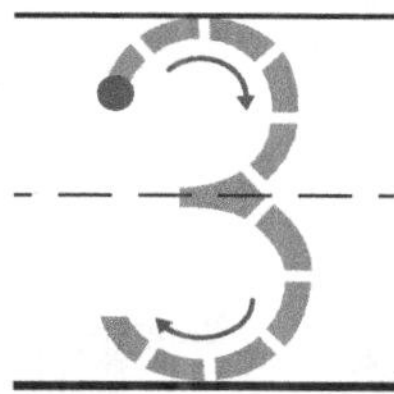

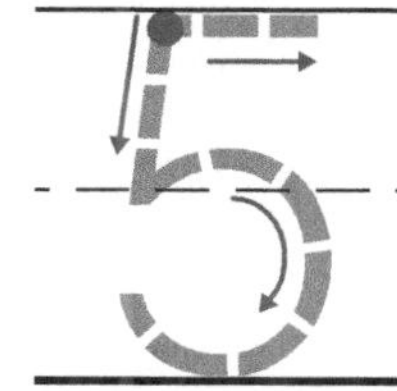

DIRECTIONS There are three boats. Some more boats come. Now there are five boats. How many more boats come? **1.** Circle the boats you start with. Trace the number. How many boats are being added to the set? Write the number. **2.** How many boats are there now? Write the number. **3.** Trace the numbers and symbols to show this as an addition sentence.

Name ____________________

Lesson **61**
CC.K.OA.5

$1 + \_\_\_ = 5$

1	2	3	4
○	○	○	○

$2 + \_\_\_ = 4$

1	2	3	4
○	○	○	○

$3 + \_\_\_ = 4$

1	2	3	4
○	○	○	○

$2 + \_\_\_ = 5$

DIRECTIONS **1–3.** Mark under the number that would complete the addition sentence. **4.** Ian has 2 apples. Then he buys more apples. Now he has 5 apples. How many apples does Ian buy? Complete the addition sentence.

Name ____________________

Lesson 62

COMMON CORE STANDARD CC.K.OA.5

Lesson Objective: Use objects and drawings to solve subtraction word problems within 5.

Algebra • Model and Draw Subtraction Problems

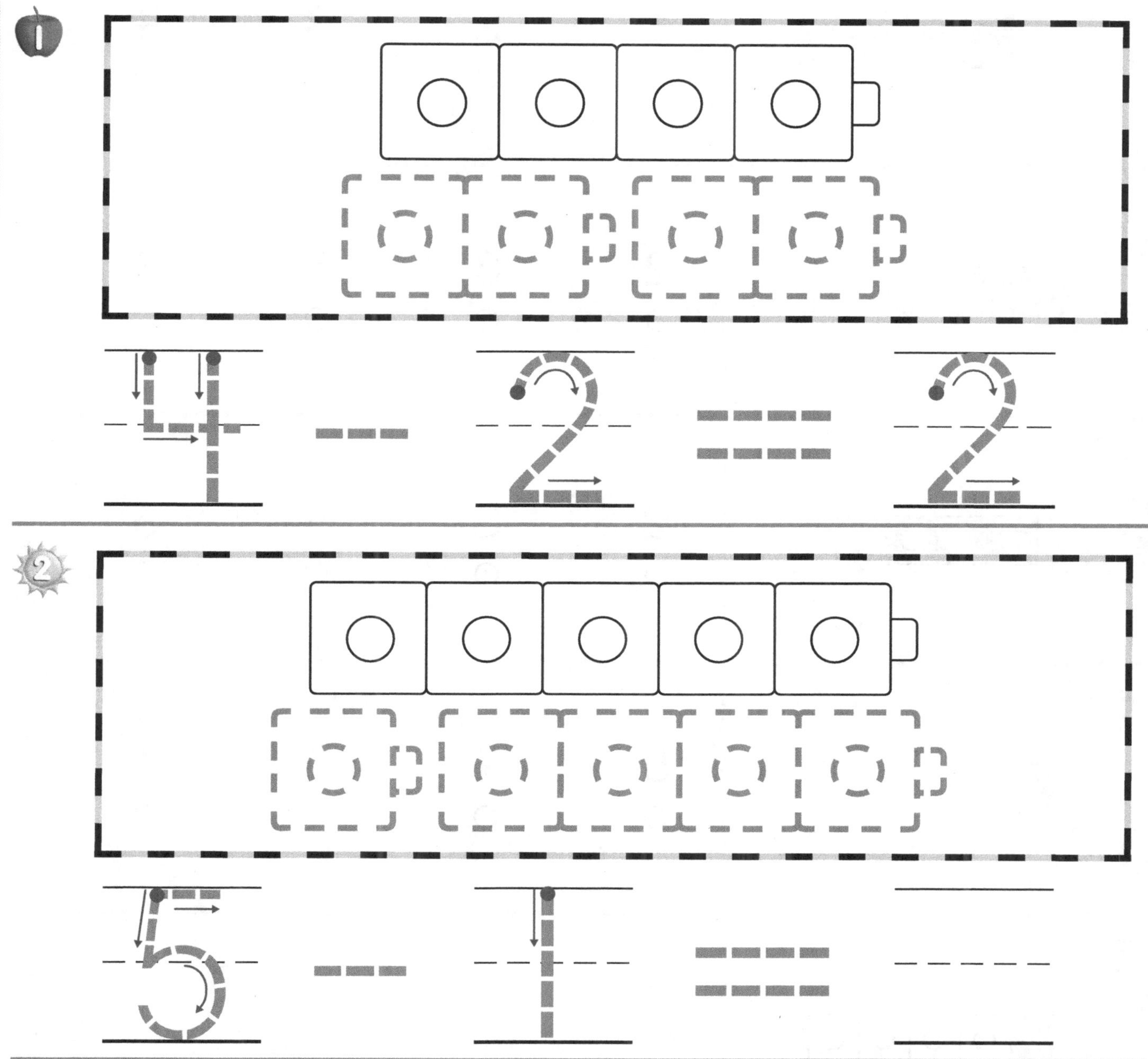

DIRECTIONS Model the subtraction word problem with cubes. **1.** There are four race cars. Two race cars are blue and the rest are green. How many race cars are green? Start with four cubes. Take apart a two-cube train. How many cubes are left? Trace the cube trains. Trace to complete the subtraction sentence. **2.** There are five rockets. One rocket is orange and the rest are red. How many rockets are red? Start with a five-cube train. Take apart one cube. How many cubes are left? Trace the cube trains. Trace and write to complete the subtraction sentence.

Name ______________________

Lesson 62
CC.K.OA.5

1

1	2	3	4
○	○	○	○

2

2	3	5	7
○	○	○	○

3

2	3	4	5
○	○	○	○

4

5	4	2	1
○	○	○	○

5

5 − 1 = ____

DIRECTIONS 1–4. Mark under the number that shows how many gray cubes are left after the cubes have been taken apart. **5.** One cube is gray and the rest are white. How many cubes are white? Trace and write to complete the subtraction sentence.

Name ____________________

Lesson 63

COMMON CORE STANDARD CC.K.OA.5

Lesson Objective: Solve subtraction word problems within 5 and record the equation.

Algebra • Write Subtraction Sentences

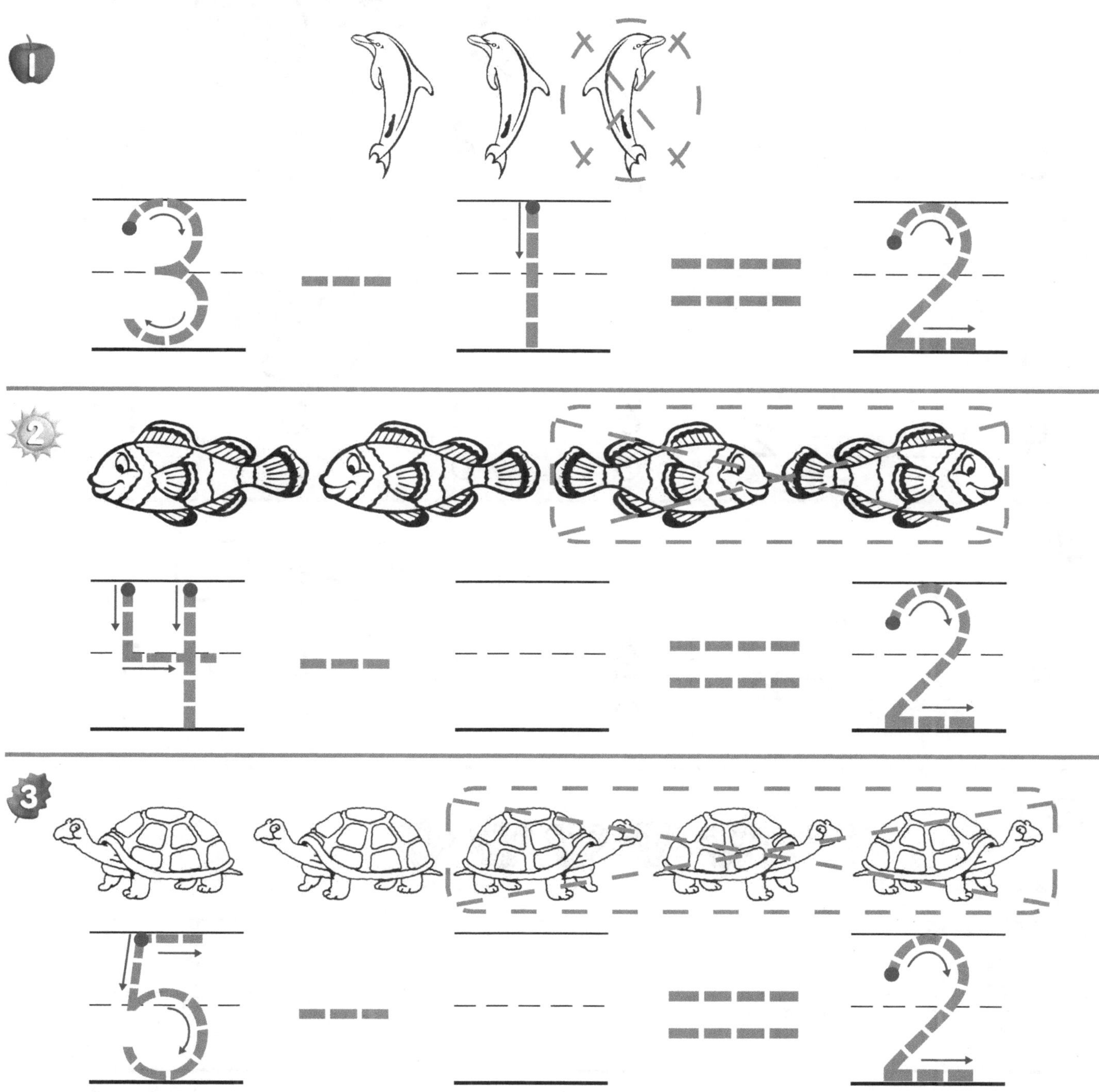

DIRECTIONS **1.** Listen to the subtraction word problem. I saw three dolphins. Some swam away. Then there were only two. How many dolphins swam away? Trace the circle and X to show one dolphin is being taken from the set. Trace to complete the subtraction sentence. **2–3.** Tell what is happening. Trace the circle and X to show how many are being taken from the set. Trace and write to complete the subtraction sentence.

Name ____________________

Lesson 63
CC.K.OA.5

$3 - \_\_\_ = 2$

1 ○ 2 ○ 3 ○ 4 ○

$4 - \_\_\_ = 2$

6 ○ 3 ○ 2 ○ 1 ○

$5 - \_\_\_ = 2$

2 ○ 3 ○ 5 ○ 8 ○

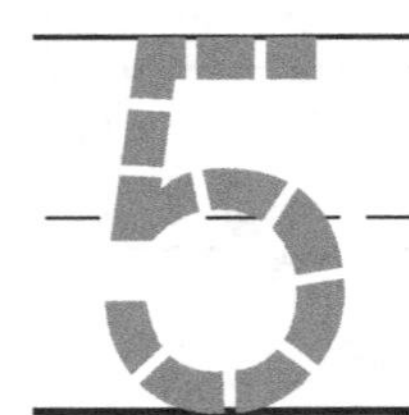 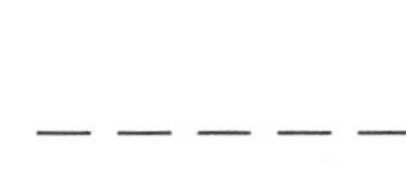  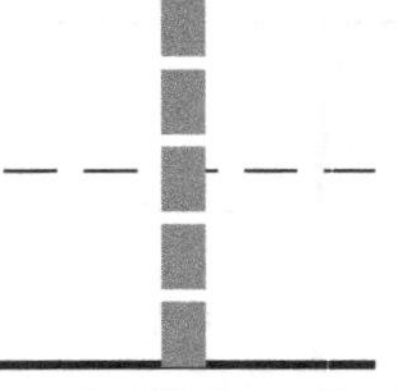

5 – ___ = 1

DIRECTIONS 1. Mark under the number that shows how many penguins are being taken from the set. 2. Mark under the number that shows how many dolphins are being taken from the set. 3. Mark under the number that shows how many fish are being taken from the set. 4. Circle and mark an X to show how many shells are being taken from the set. Trace and write to complete the subtraction sentence.

Name ______________________

Lesson 64

COMMON CORE STANDARD CC.K.NBT.1

Lesson Objective: Use objects to decompose the numbers 11 and 12 into ten ones and some further ones.

Model and Count 11 and 12

11
eleven

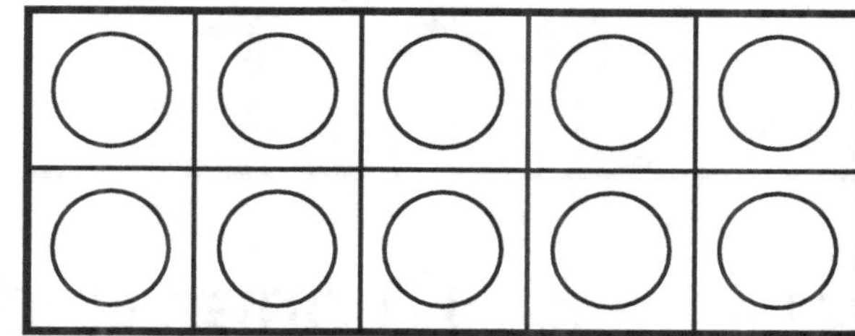

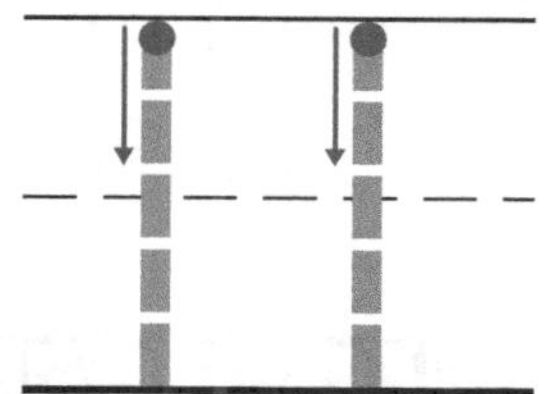

12
twelve

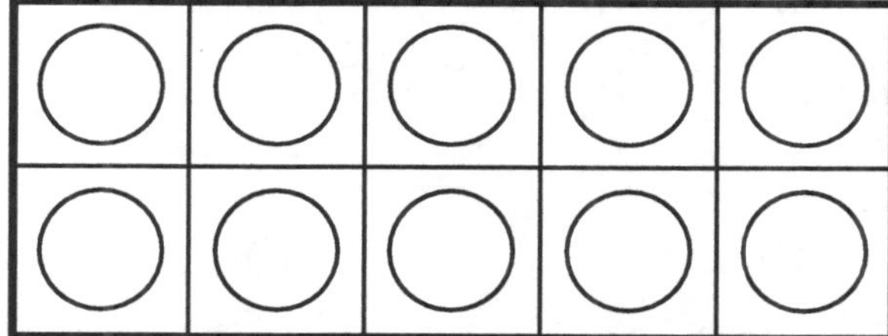

DIRECTIONS 1. How many counters are in the ten frame? Draw a dot on each counter as you count. Trace the counter below to show 11. Trace the number. **2.** How many counters are in the ten frame? Draw a dot on each counter as you count. Draw counters below to show 12. Write the number.

Name ______________________

Lesson 64
CC.K.NBT.1

○ ○ ○ ○

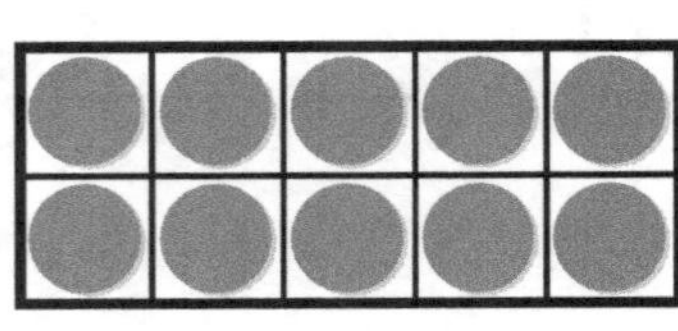

○ 10 ones and 0 ones
○ 10 ones and 1 one
○ 10 ones and 2 ones
○ 10 ones and 3 ones

○ ○ ○ ○

Write the answer.

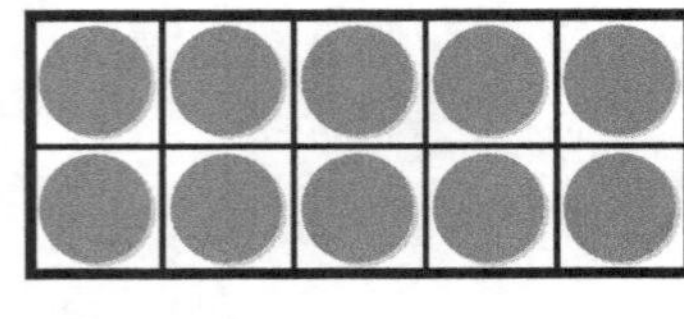

10 ones and ______ ones

DIRECTIONS 1. Mark under the set that shows 11. **2.** Look at the counters. How many ones are in the ten frame? How many more ones are there? Mark next to your answer. **3.** Mark under the set that shows 12. **4.** Look at the counters. How many more ones than 10 ones are there? Write the number.

Name ______________________

Lesson 65

COMMON CORE STANDARD CC.K.NBT.1

Lesson Objective: Use objects to decompose the numbers 13 and 14 into ten ones and some further ones.

Model and Count 13 and 14

13
thirteen

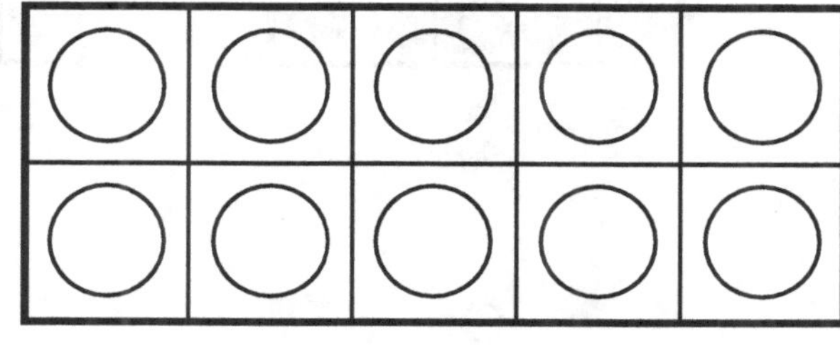

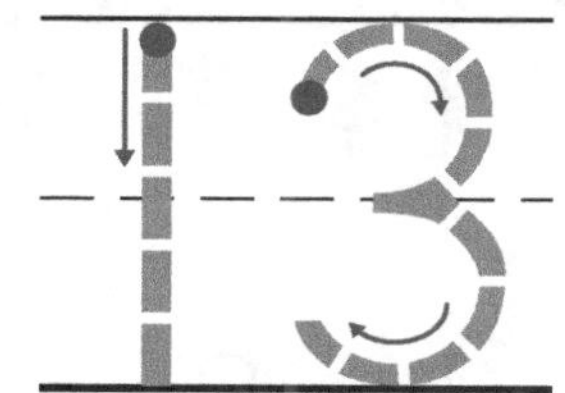

fourteen

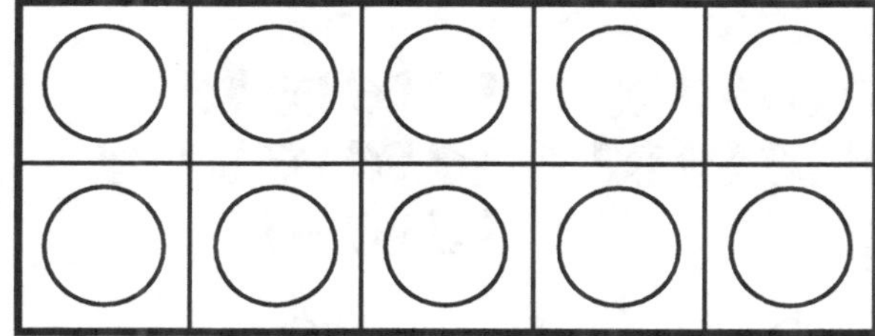

DIRECTIONS **1.** How many counters are in the ten frame? Draw a dot on each counter as you count. Trace the counters below to show 13. Trace the number. **2.** How many counters are in the ten frame? Draw a dot on each counter as you count. Draw counters below to show 14. Write the number.

Name ____________________

Lesson 65
CC.K.NBT.1

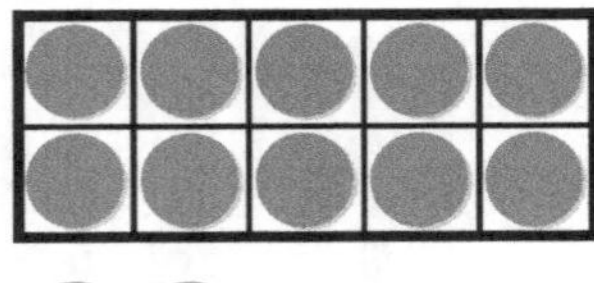 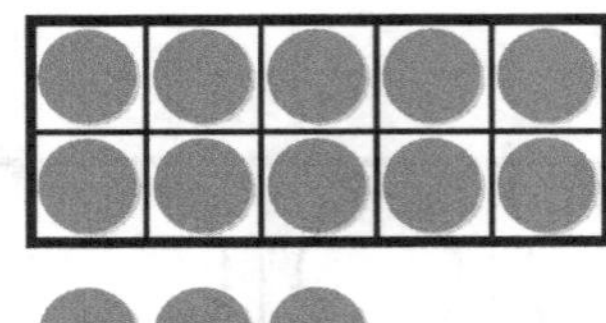 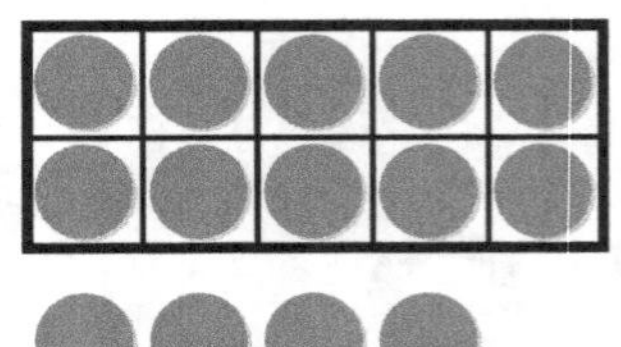

○ ○ ○

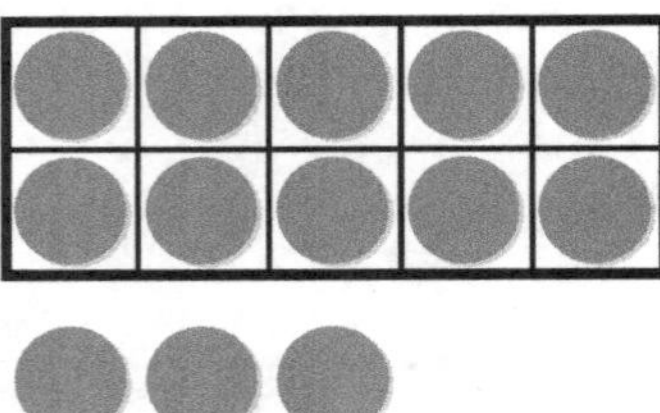

○ 10 ones and 1 one
○ 10 ones and 2 ones
○ 10 ones and 3 ones
○ 10 ones and 4 ones

○ ○ ○ ○

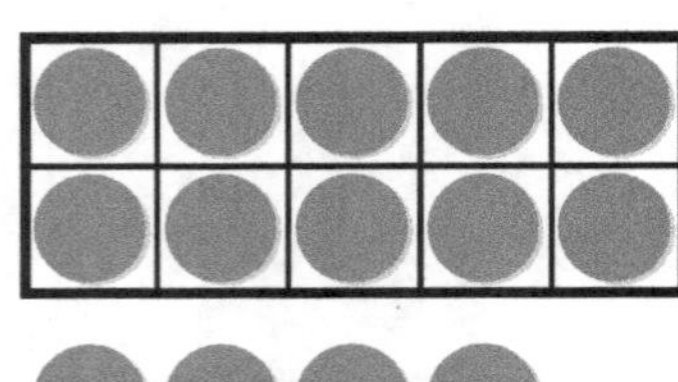

10 ones and ______ ones

DIRECTIONS 1. Mark under the set of counters that shows 14. **2.** Look at the counters. How many ones are in the ten frame? How many more ones are there? Mark next to your answer. **3.** Mark under the set that shows 13. **4.** Look at the counters. How many more ones than 10 ones are there? Write the number.

Name ________________________

Lesson 66

COMMON CORE STANDARD CC.K.NBT.1

Lesson Objective: Use objects to decompose 15 into ten ones and some further ones and represent 15 with a number name and a written numeral.

Model, Count, and Write 15

1

15
fifteen

☆ ☆ ☆ ☆ ☆
☆ ☆ ☆ ☆ ☆

☆ ☆ ☆ ☆ ☆

15

2

☆ ☆ ☆ ☆ ☆
☆ ☆ ☆ ☆ ☆

3

☆ ☆ ☆ ☆ ☆

4

____ + ____ = ____

DIRECTIONS 1. Count and tell how many. Draw a dot on each object as you count. Trace the number. **2.** Look at the objects in the ten frame in Exercise 1. Count and write the number. **3.** Look at the objects below the ten frame in Exercise 1. Count and write the number. **4.** Look at the ten ones and some more ones in Exercise 1. Complete the addition sentence to match.

Name ______________________

Lesson 66
CC.K.NBT.1

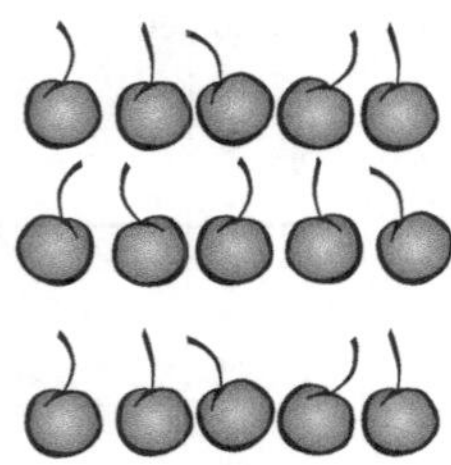

12	13	14	15
○	○	○	○

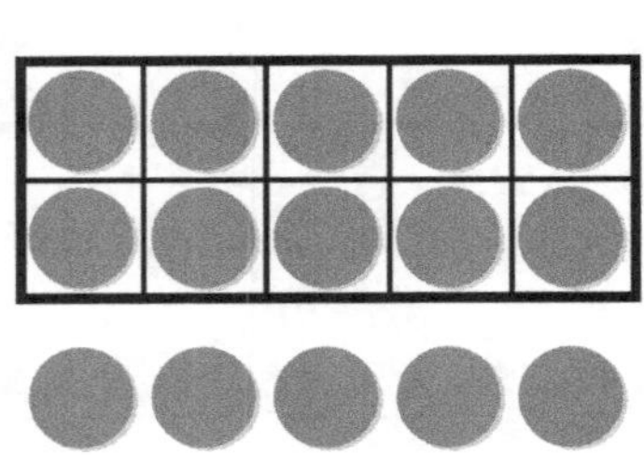

- ○ 10 ones and 2 ones
- ○ 10 ones and 3 ones
- ○ 10 ones and 4 ones
- ○ 10 ones and 5 ones

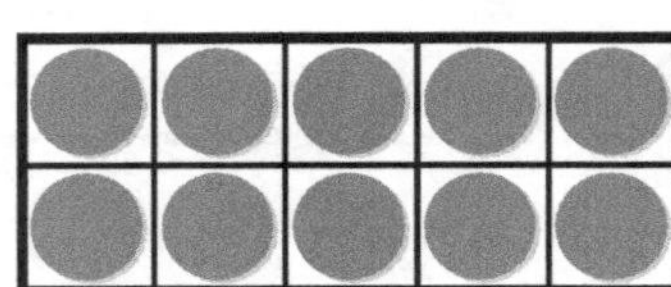 

○ $10 + 5 = 15$ ○ $10 + 4 = 14$
○ $10 + 3 = 13$ ○ $10 + 2 = 12$

______

DIRECTIONS 1. Count. Mark under the number that tells how many. 2. Look at the counters. How many ones are in the ten frame? How many more ones are there? Mark next to your answer. 3. Look at the ten ones and some more ones. Mark next to the addition sentence that matches. 4. Count. Write the number that tells how many.

Name ______________________

Lesson 67

COMMON CORE STANDARD CC.K.NBT.1

Lesson Objective: Use objects to decompose the numbers 16 and 17 into ten ones and some further ones.

Model and Count 16 and 17

16

sixteen

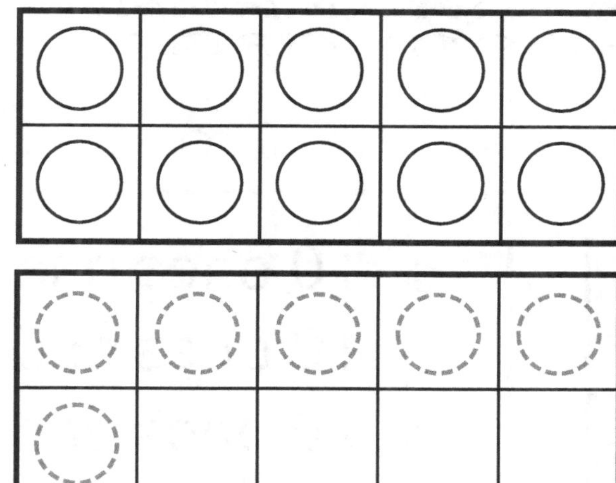

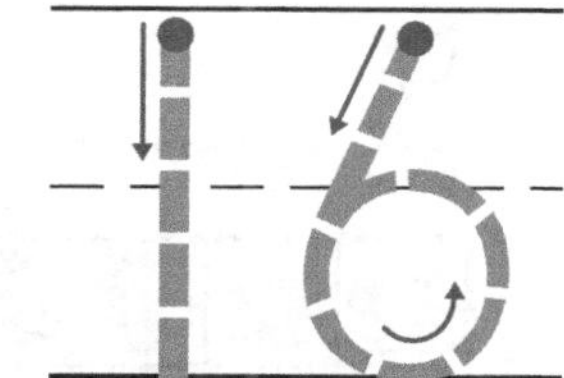

17

seventeen

DIRECTIONS 1. How many counters are in the top ten frame? Draw a dot on each counter as you count. Trace the counters in the ten frame below to show 16. Trace the number. **2.** How many counters are in the top ten frame? Draw a dot on each counter as you count. Draw counters in the ten frame below to show 17. Write the number.

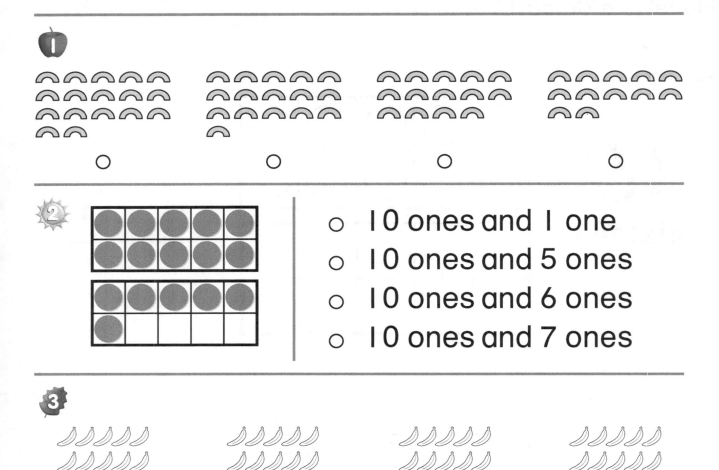

Name ______________________________

Lesson 67
CC.K.NBT.1

1

○ ○ ○ ○

2

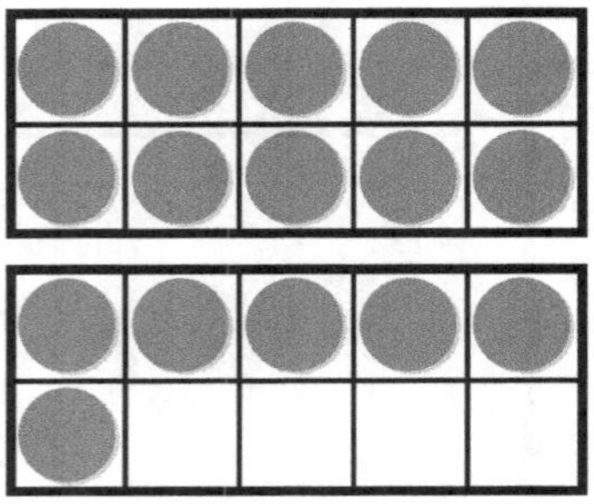

○ 10 ones and 1 one
○ 10 ones and 5 ones
○ 10 ones and 6 ones
○ 10 ones and 7 ones

3

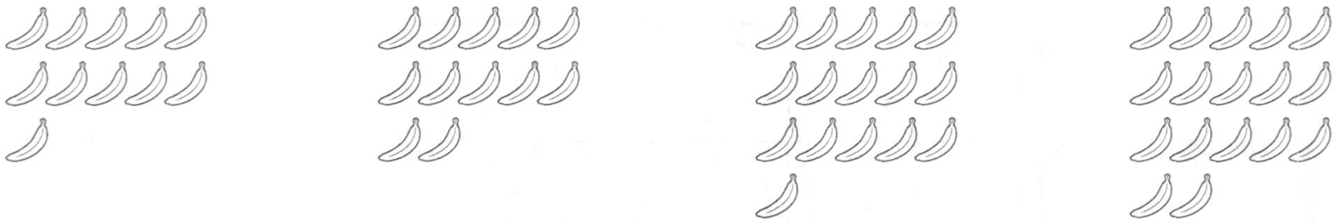

○ ○ ○ ○

4

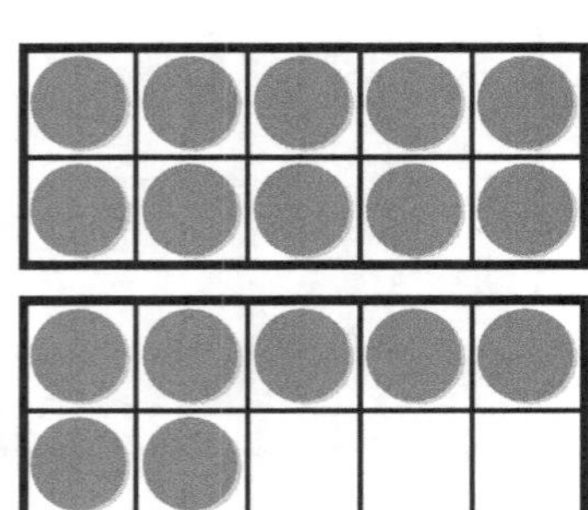

______

10 ones and ______ ones

DIRECTIONS 1. Mark under the set that shows 17. **2.** Look at the counters. How many ones are in the top ten frame? How many ones are in the bottom ten frame? Mark next to your answer. **3.** Mark under the set that shows 16. **4.** Look at the counters. How many ones are in the bottom ten frame? Write the number.

Name ______________________

Lesson 68

COMMON CORE STANDARD CC.K.NBT.1

Lesson Objective: Use objects to decompose the numbers 18 and 19 into ten ones and some further ones.

Model and Count 18 and 19

1

18

eighteen

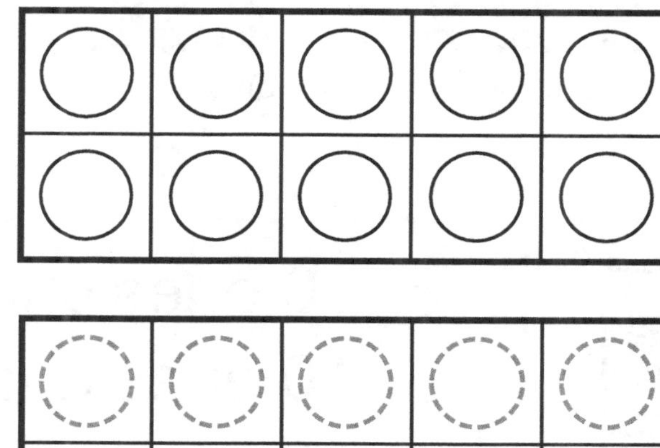

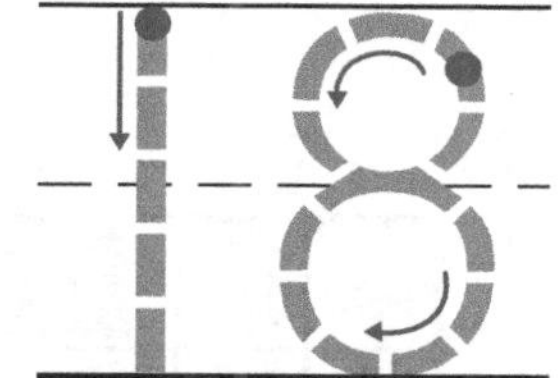

19

nineteen

DIRECTIONS 1. How many counters are in the top ten frame? Draw a dot on each counter as you count. Trace the counters in the ten frame below to show 18. Trace the number. **2.** How many counters are in the top ten frame? Draw a dot on each counter as you count. Draw counters in the ten frame to show 19. Write the number.

Name ____________________

Lesson 68
CC.K.NBT.1

○ ○ ○ ○

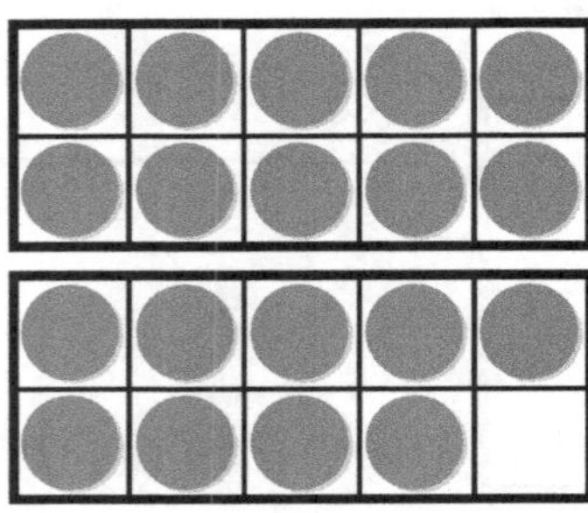

○ 10 ones and 4 ones
○ 10 ones and 5 ones
○ 10 ones and 8 ones
○ 10 ones and 9 ones

○ ○ ○ ○

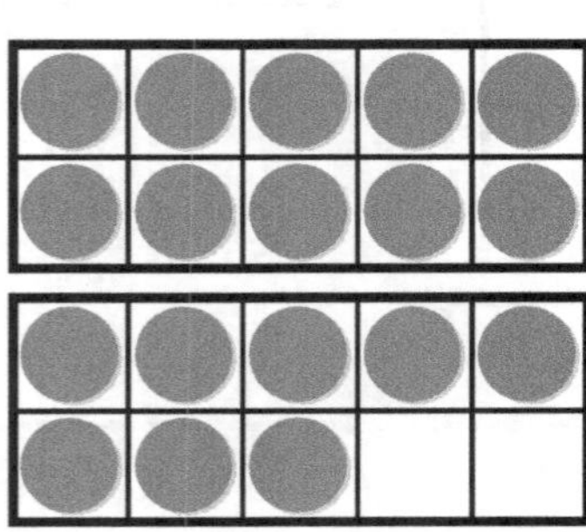

10 ones and ______ ones

DIRECTIONS **1.** Mark under the set that shows 18. **2.** Look at the counters. How many ones are in the top ten frame? How many ones are in the bottom ten frame? Mark next to your answer. **3.** Mark under the set that shows 19. **4.** Look at the counters. How many ones are in the bottom ten frame? Write the number.

Name ______________________________

Lesson 69

COMMON CORE STANDARD CC.K.MD.1

Lesson Objective: Describe several measurable attributes of a single object.

Length, Height, and Weight

DIRECTIONS **1.** Use red to trace the line that shows how to measure the length. **2.** Use blue to trace the line that shows how to measure the height. **3–4.** Use red to trace the line that shows how to measure the length. Use blue to trace the line that shows how to measure the height. Talk about another way to measure the object.

Name ____________________

Lesson 69
CC.K.MD.1

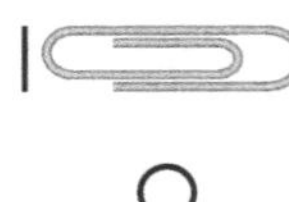
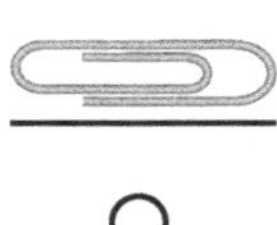
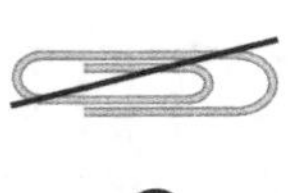
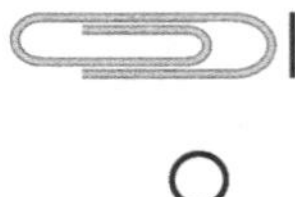

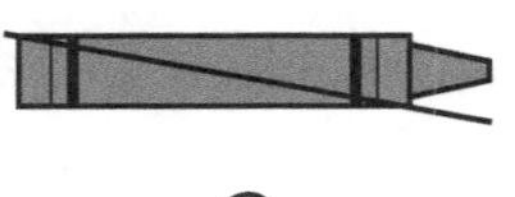

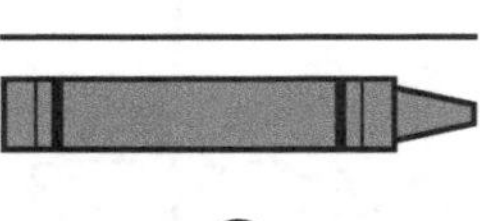
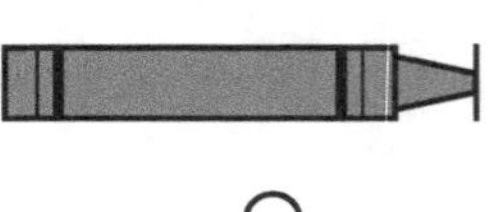

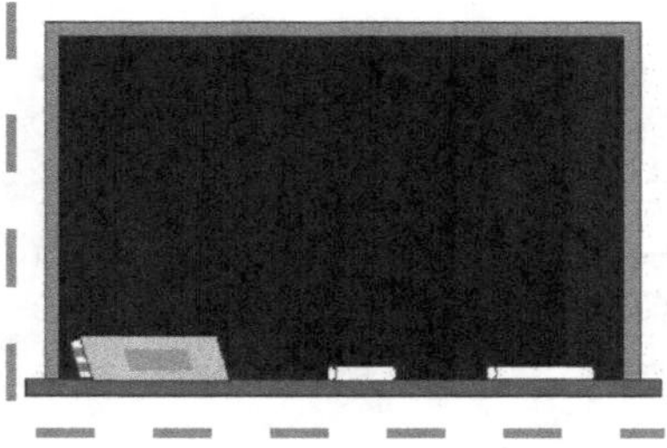

DIRECTIONS **1–2.** Mark under the picture that has a line that shows how to measure the length of the object. **3.** Mark under the picture that has a line that shows how to measure the height of the object. **4.** Circle the dashed line that shows how to measure the length. Mark an X on the dashed line that shows how to measure the height.

Name ____________________

Lesson 70

COMMON CORE STANDARD CC.K.MD.2

Lesson Objective: Directly compare the lengths of two objects.

Compare Lengths

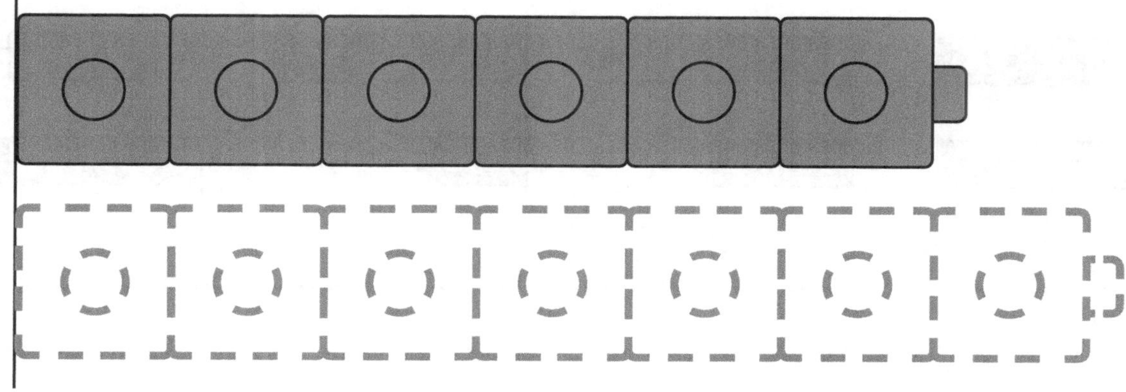

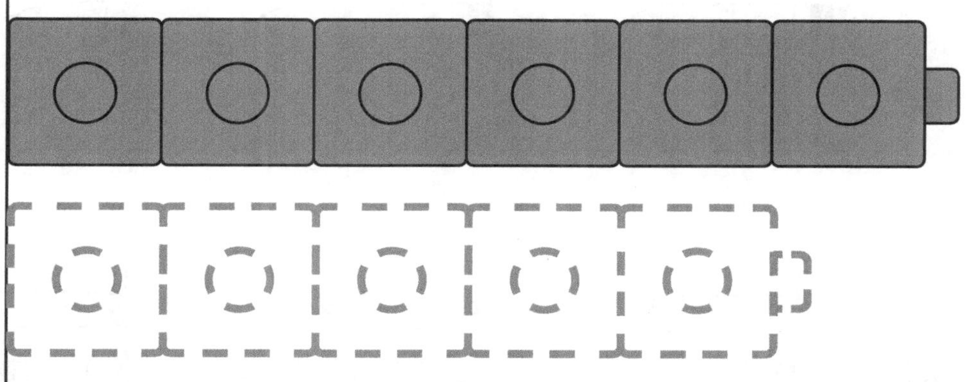

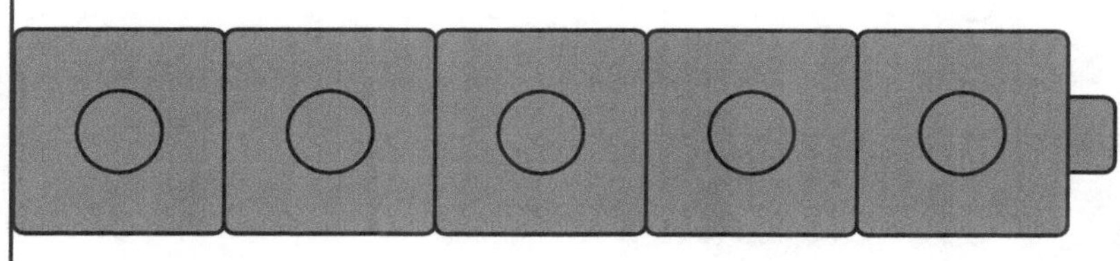

DIRECTIONS **1.** Place cubes on the longer cube train. Trace and color the cube train. **2.** Place cubes on the shorter cube train. Trace and color the cube train. **3.** Make a cube train that is longer than the cube train shown. Draw and color the cube train.

Name ______________________________

Lesson 70
CC.K.MD.2

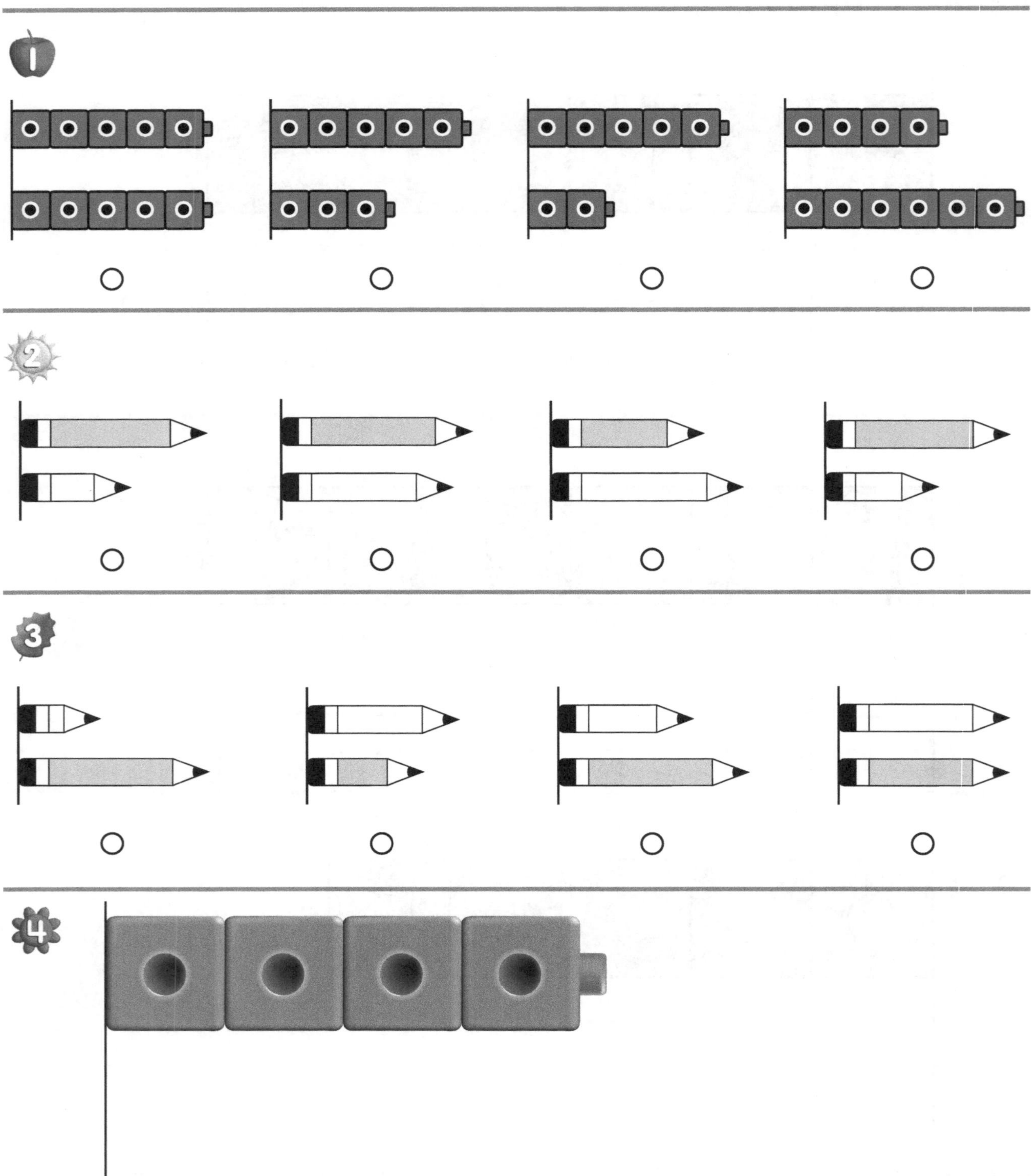

DIRECTIONS 1. Mark under the set with two cube trains that are about the same length. 2. Mark under the set that shows the gray pencil is shorter than the white pencil. 3. Mark under the set that shows the white pencil is longer than the gray pencil. 4. Draw a cube train that is longer than the cube train shown.

Name ______________________________

Lesson 71

COMMON CORE STANDARD CC.K.MD.2

Lesson Objective: Directly compare the heights of two objects.

Compare Heights

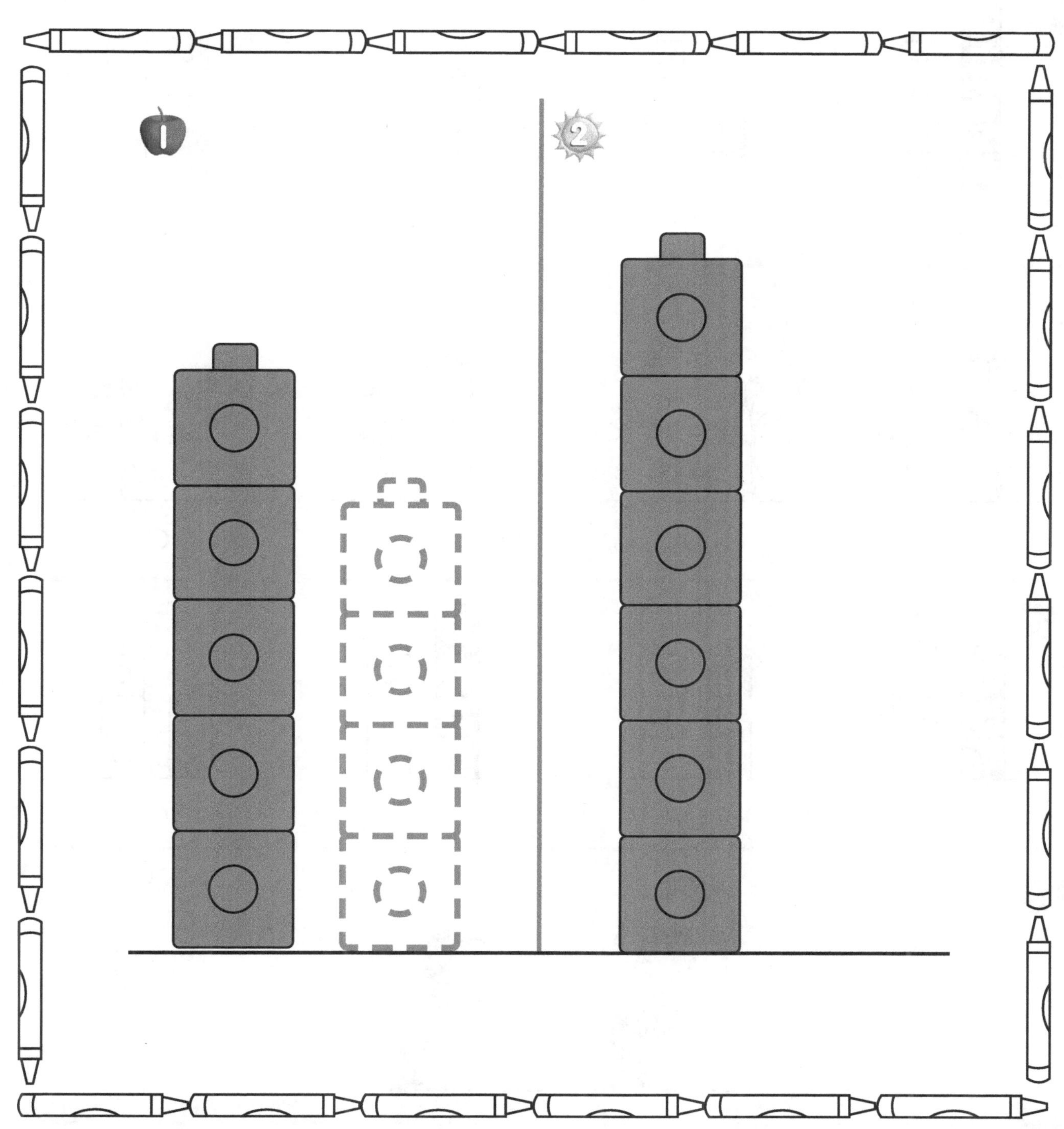

DIRECTIONS 1. Place cubes on the shorter cube tower. Trace and color the cube tower. 2. Make a cube tower that is taller than the cube tower shown. Draw and color the cube tower.

Name ______________________________

Lesson 71
CC.K.MD.2

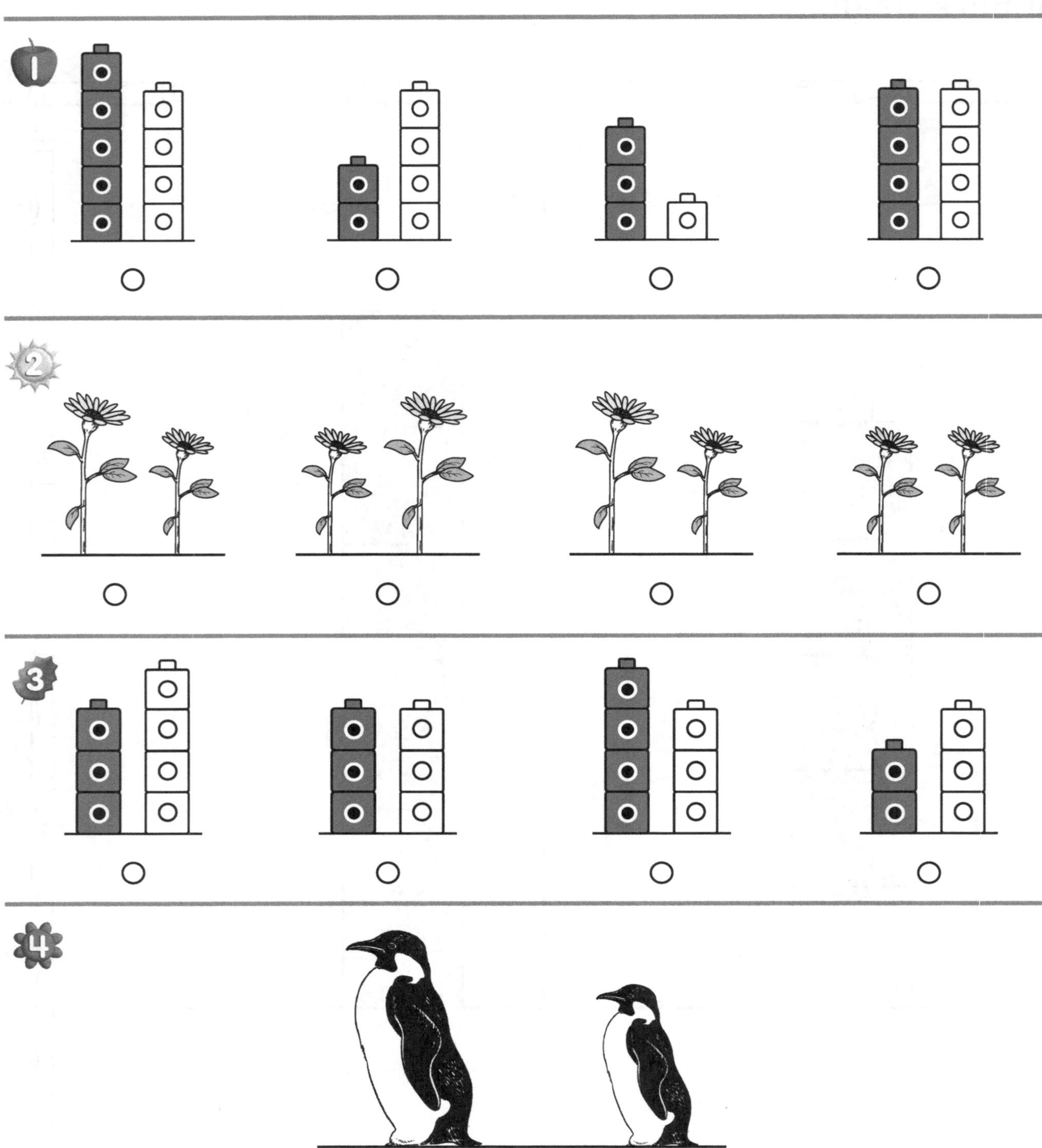

DIRECTIONS 1. Mark under the set that shows the gray cube tower is shorter than the white cube tower. 2. Mark under the set with two flowers that are about the same height. 3. Mark under the set that shows the gray cube tower is taller than the white cube tower. 4. Compare the heights of the two penguins. Circle the shorter penguin. Mark an X on the taller penguin.

Name ______________________________

Lesson 72

COMMON CORE STANDARD CC.K.MD.2

Lesson Objective: Solve problems by using the strategy *draw a picture.*

Problem Solving • Direct Comparison

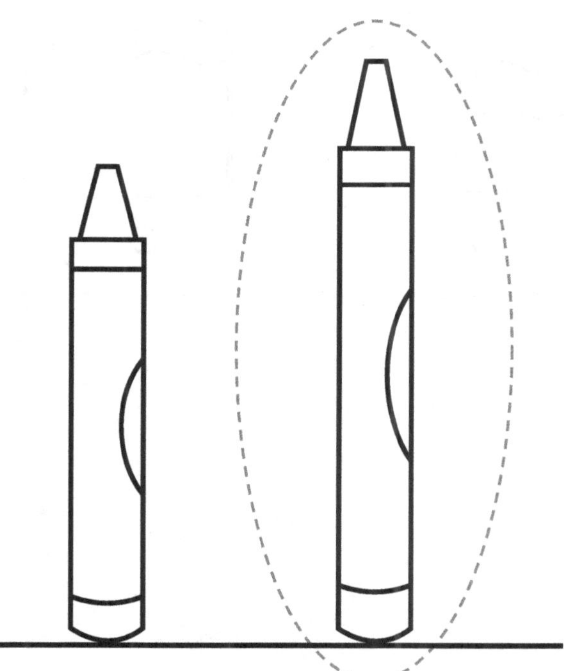

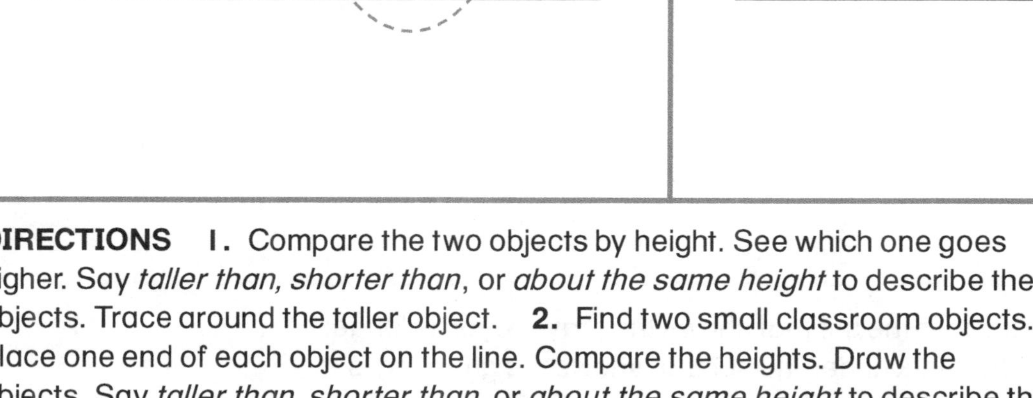

DIRECTIONS **1.** Compare the two objects by height. See which one goes higher. Say *taller than, shorter than*, or *about the same height* to describe the objects. Trace around the taller object. **2.** Find two small classroom objects. Place one end of each object on the line. Compare the heights. Draw the objects. Say *taller than, shorter than,* or *about the same height* to describe the heights. Circle the shorter object.

Name ______________________________

Lesson 72
CC.K.MD.2

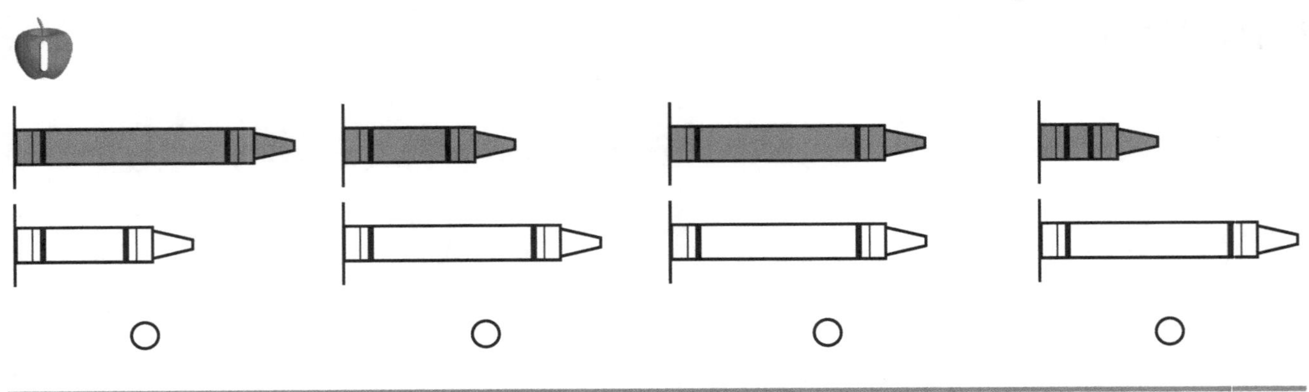

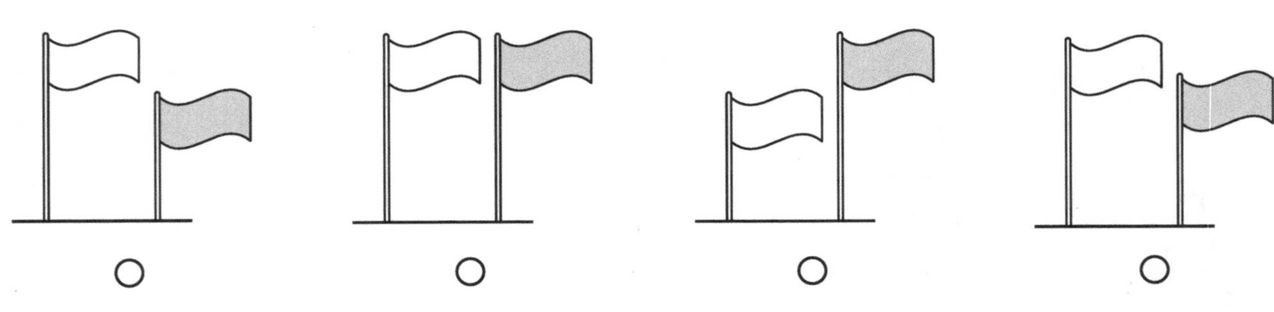

DIRECTIONS **1.** Mark under the set that shows the gray crayon is longer than the white crayon. **2.** Mark under the set that shows the gray flag is taller than the white flag. **3.** Draw two classroom objects. Place one end of each object on the line. Compare the lengths. Circle the shorter object.

Name ____________________

Lesson 73

COMMON CORE STANDARD CC.K.MD.2

Lesson Objective: Directly compare the weights of two objects.

Compare Weights

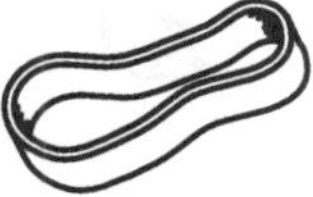

DIRECTIONS 1–4. Find the objects. Hold one in each hand. Circle the object that is heavier. Mark an X on the object that is lighter.

Name ______________________________

Lesson 73

CC.K.MD.2

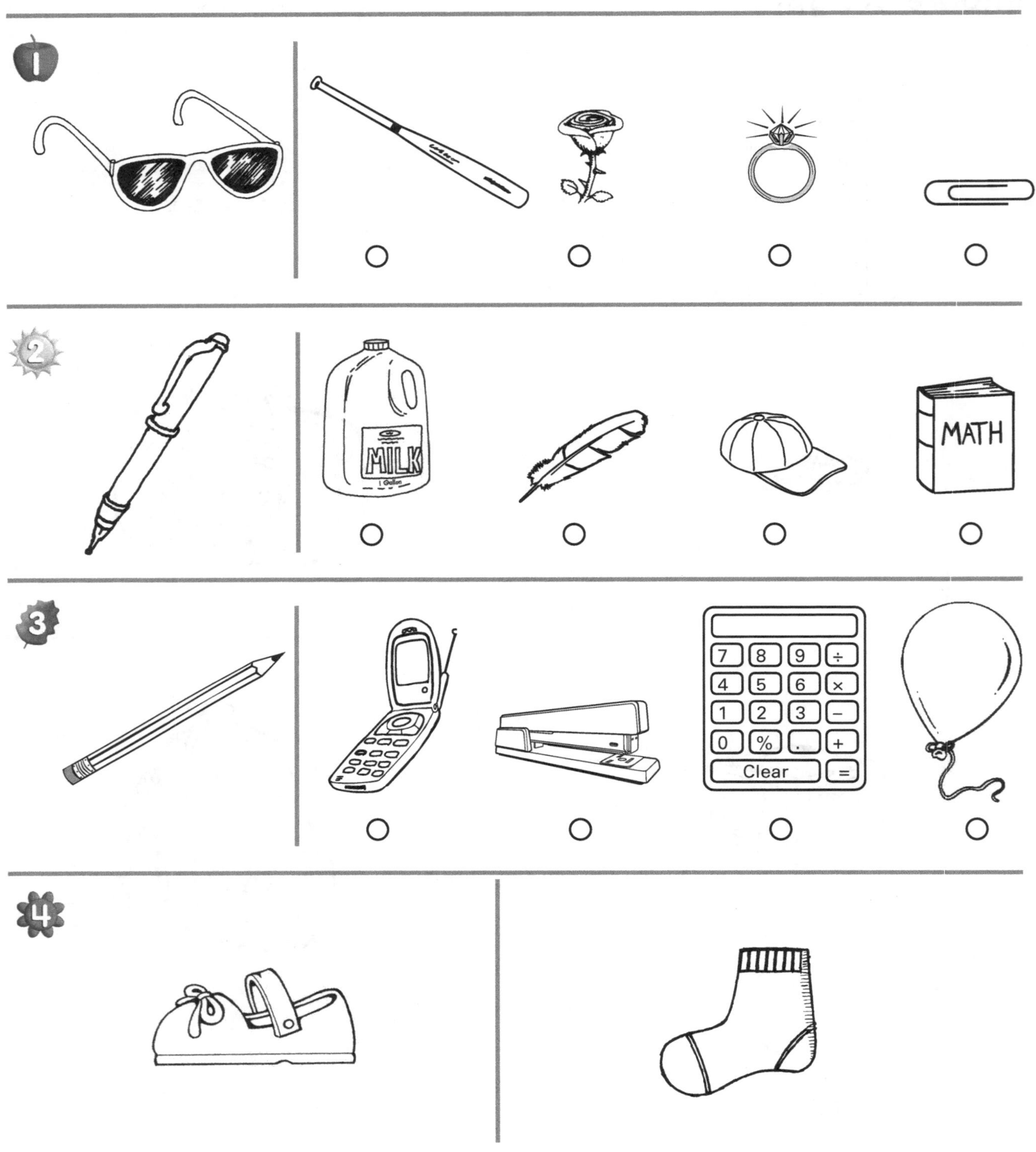

DIRECTIONS **1.** Mark under the object that is heavier than the object at the beginning of the row. **2–3.** Mark under the object that is lighter than the object at the beginning of the row. **4.** Look at the two objects. Circle the lighter object. Mark an X on the heavier object.

Name ____________________

Lesson 74

COMMON CORE STANDARD CC.K.MD.3

Lesson Objective: Classify and count objects by color.

Algebra • Classify and Count by Color

1

blue	green
yellow	red

DIRECTIONS 1. Place a green triangle, red triangle, blue circle, yellow square, blue rectangle, red rectangle, and green triangle at the top of the page as shown. Sort and classify the shapes by the category of color. Trace and color a shape in each category. Draw and color the rest of the shapes.

Name ______________________________

Lesson 74
CC.K.MD.3

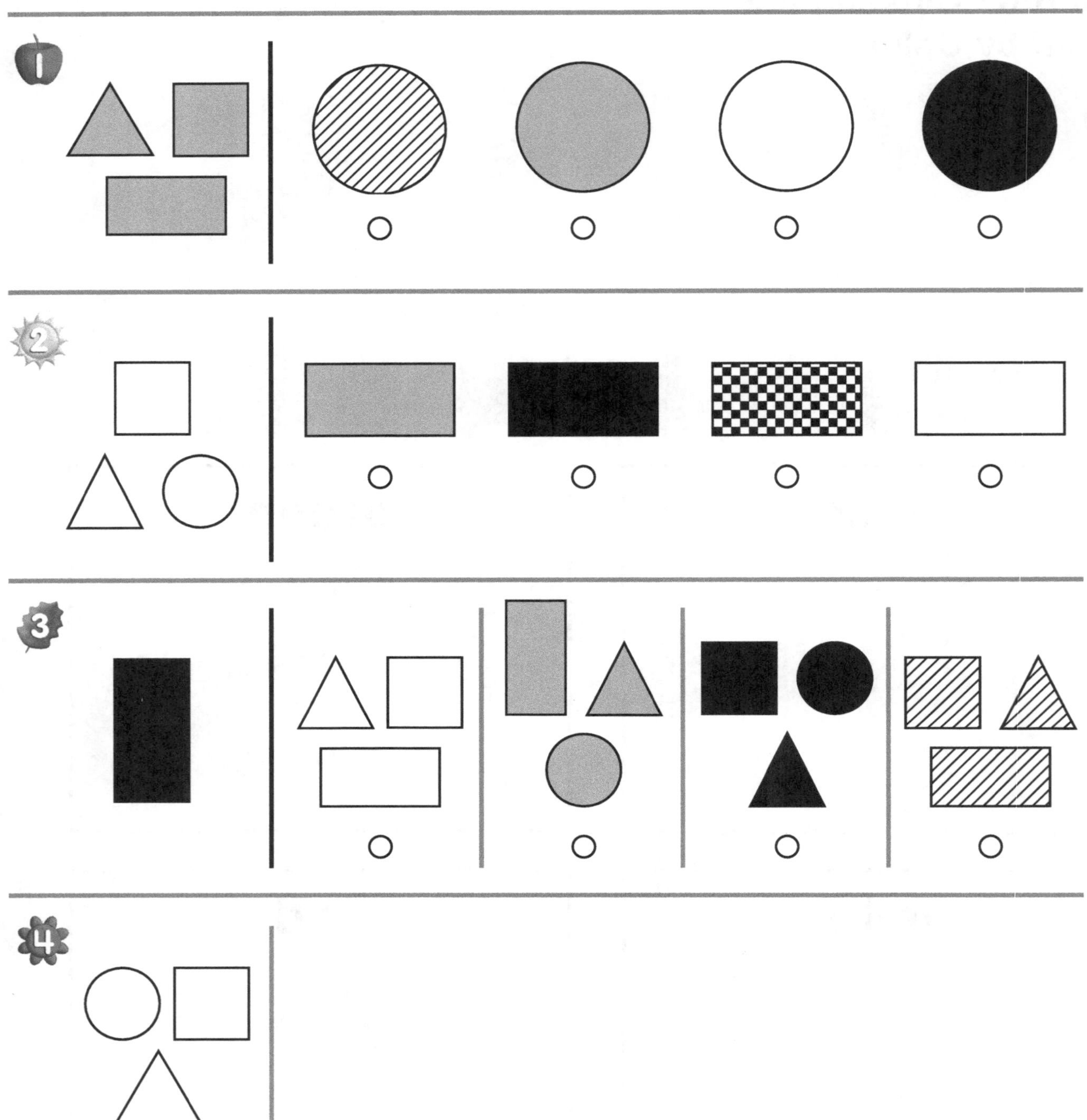

DIRECTIONS **1–2.** Look at the set of shapes at the beginning of the row. Mark under the shape that belongs in that set. **3.** Look at the shape at the beginning of the row. Mark under the set of shapes in which it belongs. **4.** Look at the shapes at the beginning of the row. Draw two shapes that would be in the same category.

Name ______________________________

Lesson 75

COMMON CORE STANDARD CC.K.MD.3

Lesson Objective: Classify and count objects by shape.

Algebra • Classify and Count by Shape

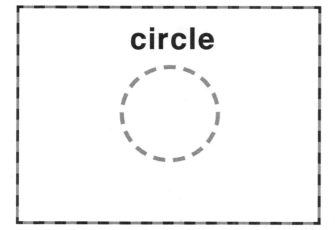

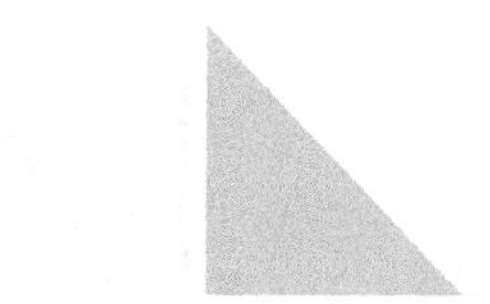

rectangle

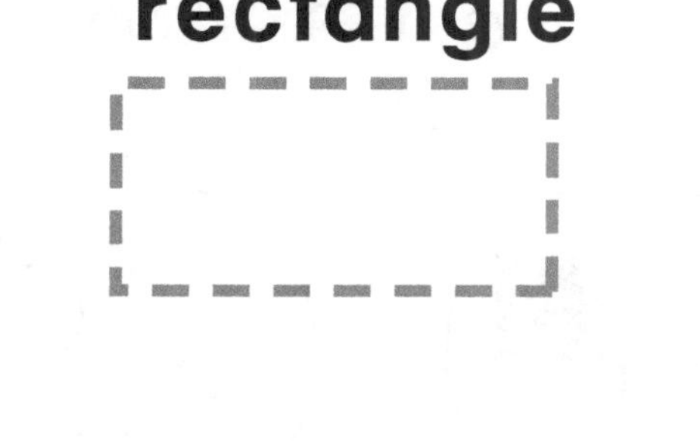

triangle

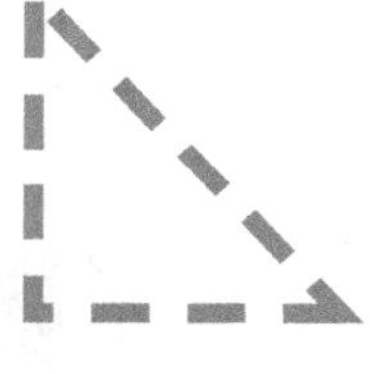

circle

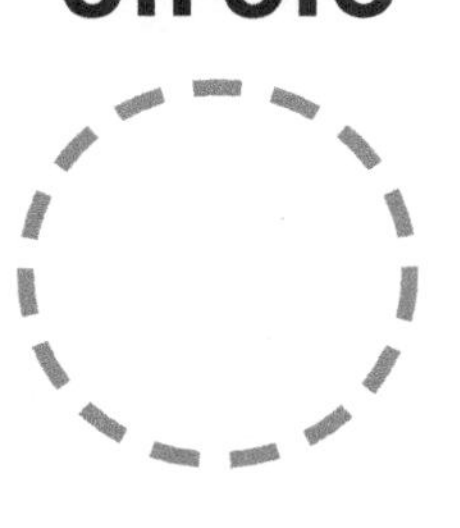

square

DIRECTIONS Place a green triangle, red triangle, blue circle, yellow square, blue rectangle, red rectangle, and green triangle at the top of the page as shown. Sort and classify the shapes by the category of shape. Trace and color a shape in each category. Draw and color the rest of the shapes.

Name ____________________

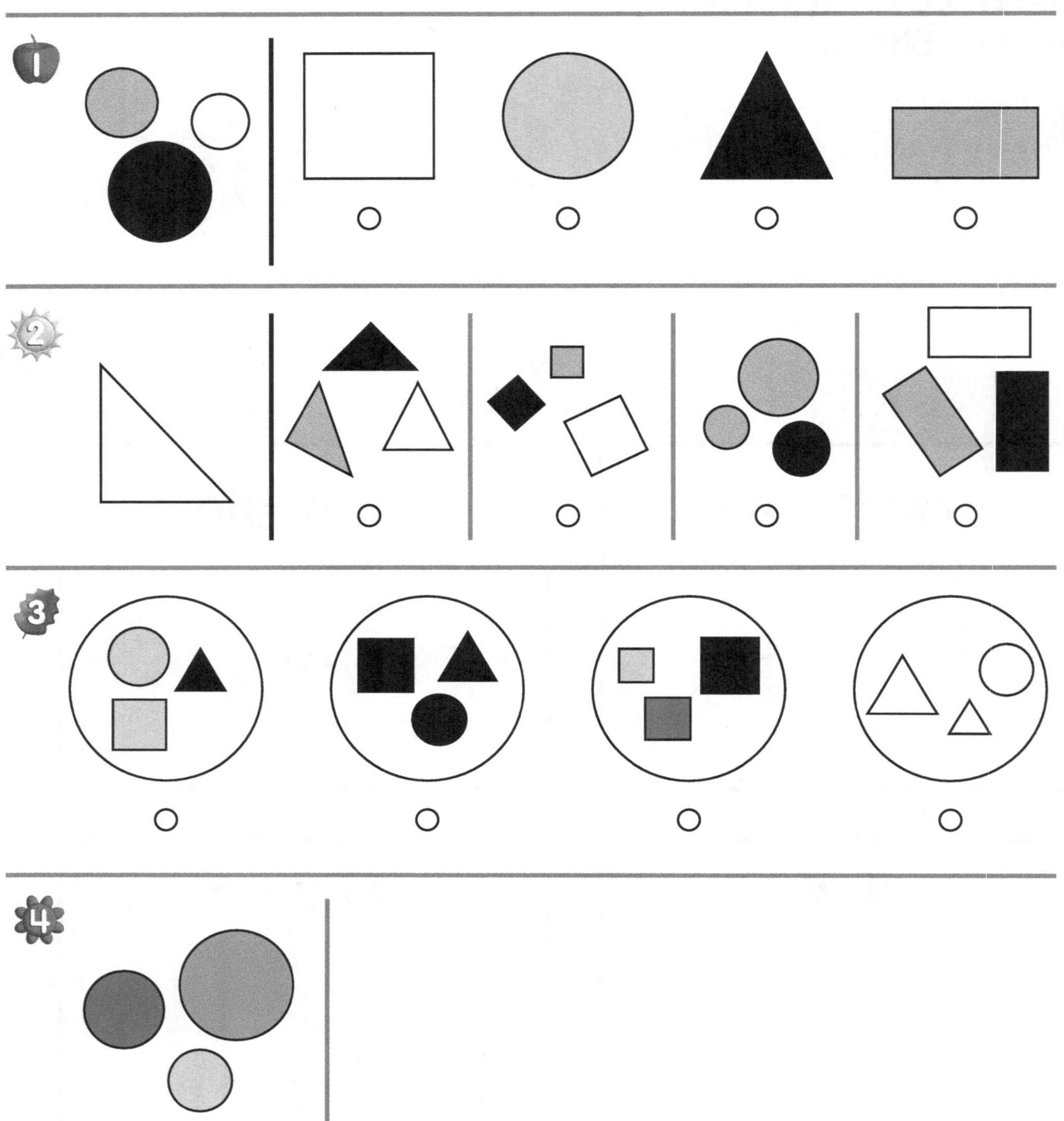

DIRECTIONS **1.** Look at the set of shapes at the beginning of the row. Mark under the shape that belongs in that set. **2.** Look at the shape at the beginning of the row. Mark under the set of shapes in which it belongs. **3.** Mark under the set of shapes that are sorted and classified by the category of shape. **4.** Look at the set of shapes at the beginning of the row. Draw two shapes that would be in the same category.

Name ______________________________

Lesson 76

COMMON CORE STANDARD CC.K.MD.3

Lesson Objective: Classify and count objects by size.

Algebra • Classify and Count by Size

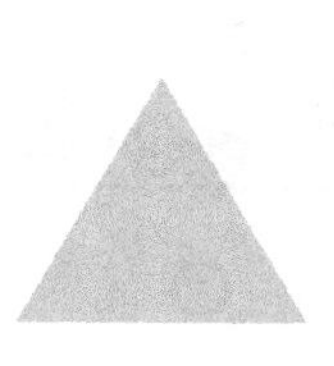

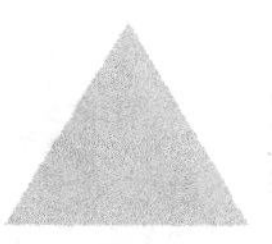

big	small
	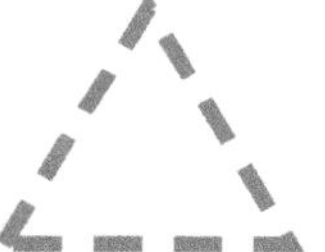

DIRECTIONS Place a green triangle, red triangle, blue circle, yellow square, blue rectangle, red rectangle, and green triangle at the top of the page as shown. Sort and classify the shapes by the category of size. Trace and color a shape in each category. Draw and color the rest of the shapes.

Name ______________________________

Lesson 76
CC.K.MD.3

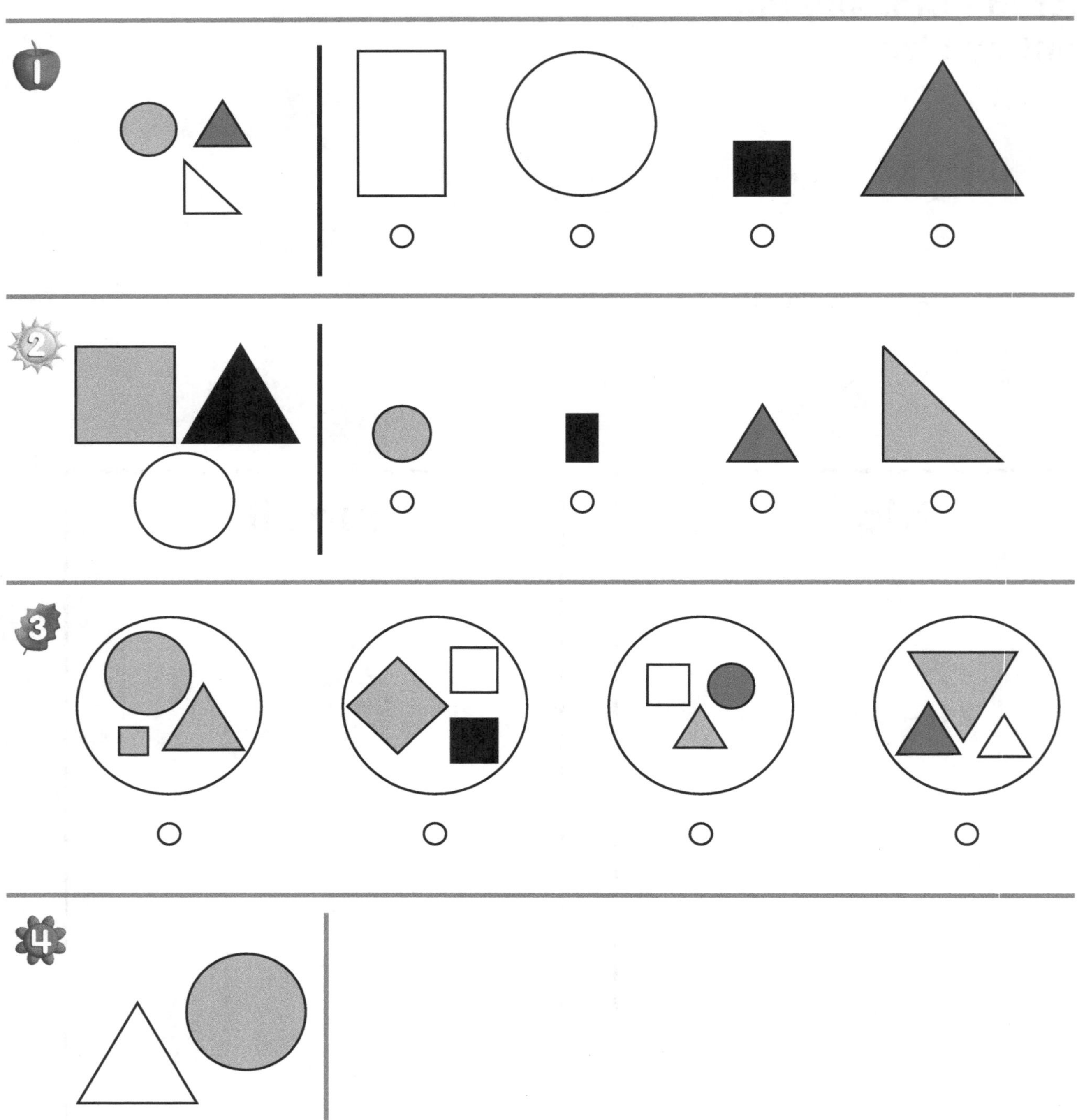

DIRECTIONS **1–2.** Look at the set of shapes at the beginning of the row. Mark under the shape that belongs in that set. **3.** Mark under the shapes that are sorted and classified by the category of size. **4.** Look at the set of shapes at the beginning of the row. Draw two shapes that would be in the same category.

Name ______________________________

Lesson 77

COMMON CORE STANDARD CC.K.MD.3

Lesson Objective: Make a graph to count objects that have been classified into categories.

Make a Concrete Graph

1

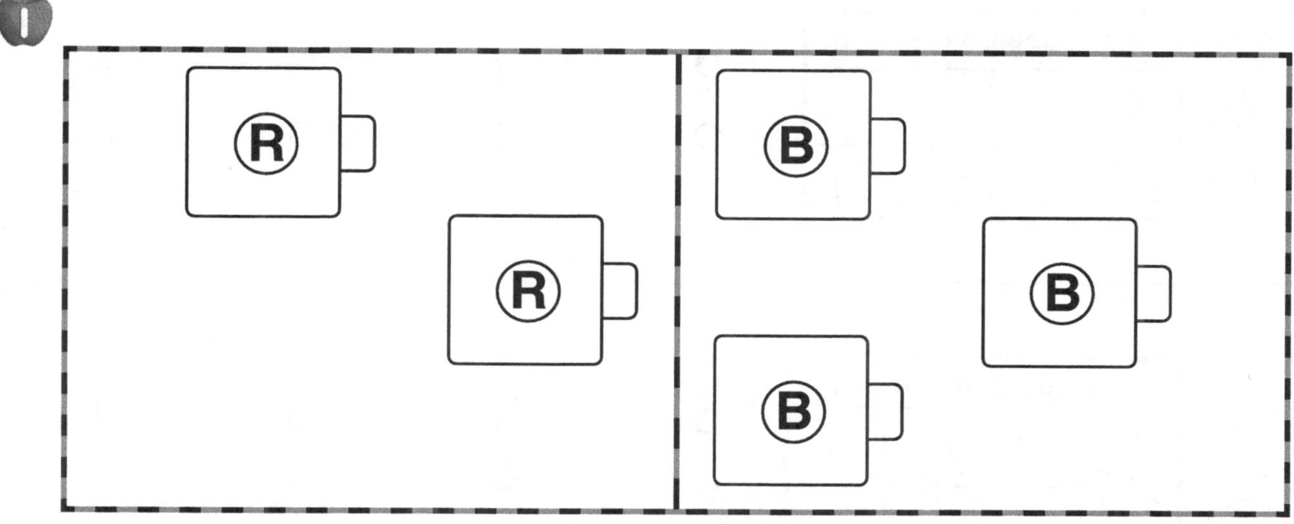

2

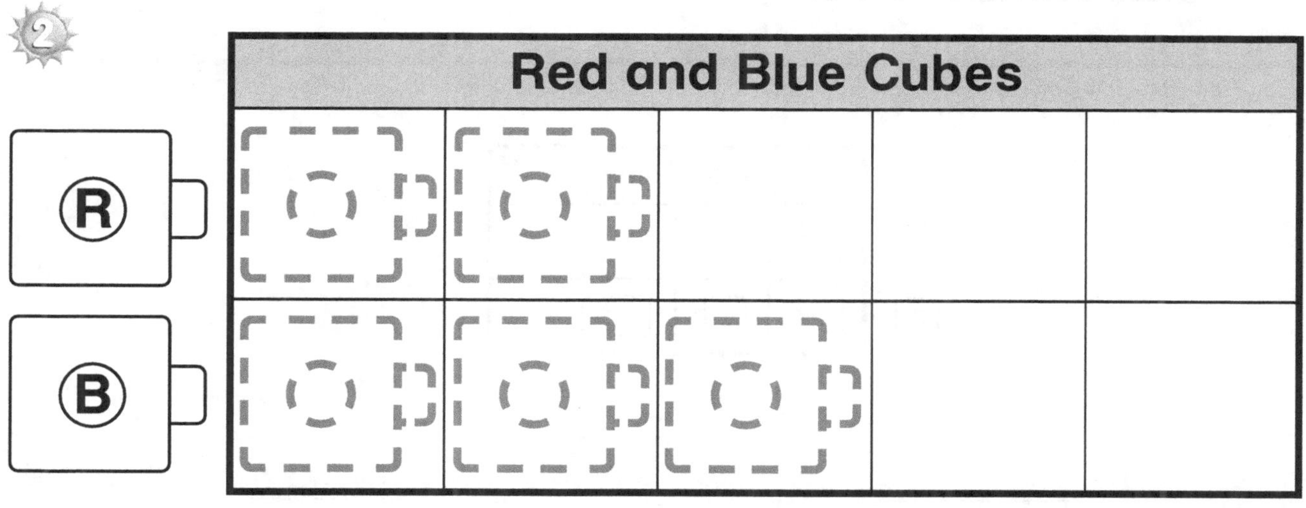

3

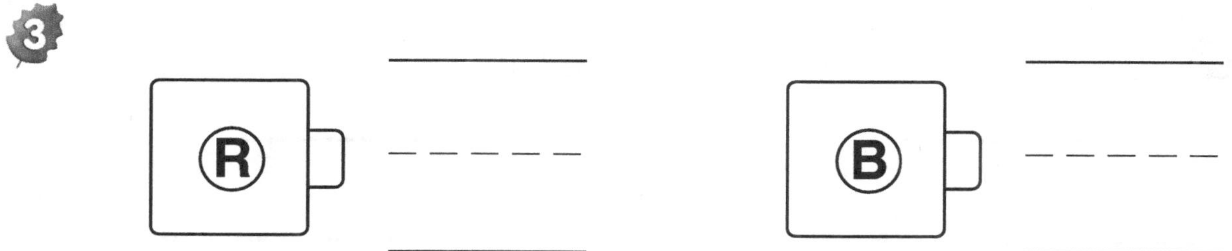

DIRECTIONS 1. Place cubes in the workspace as shown. R is for red, and B is for blue. See how the cubes are sorted and classified by the category of color. 2. Move the cubes to the graph. Trace and color the cubes. 3. Write how many of each cube.

Name ____________________

Lesson 77
CC.K.MD.3

1

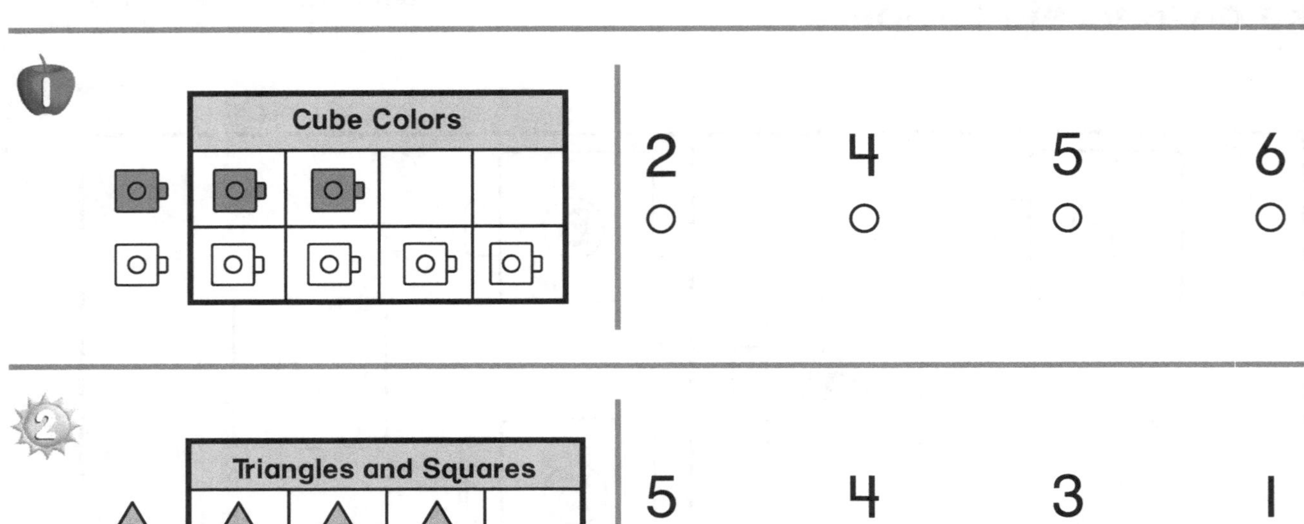

2 ○ 4 ○ 5 ○ 6 ○

2

Triangles and Squares

5 ○ 4 ○ 3 ○ 1 ○

3

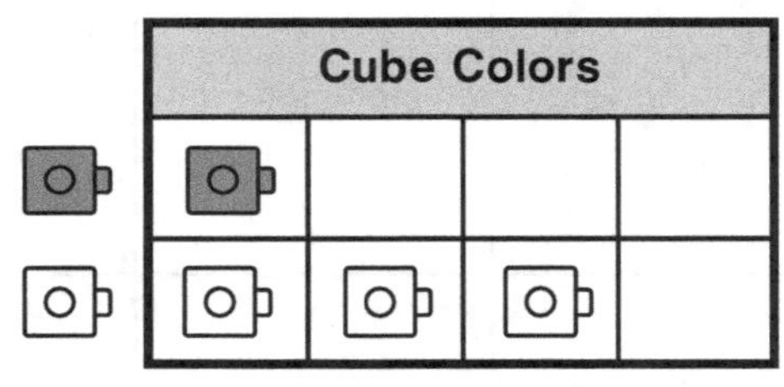

______ ______

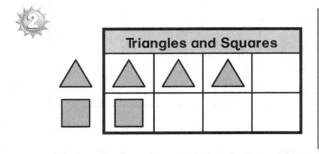

DIRECTIONS 1. Look at the graph. Mark under the number that shows how many gray cubes are on the graph. 2. Look at the graph. Mark under the number that shows how many squares are on the graph. 3. Look at the graph. How many gray cubes are on the graph? Write the number. How many white cubes are on the graph? Write the number.

Name ______________________

Lesson 78

COMMON CORE STANDARD CC.K.MD.3

Lesson Objective: Read a graph to count objects that have been classified into categories

Read a Graph

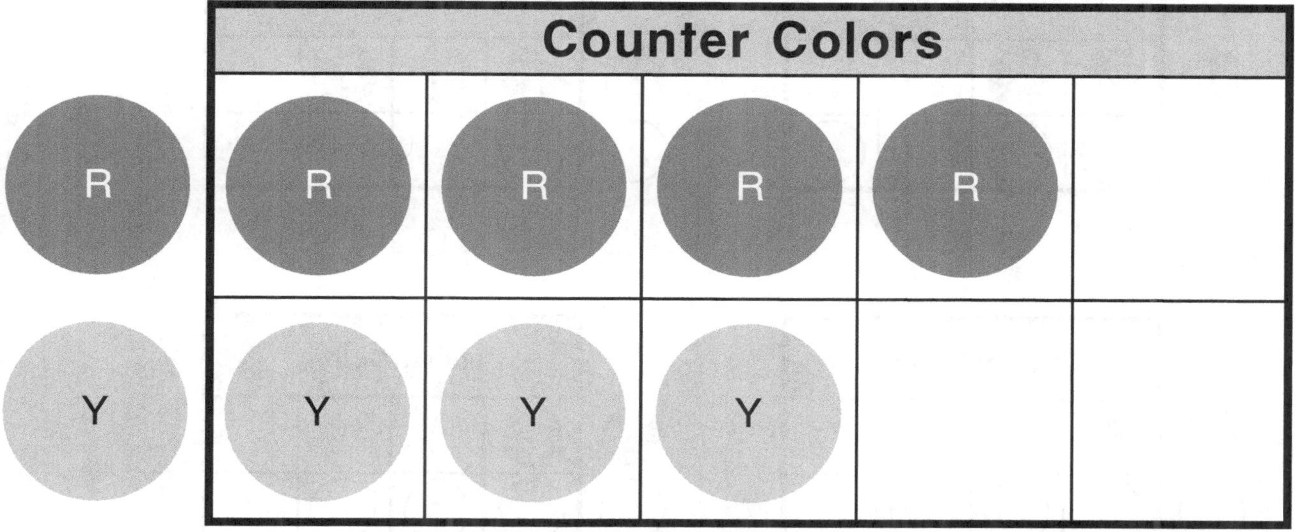

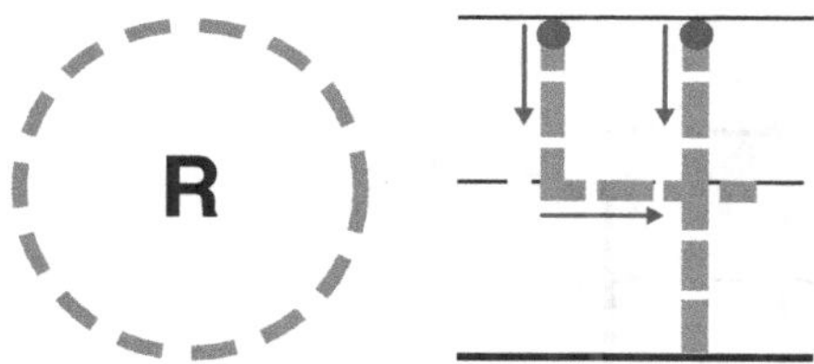

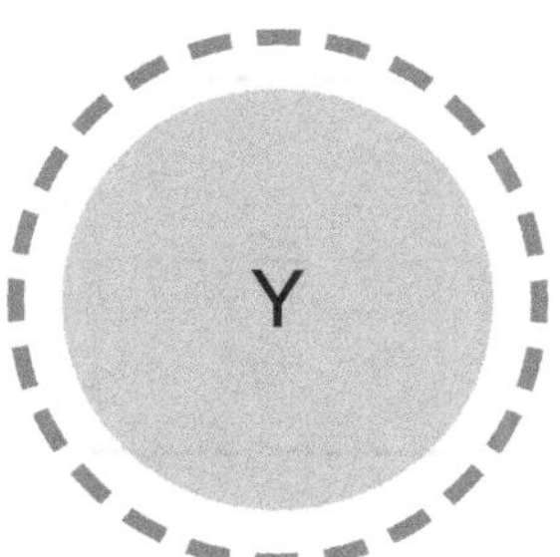

DIRECTIONS **1.** Color the counters to show the categories. R is for red, and Y is for yellow. How many counters are in each category? Draw a dot on each counter on the graph as you count. Trace or write the numbers.
2. Trace the circle around the category that has fewer counters on the graph.

Name ______________________

Lesson **78**
CC.K.MD.3

1

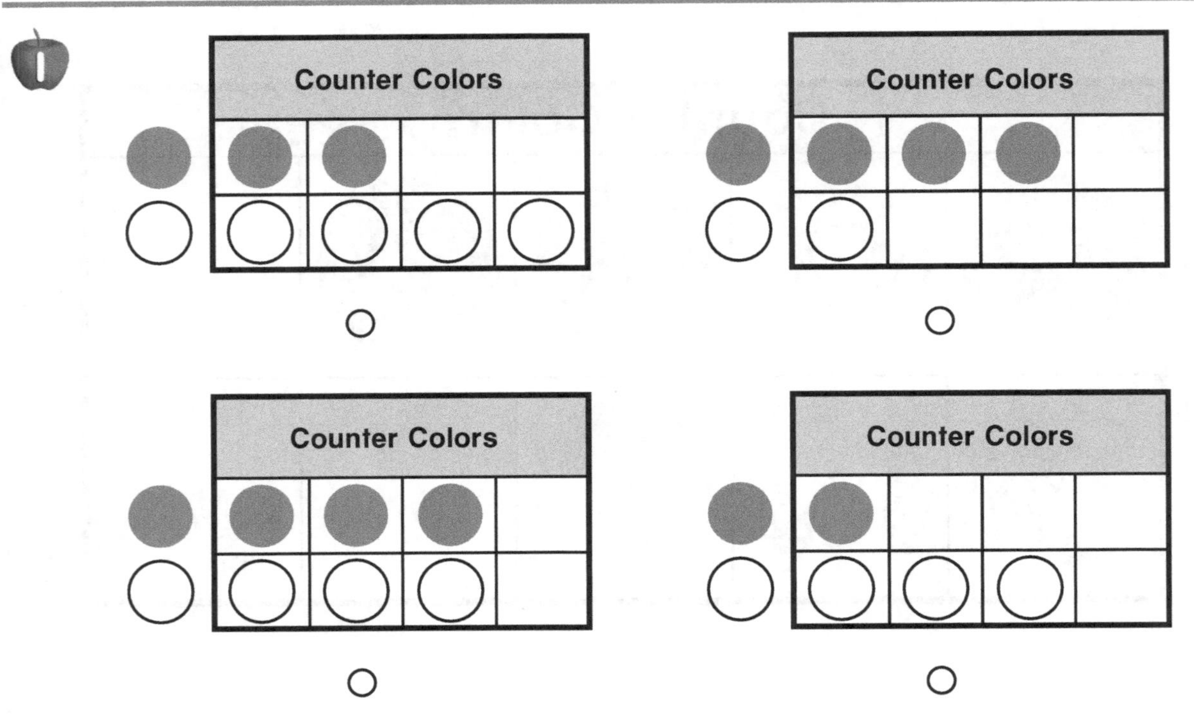

2

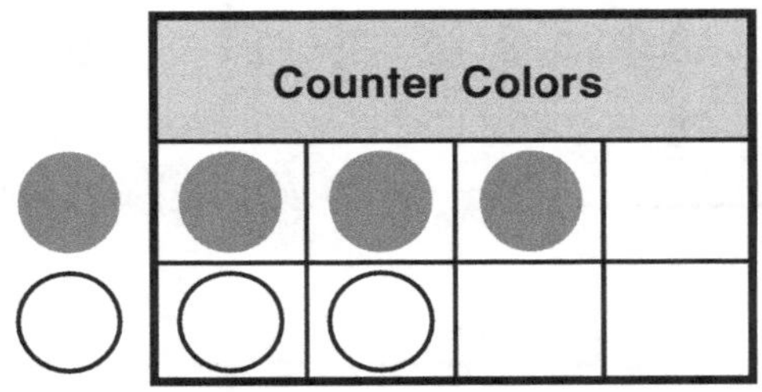

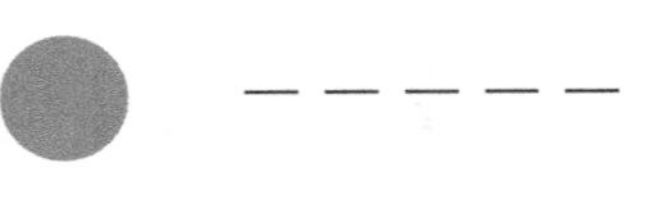

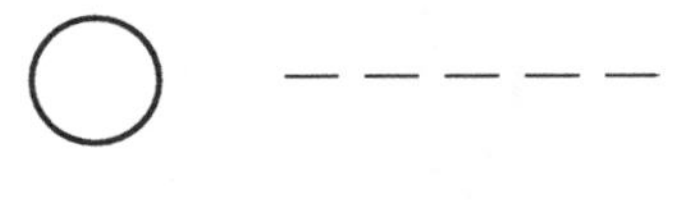

DIRECTIONS **1.** Mark under the graph that shows there are more gray counters than white counters. **2.** Look at the graph. How many gray counters are on the graph? Write the number. How many white counters are on the graph? Write the number. Which category has fewer counters on the graph? Circle the counter next to the smaller number.

Name ______________________

Lesson 79

COMMON CORE STANDARD CC.K.MD.3

Lesson Objective: Solve problems by using the strategy *use logical reasoning.*

Problem Solving • Sort and Count

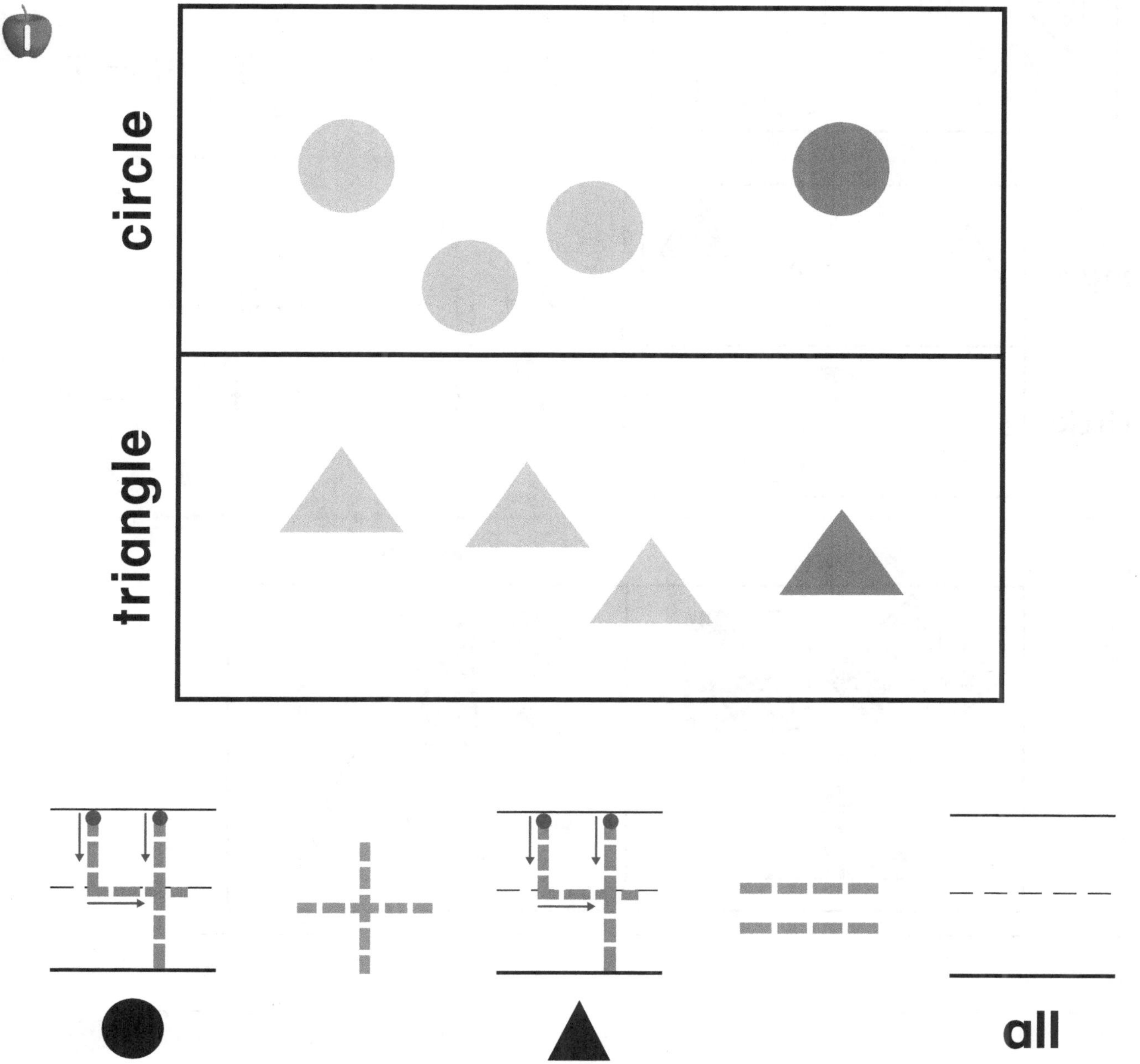

DIRECTIONS 1. Look at the sorting mat. How are the shapes sorted? How many circles are there? How many triangles are there? Draw a dot on each shape as you count. Add the two sets. Trace and write the numbers and symbols to complete the addition sentence.

Name ______________________

Lesson 79
CC.K.MD.3

1

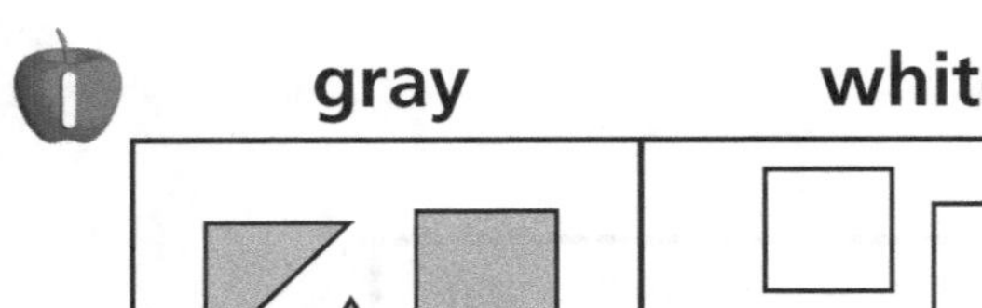

○ 2 + 3 = 5 ○ 3 + 3 = 6

○ 3 + 2 = 5 ○ 3 + 4 = 7

2

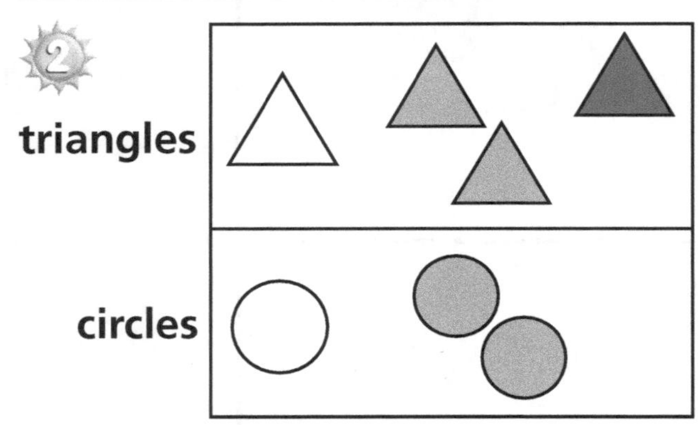

○ 2 + 3 = 5 ○ 3 + 3 = 6

○ 3 + 2 = 5 ○ 4 + 3 = 7

3

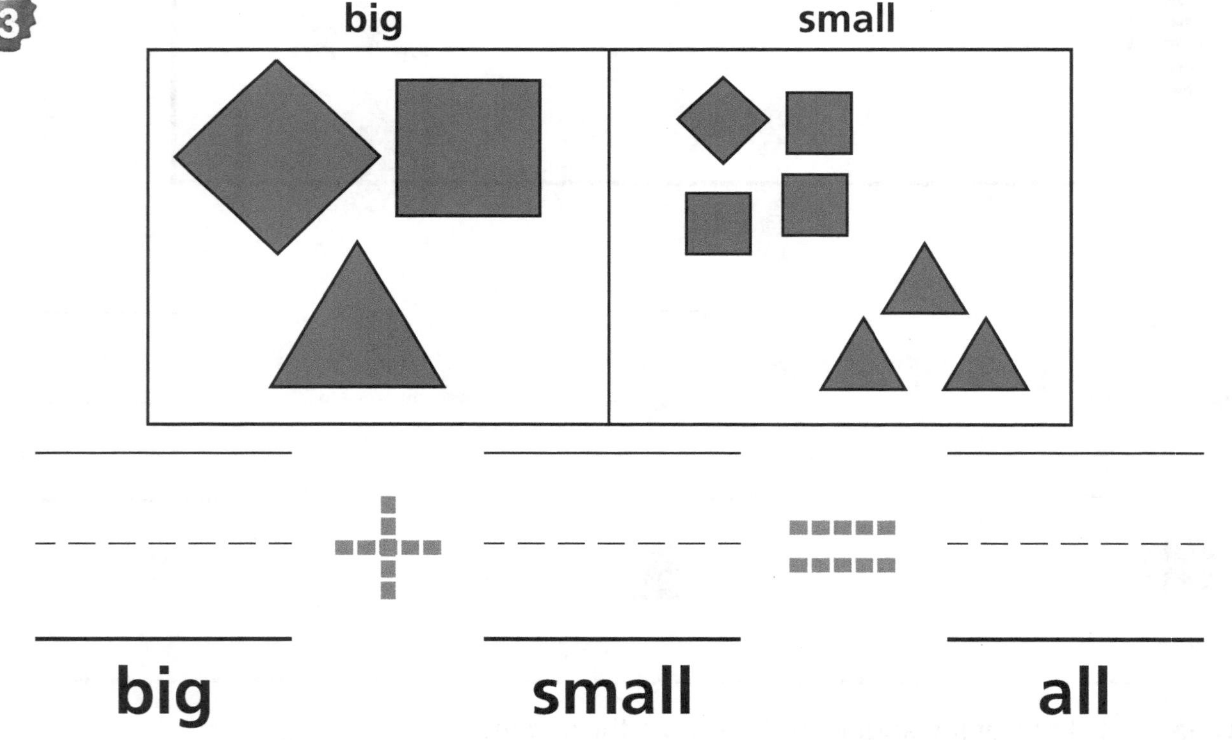

_____ + _____ = _____

big small all

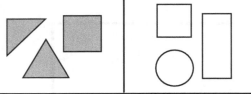

DIRECTIONS 1–2. Look at the sorting mat. Mark under the addition sentence that matches the sorted shapes. 3. Look at the sorting mat. How many big shapes? How many small shapes? Add the two sets. Write and trace to complete the addition sentence.

Name ___________________________

Lesson 80

COMMON CORE STANDARD CC.K.G.1

Lesson Objective: Use the terms *above* and *below* to describe shapes in the environment

Above and Below

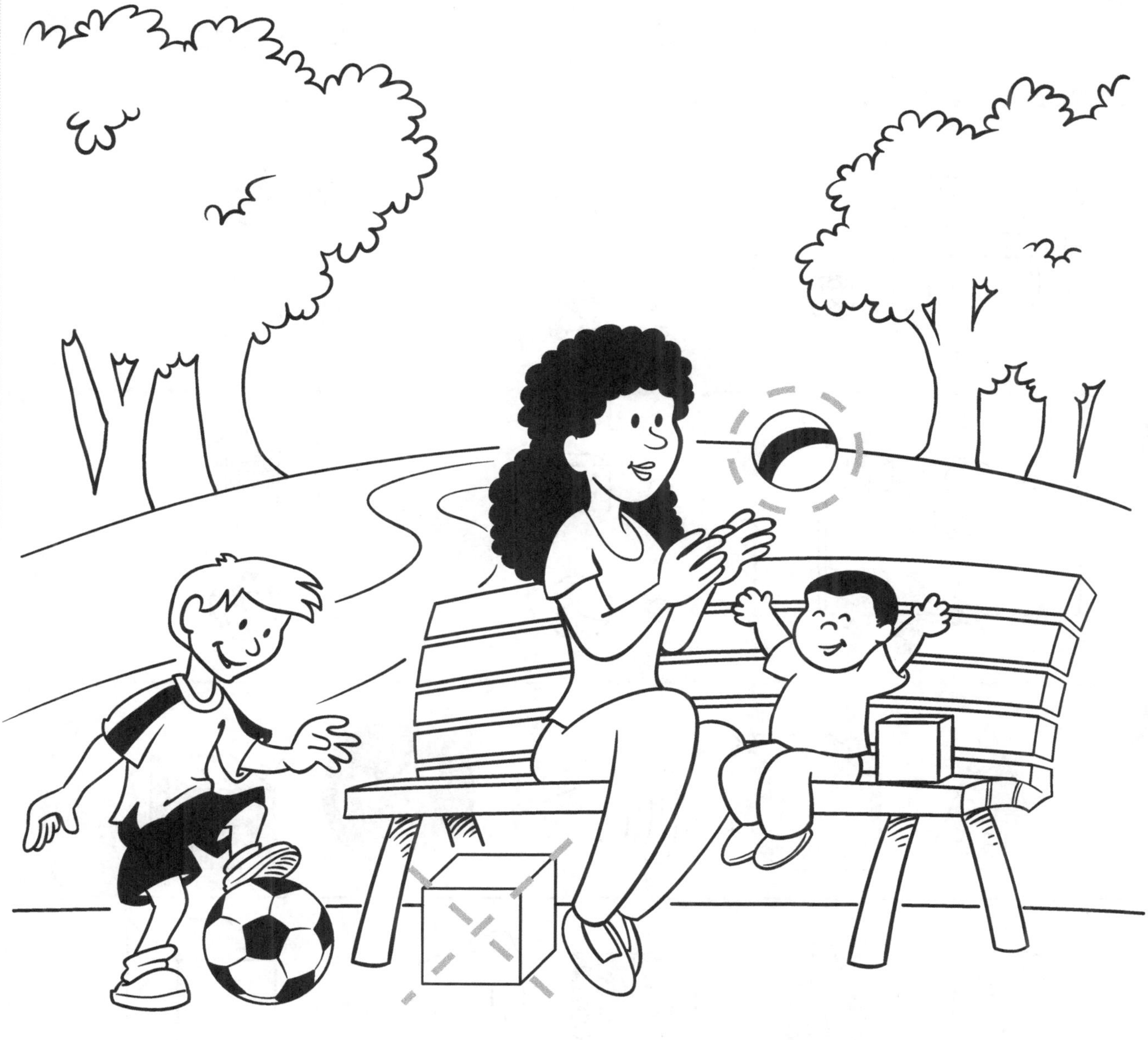

DIRECTIONS 1. Trace the circle around the object that is shaped like a sphere above the bench. Trace the X on the object that is shaped like a cube below the bench.

Name ________________________________

Lesson 80
CC.K.G.1

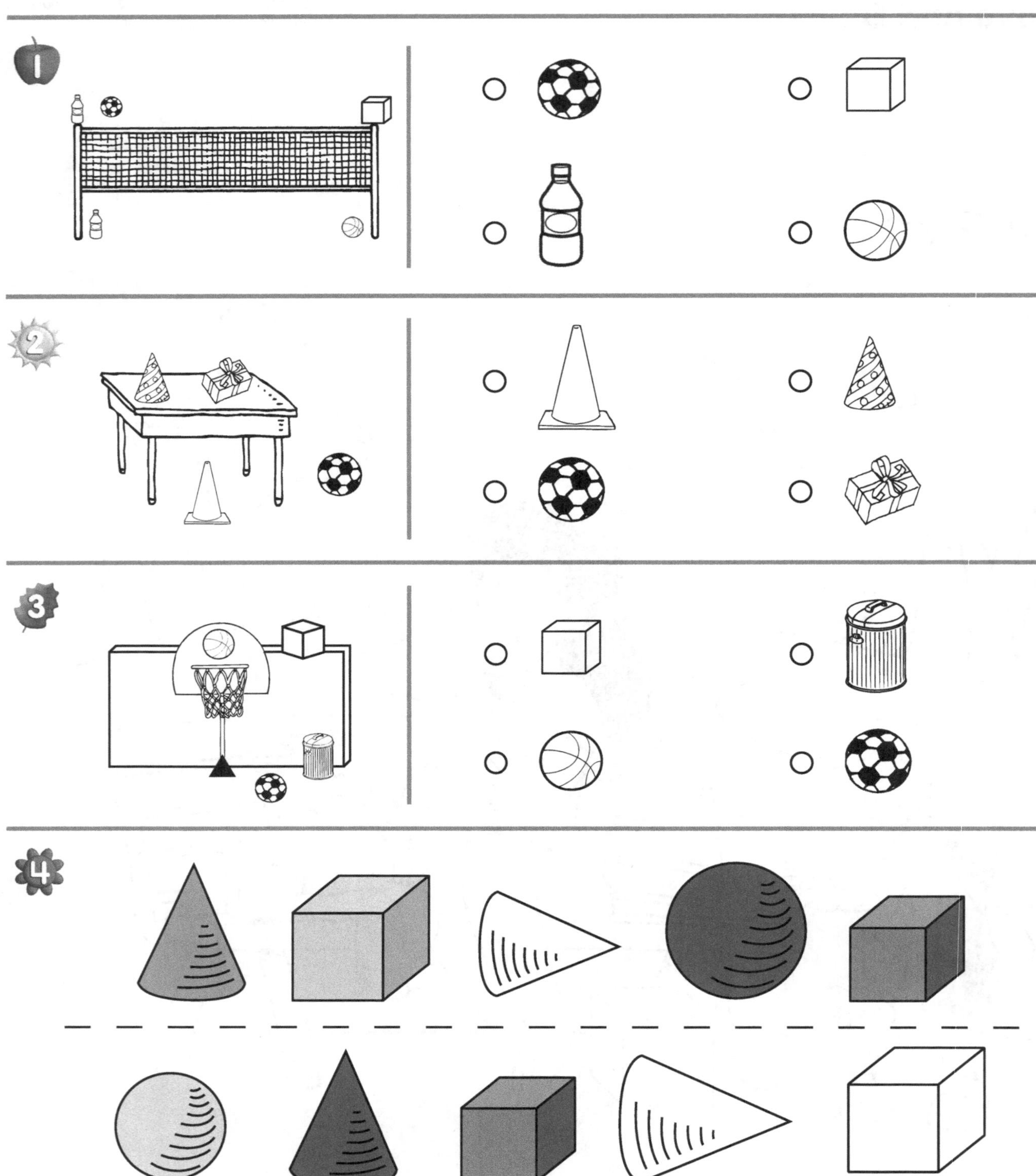

DIRECTIONS 1. Mark beside the object shaped like a sphere that is below the net. 2. Mark beside the object shaped like a cone that is below the table. 3. Mark beside the object shaped like a sphere that is above the basketball hoop. 4. Circle the cubes above the dashed line. Mark an X on the cones below the dashed line.

Name ______________________________

Lesson 81

COMMON CORE STANDARD CC.K.G.1

Lesson Objective: Use the terms *beside* and *next to* to describe shapes in the environment.

Beside and Next To

DIRECTIONS 1. Trace the X on the object shaped like a sphere that is next to the object shaped like a cylinder. Trace the circle around the object shaped like a cylinder that is beside the object shaped like a cube.

Name ______________________

Lesson 81
CC.K.G.1

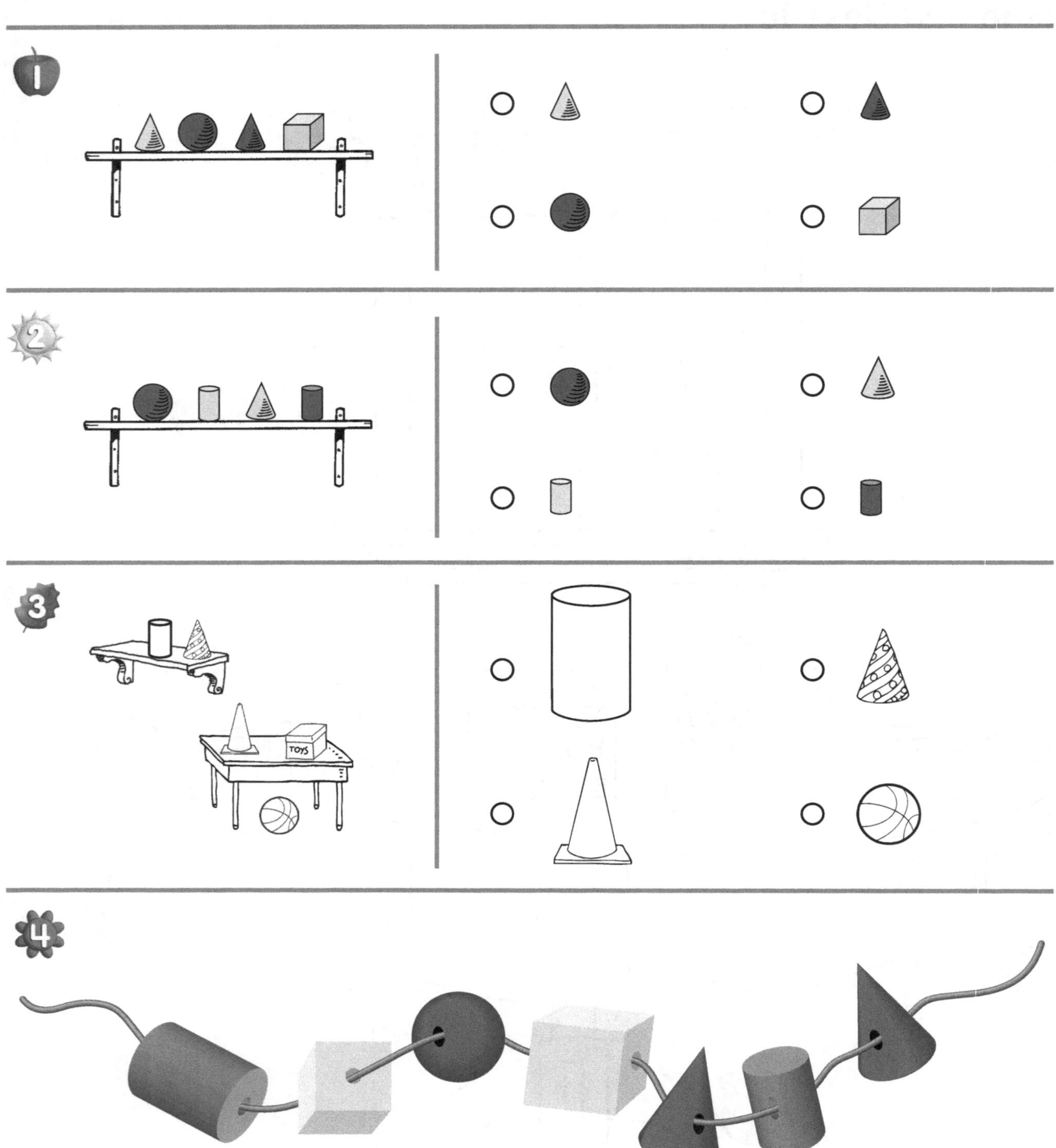

DIRECTIONS 1. Mark beside the object shaped like a cone that is next to the object shaped like a cube. 2. Mark beside the object shaped like a cylinder that is next to the object shaped like a sphere. 3. Mark beside the object shaped like a cone that is beside the object shaped like a cylinder. 4. Mark an X on the bead shaped like a cube that is next to the bead shaped like a cone.

Name ____________________

In Front Of and Behind

Lesson 82

COMMON CORE STANDARD CC.K.G.1

Lesson Objective: Use the terms *in front of* and *behind* to describe shapes in the environment.

1

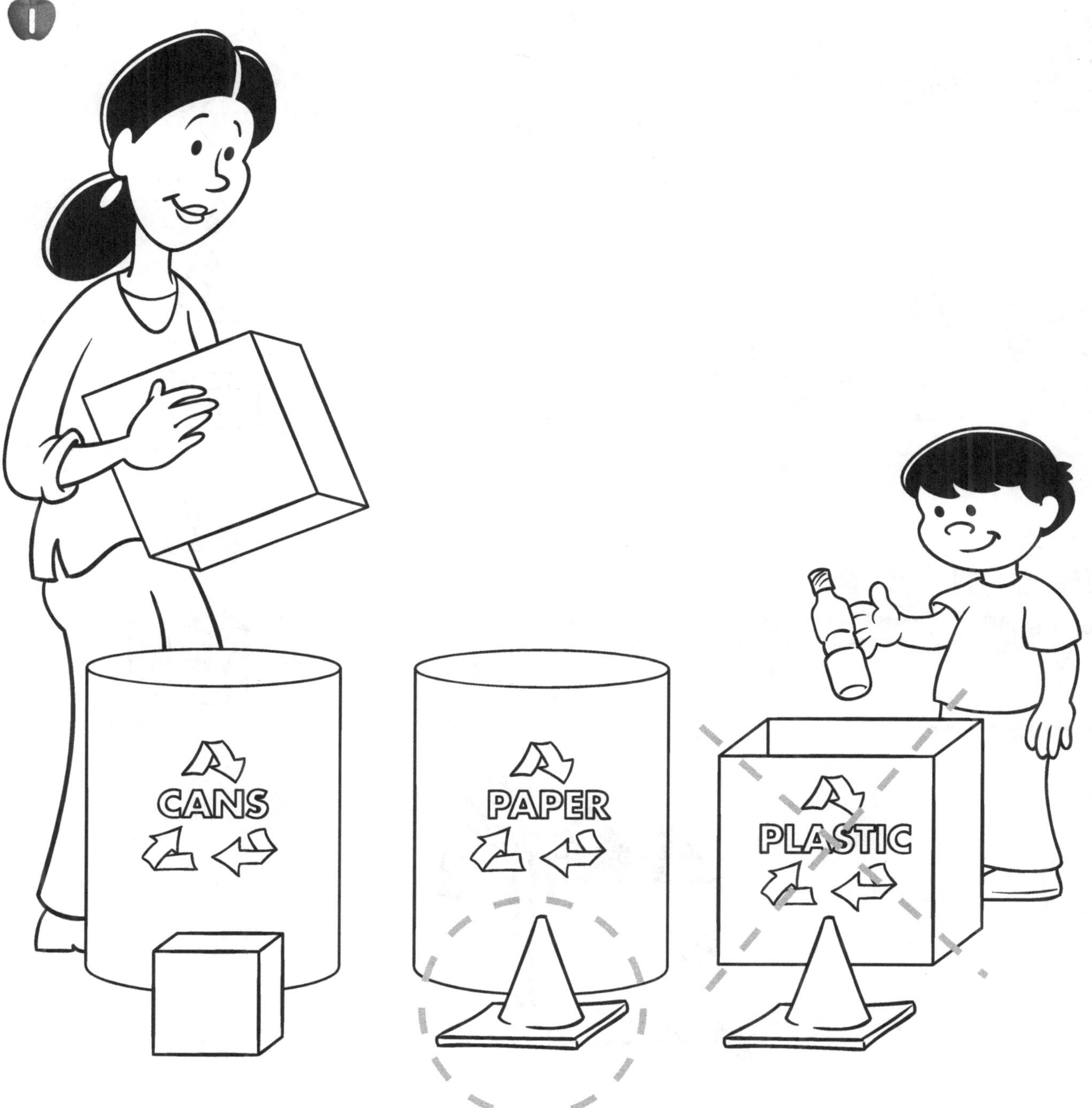

DIRECTIONS 1. Trace the X on the object shaped like a cube that is behind the object shaped like a cone. Trace the circle around the object shaped like a cone that is in front of the object shaped like a cylinder.

Name ___________________________

Lesson 82
CC.K.G.1

DIRECTIONS 1. Mark beside the object shaped like a cone that is behind the object shaped like a sphere. 2. Mark beside the object shaped like a cube that is in front of the object shaped like a sphere. 3. Mark beside the object that is in front of the sphere in the truck. 4. Mark an X on the object shaped like a cone that is behind the object shaped like a cube. Draw a circle around the object shaped like a cone that is in front of the object shaped like a cube.

Name ___________________________

Lesson 83

COMMON CORE STANDARD CC.K.G.2

Lesson Objective: Identify and name two-dimensional shapes including circles.

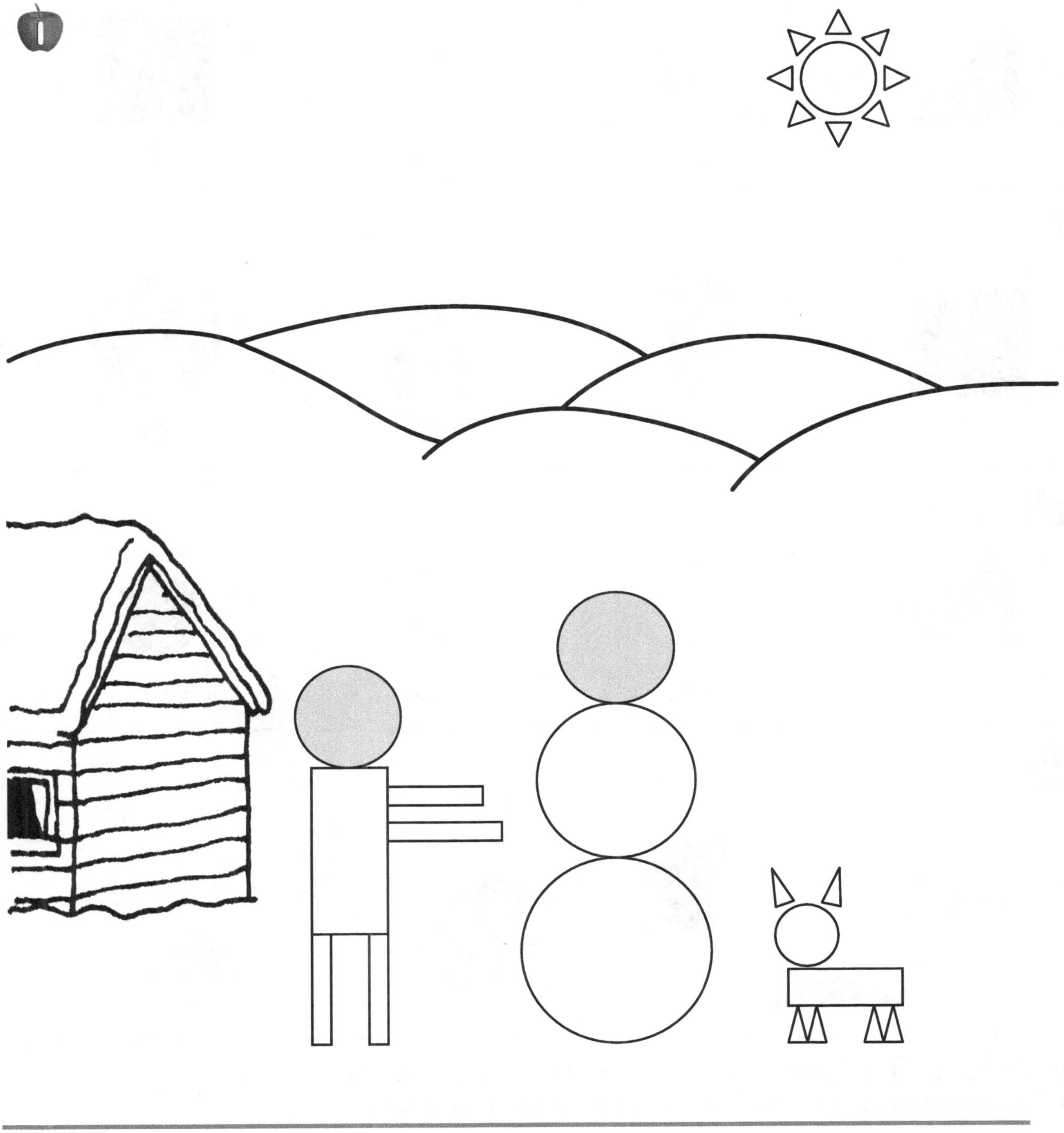

Identify and Name Circles

DIRECTIONS 1. Place a circle on each shaded circle. Color the other circles in the picture.

Name ______________________________

Lesson 83
CC.K.G.2

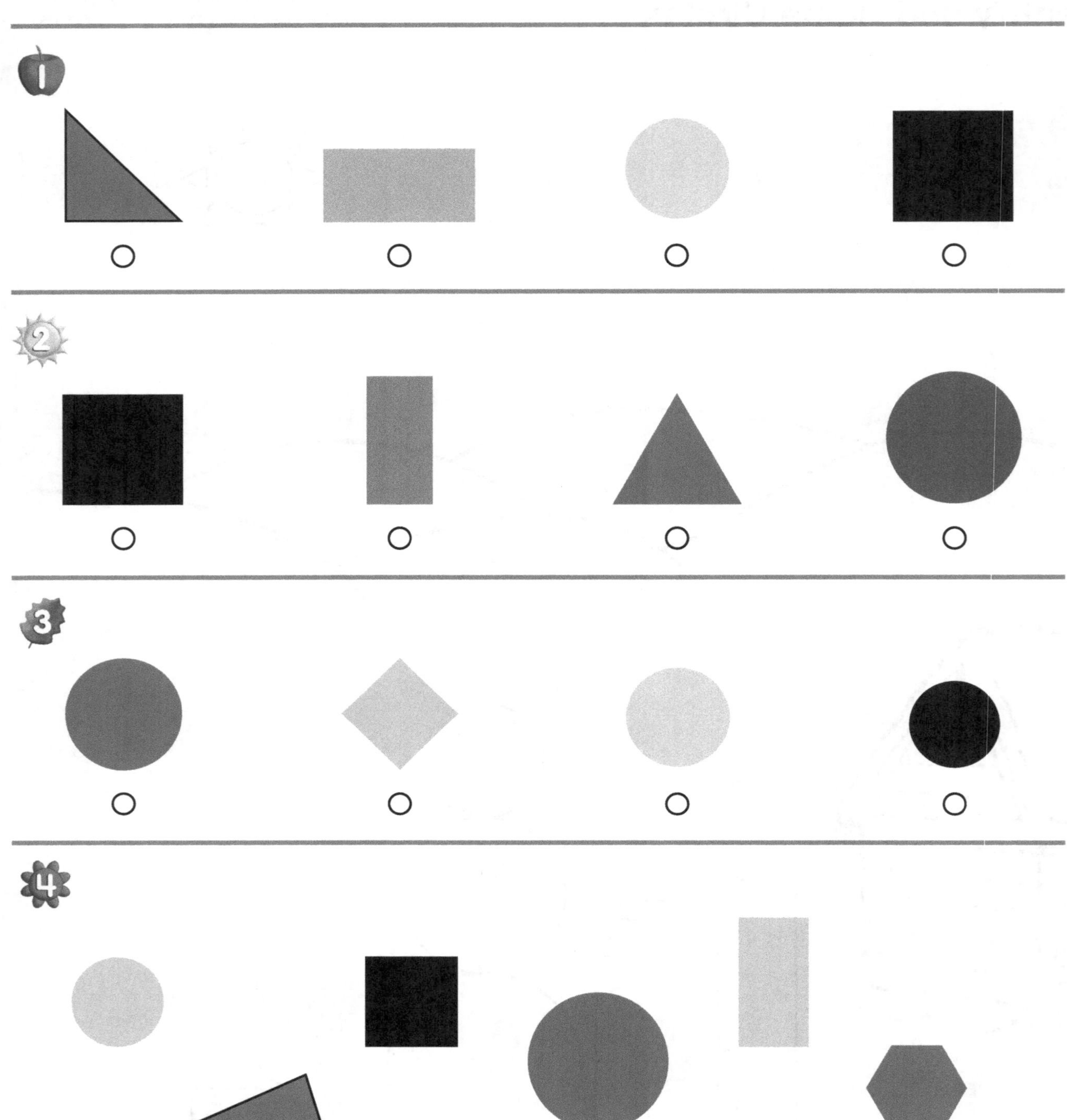

DIRECTIONS **1–2.** Mark under the shape that is a circle. **3.** Mark under the shape that is **not** a circle. **4.** Mark an X on all of the circles.

Name ____________________

Lesson 84

COMMON CORE STANDARD CC.K.G.2

Lesson Objective: Identify and name two-dimensional shapes including squares.

Identify and Name Squares

DIRECTIONS 1. Place a square on each shaded square. Color the other squares in the picture.

Name ____________________

Lesson 84
CC.K.G.2

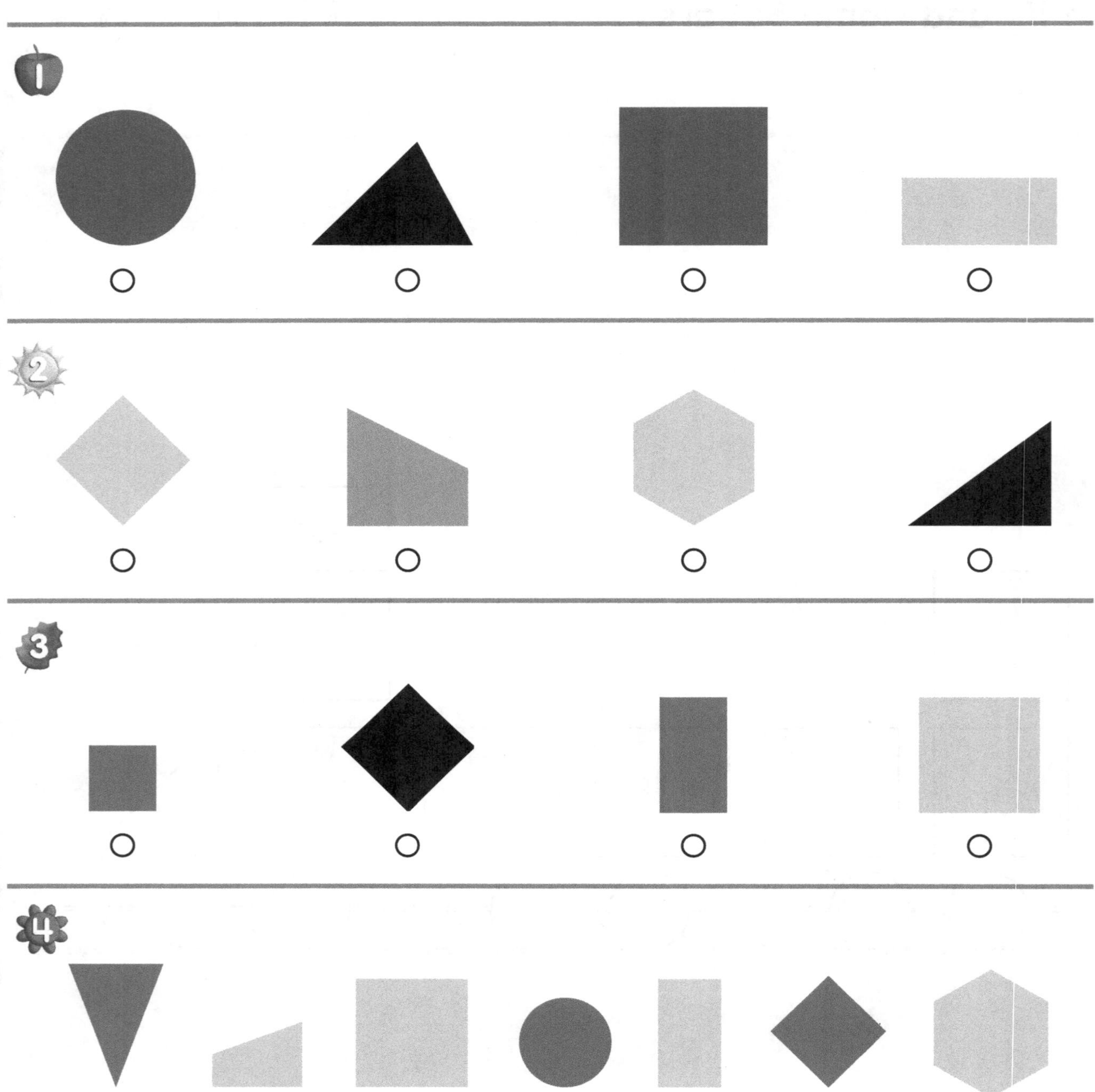

DIRECTIONS **1–2.** Mark under the shape that is a square. **3.** Mark under the shape that is **not** a square. **4.** Mark an X on all of the squares.

Name ____________________

Lesson 85

COMMON CORE STANDARD CC.K.G.2

Lesson Objective: Identify and name two-dimensional shapes including triangles.

Identify and Name Triangles

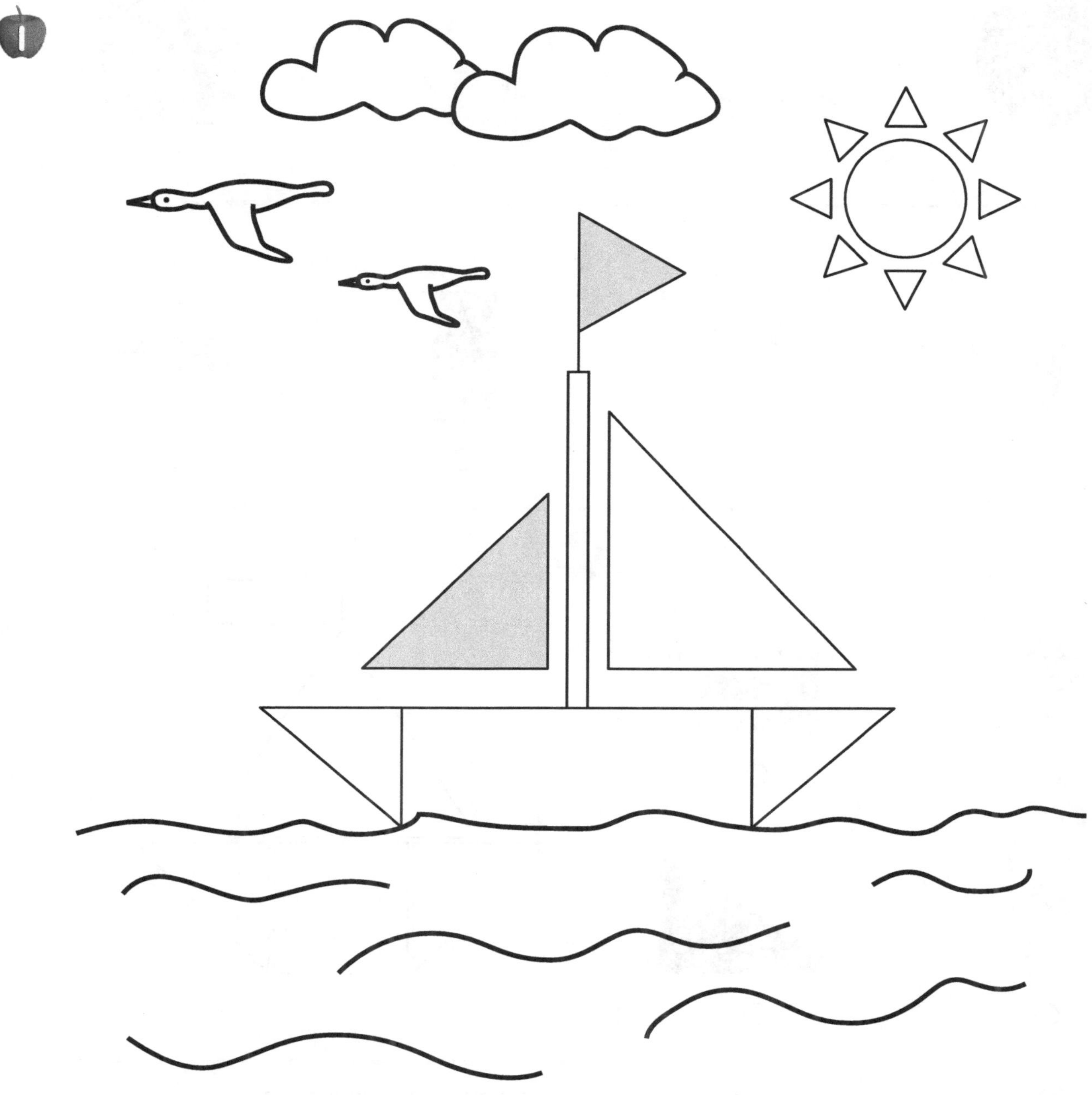

DIRECTIONS 1. Place a triangle on each shaded triangle. Color the other triangles in the picture.

Name ________________________________

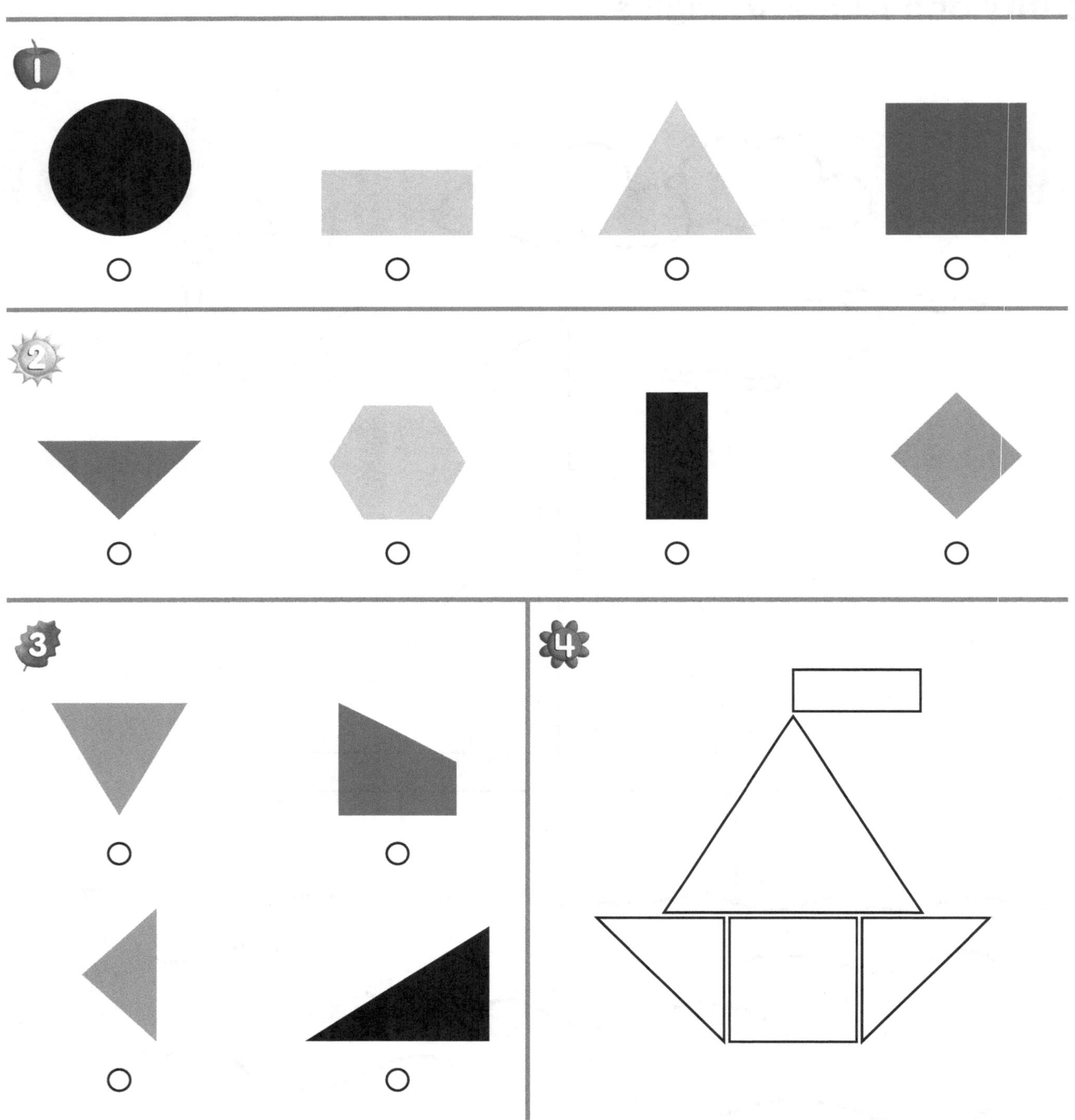

DIRECTIONS **1–2.** Mark under the shape that is a triangle. **3.** Mark under the shape that is **not** a triangle. **4.** Color the triangles in the picture.

Name ___________________________

Lesson 86

COMMON CORE STANDARD CC.K.G.2

Lesson Objective: Identify and name two-dimensional shapes including rectangles.

Identify and Name Rectangles

1

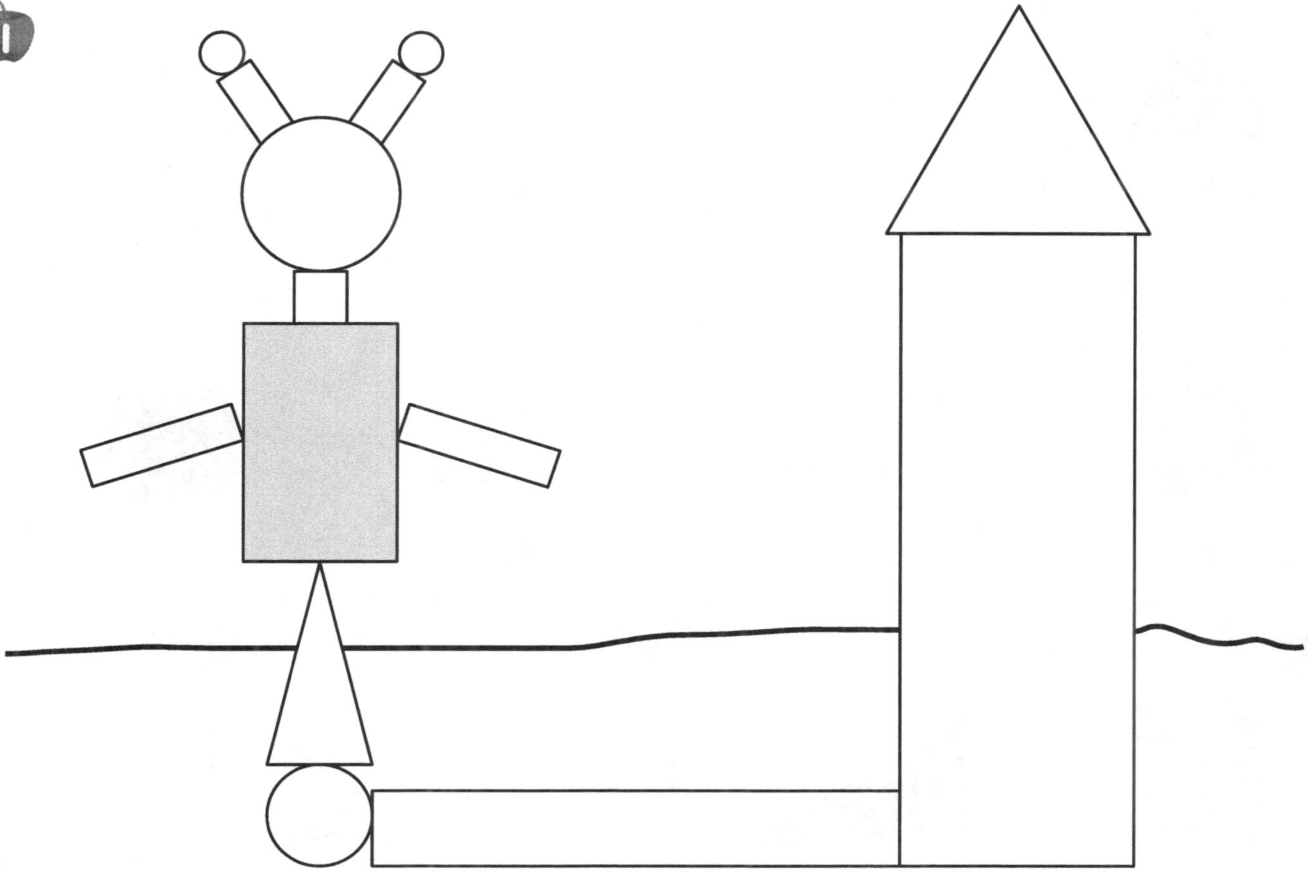

DIRECTIONS 1. Place a rectangle on the shaded rectangle. Color the other rectangles in the picture.

Name ____________________

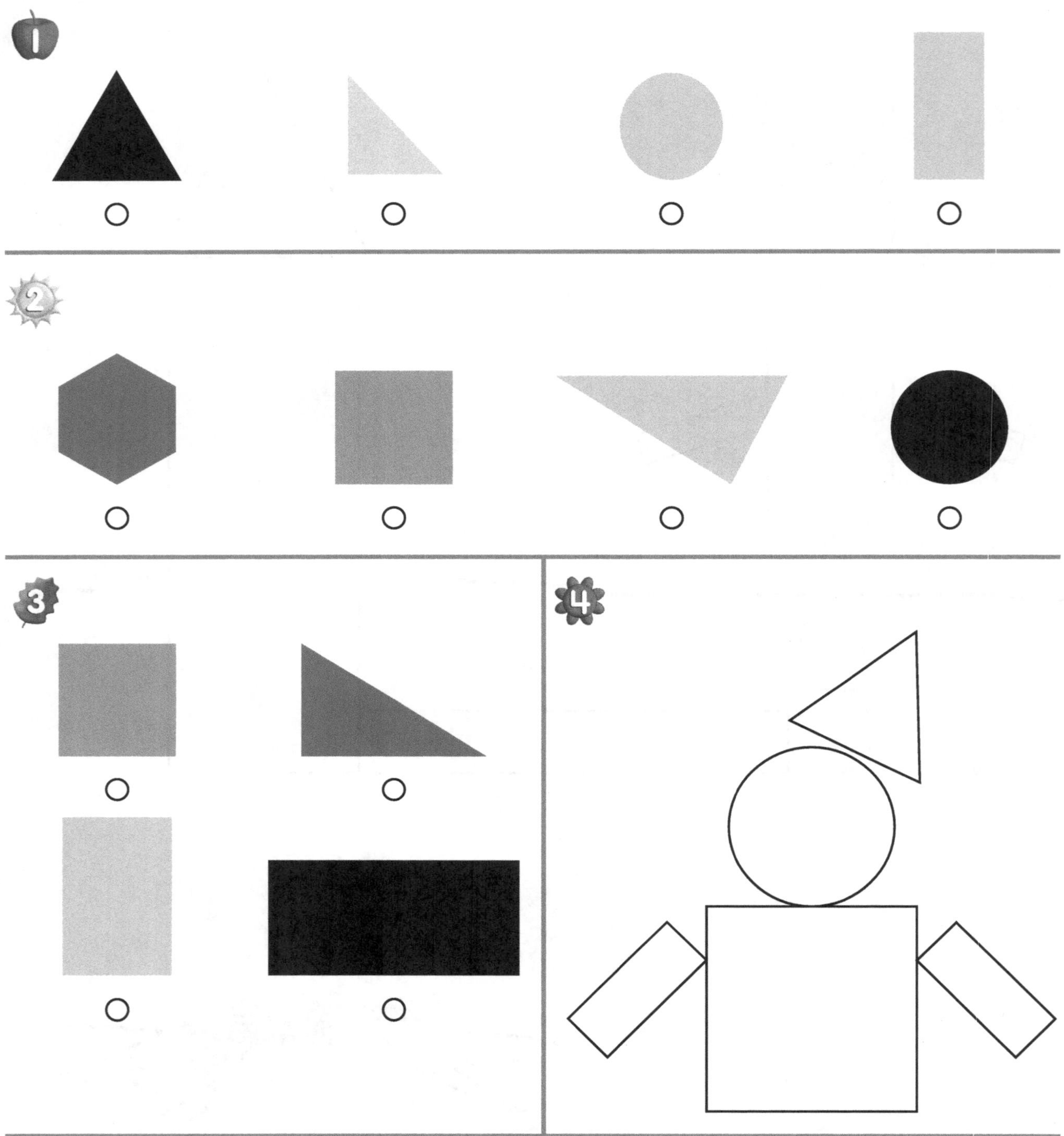

DIRECTIONS **1–2.** Mark under the shape that is a rectangle. **3.** Mark under the shape that is **not** a rectangle. **4.** Color the rectangles in the picture.

Name ___________________________

Lesson 87

COMMON CORE STANDARD CC.K.G.2

Lesson Objective: Identify and name two-dimensional shapes including hexagons.

Identify and Name Hexagons

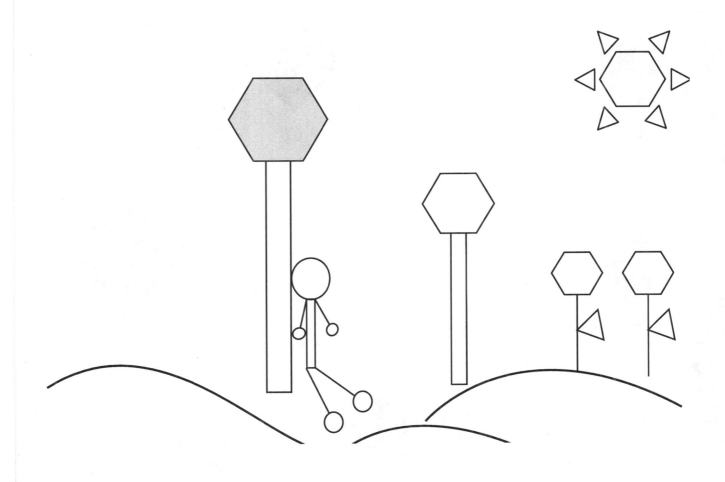

DIRECTIONS 1. Place a hexagon on the shaded hexagon. Color the other hexagons in the picture.

Name ______________________

Lesson 87
CC.K.G.2

1

○ ○ ○ ○

2

○ ○ ○ ○

3

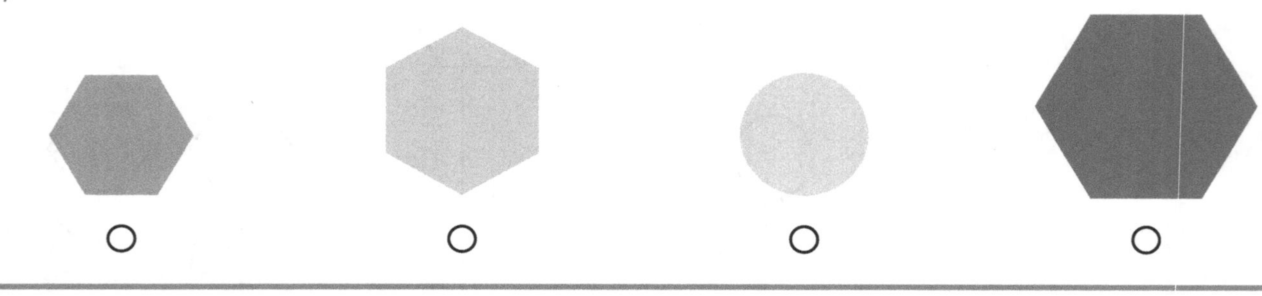

○ ○ ○ ○

4

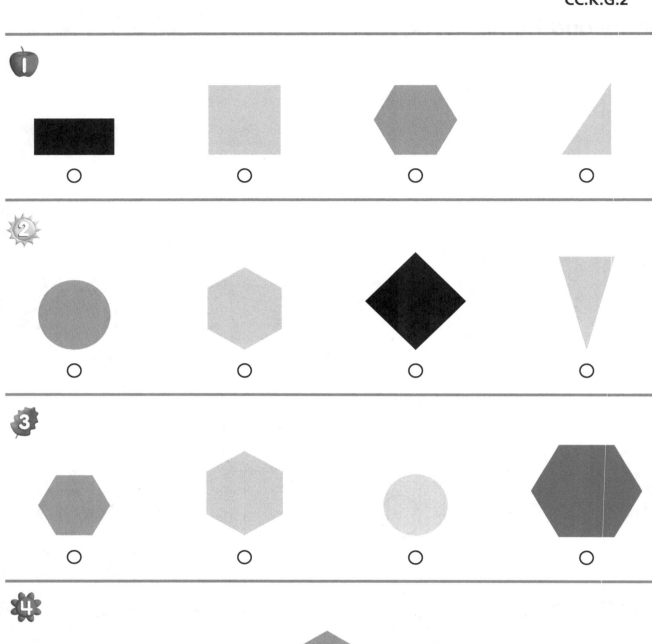

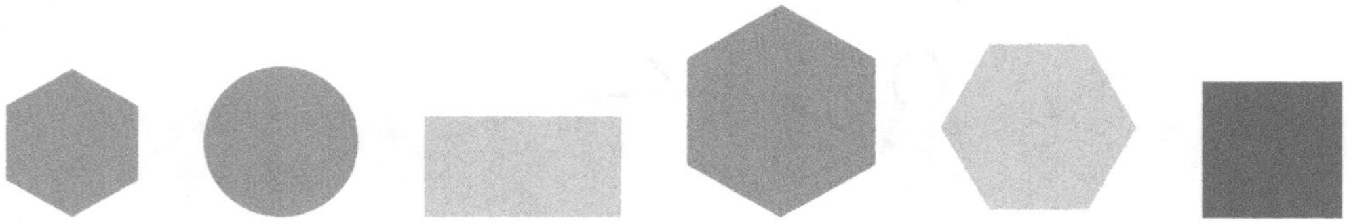

DIRECTIONS **1–2.** Mark under the shape that is a hexagon. **3.** Mark under the shape that is **not** a hexagon. **4.** Mark an X on all of the hexagons.

Name ______________________________

Lesson 88

COMMON CORE STANDARD CC.K.G.2

Lesson Objective: Identify, name, and describe three-dimensional shapes including spheres.

Identify, Name, and Describe Spheres

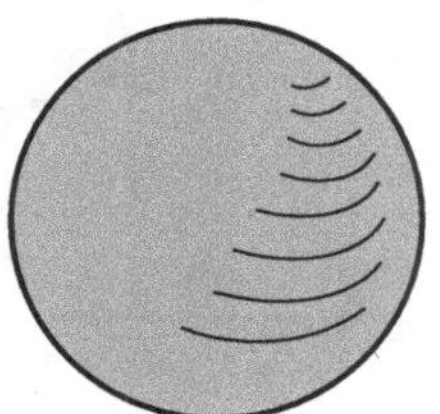

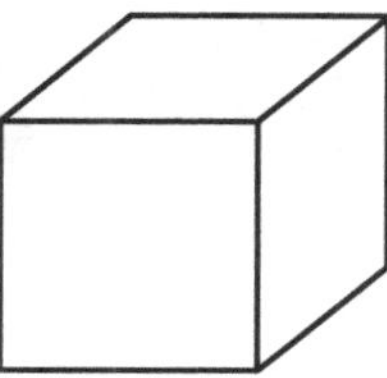

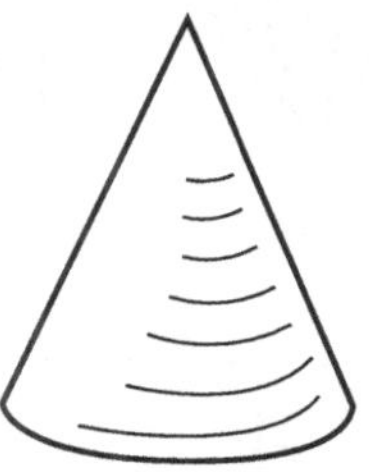

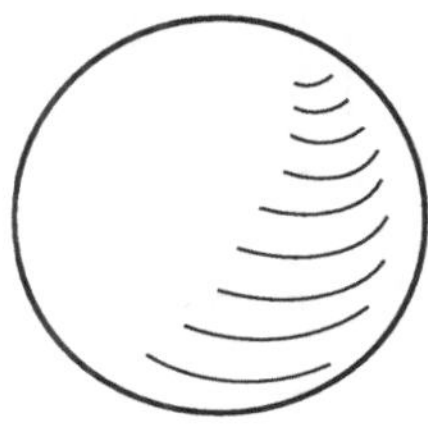

DIRECTIONS A sphere has a curved surface and no flat surfaces. Trace the shapes with your finger. **1.** Trace the gray sphere with your crayon. **2–4.** Color the spheres.

Name ______________________________

Lesson 88
CC.K.G.2

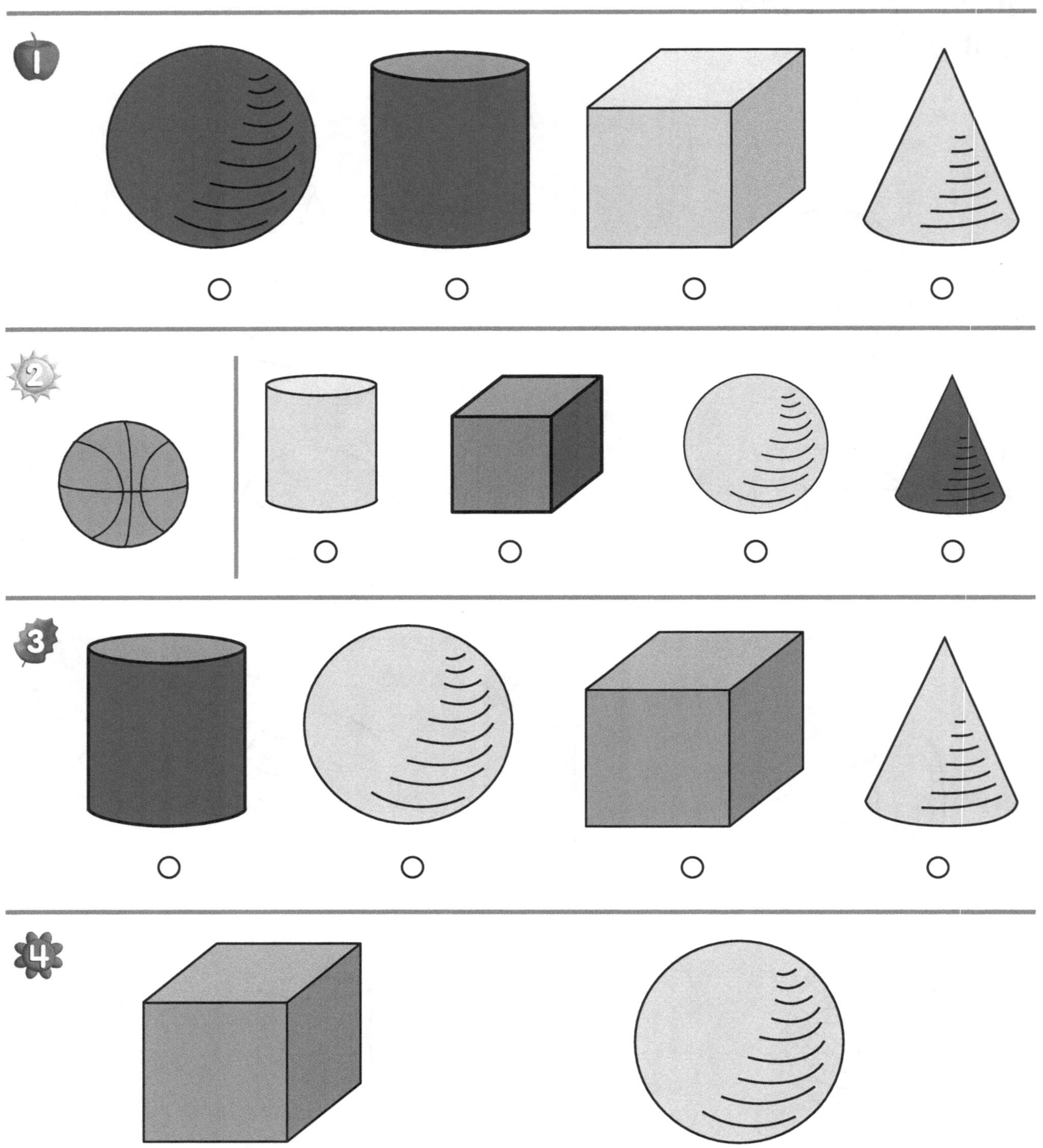

DIRECTIONS 1. Mark under the sphere. 2. Mark under the shape that is the same shape as the object at the beginning of the row. 3. Mark under the sphere. 4. Mark an X on the shape that has a curved surface.

Name ______________________________

Lesson 89

COMMON CORE STANDARD CC.K.G.2

Lesson Objective: Identify, name, and describe three-dimensional shapes including cubes.

Identify, Name, and Describe Cubes

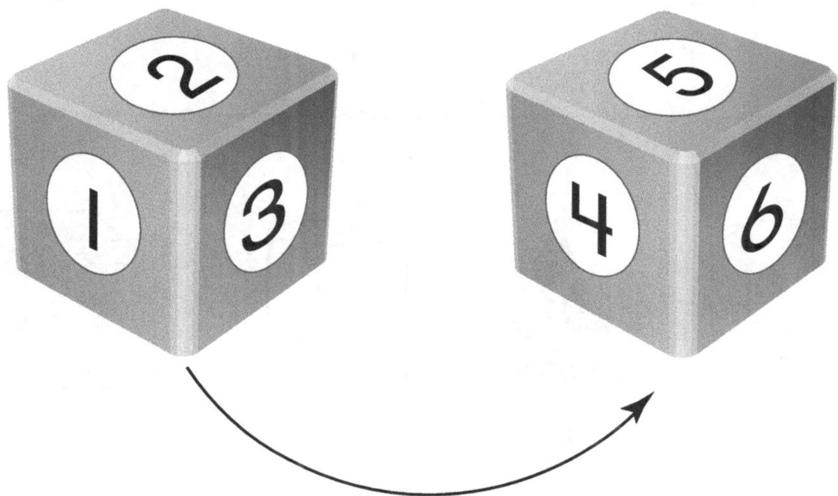

2

______

______ **flat surfaces**

DIRECTIONS 1. Look at the pictures that show all the flat surfaces on one cube. Count how many flat surfaces. Touch each number as you count. **2.** Write the number that shows how many flat surfaces.

Name ______________________________

Lesson 89
CC.K.G.2

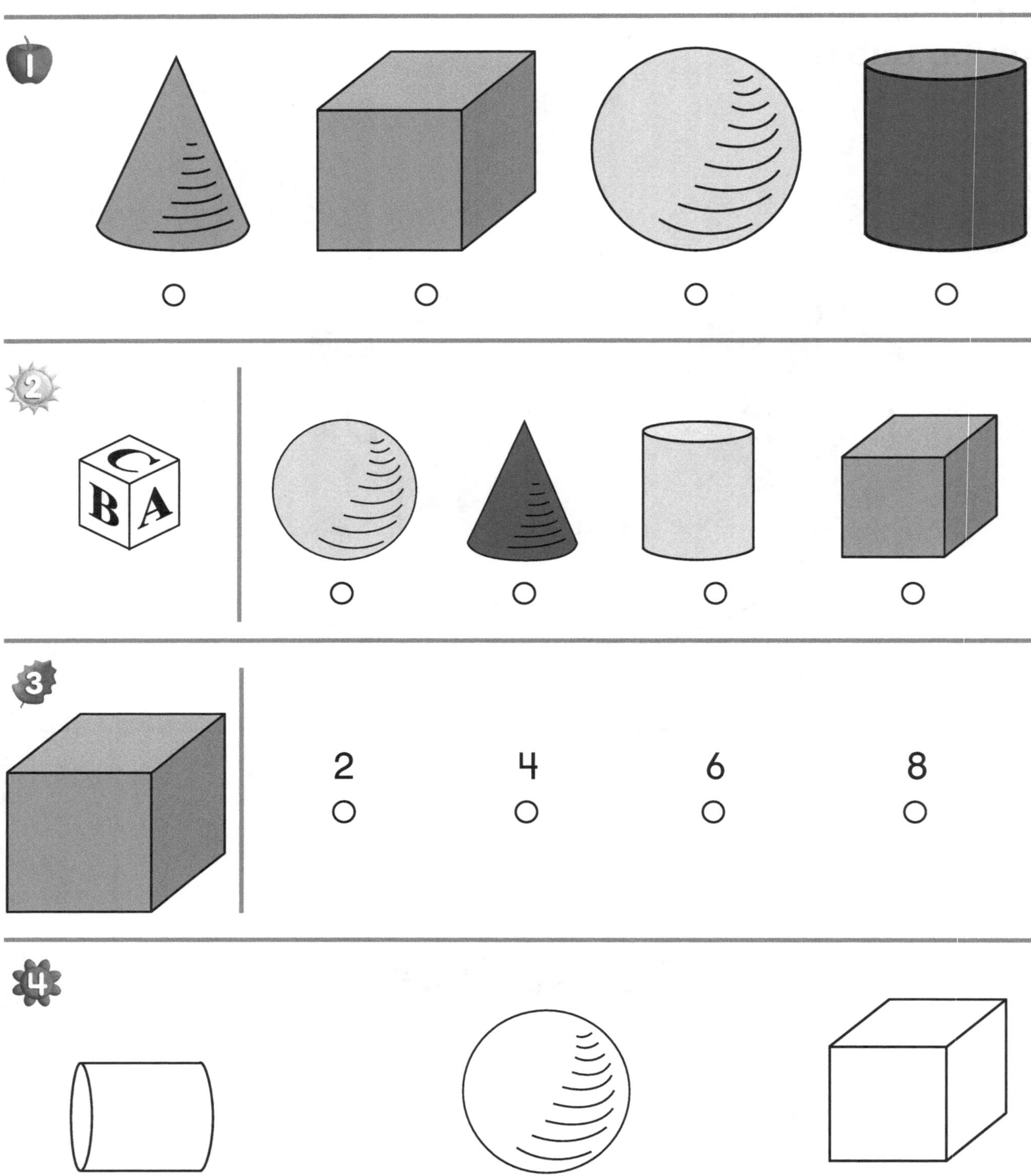

DIRECTIONS 1. Mark under the cube. 2. Mark under the shape that is the same shape as the object at the beginning of the row. 3. Mark under the number that shows how many flat surfaces the cube has. 4. Mark an X on the cube.

Name ______________________________

COMMON CORE STANDARD CC.K.G.2

Lesson Objective: Identify, name, and describe three-dimensional shapes including cylinders.

Identify, Name, and Describe Cylinders

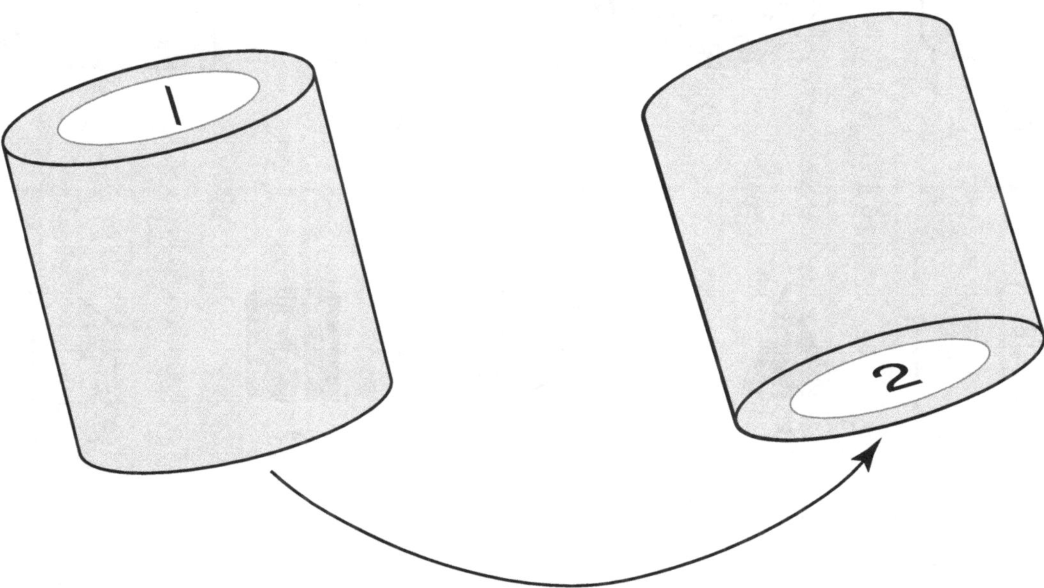

______

_ _ _ _ _

______ **flat surfaces**

DIRECTIONS **1.** Look at the pictures that show the flat surfaces on one cylinder. Count how many flat surfaces. Touch each number as you count. **2.** Write the number that shows how many flat surfaces.

Name ______________________________

Lesson 90
CC.K.G.2

1

○ ○ ○ ○

2

○ ○ ○ ○

3

2	3	4	5
○	○	○	○

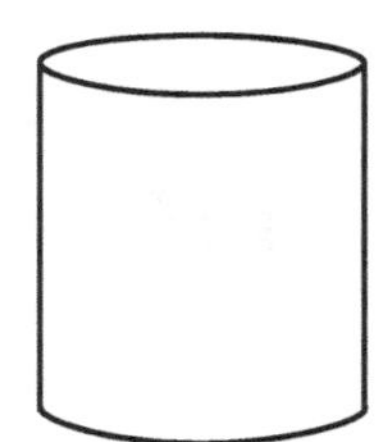

DIRECTIONS 1. Mark under the cylinder. **2.** Mark under the shape that is the same shape as the object at the beginning of the row. **3.** Mark under the number that shows how many flat surfaces the cylinder has. **4.** Mark an X on the cylinder.

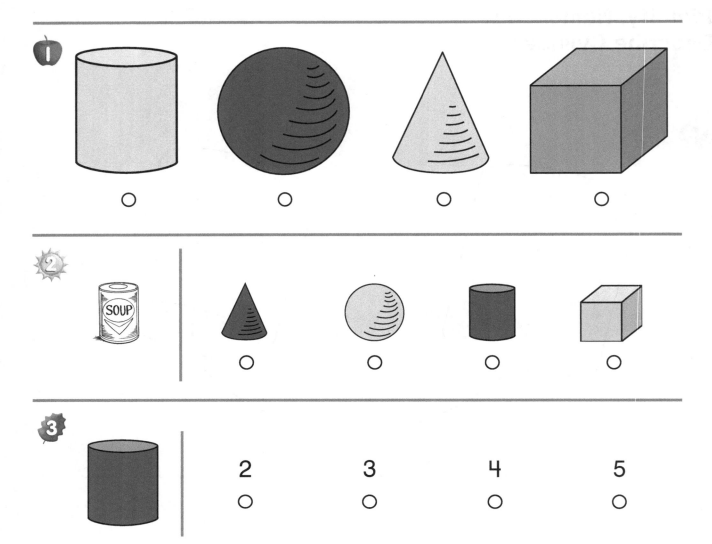

Name ______________________________

Lesson 91

COMMON CORE STANDARD CC.K.G.2

Lesson Objective: Identify, name, and describe three-dimensional shapes including cones.

Identify, Name, and Describe Cones

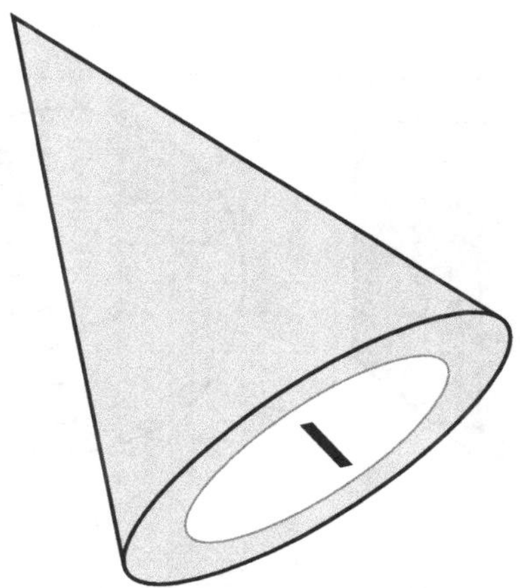

______

_ _ _ _ _

______ **flat surface**

DIRECTIONS 1. Look at the picture that shows the flat surface on one cone. Count how many flat surfaces. Touch the number as you count. **2.** Write the number that shows how many flat surfaces.

Name ______________________________

Lesson 91
CC.K.G.2

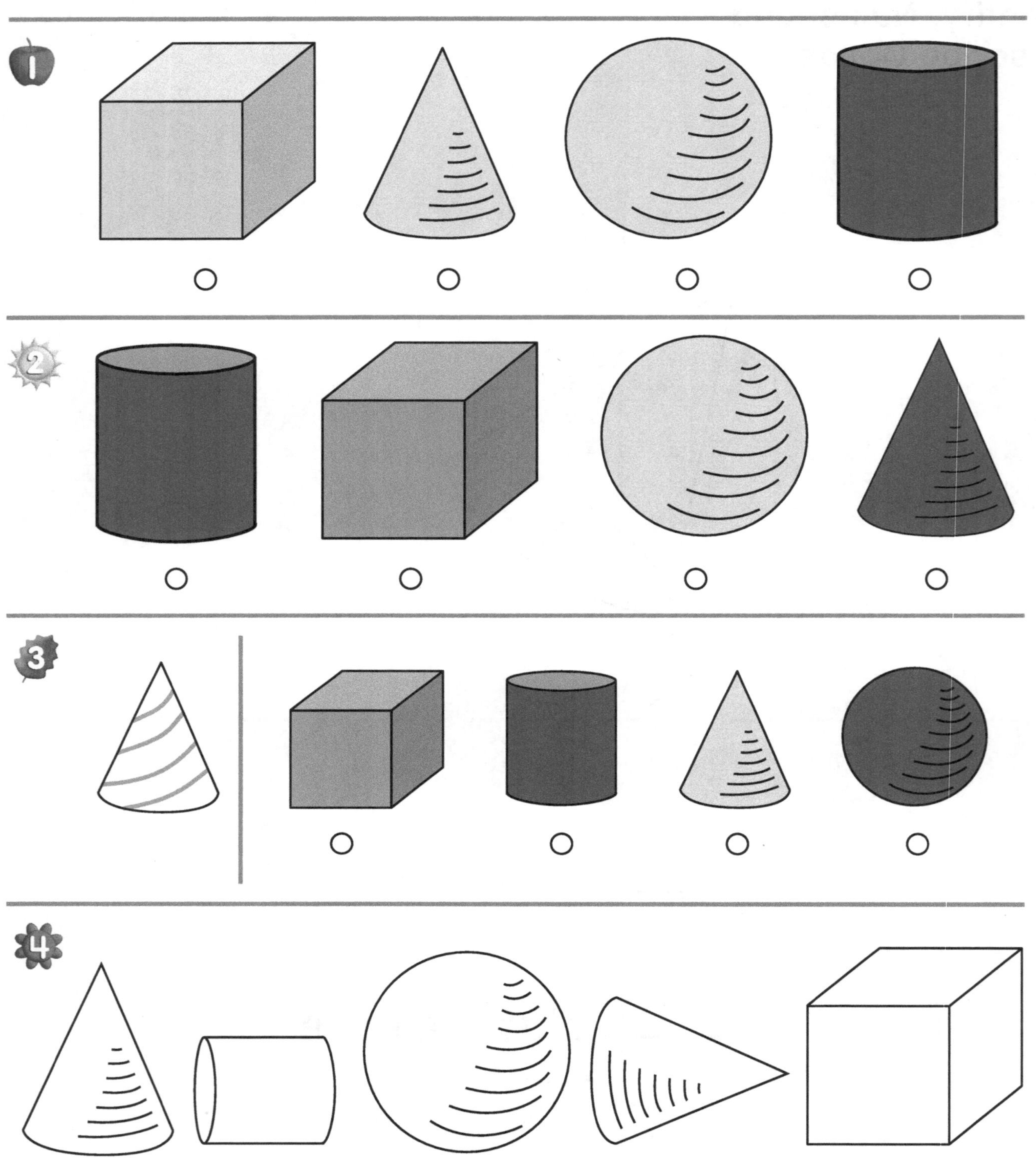

DIRECTIONS 1. Mark under the cone. 2. Mark under the shape that has one flat surface and a curved surface. 3. Mark under the shape that is the same shape as the object at the beginning of the row. 4. Color all of the cones.

Name ______________________________

Lesson 92

COMMON CORE STANDARD CC.K.G.3

Lesson Objective: Solve problems by using the strategy *use logical reasoning.*

Problem Solving • Two- and Three-Dimensional Shapes

red

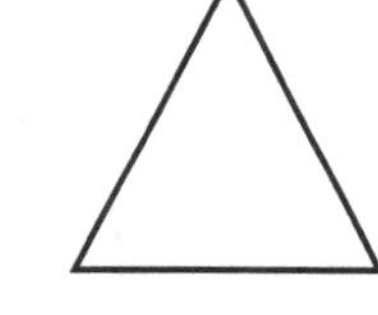

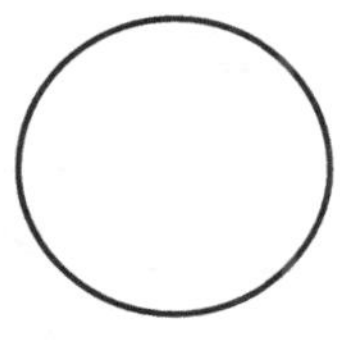

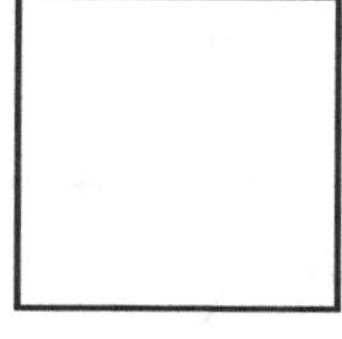

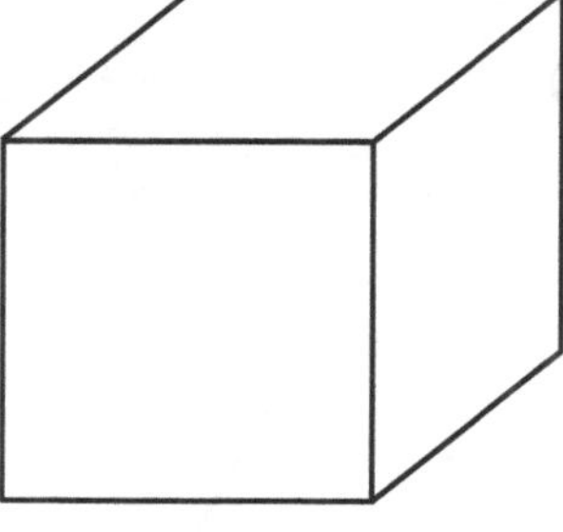

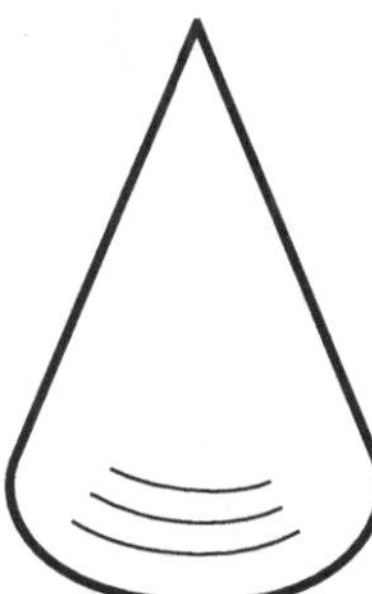

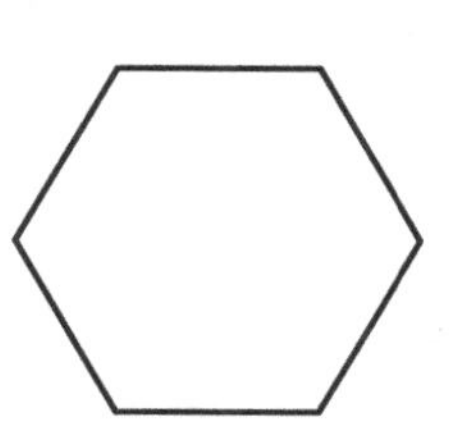

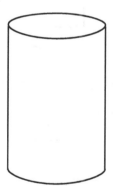

DIRECTIONS **1.** Use red to color the two-dimensional, or flat, shape. Use blue to color the three-dimensional, or solid, shape. **2.** Look at the shape you colored red in Exercise 1. Use red to color the flat shapes. Look at the shape you colored blue in Exercise 1. Use blue to color the solid shapes.

Name ______________________________

Lesson 92
CC.K.G.3

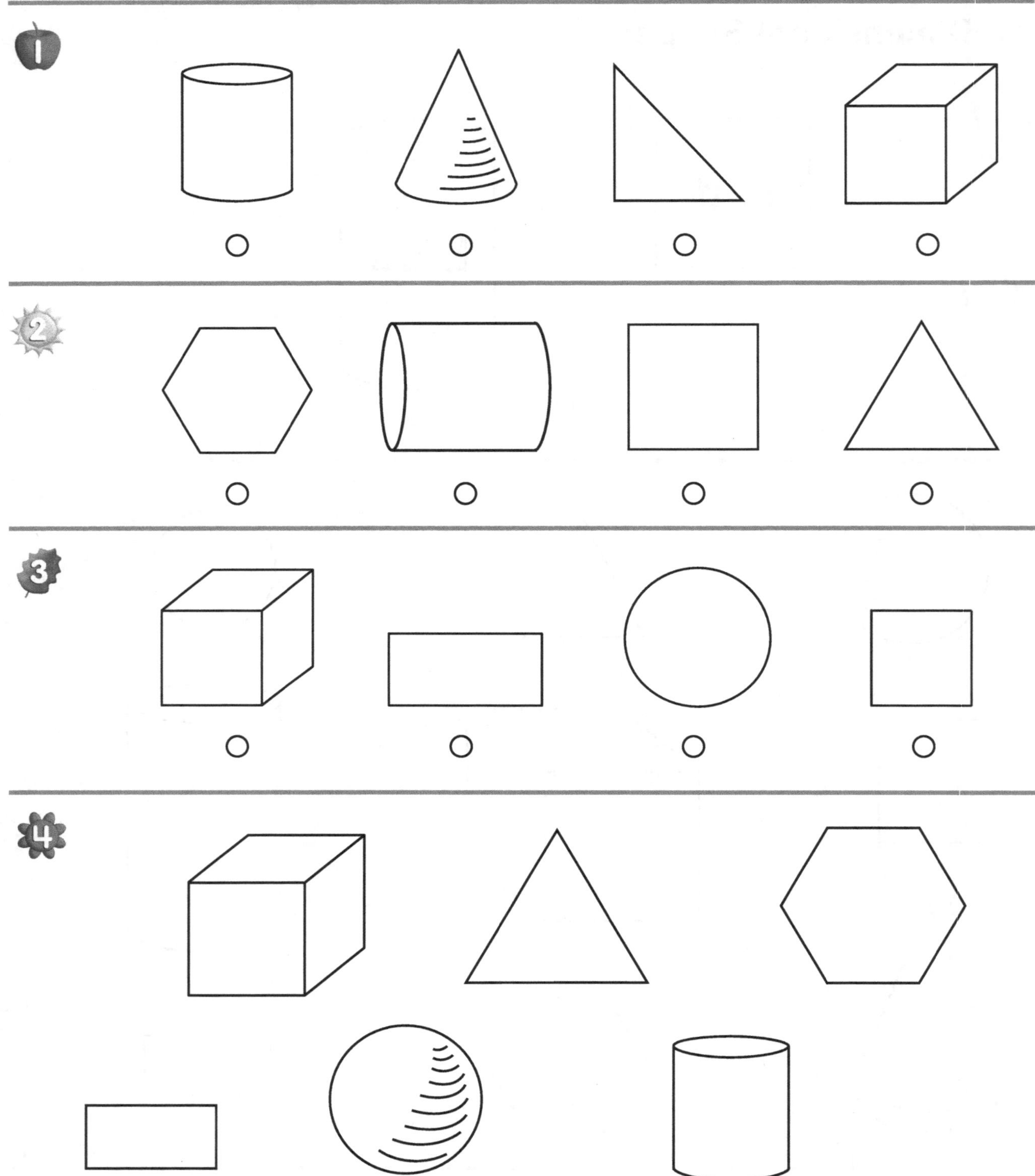

DIRECTIONS 1. Mark under the two-dimensional, or flat, shape. **2–3.** Mark under the three-dimensional, or solid, shape. **4.** Circle the two-dimensional, or flat, shapes. Mark an X on the three-dimensional, or solid, shapes.

Name ______________________________

Lesson 93

COMMON CORE STANDARD CC.K.G.4

Lesson Objective: Describe attributes of circles.

Describe Circles

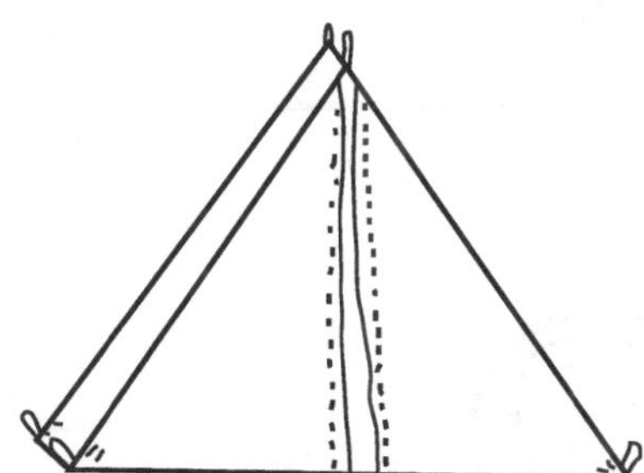

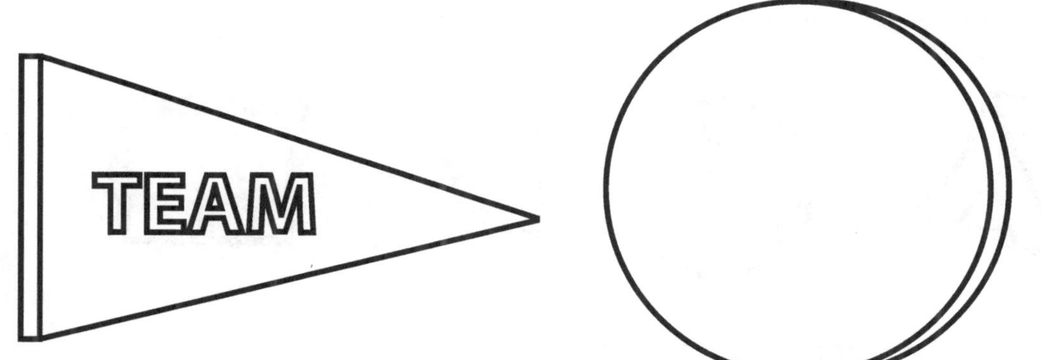

DIRECTIONS 1. Finish coloring the object that is shaped like a circle. 2. Color the object that is shaped like a circle.

Name ____________________

Lesson 93
CC.K.G.4

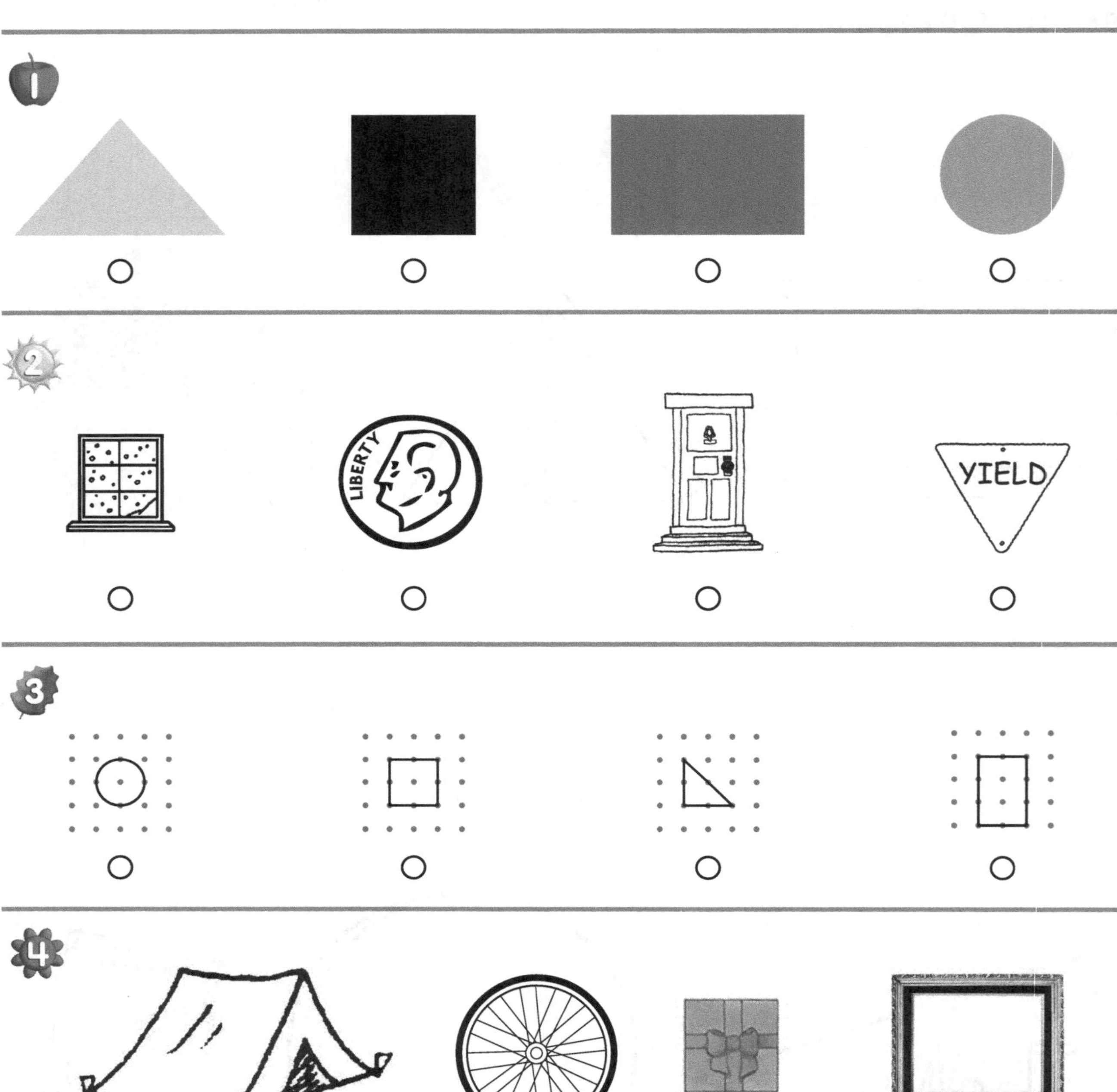

DIRECTIONS **1.** Mark under the shape that has a curve. **2.** Mark under the object that is shaped like a circle. **3.** Kristin drew a circle. Mark under the shape that Kristin drew. **4.** Color the object that is shaped like a circle.

Name ______________________

Lesson 94

COMMON CORE STANDARD CC.K.G.4

Lesson Objective: Describe attributes of squares.

Describe Squares

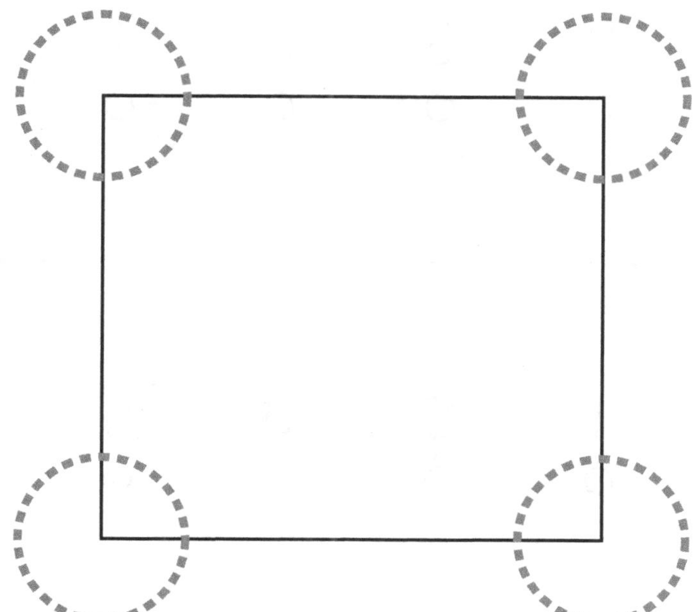

______ vertices

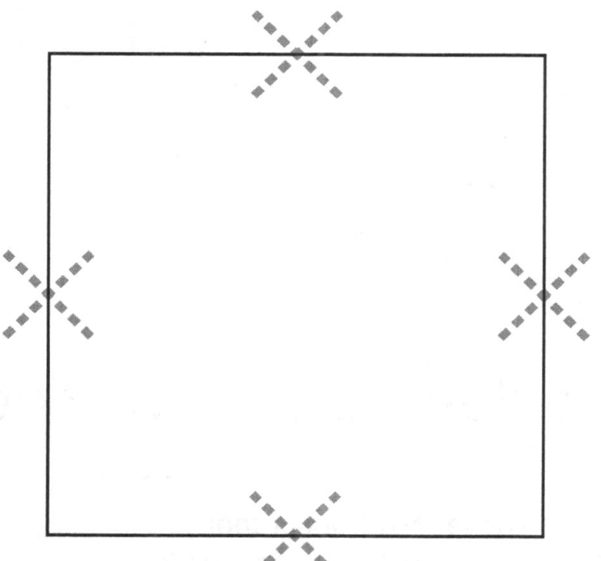

______ sides

DIRECTIONS **1.** Trace the circle around each corner, or vertex. Draw a dot in each circle as you count. Write how many corners, or vertices. **2.** Trace the X on each side. Draw a dot on each X as you count. Write how many sides.

Name ____________________

Lesson 94
CC.K.G.4

4 ○ 3 ○ 2 ○ 1 ○

1 ○ 2 ○ 3 ○ 4 ○

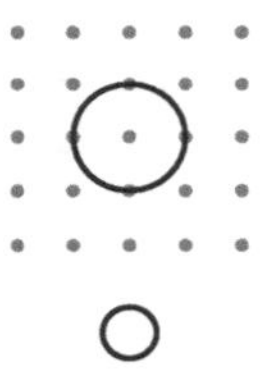

○ ○ ○ ○

_____ sides _____ vertices

DIRECTIONS **1.** How many sides does the square have? Mark under that number. **2.** How many corners, or vertices, does the square have? Mark under that number. **3.** Juan drew a shape with 4 sides of equal length and 4 vertices. Mark under the shape that Juan drew. **4.** Write how many sides the square has. Then write how many corners, or vertices, the square has.

Name ___________________________

Lesson 95

COMMON CORE STANDARD CC.K.G.4

Lesson Objective: Describe attributes of triangles.

Describe Triangles

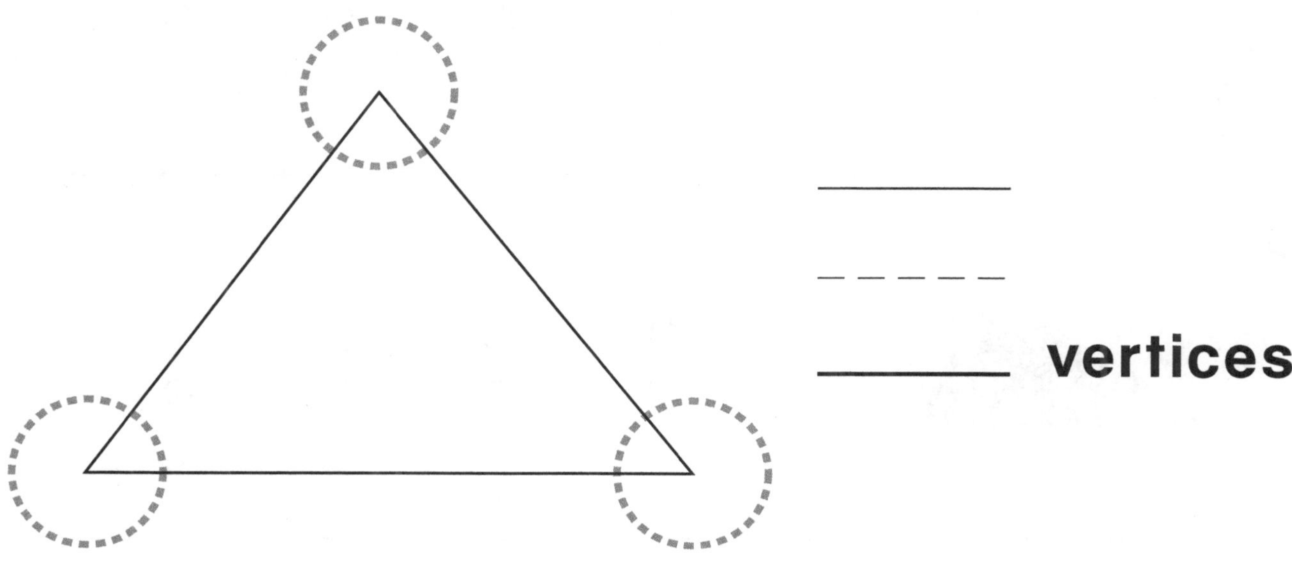

______ **vertices**

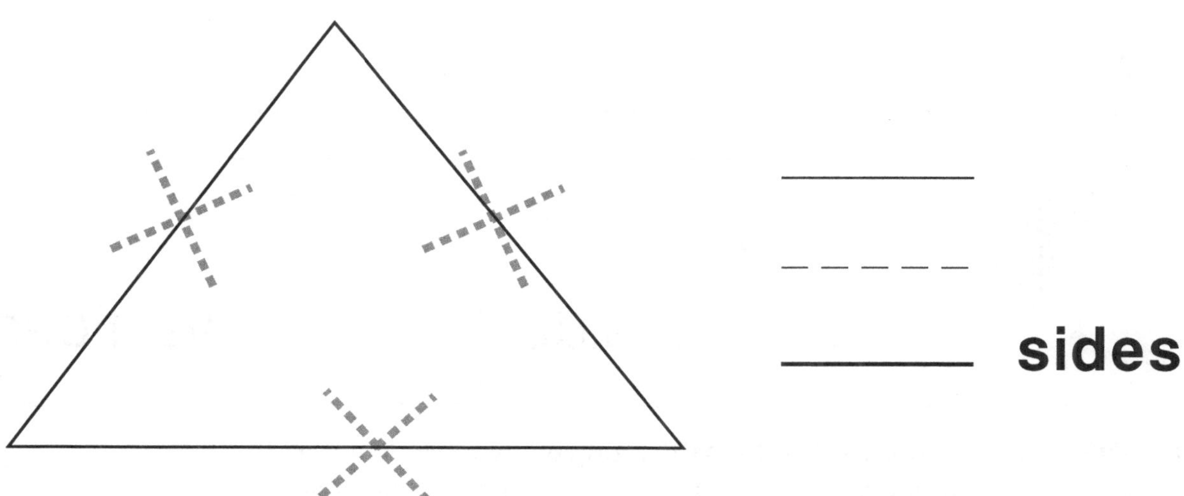

______ **sides**

DIRECTIONS **1.** Trace the circle around each corner, or vertex. Draw a dot in each circle as you count. Write how many corners, or vertices. **2.** Trace the X on each side. Draw a dot on each X as you count. Write how many sides.

Name ___________________________

Lesson 95
CC.K.G.4

1	2	3	4
○	○	○	○

4	3	2	1
○	○	○	○

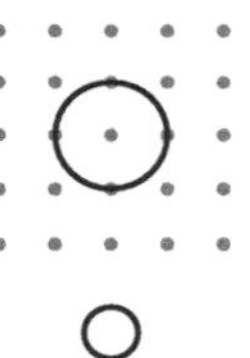

○

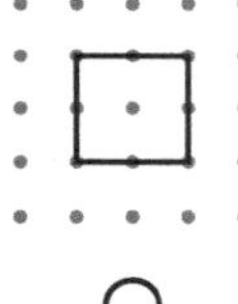

○

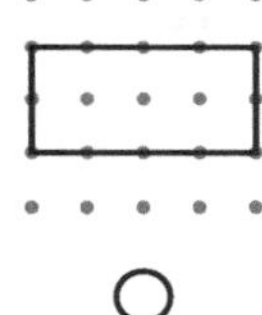

○

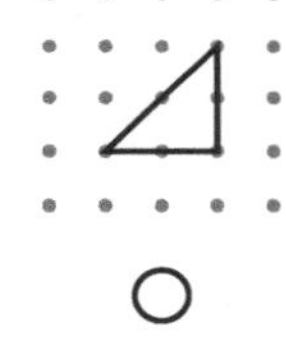

○

______ sides ______ vertices

DIRECTIONS 1. How many sides does the triangle have? Mark under that number. **2.** How many corners, or vertices, does the triangle have? Mark under that number. **3.** Tito drew a shape with 3 sides and 3 vertices. Mark under the shape that Tito drew. **4.** Write how many sides the triangle has. Then write how many corners, or vertices, the triangle has.

Name ______________________

Describe Rectangles

Lesson 96

COMMON CORE STANDARD CC.K.G.4

Lesson Objective: Describe attributes of rectangles.

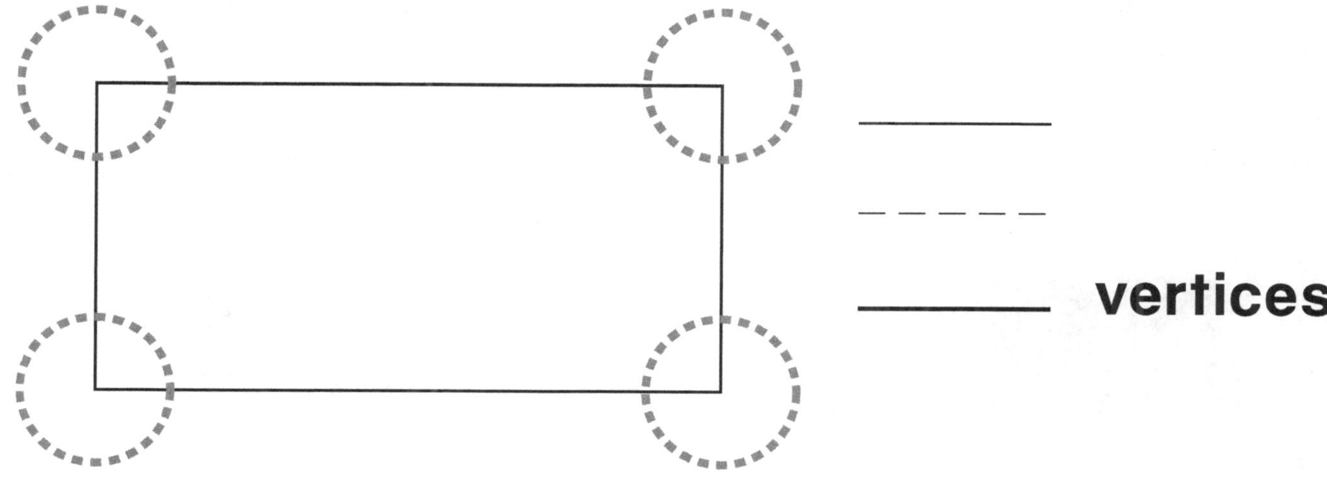

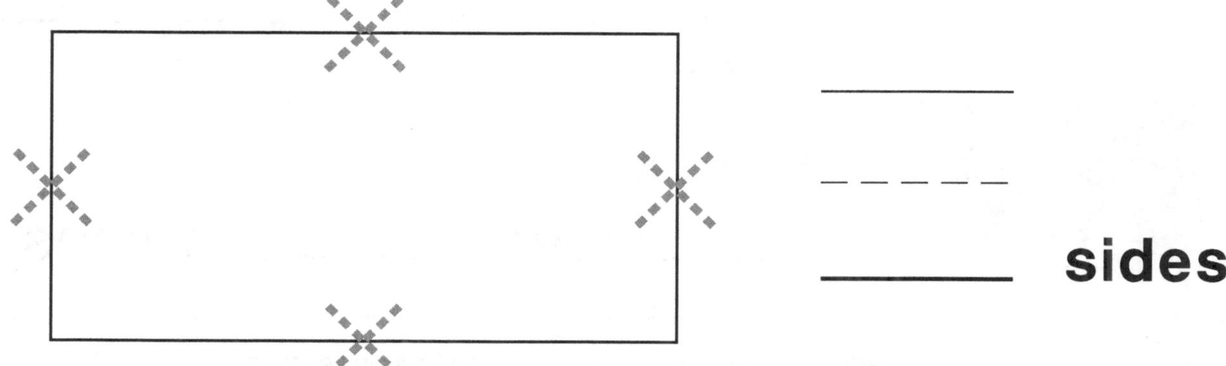

DIRECTIONS **1.** Trace the circle around each corner, or vertex. Draw a dot in each circle as you count. Write how many corners, or vertices. **2.** Trace the X on each side. Draw a dot on each X as you count. Write how many sides.

Name ___________________________

Lesson 96
CC.K.G.4

4 3 2 1

○ ○ ○ ○

1 2 3 4

○ ○ ○ ○

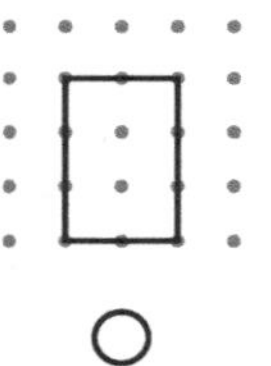

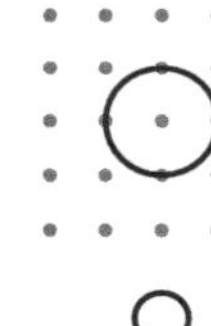

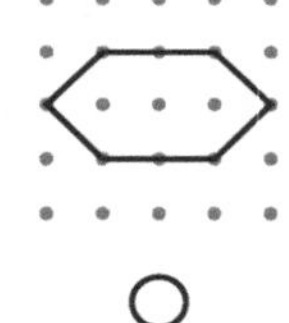

○ ○ ○ ○

______ sides ______ vertices

DIRECTIONS 1. How many sides does the rectangle have? Mark under that number. **2.** How many corners, or vertices, does the rectangle have? Mark under that number. **3.** Rita drew a shape with 4 sides and 4 vertices. Mark under the shape that Rita drew. **4.** Write how many sides the rectangle has. Then write how many corners, or vertices, the rectangle has.

Name ____________________

COMMON CORE STANDARD CC.K.G.4

Lesson Objective: Describe attributes of hexagons.

Describe Hexagons

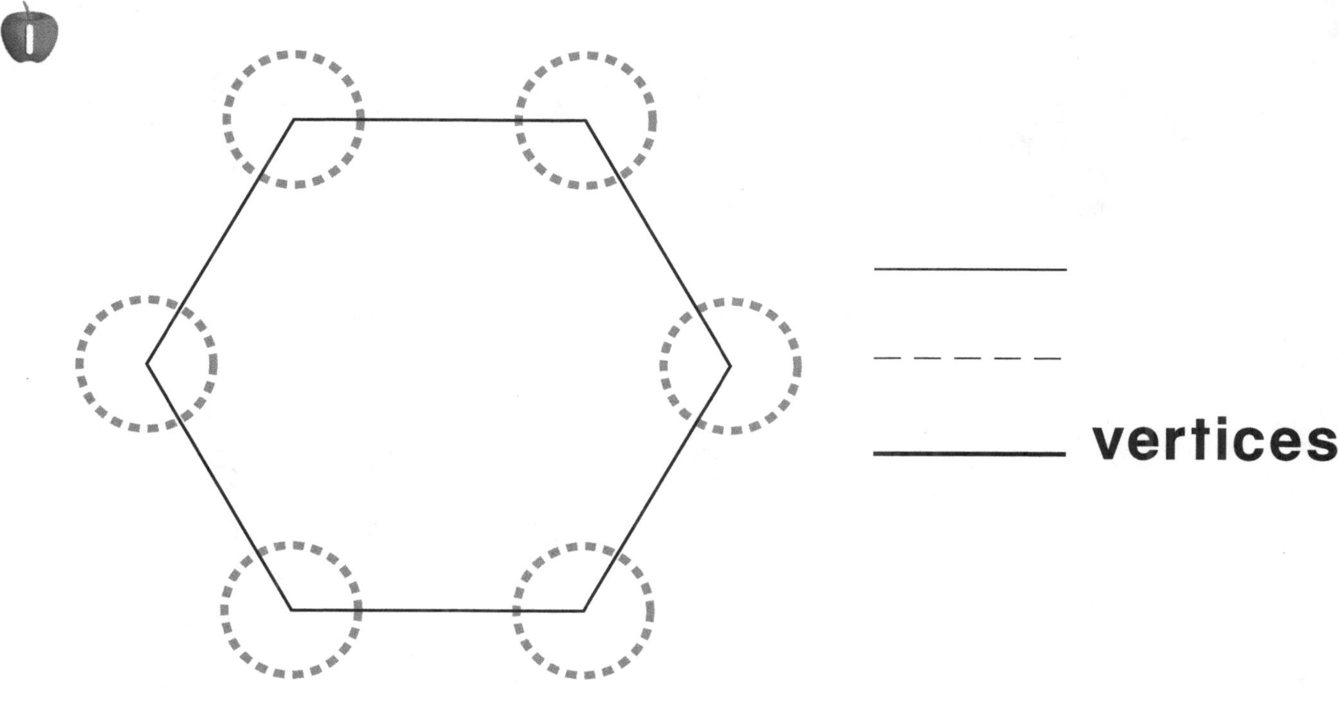

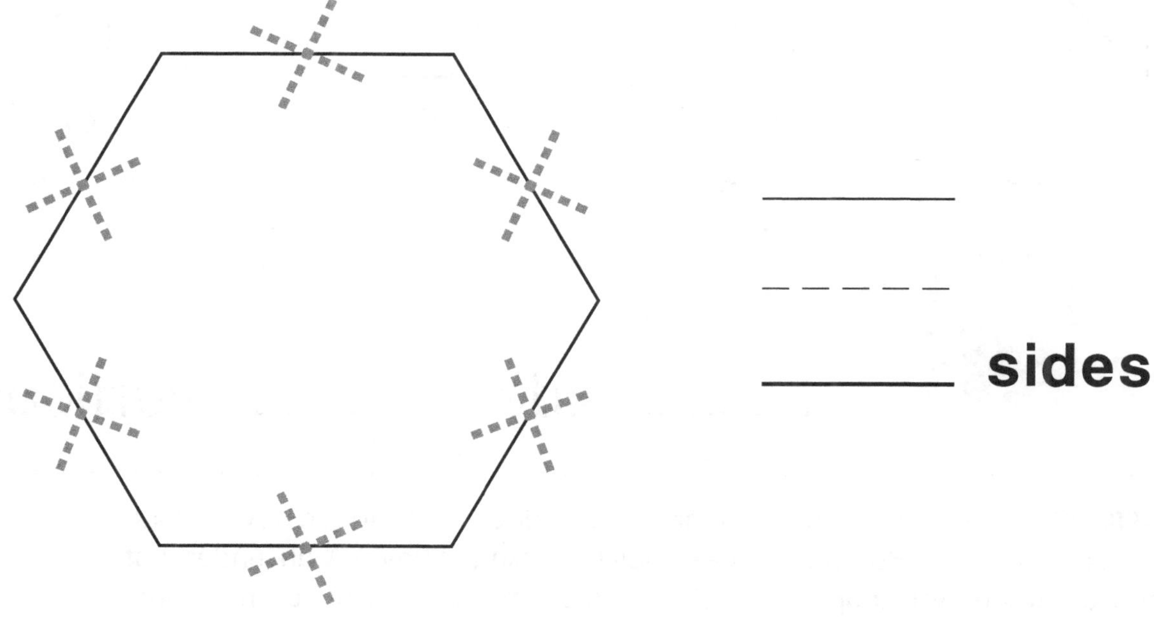

DIRECTIONS 1. Trace the circle around each corner, or vertex. Draw a dot in each circle as you count. Write how many corners, or vertices. **2.** Trace the X on each side. Draw a dot on each X as you count. Write how many sides.

Name ______________________

Lesson 97
CC.K.G.4

8 6 4 3

○ ○ ○ ○

3 4 5 6

○ ○ ○ ○

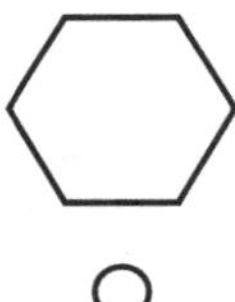

○ ○ ○ ○

______ sides ______ vertices

DIRECTIONS **1.** How many corners, or vertices, does the hexagon have? Mark under that number. **2.** How many sides does the hexagon have? Mark under that number. **3.** Alex drew a shape with 6 sides and 6 vertices. Mark under the shape that Alex drew. **4.** Write how many sides the hexagon has. Then write how many corners, or vertices, the hexagon has.

Name ______________________________

Lesson 98

COMMON CORE STANDARD CC.K.G.4

Lesson Objective: Use the words *alike* and *different* to compare two-dimensional shapes by attributes.

Algebra • Compare Two-Dimensional Shapes

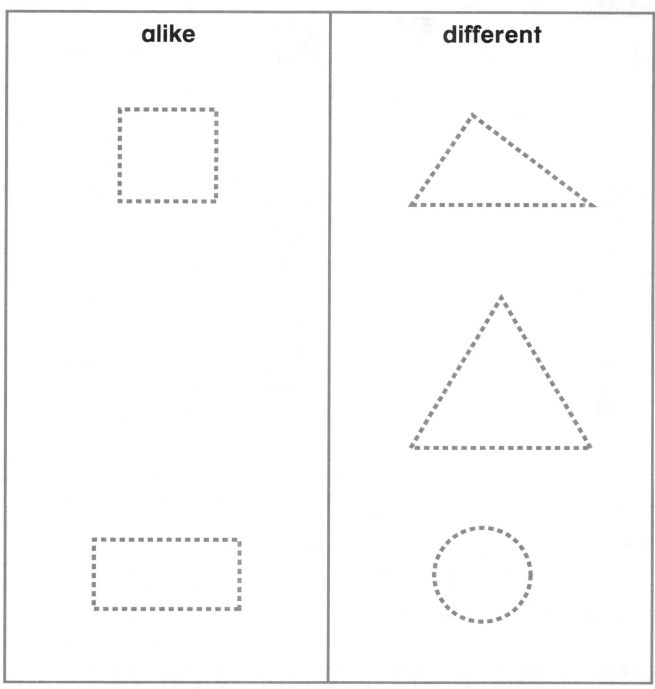

alike	different

DIRECTIONS 1. Sort two-dimensional shapes by number of vertices as shown. Trace the shapes that have four vertices. Tell a friend why the shapes are alike. Trace the other shapes. Tell a friend why they are different.

Name ______________________________

Lesson 98
CC.K.G.4

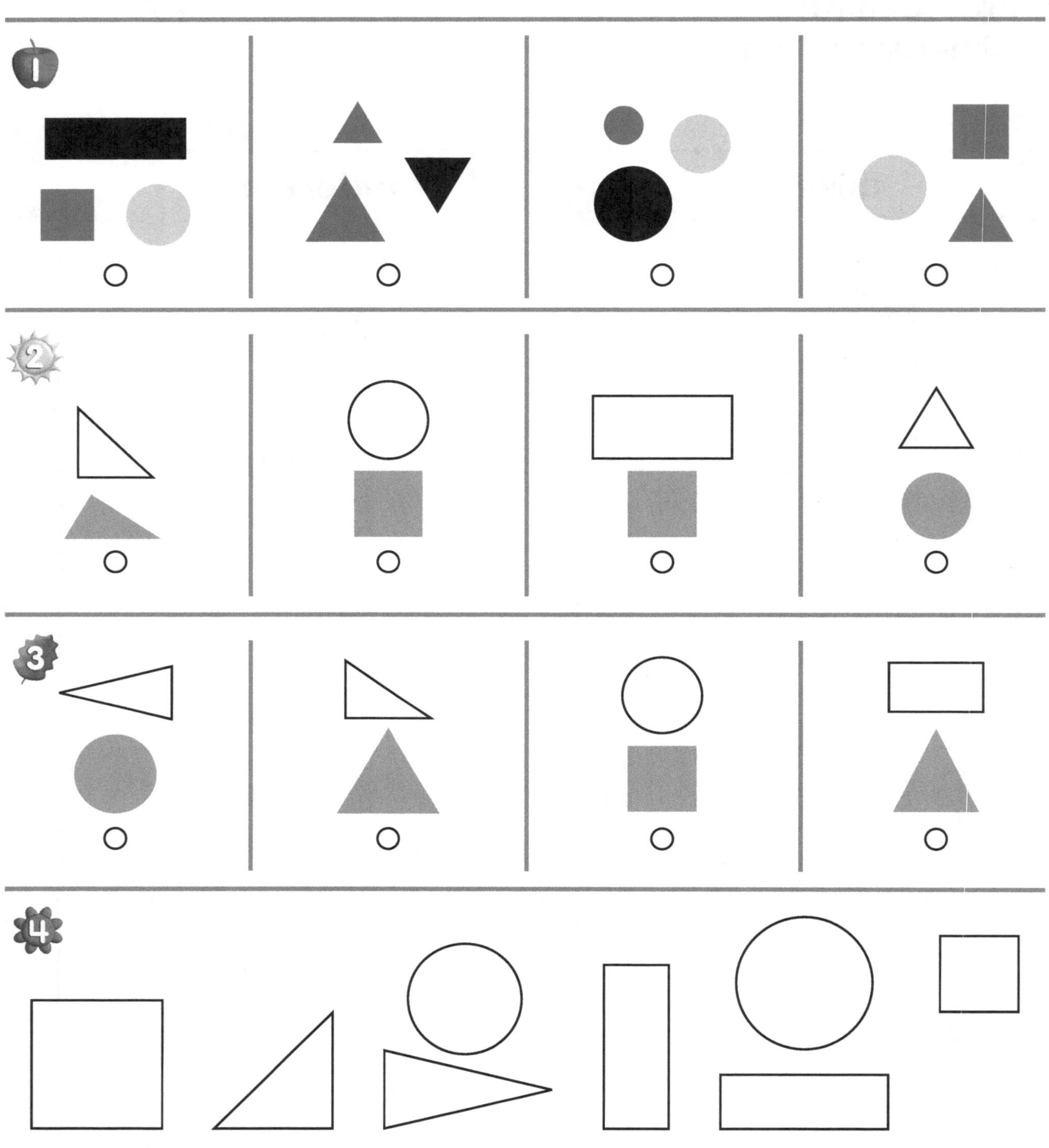

DIRECTIONS **1.** Which set is made up of shapes that are **alike** because they all have 3 sides? Mark under that set. **2.** Which set is made up of shapes that are **alike** because they have 4 corners, or vertices? Mark under that set. **3.** Which set is made up of shapes that are **alike** because they have the same number of sides? Mark under that set. **4.** Color all of the shapes that are **alike** because they have 4 vertices and 4 sides.

Name ______________________________

Lesson 99

COMMON CORE STANDARD CC.K.G.4

Lesson Objective: Analyze and compare three-dimensional shapes by attributes.

Three-Dimensional Shapes

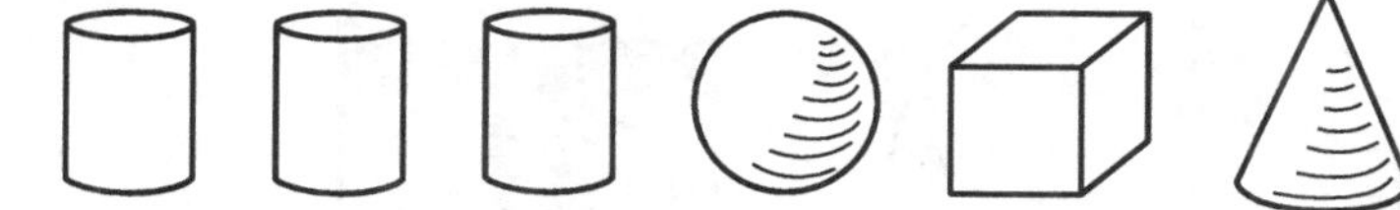

stack

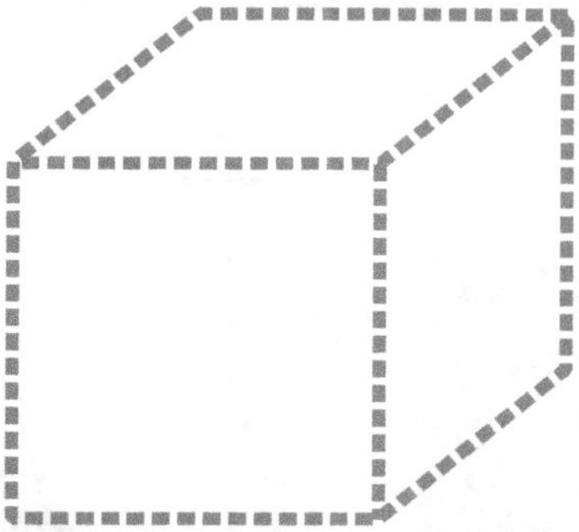

roll

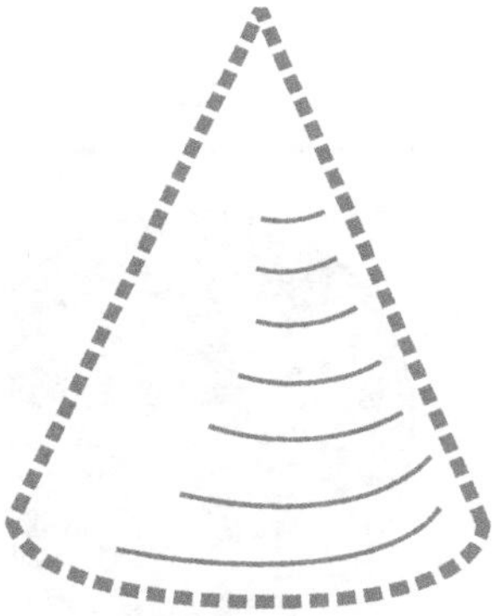

roll and stack

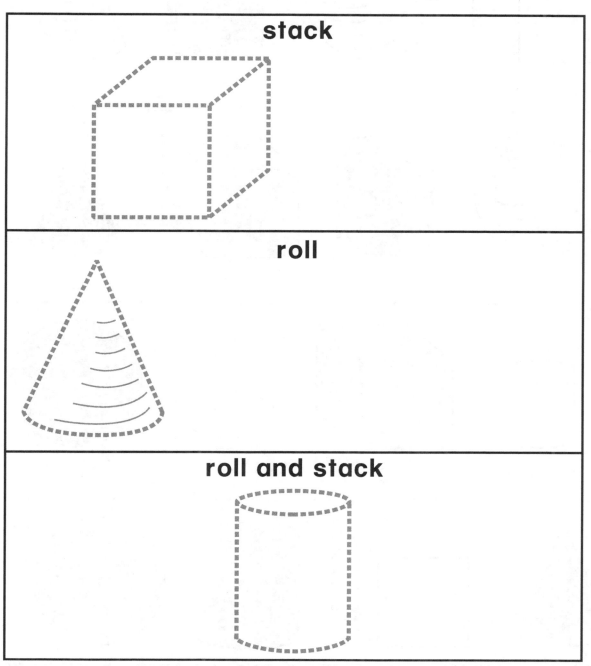

DIRECTIONS 1. Place three-dimensional shapes on the page. Sort the shapes by whether they roll or stack. Describe the shapes. Match a picture of each shape to the shapes. Glue the shape pictures on the page.

Name ________________________________

Lesson 99
CC.K.G.4

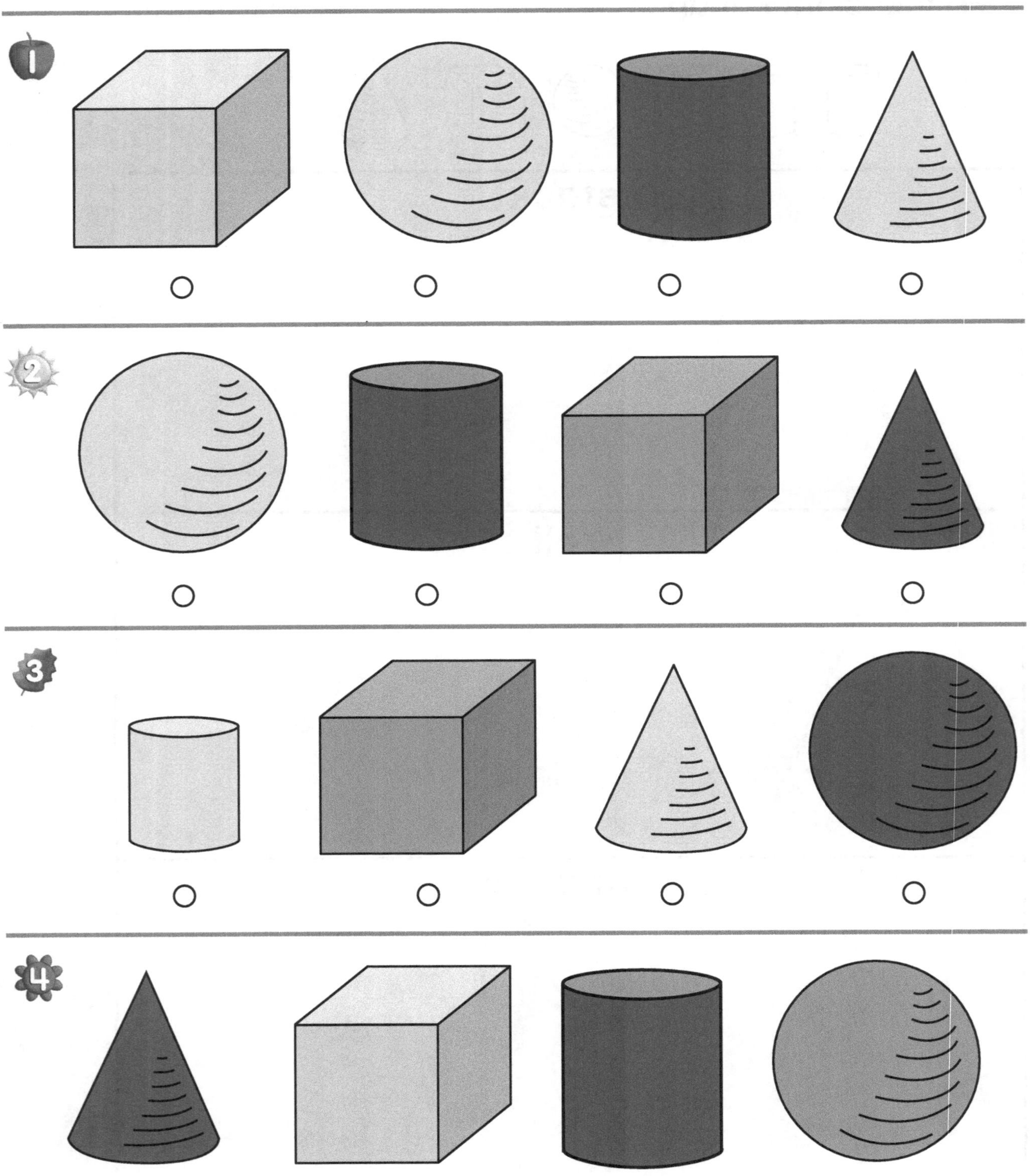

DIRECTIONS 1. Mark under the shape that stacks but does not roll. **2.** Mark under the shape that rolls and stacks. **3.** Mark under the shape that does not slide. **4.** Mark an X on the shapes that roll but do not stack.

Name ______________________________

Lesson 100

COMMON CORE STANDARD CC.K.G.5

Lesson Objective: Use objects to build models of real-world shapes.

Build Models

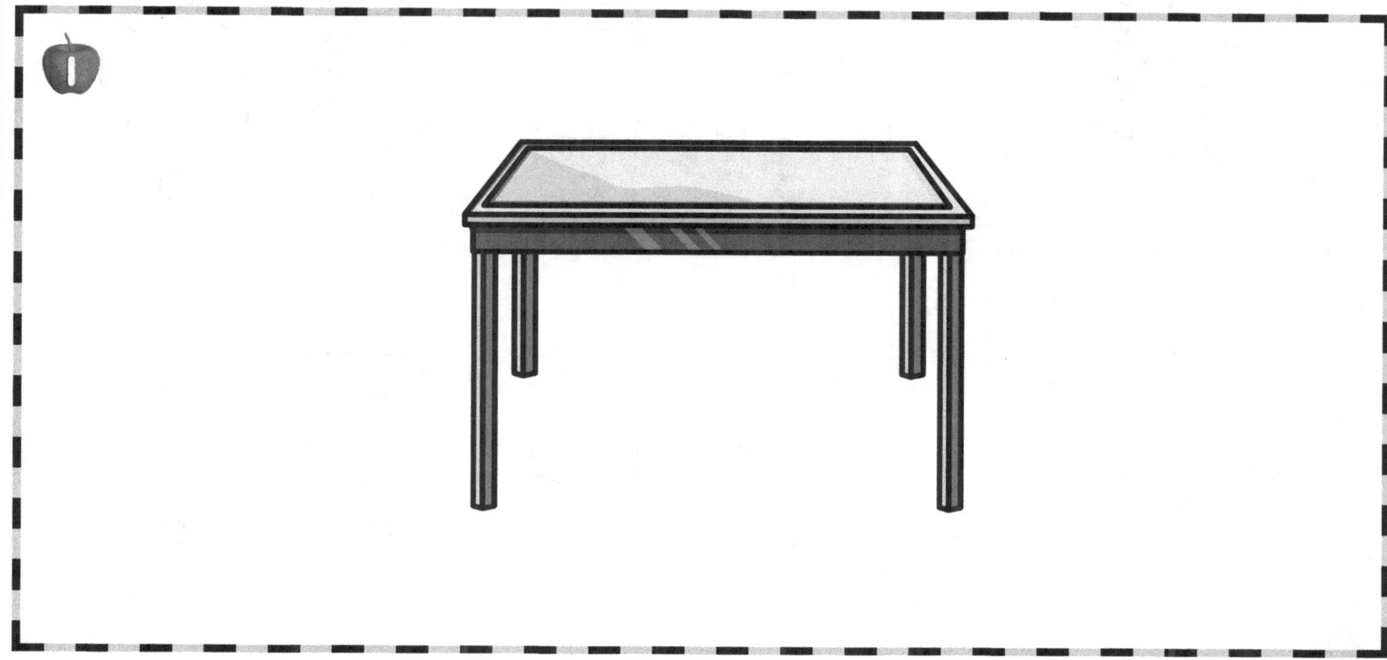

DIRECTIONS 1–2. Make a model of the object with blocks.

Name ______________________

Lesson 100
CC.K.G.5

4

DIRECTIONS **1–3.** Look at the picture at the beginning of the row. Mark under the shape that is most like the shape at the beginning of the row. **4.** Draw a picture of a shape that looks like a basketball.

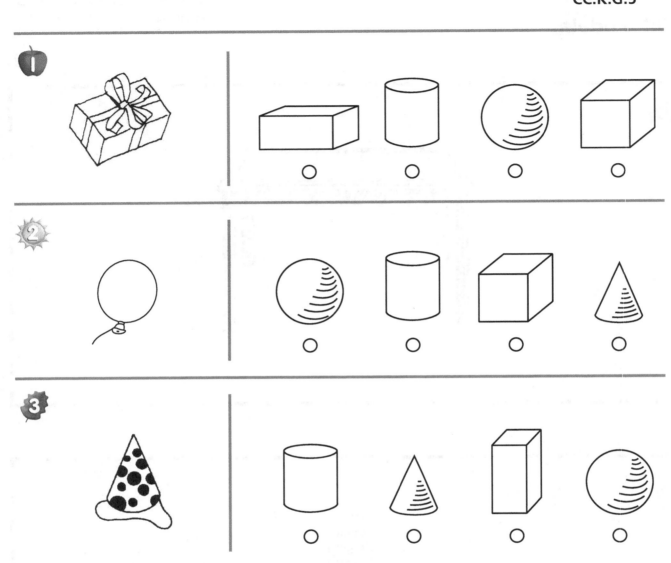

Name ______________________

Lesson 101

COMMON CORE STANDARD CC.K.G.6

Lesson Objective: Make larger shapes from smaller shapes.

Make Shapes

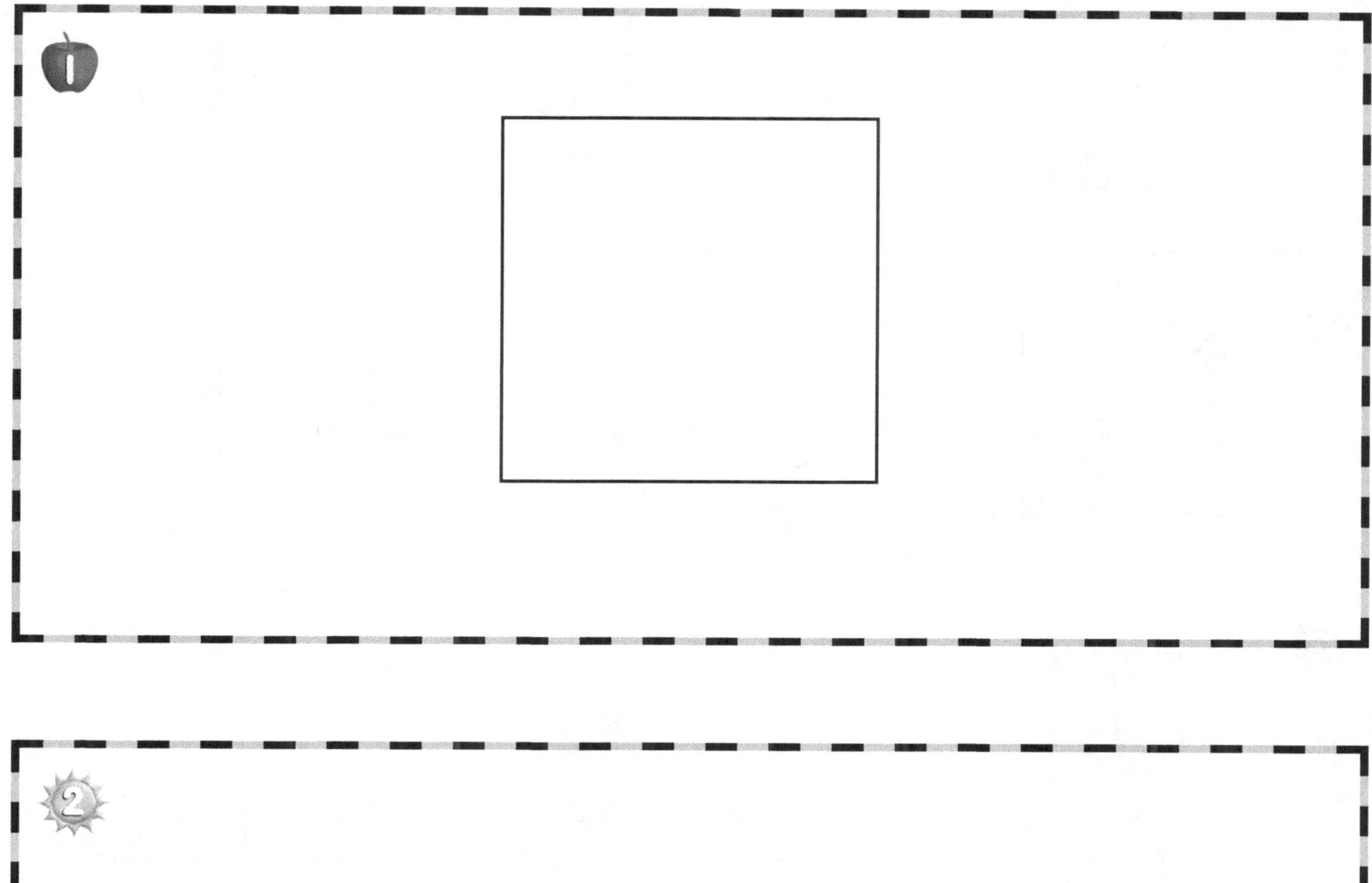

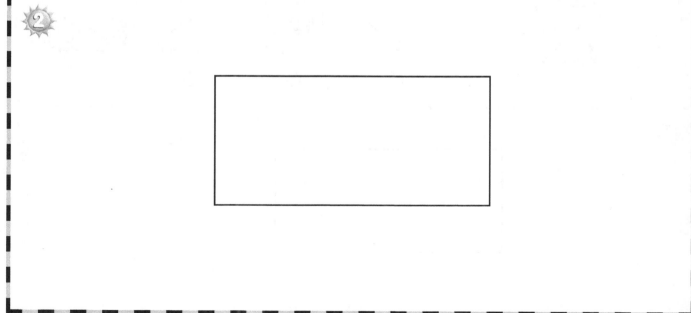

DIRECTIONS 1–2. Make the shape with triangles. Then trace the shapes you used.

Name ______________________________

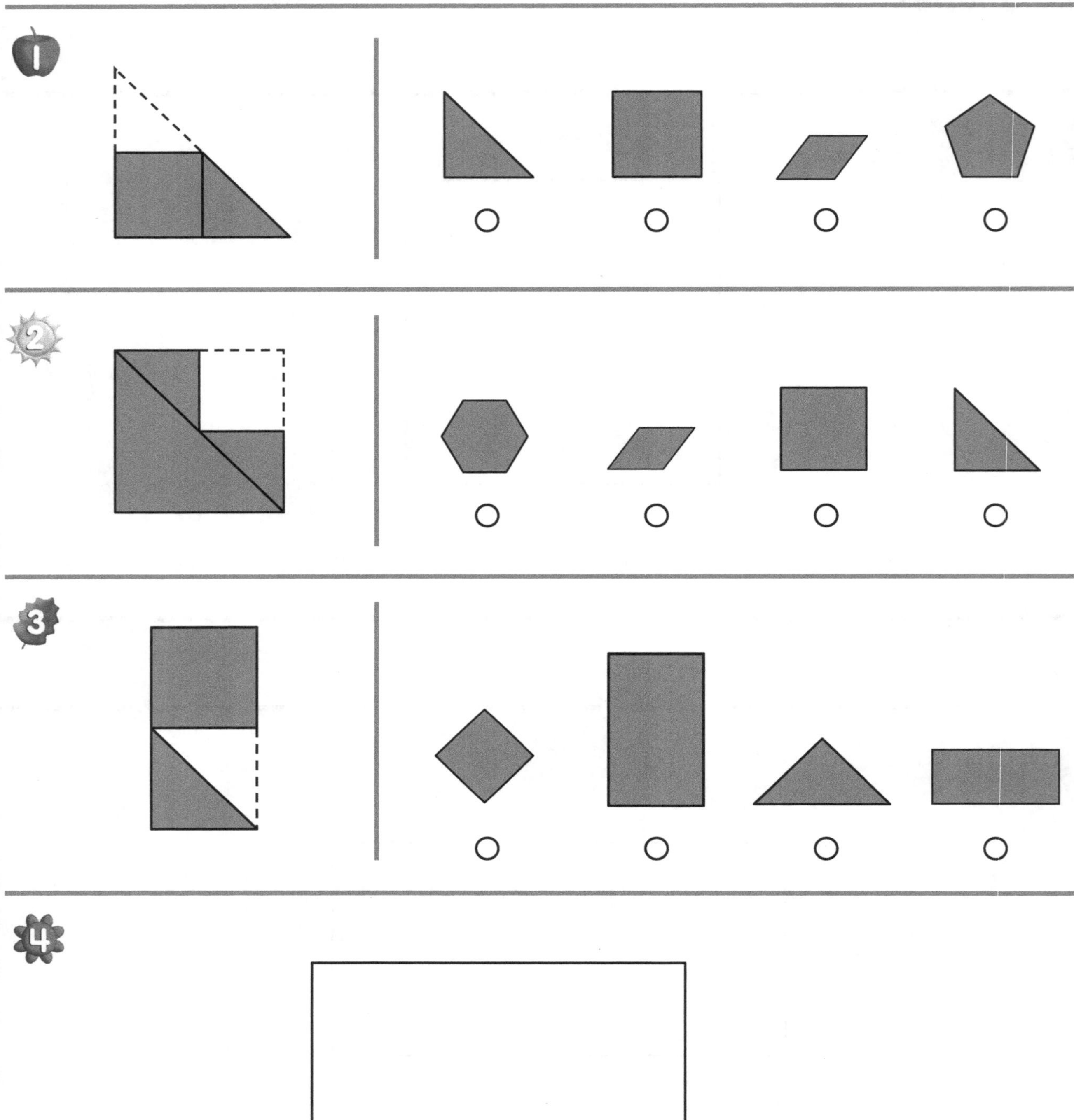

DIRECTIONS **1–3.** Look at the shape at the beginning of the row. Mark under the shape that matches the white part of the shape. **4.** Draw on the shape to show how you could use smaller shapes to make it.

Name ______________________________

Lesson 102

COMMON CORE STANDARD CC.K.G.6

Lesson Objective: Solve problems by using the strategy *draw a picture.*

Problem Solving • Draw to Join Shapes

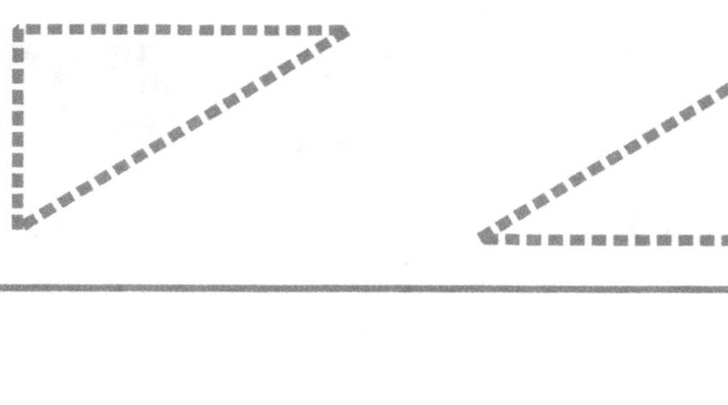

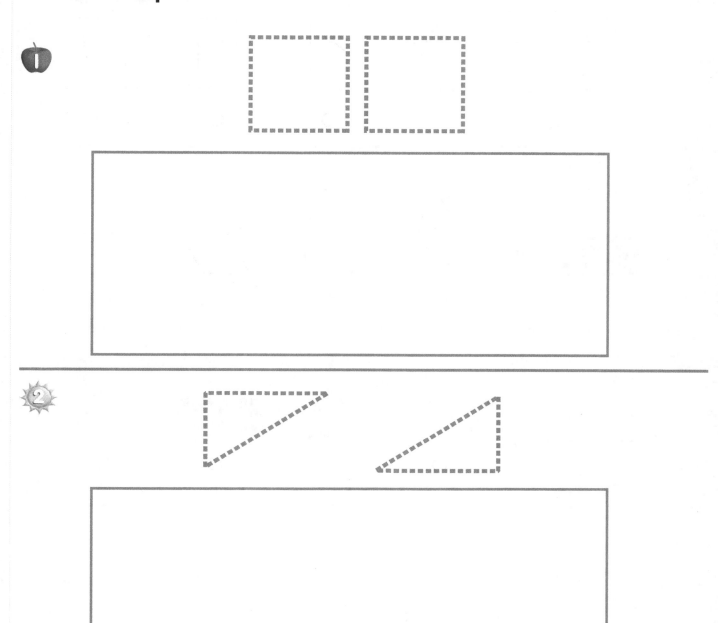

DIRECTIONS Place two-dimensional shapes on the page as shown. **1.** How can you use the two squares to make a rectangle? Trace around the squares to draw the rectangle. **2.** How can you use the two triangles to make a rectangle? Trace around the triangles to draw the rectangle.

Name ______________________________

Lesson 102
CC.K.G.6

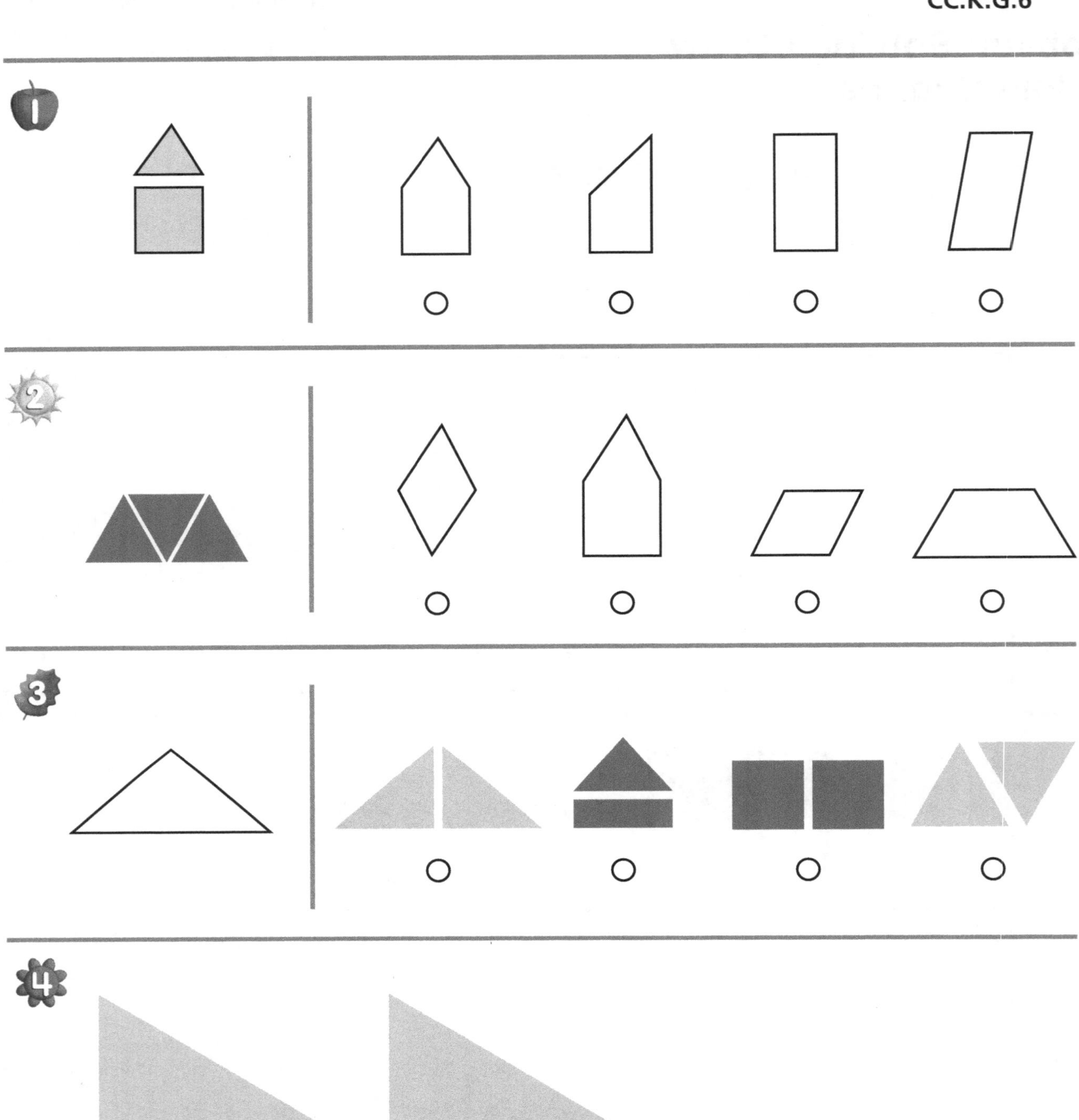

DIRECTIONS 1. Which shape can be made by joining the shapes at the beginning of the row? Mark under that shape. **2.** Which shape can be made by joining the triangles at the beginning of the row? Mark under that shape. **3.** Which set of shapes can be joined to make the triangle at the beginning of the row? Mark under that set. **4.** How can you join the two triangles to make a rectangle? Draw and color the triangles you used.

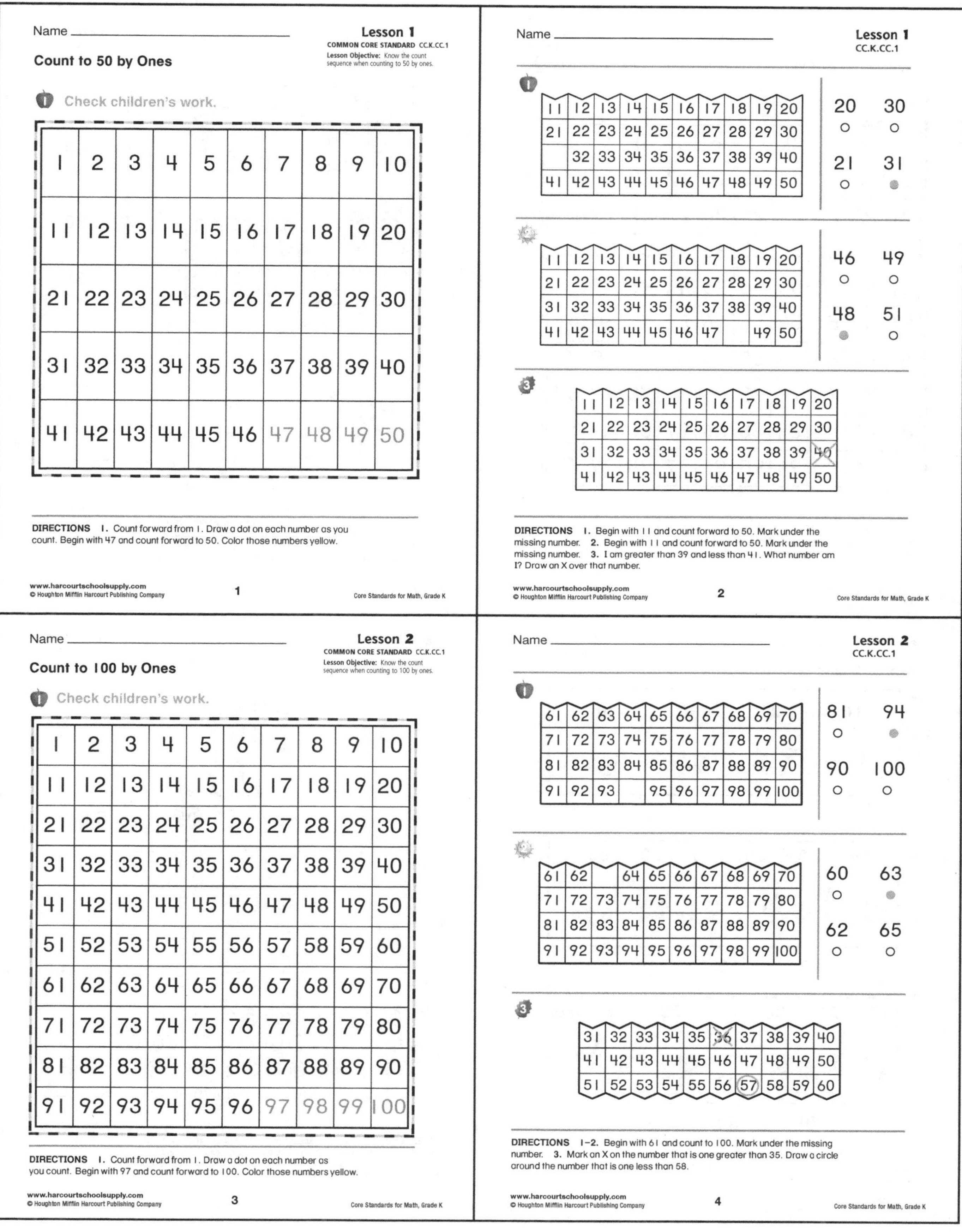

Name ______________________

Lesson 1
COMMON CORE STANDARD CC.K.CC.1
Lesson Objective: Know the count sequence when counting to 50 by ones.

Count to 50 by Ones

1. Check children's work.

1	2	3	4	5	6	7	8	9	10
11	12	13	14	15	16	17	18	19	20
21	22	23	24	25	26	27	28	29	30
31	32	33	34	35	36	37	38	39	40
41	42	43	44	45	46	47	48	49	50

DIRECTIONS 1. Count forward from 1. Draw a dot on each number as you count. Begin with 47 and count forward to 50. Color those numbers yellow.

Name ______________________

Lesson 1
CC.K.CC.1

1.

11	12	13	14	15	16	17	18	19	20
21	22	23	24	25	26	27	28	29	30
	32	33	34	35	36	37	38	39	40
41	42	43	44	45	46	47	48	49	50

20 ○ 30 ○
21 ○ 31 ●

2.

11	12	13	14	15	16	17	18	19	20
21	22	23	24	25	26	27	28	29	30
31	32	33	34	35	36	37	38	39	40
41	42	43	44	45	46	47		49	50

46 ○ 49 ○
48 ● 51 ○

3.

11	12	13	14	15	16	17	18	19	20
21	22	23	24	25	26	27	28	29	30
31	32	33	34	35	36	37	38	39	40 (X)
41	42	43	44	45	46	47	48	49	50

DIRECTIONS 1. Begin with 11 and count forward to 50. Mark under the missing number. 2. Begin with 11 and count forward to 50. Mark under the missing number. 3. I am greater than 39 and less than 41. What number am I? Draw an X over that number.

Name ______________________

Lesson 2
COMMON CORE STANDARD CC.K.CC.1
Lesson Objective: Know the count sequence when counting to 100 by ones.

Count to 100 by Ones

1. Check children's work.

1	2	3	4	5	6	7	8	9	10
11	12	13	14	15	16	17	18	19	20
21	22	23	24	25	26	27	28	29	30
31	32	33	34	35	36	37	38	39	40
41	42	43	44	45	46	47	48	49	50
51	52	53	54	55	56	57	58	59	60
61	62	63	64	65	66	67	68	69	70
71	72	73	74	75	76	77	78	79	80
81	82	83	84	85	86	87	88	89	90
91	92	93	94	95	96	97	98	99	100

DIRECTIONS 1. Count forward from 1. Draw a dot on each number as you count. Begin with 97 and count forward to 100. Color those numbers yellow.

Name ______________________

Lesson 2
CC.K.CC.1

1.

61	62	63	64	65	66	67	68	69	70
71	72	73	74	75	76	77	78	79	80
81	82	83	84	85	86	87	88	89	90
91	92	93		95	96	97	98	99	100

81 ○ 94 ●
90 ○ 100 ○

2.

61	62		64	65	66	67	68	69	70
71	72	73	74	75	76	77	78	79	80
81	82	83	84	85	86	87	88	89	90
91	92	93	94	95	96	97	98	99	100

60 ○ 63 ●
62 ○ 65 ○

3.

31	32	33	34	35	36 (X)	37	38	39	40
41	42	43	44	45	46	47	48	49	50
51	52	53	54	55	56	57 (circled)	58	59	60

DIRECTIONS 1–2. Begin with 61 and count to 100. Mark under the missing number. 3. Mark an X on the number that is one greater than 35. Draw a circle around the number that is one less than 58.

Answer Key

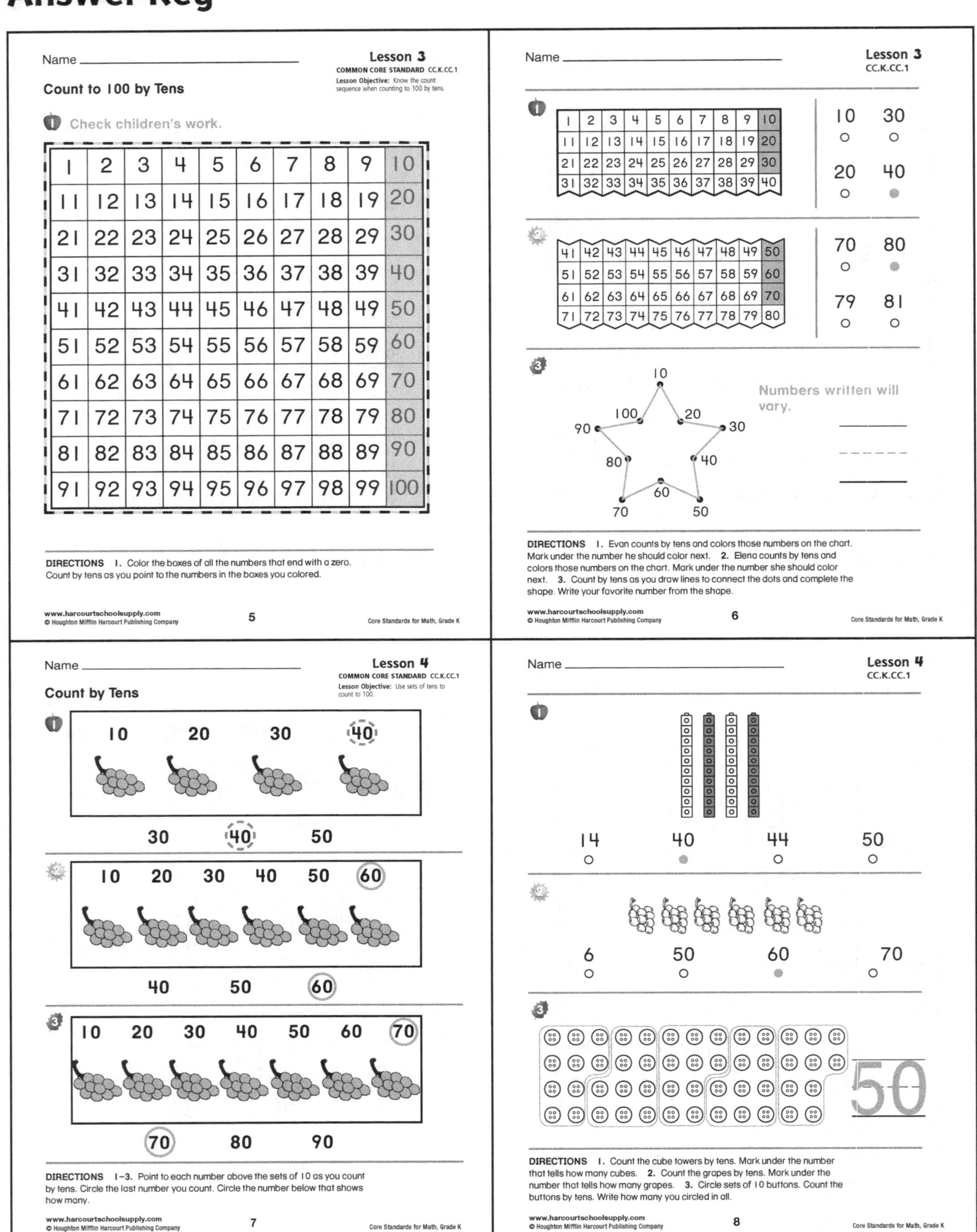

Name ______________________

Lesson 3
COMMON CORE STANDARD CC.K.CC.1
Lesson Objective: Know the count sequence when counting to 100 by tens.

Count to 100 by Tens

1 Check children's work.

1	2	3	4	5	6	7	8	9	10
11	12	13	14	15	16	17	18	19	20
21	22	23	24	25	26	27	28	29	30
31	32	33	34	35	36	37	38	39	40
41	42	43	44	45	46	47	48	49	50
51	52	53	54	55	56	57	58	59	60
61	62	63	64	65	66	67	68	69	70
71	72	73	74	75	76	77	78	79	80
81	82	83	84	85	86	87	88	89	90
91	92	93	94	95	96	97	98	99	100

DIRECTIONS **1.** Color the boxes of all the numbers that end with a zero. Count by tens as you point to the numbers in the boxes you colored.

www.harcourtschoolsupply.com
© Houghton Mifflin Harcourt Publishing Company — 5 — Core Standards for Math, Grade K

Name ______________________

Lesson 3
CC.K.CC.1

1

1	2	3	4	5	6	7	8	9	10
11	12	13	14	15	16	17	18	19	20
21	22	23	24	25	26	27	28	29	30
31	32	33	34	35	36	37	38	39	40

10 ○ 30 ○ 20 ○ 40 ●

2

41	42	43	44	45	46	47	48	49	50
51	52	53	54	55	56	57	58	59	60
61	62	63	64	65	66	67	68	69	70
71	72	73	74	75	76	77	78	79	80

70 ○ 80 ● 79 ○ 81 ○

3

10, 20, 30, 40, 50, 60, 70, 80, 90, 100

Numbers written will vary.

DIRECTIONS **1.** Evan counts by tens and colors those numbers on the chart. Mark under the number he should color next. **2.** Elena counts by tens and colors those numbers on the chart. Mark under the number she should color next. **3.** Count by tens as you draw lines to connect the dots and complete the shape. Write your favorite number from the shape.

www.harcourtschoolsupply.com
© Houghton Mifflin Harcourt Publishing Company — 6 — Core Standards for Math, Grade K

Name ______________________

Lesson 4
COMMON CORE STANDARD CC.K.CC.1
Lesson Objective: Use sets of tens to count to 100.

Count by Tens

1 10 20 30 (40)

30 (40) 50

2 10 20 30 40 50 (60)

40 50 (60)

3 10 20 30 40 50 60 (70)

(70) 80 90

DIRECTIONS **1–3.** Point to each number above the sets of 10 as you count by tens. Circle the last number you count. Circle the number below that shows how many.

www.harcourtschoolsupply.com
© Houghton Mifflin Harcourt Publishing Company — 7 — Core Standards for Math, Grade K

Name ______________________

Lesson 4
CC.K.CC.1

1

14 ○ 40 ● 44 ○ 50 ○

2

6 ○ 50 ○ 60 ● 70 ○

3

50

DIRECTIONS **1.** Count the cube towers by tens. Mark under the number that tells how many cubes. **2.** Count the grapes by tens. Mark under the number that tells how many grapes. **3.** Circle sets of 10 buttons. Count the buttons by tens. Write how many you circled in all.

www.harcourtschoolsupply.com
© Houghton Mifflin Harcourt Publishing Company — 8 — Core Standards for Math, Grade K

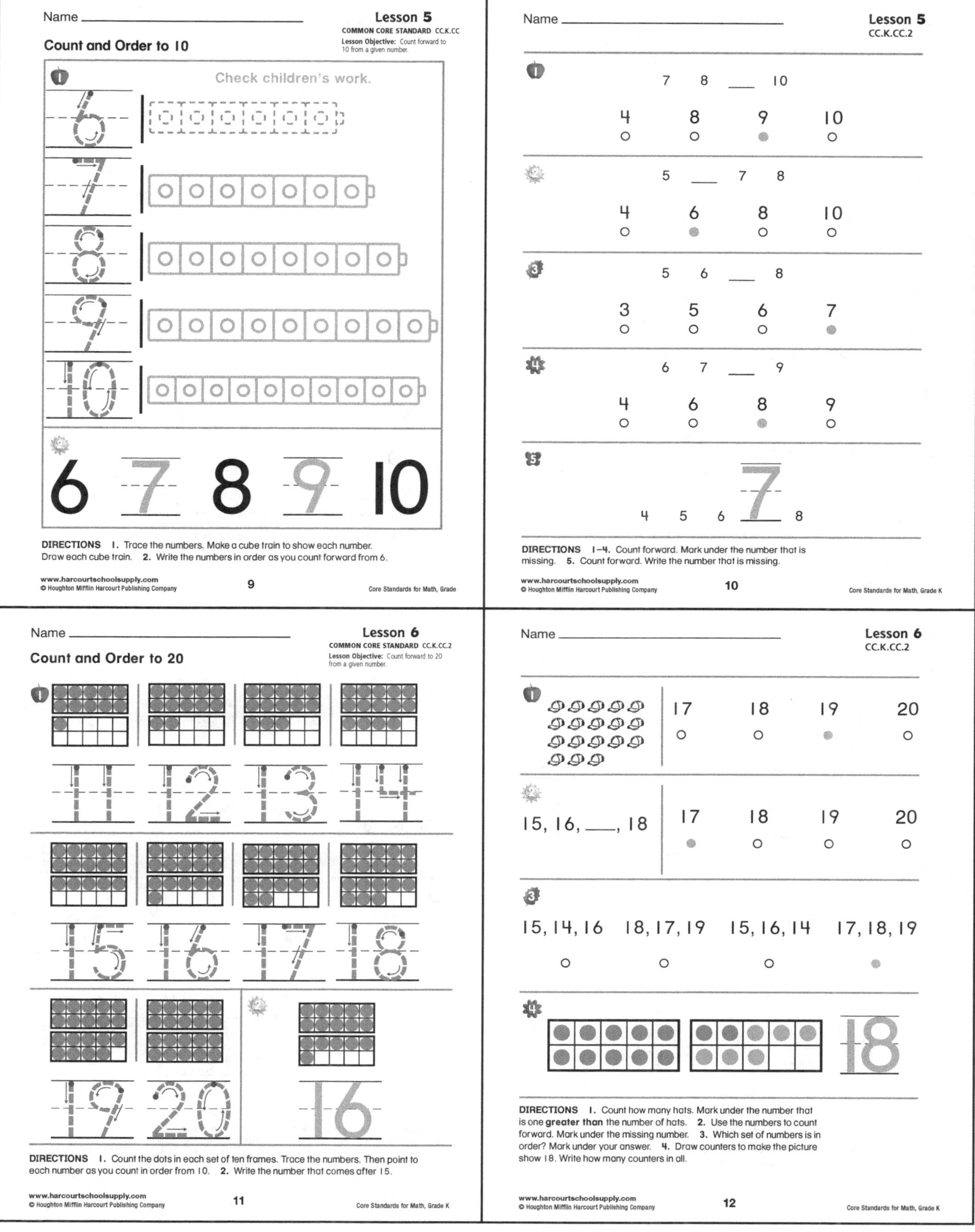

Name ______________________

Lesson 5
COMMON CORE STANDARD CC.K.CC
Lesson Objective: Count forward to 10 from a given number.

Count and Order to 10

1 Check children's work.

6 7 8 9 10

2 6 7 8 9 10

DIRECTIONS 1. Trace the numbers. Make a cube train to show each number. Draw each cube train. 2. Write the numbers in order as you count forward from 6.

www.harcourtschoolsupply.com
© Houghton Mifflin Harcourt Publishing Company
9
Core Standards for Math, Grade

Name ______________________

Lesson 5
CC.K.CC.2

1 7 8 ___ 10
4 8 9 10

2 5 ___ 7 8
4 6 8 10

3 5 6 ___ 8
3 5 6 7

4 6 7 ___ 9
4 6 8 9

5 4 5 6 7 8

DIRECTIONS 1–4. Count forward. Mark under the number that is missing. 5. Count forward. Write the number that is missing.

www.harcourtschoolsupply.com
© Houghton Mifflin Harcourt Publishing Company
10
Core Standards for Math, Grade K

Name ______________________

Lesson 6
COMMON CORE STANDARD CC.K.CC.2
Lesson Objective: Count forward to 20 from a given number.

Count and Order to 20

1 11 12 13 14

15 16 17 18

19 20

2 16

DIRECTIONS 1. Count the dots in each set of ten frames. Trace the numbers. Then point to each number as you count in order from 10. 2. Write the number that comes after 15.

www.harcourtschoolsupply.com
© Houghton Mifflin Harcourt Publishing Company
11
Core Standards for Math, Grade K

Name ______________________

Lesson 6
CC.K.CC.2

1 17 18 19 20

2 15, 16, ___, 18
17 18 19 20

3 15, 14, 16 18, 17, 19 15, 16, 14 17, 18, 19

4 18

DIRECTIONS 1. Count how many hats. Mark under the number that is one **greater than** the number of hats. 2. Use the numbers to count forward. Mark under the missing number. 3. Which set of numbers is in order? Mark under your answer. 4. Draw counters to make the picture show 18. Write how many counters in all.

www.harcourtschoolsupply.com
© Houghton Mifflin Harcourt Publishing Company
12
Core Standards for Math, Grade K

Answer Key

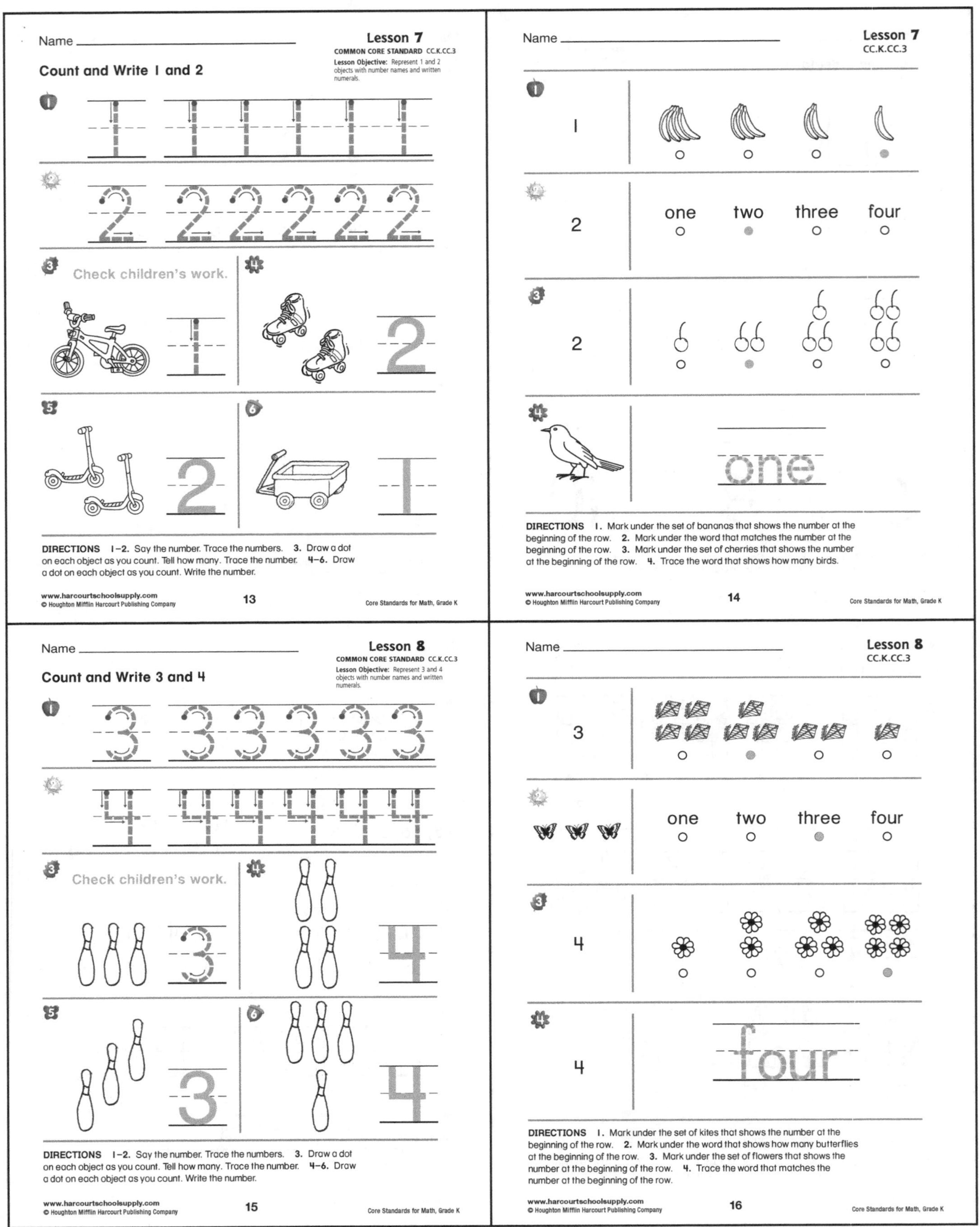

Name

Lesson 7

COMMON CORE STANDARD CC.K.CC.3

Lesson Objective: Represent 1 and 2 objects with number names and written numerals.

Count and Write 1 and 2

1. 1 1 1 1 1 1
2. 2 2 2 2 2 2
3. Check children's work. 1
4. 2
5. 2
6. 1

DIRECTIONS 1–2. Say the number. Trace the numbers. 3. Draw a dot on each object as you count. Tell how many. Trace the number. 4–6. Draw a dot on each object as you count. Write the number.

www.harcourtschoolsupply.com
© Houghton Mifflin Harcourt Publishing Company 13 Core Standards for Math, Grade K

Name

Lesson 7

CC.K.CC.3

1. 1
2. 2 — one, two, three, four
3. 2
4. one

DIRECTIONS 1. Mark under the set of bananas that shows the number at the beginning of the row. 2. Mark under the word that matches the number at the beginning of the row. 3. Mark under the set of cherries that shows the number at the beginning of the row. 4. Trace the word that shows how many birds.

www.harcourtschoolsupply.com
© Houghton Mifflin Harcourt Publishing Company 14 Core Standards for Math, Grade K

Name

Lesson 8

COMMON CORE STANDARD CC.K.CC.3

Lesson Objective: Represent 3 and 4 objects with number names and written numerals.

Count and Write 3 and 4

1. 3 3 3 3 3 3
2. 4 4 4 4 4 4
3. Check children's work. 3
4. 4
5. 3
6. 4

DIRECTIONS 1–2. Say the number. Trace the numbers. 3. Draw a dot on each object as you count. Tell how many. Trace the number. 4–6. Draw a dot on each object as you count. Write the number.

www.harcourtschoolsupply.com
© Houghton Mifflin Harcourt Publishing Company 15 Core Standards for Math, Grade K

Name

Lesson 8

CC.K.CC.3

1. 3
2. one, two, three, four
3. 4
4. 4 — four

DIRECTIONS 1. Mark under the set of kites that shows the number at the beginning of the row. 2. Mark under the word that shows how many butterflies at the beginning of the row. 3. Mark under the set of flowers that shows the number at the beginning of the row. 4. Trace the word that matches the number at the beginning of the row.

www.harcourtschoolsupply.com
© Houghton Mifflin Harcourt Publishing Company 16 Core Standards for Math, Grade K

Answer Key

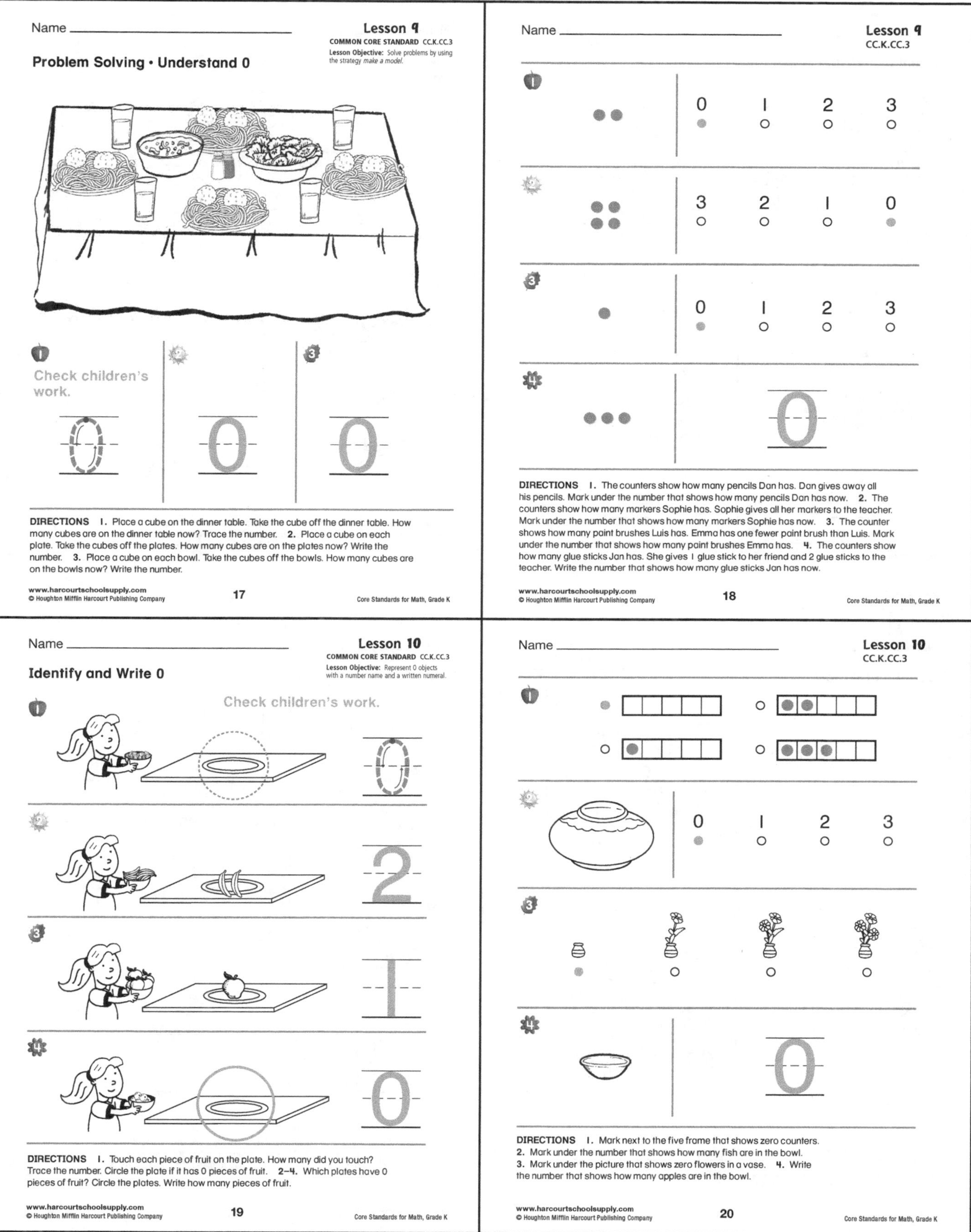

Name
Lesson 9
COMMON CORE STANDARD CC.K.CC.3
Lesson Objective: Solve problems by using the strategy make a model.
Problem Solving • Understand 0
Check children's work.
DIRECTIONS 1. Place a cube on the dinner table. Take the cube off the dinner table. How many cubes are on the dinner table now? Trace the number. 2. Place a cube on each plate. Take the cubes off the plates. How many cubes are on the plates now? Write the number. 3. Place a cube on each bowl. Take the cubes off the bowls. How many cubes are on the bowls now? Write the number.
www.harcourtschoolsupply.com
© Houghton Mifflin Harcourt Publishing Company
17
Core Standards for Math, Grade K
Name
Lesson 9
CC.K.CC.3
DIRECTIONS 1. The counters show how many pencils Dan has. Dan gives away all his pencils. Mark under the number that shows how many pencils Dan has now. 2. The counters show how many markers Sophie has. Sophie gives all her markers to the teacher. Mark under the number that shows how many markers Sophie has now. 3. The counter shows how many paint brushes Luis has. Emma has one fewer paint brush than Luis. Mark under the number that shows how many paint brushes Emma has. 4. The counters show how many glue sticks Jan has. She gives 1 glue stick to her friend and 2 glue sticks to the teacher. Write the number that shows how many glue sticks Jan has now.
www.harcourtschoolsupply.com
© Houghton Mifflin Harcourt Publishing Company
18
Core Standards for Math, Grade K
Name
Lesson 10
COMMON CORE STANDARD CC.K.CC.3
Lesson Objective: Represent 0 objects with a number name and a written numeral.
Identify and Write 0
Check children's work.
DIRECTIONS 1. Touch each piece of fruit on the plate. How many did you touch? Trace the number. Circle the plate if it has 0 pieces of fruit. 2–4. Which plates have 0 pieces of fruit? Circle the plates. Write how many pieces of fruit.
www.harcourtschoolsupply.com
© Houghton Mifflin Harcourt Publishing Company
19
Core Standards for Math, Grade K
Name
Lesson 10
CC.K.CC.3
DIRECTIONS 1. Mark next to the five frame that shows zero counters. 2. Mark under the number that shows how many fish are in the bowl. 3. Mark under the picture that shows zero flowers in a vase. 4. Write the number that shows how many apples are in the bowl.
www.harcourtschoolsupply.com
© Houghton Mifflin Harcourt Publishing Company
20
Core Standards for Math, Grade K

Answer Key

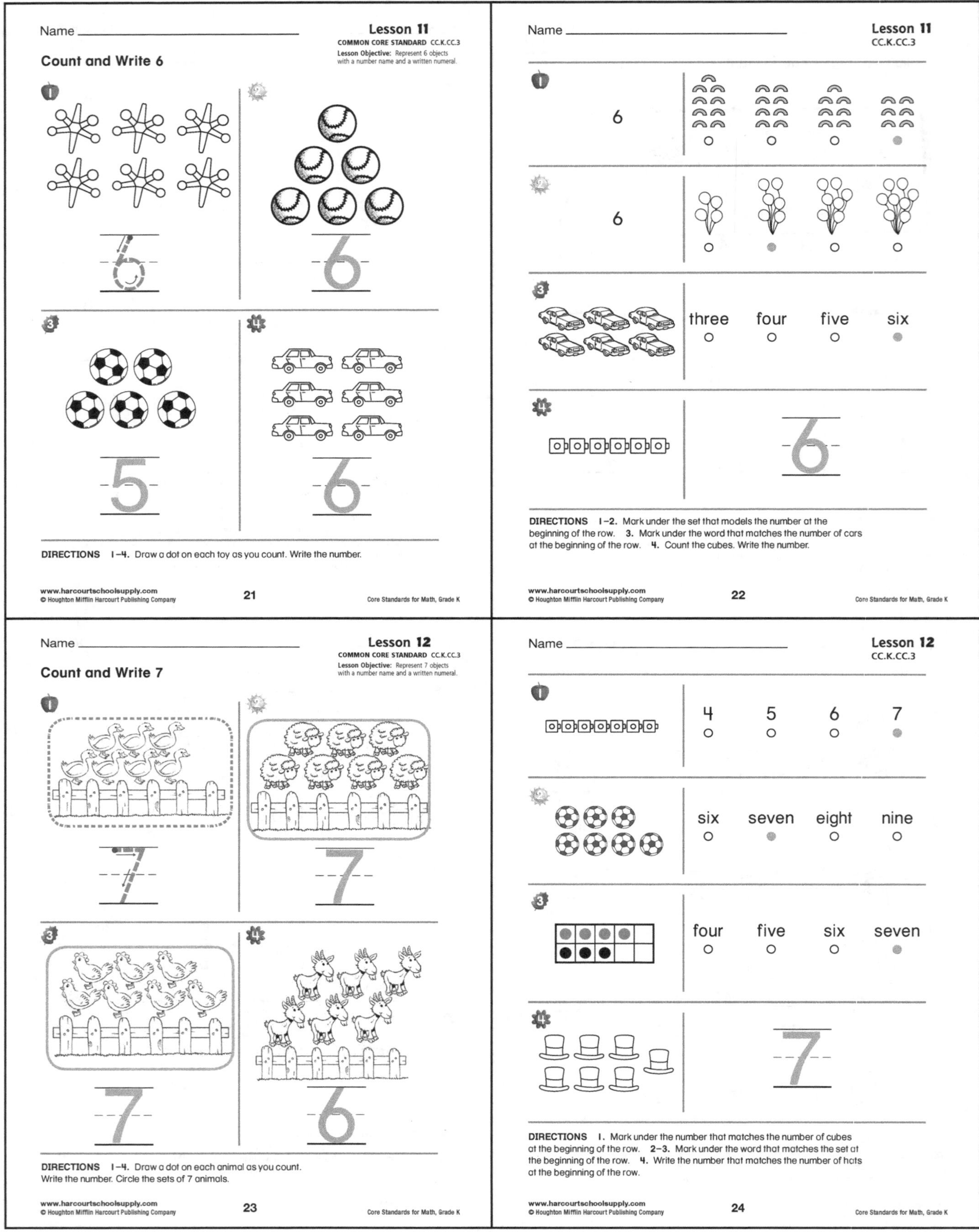

Name
Lesson 11
COMMON CORE STANDARD CC.K.CC.3
Lesson Objective: Represent 6 objects with a number name and a written numeral.
Count and Write 6
6
6
5
6
DIRECTIONS 1–4. Draw a dot on each toy as you count. Write the number.
www.harcourtschoolsupply.com
© Houghton Mifflin Harcourt Publishing Company
21
Core Standards for Math, Grade K
Name
Lesson 11
CC.K.CC.3
6
6
three
four
five
six
6
DIRECTIONS 1–2. Mark under the set that models the number at the beginning of the row. 3. Mark under the word that matches the number of cars at the beginning of the row. 4. Count the cubes. Write the number.
www.harcourtschoolsupply.com
© Houghton Mifflin Harcourt Publishing Company
22
Core Standards for Math, Grade K
Name
Lesson 12
COMMON CORE STANDARD CC.K.CC.3
Lesson Objective: Represent 7 objects with a number name and a written numeral.
Count and Write 7
7
7
7
6
DIRECTIONS 1–4. Draw a dot on each animal as you count. Write the number. Circle the sets of 7 animals.
www.harcourtschoolsupply.com
© Houghton Mifflin Harcourt Publishing Company
23
Core Standards for Math, Grade K
Name
Lesson 12
CC.K.CC.3
4
5
6
7
six
seven
eight
nine
four
five
six
seven
7
DIRECTIONS 1. Mark under the number that matches the number of cubes at the beginning of the row. 2–3. Mark under the word that matches the set at the beginning of the row. 4. Write the number that matches the number of hats at the beginning of the row.
www.harcourtschoolsupply.com
© Houghton Mifflin Harcourt Publishing Company
24
Core Standards for Math, Grade K

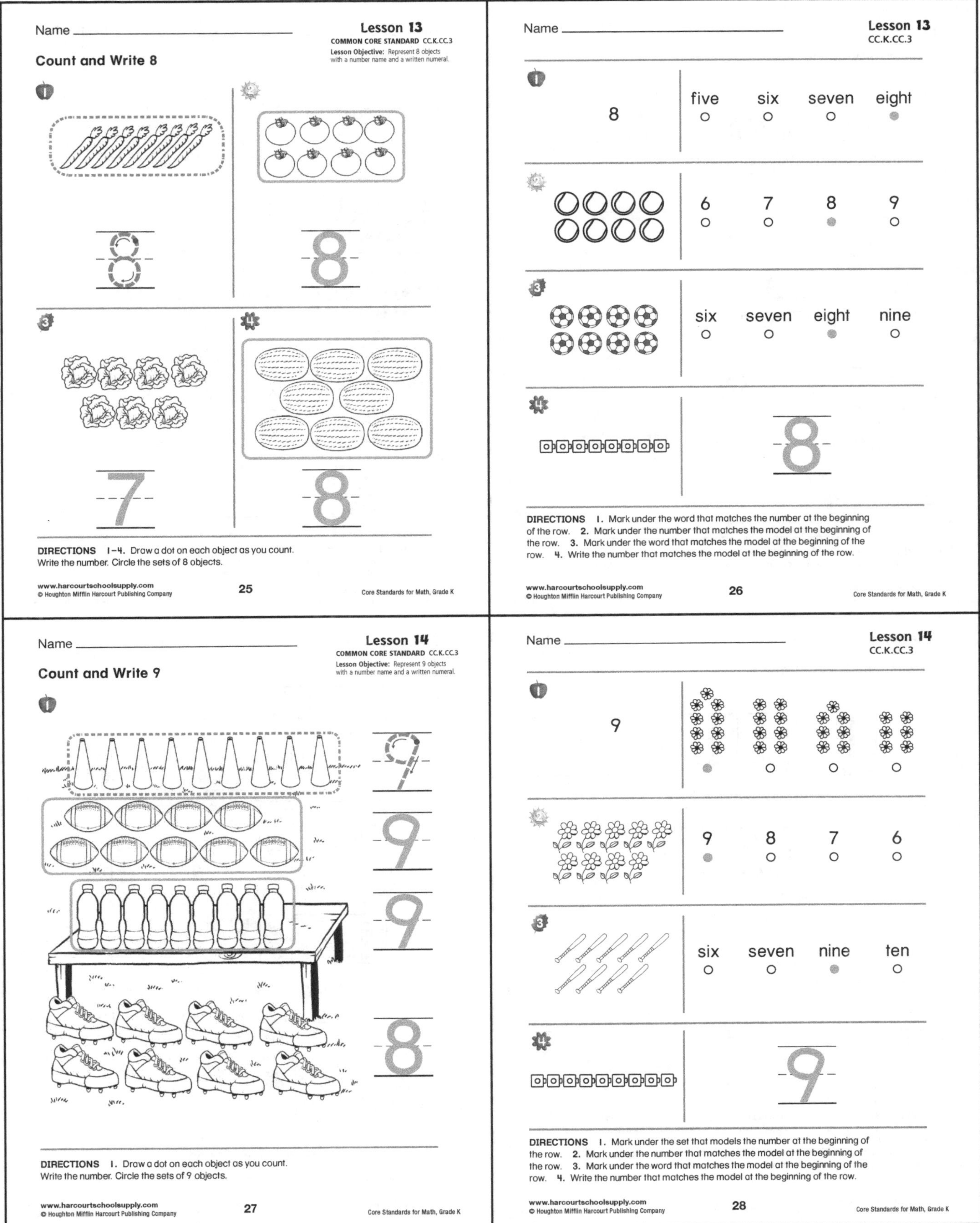

Name ______________________

Lesson 13
COMMON CORE STANDARD CC.K.CC.3
Lesson Objective: Represent 8 objects with a number name and a written numeral.

Count and Write 8

1. 8
2. 8
3. 7
4. 8

DIRECTIONS 1–4. Draw a dot on each object as you count. Write the number. Circle the sets of 8 objects.

www.harcourtschoolsupply.com
© Houghton Mifflin Harcourt Publishing Company
25
Core Standards for Math, Grade K

Name ______________________

Lesson 13
CC.K.CC.3

1. 8 — five, six, seven, eight
2. 6, 7, 8, 9
3. six, seven, eight, nine
4. 8

DIRECTIONS 1. Mark under the word that matches the number at the beginning of the row. 2. Mark under the number that matches the model at the beginning of the row. 3. Mark under the word that matches the model at the beginning of the row. 4. Write the number that matches the model at the beginning of the row.

www.harcourtschoolsupply.com
© Houghton Mifflin Harcourt Publishing Company
26
Core Standards for Math, Grade K

Name ______________________

Lesson 14
COMMON CORE STANDARD CC.K.CC.3
Lesson Objective: Represent 9 objects with a number name and a written numeral.

Count and Write 9

1. 9
9
9
8

DIRECTIONS 1. Draw a dot on each object as you count. Write the number. Circle the sets of 9 objects.

www.harcourtschoolsupply.com
© Houghton Mifflin Harcourt Publishing Company
27
Core Standards for Math, Grade K

Name ______________________

Lesson 14
CC.K.CC.3

1. 9
2. 9, 8, 7, 6
3. six, seven, nine, ten
4. 9

DIRECTIONS 1. Mark under the set that models the number at the beginning of the row. 2. Mark under the number that matches the model at the beginning of the row. 3. Mark under the word that matches the model at the beginning of the row. 4. Write the number that matches the model at the beginning of the row.

www.harcourtschoolsupply.com
© Houghton Mifflin Harcourt Publishing Company
28
Core Standards for Math, Grade K

Answer Key

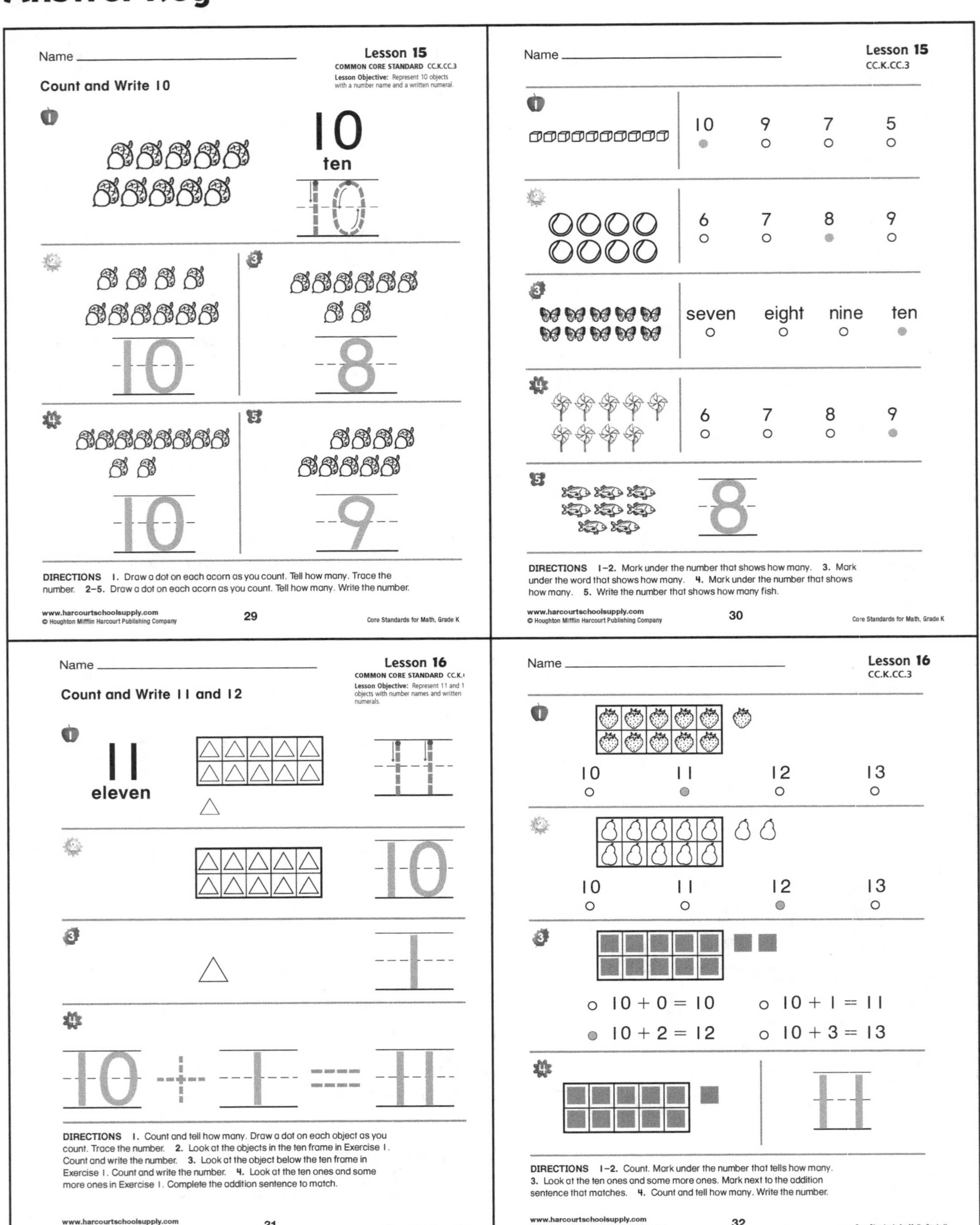

Name ____________________

Lesson 15

COMMON CORE STANDARD CC.K.CC.3

Lesson Objective: Represent 10 objects with a number name and a written numeral.

Count and Write 10

1. 10 ten — 10
2. 10
3. 8
4. 10
5. 9

DIRECTIONS 1. Draw a dot on each acorn as you count. Tell how many. Trace the number. 2–5. Draw a dot on each acorn as you count. Tell how many. Write the number.

www.harcourtschoolsupply.com
© Houghton Mifflin Harcourt Publishing Company — 29 — Core Standards for Math, Grade K

Name ____________________

Lesson 15

CC.K.CC.3

1. 10 ● 9 ○ 7 ○ 5 ○
2. 6 ○ 7 ○ 8 ● 9 ○
3. seven ○ eight ○ nine ○ ten ●
4. 6 ○ 7 ○ 8 ○ 9 ●
5. 8

DIRECTIONS 1–2. Mark under the number that shows how many. 3. Mark under the word that shows how many. 4. Mark under the number that shows how many. 5. Write the number that shows how many fish.

www.harcourtschoolsupply.com
© Houghton Mifflin Harcourt Publishing Company — 30 — Core Standards for Math, Grade K

Name ____________________

Lesson 16

COMMON CORE STANDARD CC.K.

Lesson Objective: Represent 11 and 1 objects with number names and written numerals.

Count and Write 11 and 12

1. 11 eleven — 11
2. 10
3. 1
4. 10 + 1 = 11

DIRECTIONS 1. Count and tell how many. Draw a dot on each object as you count. Trace the number. 2. Look at the objects in the ten frame in Exercise 1. Count and write the number. 3. Look at the object below the ten frame in Exercise 1. Count and write the number. 4. Look at the ten ones and some more ones in Exercise 1. Complete the addition sentence to match.

www.harcourtschoolsupply.com
© Houghton Mifflin Harcourt Publishing Company — 31 — Core Standards for Math, Gra

Name ____________________

Lesson 16

CC.K.CC.3

1. 10 ○ 11 ● 12 ○ 13 ○
2. 10 ○ 11 ○ 12 ● 13 ○
3. ○ 10 + 0 = 10 ○ 10 + 1 = 11 ● 10 + 2 = 12 ○ 10 + 3 = 13
4. 11

DIRECTIONS 1–2. Count. Mark under the number that tells how many. 3. Look at the ten ones and some more ones. Mark next to the addition sentence that matches. 4. Count and tell how many. Write the number.

www.harcourtschoolsupply.com
© Houghton Mifflin Harcourt Publishing Company — 32 — Core Standards for Math, Grade K

Name ______________________

Lesson 17
COMMON CORE STANDARD CC.K.CC.3
Lesson Objective: Represent 13 and 14 objects with number names and written numerals.

Count and Write 13 and 14

1. 13 thirteen — 13

2. 10

3. 3

4. 10 + 3 = 13

DIRECTIONS 1. Count and tell how many. Draw a dot on each object as you count. Trace the number. 2. Look at the objects in the ten frame in Exercise 1. Count and write the number. 3. Look at the objects below the ten frame in Exercise 1. Count and write the number. 4. Look at the ten ones and some more ones in Exercise 1. Complete the addition sentence to match.

Name ______________________

Lesson 17
CC.K.CC.3

1. 14 ● 13 ○ 12 ○ 11 ○

2. 10 ○ 11 ○ 12 ○ 13 ●

3.
- ○ 10 + 1 = 11
- ○ 10 + 2 = 12
- ● 10 + 3 = 13
- ○ 10 + 4 = 14

4. 14

DIRECTIONS 1–2. Count. Mark under the number that tells how many. 3. Look at the ten ones and some more ones. Mark next to the addition sentence that matches. 4. Count. Write the number that tells how many.

Name ______________________

Lesson 18
COMMON CORE STANDARD CC.K.CC.3
Lesson Objective: Solve problems by using the strategy *draw a picture*.

Problem Solving • Use Numbers to 15

1.

B	B	B	G	G
B	B	B	G	G
B	B	B	G	G

9 boys

2. Check children's work.

3 girls

DIRECTIONS 1. There are 15 children in Mrs. Joiner's class. They sit in rows of 5. There are 3 boys and 2 girls in each row. How many boys are in the class? Trace the 3 rows of 5 circles. *B* is for boy and *G* is for girl. Count the boys. Write the number. 2. There are 15 children in Mr. Gilbert's class. They sit in rows of 5. There are 4 boys and 1 girl in each row. How many girls are in the class? Draw to solve the problem.

Name ______________________

Lesson 18
CC.K.CC.3

1. 12 cups ○ 13 cups ○ 14 cups ○ 15 cups ●

2.
- ○ 3 more apples
- ○ 4 more apples
- ● 5 more apples
- ○ 6 more apples

3. Check children's work.

3 blue blocks

DIRECTIONS 1. There are 13 cups with juice in them. There are 2 cups with no juice. How many cups are there? Mark under the number that shows how many cups there are. 2. Kate has 15 baskets. Ten baskets have 1 apple in them. How many more apples would Kate need to have 1 apple in each basket? Mark next to the number that shows how many more apples. 3. Kevin has 15 blocks. He puts them in rows of 5. There are 4 red blocks and 1 blue block in each row. How many blue blocks does Kevin have? Draw to solve the problem. Write how many blue blocks.

Answer Key

Name ____________________

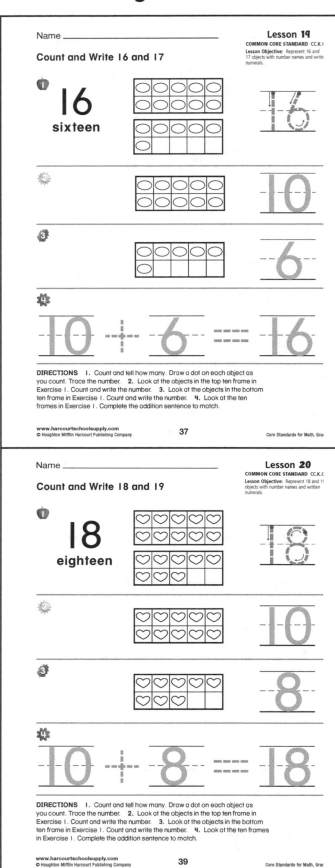

Lesson 19
COMMON CORE STANDARD CC.K.CC.3
Lesson Objective: Represent 16 and 17 objects with number names and written numerals.

Count and Write 16 and 17

1. 16 **sixteen** — 16

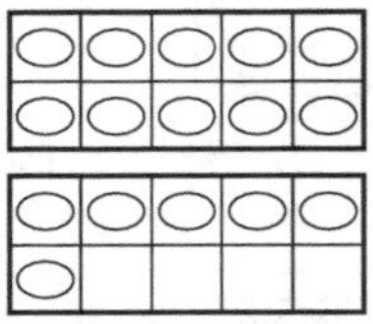

2. 10

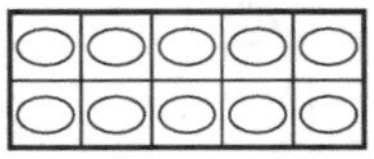

3. 6

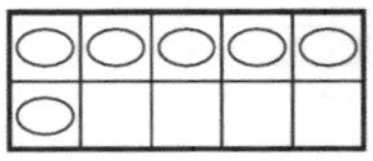

4. 10 + 6 = 16

DIRECTIONS 1. Count and tell how many. Draw a dot on each object as you count. Trace the number. 2. Look at the objects in the top ten frame in Exercise 1. Count and write the number. 3. Look at the objects in the bottom ten frame in Exercise 1. Count and write the number. 4. Look at the ten frames in Exercise 1. Complete the addition sentence to match.

Name ____________________

Lesson 19
CC.K.CC.3

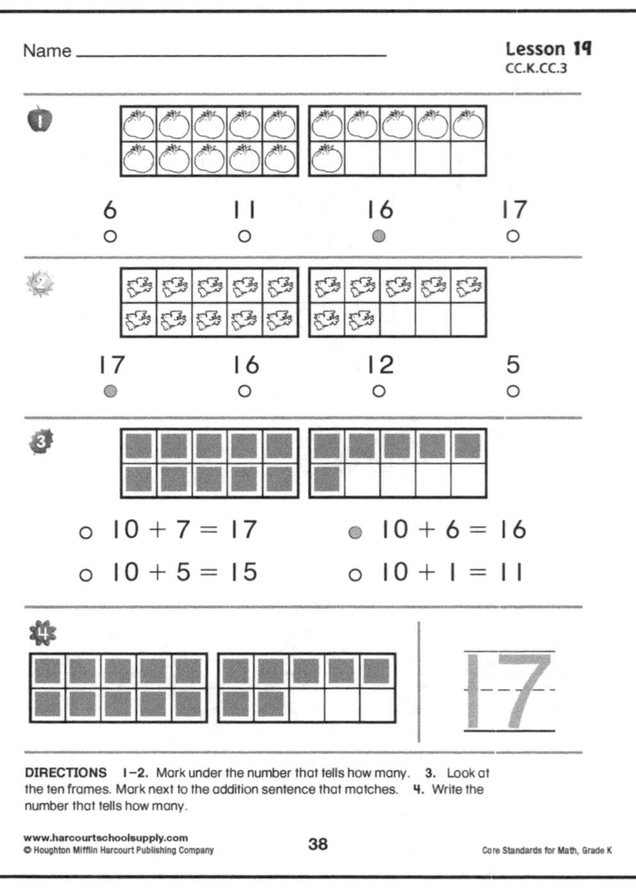

1. 6 ○ 11 ○ 16 ● 17 ○

2. 17 ● 16 ○ 12 ○ 5 ○

3. ○ 10 + 7 = 17 ● 10 + 6 = 16
○ 10 + 5 = 15 ○ 10 + 1 = 11

4. 17

DIRECTIONS 1–2. Mark under the number that tells how many. 3. Look at the ten frames. Mark next to the addition sentence that matches. 4. Write the number that tells how many.

Name ____________________

Lesson 20
COMMON CORE STANDARD CC.K.CC.3
Lesson Objective: Represent 18 and 19 objects with number names and written numerals.

Count and Write 18 and 19

1. 18 **eighteen** — 18

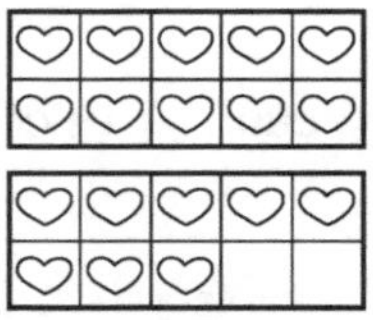

2. 10

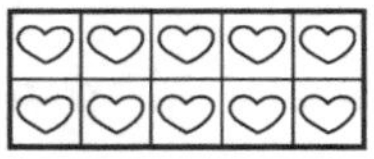

3. 8

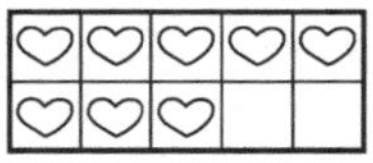

4. 10 + 8 = 18

DIRECTIONS 1. Count and tell how many. Draw a dot on each object as you count. Trace the number. 2. Look at the objects in the top ten frame in Exercise 1. Count and write the number. 3. Look at the objects in the bottom ten frame in Exercise 1. Count and write the number. 4. Look at the ten frames in Exercise 1. Complete the addition sentence to match.

Name ____________________

Lesson 20
CC.K.CC.3

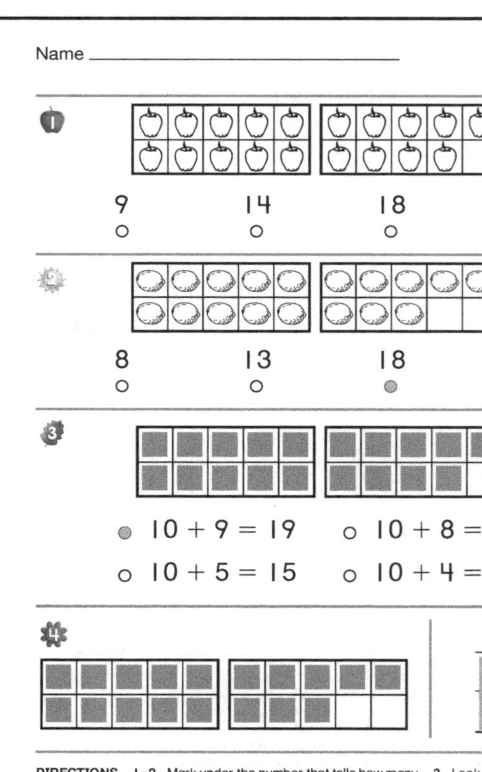

1. 9 ○ 14 ○ 18 ○ 19 ●

2. 8 ○ 13 ○ 18 ● 19 ○

3. ● 10 + 9 = 19 ○ 10 + 8 = 18
○ 10 + 5 = 15 ○ 10 + 4 = 14

4. 18

DIRECTIONS 1–2. Mark under the number that tells how many. 3. Look at the ten frames. Mark next to the addition sentence that matches. 4. Write the number that tells how many.

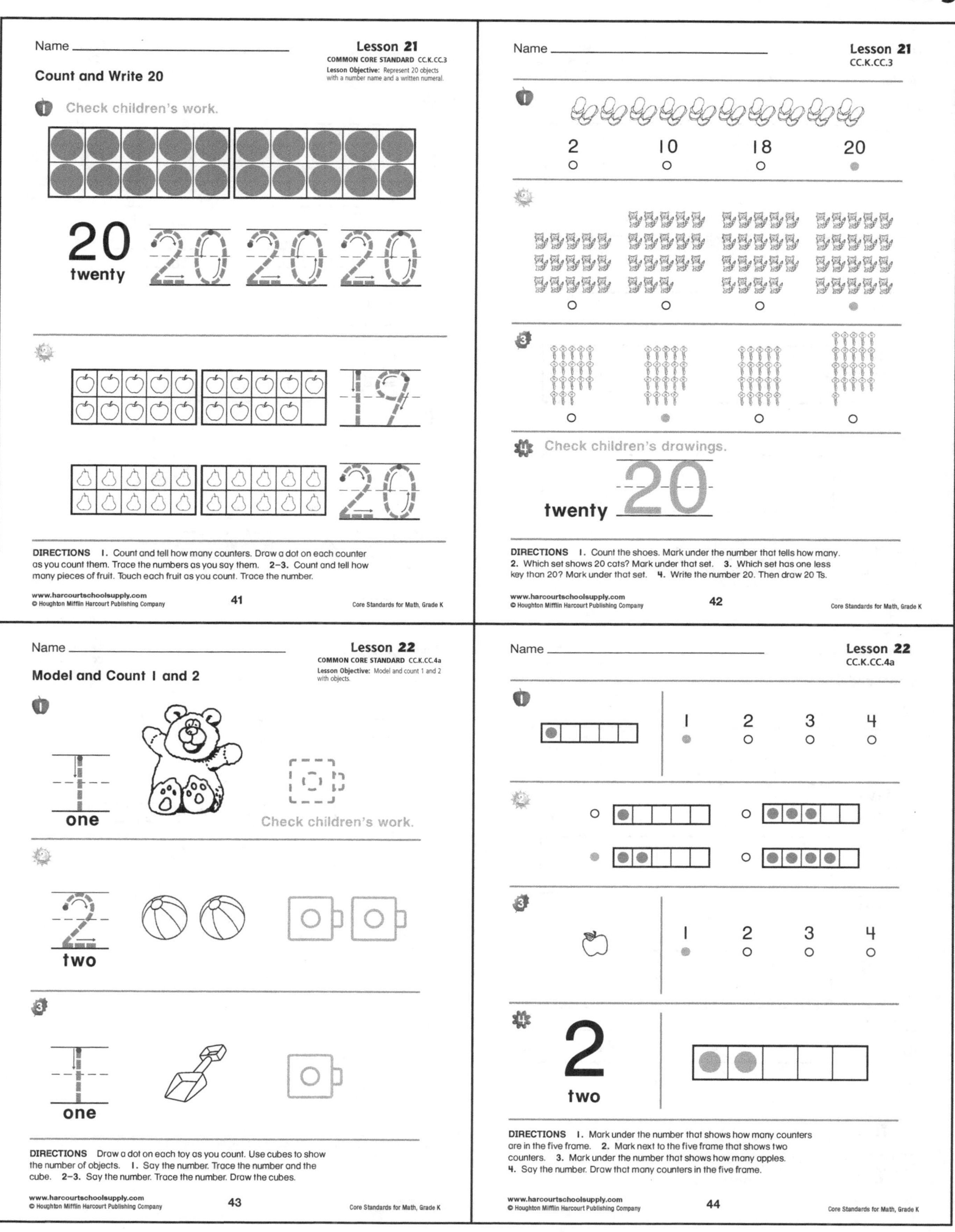

Name
Lesson 21
COMMON CORE STANDARD CC.K.CC.3
Lesson Objective: Represent 20 objects with a number name and a written numeral.
Count and Write 20
Check children's work.
20
twenty
DIRECTIONS 1. Count and tell how many counters. Draw a dot on each counter as you count them. Trace the numbers as you say them. 2–3. Count and tell how many pieces of fruit. Touch each fruit as you count. Trace the number.
www.harcourtschoolsupply.com
© Houghton Mifflin Harcourt Publishing Company
41
Core Standards for Math, Grade K
Name
Lesson 21
CC.K.CC.3
2 10 18 20
Check children's drawings.
twenty 20
DIRECTIONS 1. Count the shoes. Mark under the number that tells how many. 2. Which set shows 20 cats? Mark under that set. 3. Which set has one less key than 20? Mark under that set. 4. Write the number 20. Then draw 20 Ts.
www.harcourtschoolsupply.com
© Houghton Mifflin Harcourt Publishing Company
42
Core Standards for Math, Grade K
Name
Lesson 22
COMMON CORE STANDARD CC.K.CC.4a
Lesson Objective: Model and count 1 and 2 with objects.
Model and Count 1 and 2
one
Check children's work.
two
one
DIRECTIONS Draw a dot on each toy as you count. Use cubes to show the number of objects. 1. Say the number. Trace the number and the cube. 2–3. Say the number. Trace the number. Draw the cubes.
www.harcourtschoolsupply.com
© Houghton Mifflin Harcourt Publishing Company
43
Core Standards for Math, Grade K
Name
Lesson 22
CC.K.CC.4a
1 2 3 4
1 2 3 4
2
two
DIRECTIONS 1. Mark under the number that shows how many counters are in the five frame. 2. Mark next to the five frame that shows two counters. 3. Mark under the number that shows how many apples. 4. Say the number. Draw that many counters in the five frame.
www.harcourtschoolsupply.com
© Houghton Mifflin Harcourt Publishing Company
44
Core Standards for Math, Grade K

Answer Key

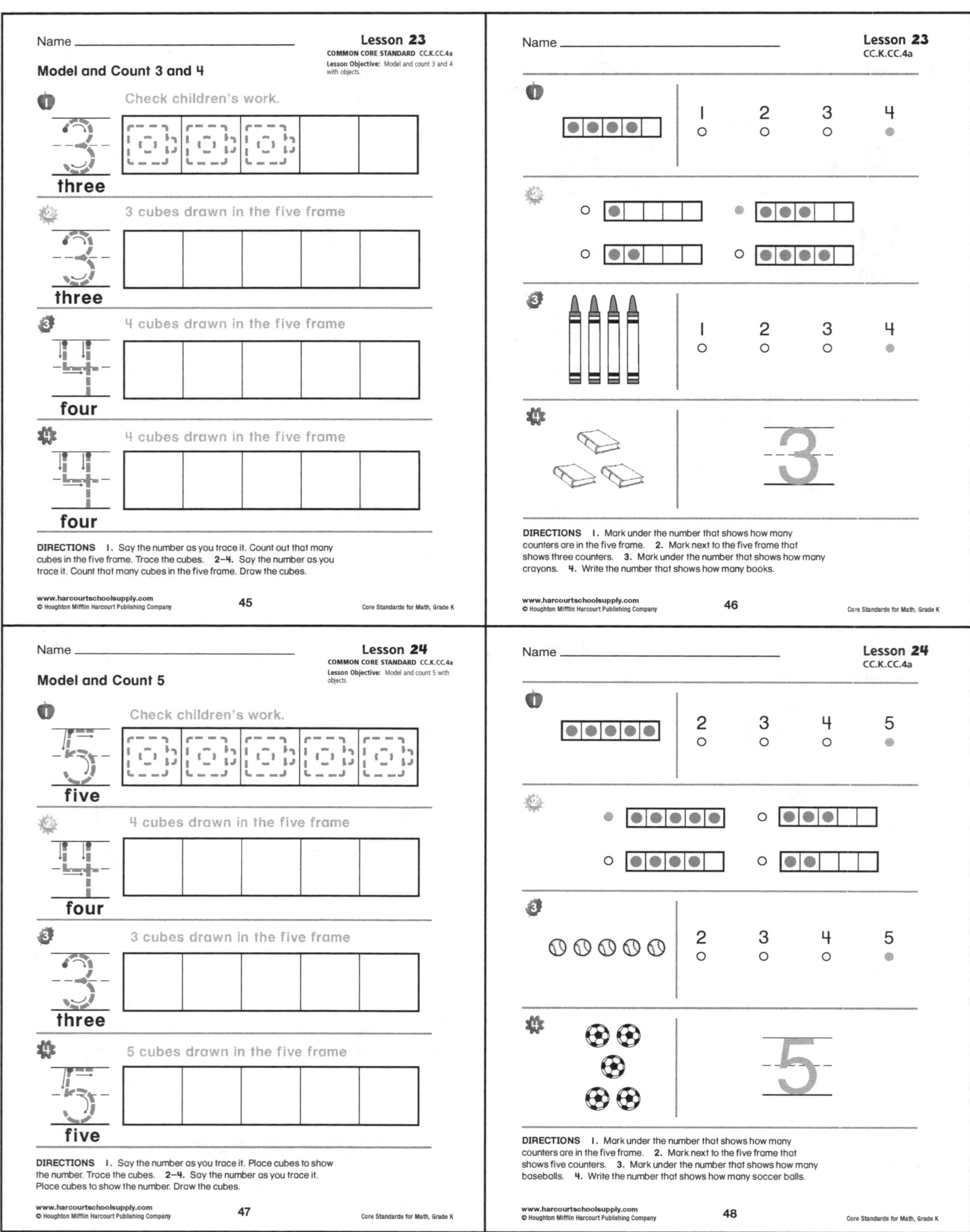

Name
Lesson 23
COMMON CORE STANDARD CC.K.CC.4a
Lesson Objective: Model and count 3 and 4 with objects.
Model and Count 3 and 4
Check children's work.
three
3 cubes drawn in the five frame
three
4 cubes drawn in the five frame
four
4 cubes drawn in the five frame
four
DIRECTIONS 1. Say the number as you trace it. Count out that many cubes in the five frame. Trace the cubes. 2–4. Say the number as you trace it. Count that many cubes in the five frame. Draw the cubes.
www.harcourtschoolsupply.com
© Houghton Mifflin Harcourt Publishing Company
45
Core Standards for Math, Grade K
Name
Lesson 23
CC.K.CC.4a
1 2 3 4
1 2 3 4
3
DIRECTIONS 1. Mark under the number that shows how many counters are in the five frame. 2. Mark next to the five frame that shows three counters. 3. Mark under the number that shows how many crayons. 4. Write the number that shows how many books.
www.harcourtschoolsupply.com
© Houghton Mifflin Harcourt Publishing Company
46
Core Standards for Math, Grade K
Name
Lesson 24
COMMON CORE STANDARD CC.K.CC.4a
Lesson Objective: Model and count 5 with objects.
Model and Count 5
Check children's work.
five
4 cubes drawn in the five frame
four
3 cubes drawn in the five frame
three
5 cubes drawn in the five frame
five
DIRECTIONS 1. Say the number as you trace it. Place cubes to show the number. Trace the cubes. 2–4. Say the number as you trace it. Place cubes to show the number. Draw the cubes.
www.harcourtschoolsupply.com
© Houghton Mifflin Harcourt Publishing Company
47
Core Standards for Math, Grade K
Name
Lesson 24
CC.K.CC.4a
2 3 4 5
2 3 4 5
5
DIRECTIONS 1. Mark under the number that shows how many counters are in the five frame. 2. Mark next to the five frame that shows five counters. 3. Mark under the number that shows how many baseballs. 4. Write the number that shows how many soccer balls.
www.harcourtschoolsupply.com
© Houghton Mifflin Harcourt Publishing Company
48
Core Standards for Math, Grade K

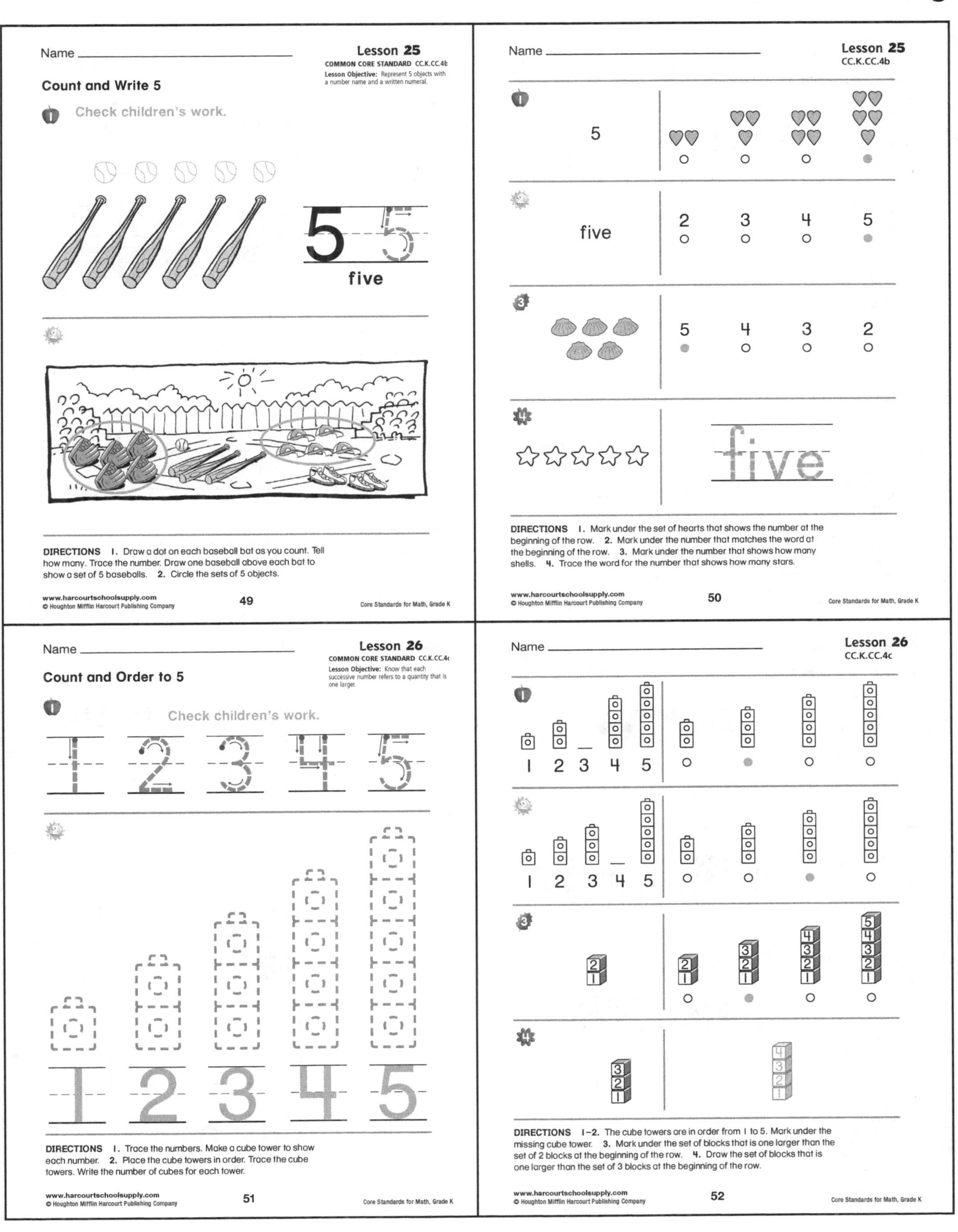
Name
Lesson 25
COMMON CORE STANDARD CC.K.CC.4b
Lesson Objective: Represent 5 objects with a number name and a written numeral.
Count and Write 5
Check children's work.
5
five
DIRECTIONS 1. Draw a dot on each baseball bat as you count. Tell how many. Trace the number. Draw one baseball above each bat to show a set of 5 baseballs. 2. Circle the sets of 5 objects.
www.harcourtschoolsupply.com
© Houghton Mifflin Harcourt Publishing Company
49
Core Standards for Math, Grade K
Name
Lesson 25
CC.K.CC.4b
5
five
2 3 4 5
5 4 3 2
five
DIRECTIONS 1. Mark under the set of hearts that shows the number at the beginning of the row. 2. Mark under the number that matches the word at the beginning of the row. 3. Mark under the number that shows how many shells. 4. Trace the word for the number that shows how many stars.
www.harcourtschoolsupply.com
© Houghton Mifflin Harcourt Publishing Company
50
Core Standards for Math, Grade K
Name
Lesson 26
COMMON CORE STANDARD CC.K.CC.4c
Lesson Objective: Know that each successive number refers to a quantity that is one larger.
Count and Order to 5
Check children's work.
1 2 3 4 5
1 2 3 4 5
DIRECTIONS 1. Trace the numbers. Make a cube tower to show each number. 2. Place the cube towers in order. Trace the cube towers. Write the number of cubes for each tower.
www.harcourtschoolsupply.com
© Houghton Mifflin Harcourt Publishing Company
51
Core Standards for Math, Grade K
Name
Lesson 26
CC.K.CC.4c
1 2 3 4 5
1 2 3 4 5
DIRECTIONS 1–2. The cube towers are in order from 1 to 5. Mark under the missing cube tower. 3. Mark under the set of blocks that is one larger than the set of 2 blocks at the beginning of the row. 4. Draw the set of blocks that is one larger than the set of 3 blocks at the beginning of the row.
www.harcourtschoolsupply.com
© Houghton Mifflin Harcourt Publishing Company
52
Core Standards for Math, Grade K

Answer Key

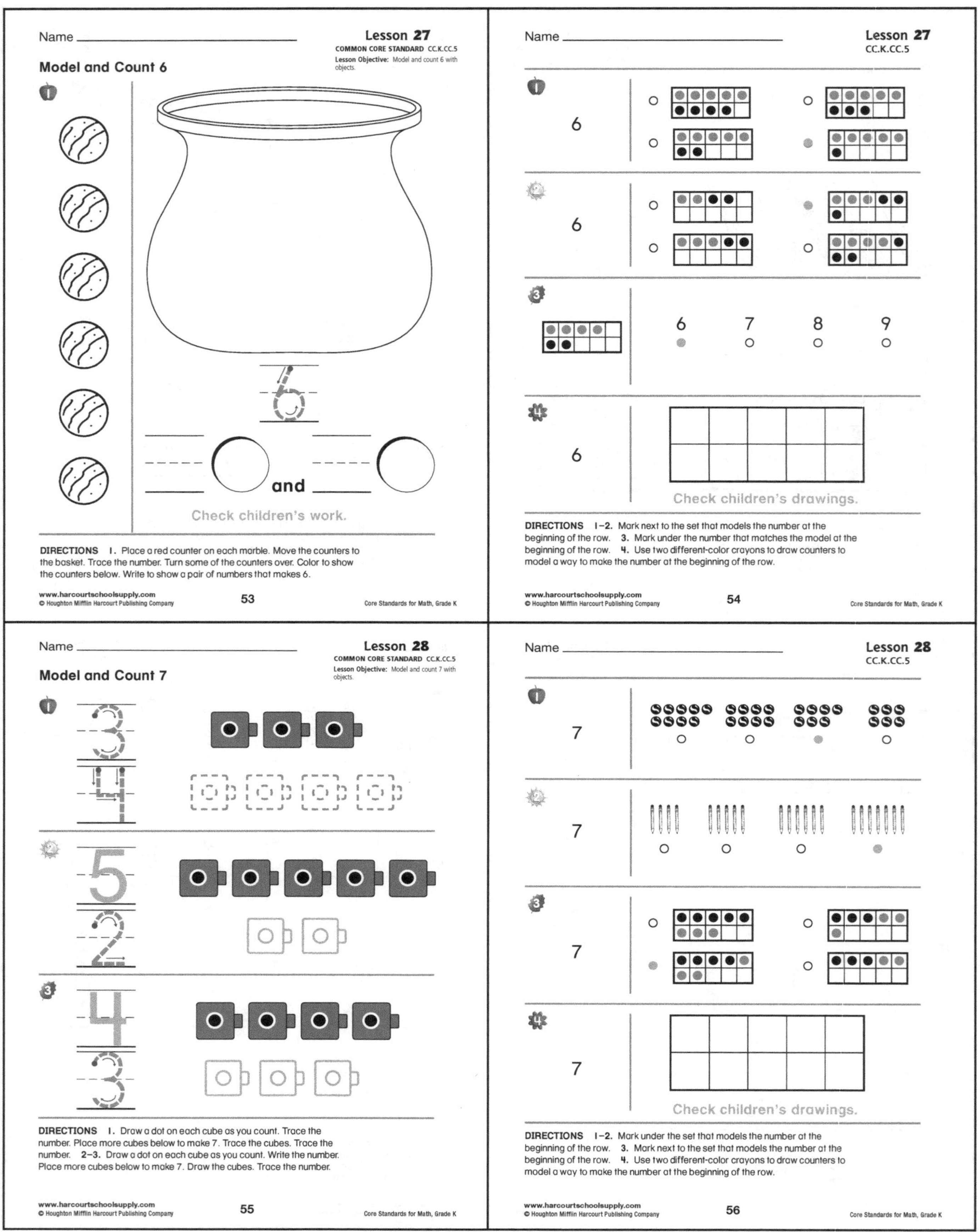

Name
Lesson 27
COMMON CORE STANDARD CC.K.CC.5
Lesson Objective: Model and count 6 with objects.
Model and Count 6
and
Check children's work.
DIRECTIONS 1. Place a red counter on each marble. Move the counters to the basket. Trace the number. Turn some of the counters over. Color to show the counters below. Write to show a pair of numbers that makes 6.
www.harcourtschoolsupply.com
© Houghton Mifflin Harcourt Publishing Company
53
Core Standards for Math, Grade K
Name
Lesson 27
CC.K.CC.5
6
6
6 7 8 9
6
Check children's drawings.
DIRECTIONS 1–2. Mark next to the set that models the number at the beginning of the row. 3. Mark under the number that matches the model at the beginning of the row. 4. Use two different-color crayons to draw counters to model a way to make the number at the beginning of the row.
www.harcourtschoolsupply.com
© Houghton Mifflin Harcourt Publishing Company
54
Core Standards for Math, Grade K
Name
Lesson 28
COMMON CORE STANDARD CC.K.CC.5
Lesson Objective: Model and count 7 with objects.
Model and Count 7
DIRECTIONS 1. Draw a dot on each cube as you count. Trace the number. Place more cubes below to make 7. Trace the cubes. Trace the number. 2–3. Draw a dot on each cube as you count. Write the number. Place more cubes below to make 7. Draw the cubes. Trace the number.
www.harcourtschoolsupply.com
© Houghton Mifflin Harcourt Publishing Company
55
Core Standards for Math, Grade K
Name
Lesson 28
CC.K.CC.5
7
7
7
7
Check children's drawings.
DIRECTIONS 1–2. Mark under the set that models the number at the beginning of the row. 3. Mark next to the set that models the number at the beginning of the row. 4. Use two different-color crayons to draw counters to model a way to make the number at the beginning of the row.
www.harcourtschoolsupply.com
© Houghton Mifflin Harcourt Publishing Company
56
Core Standards for Math, Grade K

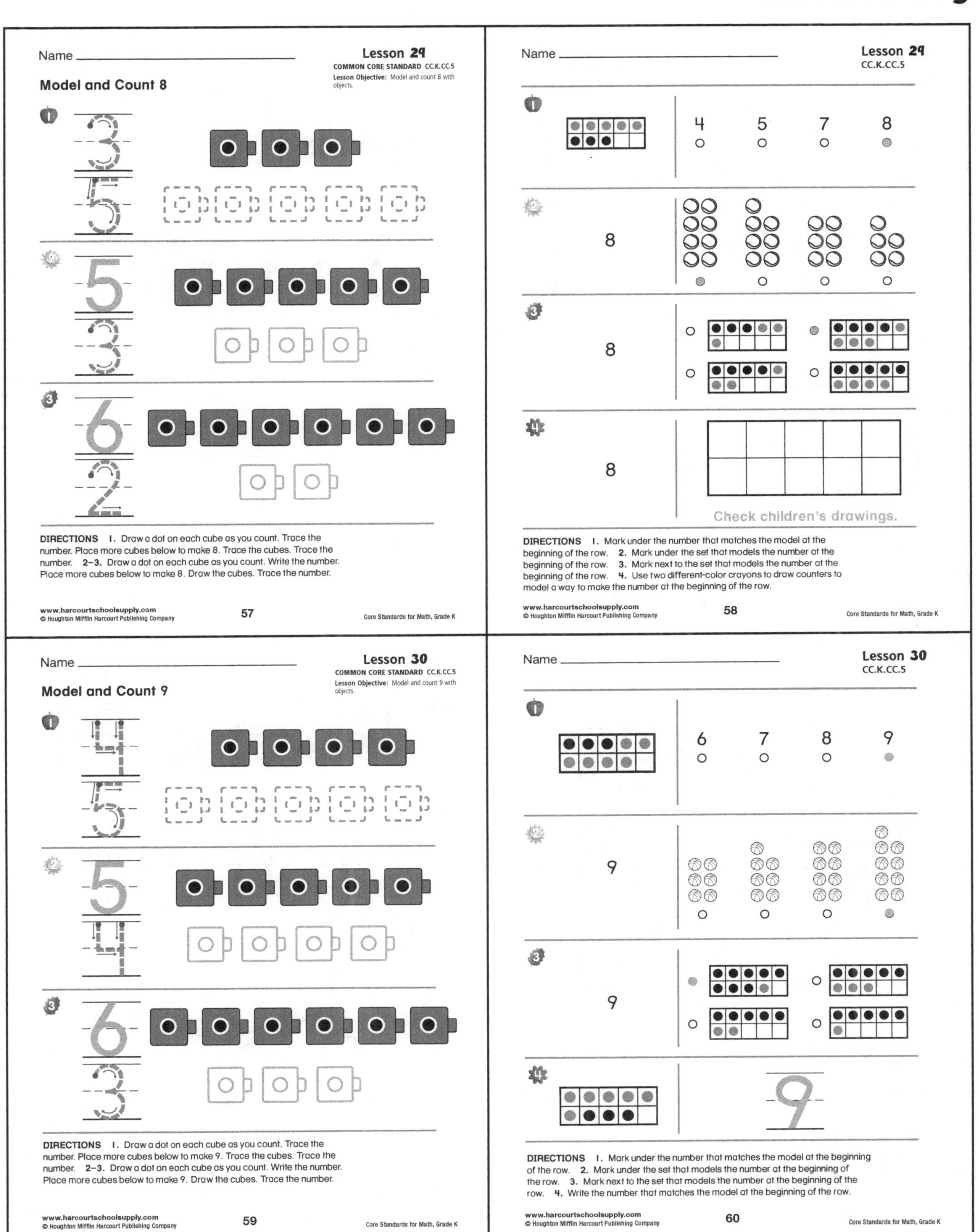

Name
Lesson 29
COMMON CORE STANDARD CC.K.CC.5
Lesson Objective: Model and count 8 with objects.
Model and Count 8
DIRECTIONS 1. Draw a dot on each cube as you count. Trace the number. Place more cubes below to make 8. Trace the cubes. Trace the number. 2–3. Draw a dot on each cube as you count. Write the number. Place more cubes below to make 8. Draw the cubes. Trace the number.
www.harcourtschoolsupply.com
© Houghton Mifflin Harcourt Publishing Company
57
Core Standards for Math, Grade K
Name
Lesson 29
CC.K.CC.5
4 5 7 8
8
8
8
Check children's drawings.
DIRECTIONS 1. Mark under the number that matches the model at the beginning of the row. 2. Mark under the set that models the number at the beginning of the row. 3. Mark next to the set that models the number at the beginning of the row. 4. Use two different-color crayons to draw counters to model a way to make the number at the beginning of the row.
www.harcourtschoolsupply.com
© Houghton Mifflin Harcourt Publishing Company
58
Core Standards for Math, Grade K
Name
Lesson 30
COMMON CORE STANDARD CC.K.CC.5
Lesson Objective: Model and count 9 with objects.
Model and Count 9
DIRECTIONS 1. Draw a dot on each cube as you count. Trace the number. Place more cubes below to make 9. Trace the cubes. Trace the number. 2–3. Draw a dot on each cube as you count. Write the number. Place more cubes below to make 9. Draw the cubes. Trace the number.
www.harcourtschoolsupply.com
© Houghton Mifflin Harcourt Publishing Company
59
Core Standards for Math, Grade K
Name
Lesson 30
CC.K.CC.5
6 7 8 9
9
9
DIRECTIONS 1. Mark under the number that matches the model at the beginning of the row. 2. Mark under the set that models the number at the beginning of the row. 3. Mark next to the set that models the number at the beginning of the row. 4. Write the number that matches the model at the beginning of the row.
www.harcourtschoolsupply.com
© Houghton Mifflin Harcourt Publishing Company
60
Core Standards for Math, Grade K

Answer Key

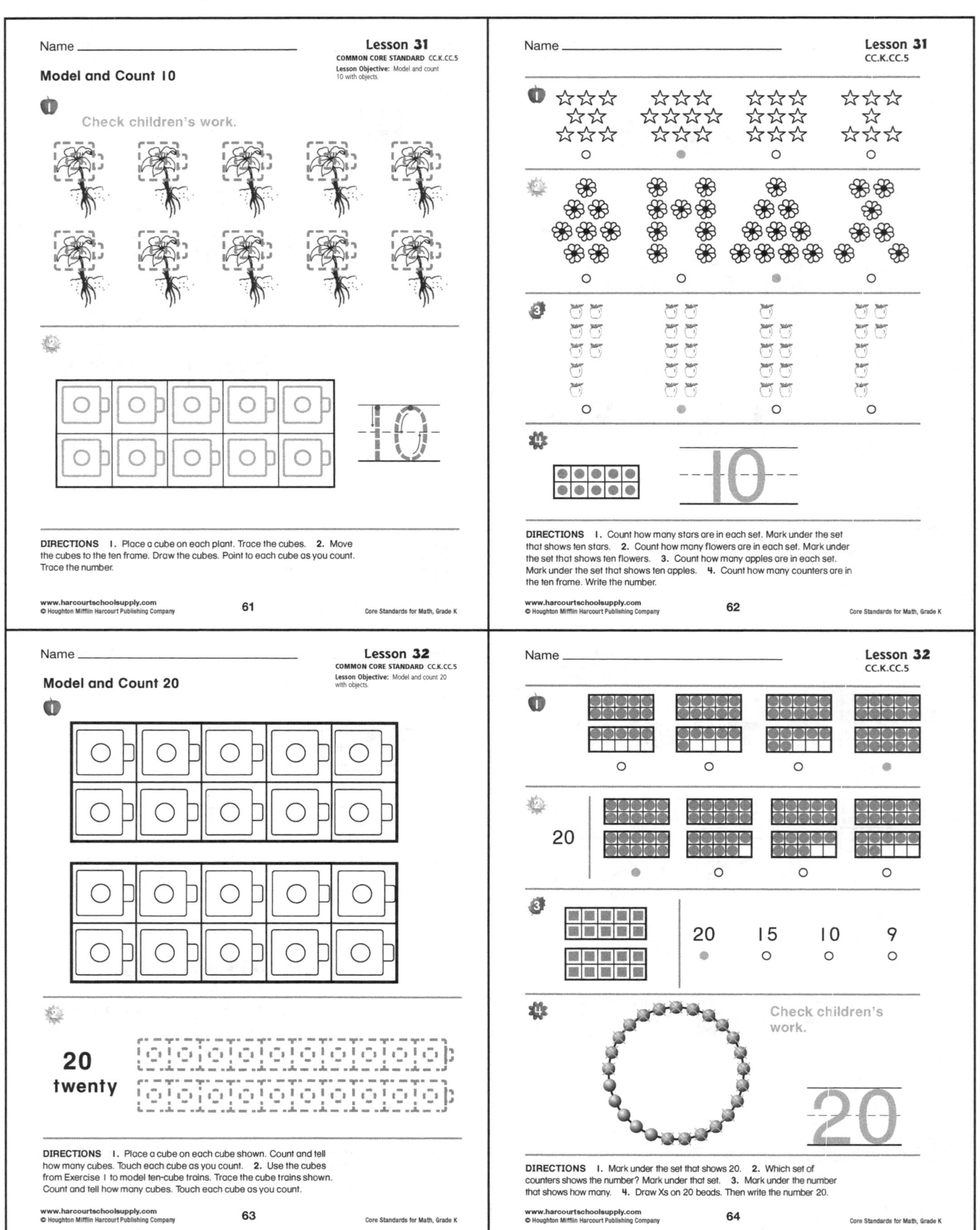

Name
Lesson 31
COMMON CORE STANDARD CC.K.CC.5
Lesson Objective: Model and count 10 with objects.
Model and Count 10
Check children's work.
DIRECTIONS 1. Place a cube on each plant. Trace the cubes. 2. Move the cubes to the ten frame. Draw the cubes. Point to each cube as you count. Trace the number.
www.harcourtschoolsupply.com
© Houghton Mifflin Harcourt Publishing Company
61
Core Standards for Math, Grade K
Name
Lesson 31
CC.K.CC.5
10
DIRECTIONS 1. Count how many stars are in each set. Mark under the set that shows ten stars. 2. Count how many flowers are in each set. Mark under the set that shows ten flowers. 3. Count how many apples are in each set. Mark under the set that shows ten apples. 4. Count how many counters are in the ten frame. Write the number.
www.harcourtschoolsupply.com
© Houghton Mifflin Harcourt Publishing Company
62
Core Standards for Math, Grade K
Name
Lesson 32
COMMON CORE STANDARD CC.K.CC.5
Lesson Objective: Model and count 20 with objects.
Model and Count 20
20
twenty
DIRECTIONS 1. Place a cube on each cube shown. Count and tell how many cubes. Touch each cube as you count. 2. Use the cubes from Exercise 1 to model ten-cube trains. Trace the cube trains shown. Count and tell how many cubes. Touch each cube as you count.
www.harcourtschoolsupply.com
© Houghton Mifflin Harcourt Publishing Company
63
Core Standards for Math, Grade K
Name
Lesson 32
CC.K.CC.5
20
20
15
10
9
Check children's work.
20
DIRECTIONS 1. Mark under the set that shows 20. 2. Which set of counters shows the number? Mark under that set. 3. Mark under the number that shows how many. 4. Draw Xs on 20 beads. Then write the number 20.
www.harcourtschoolsupply.com
© Houghton Mifflin Harcourt Publishing Company
64
Core Standards for Math, Grade K

Answer Key

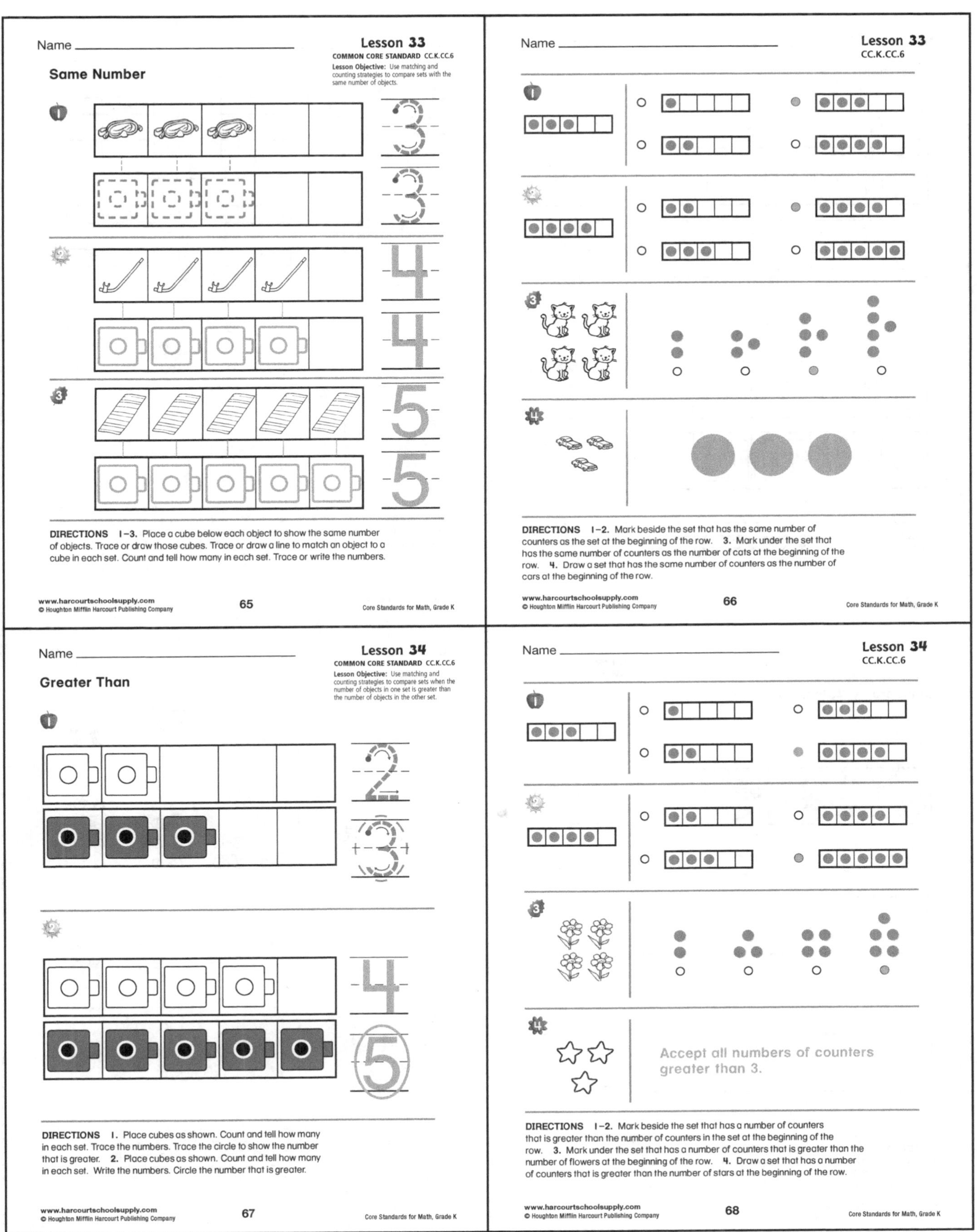

Name ____________________

Lesson 33
COMMON CORE STANDARD CC.K.CC.6
Lesson Objective: Use matching and counting strategies to compare sets with the same number of objects.

Same Number

1 3 3

2 4 4

3 5 5

DIRECTIONS 1–3. Place a cube below each object to show the same number of objects. Trace or draw those cubes. Trace or draw a line to match an object to a cube in each set. Count and tell how many in each set. Trace or write the numbers.

www.harcourtschoolsupply.com
© Houghton Mifflin Harcourt Publishing Company
65
Core Standards for Math, Grade K

Name ____________________

Lesson 33
CC.K.CC.6

DIRECTIONS 1–2. Mark beside the set that has the same number of counters as the set at the beginning of the row. **3.** Mark under the set that has the same number of counters as the number of cats at the beginning of the row. **4.** Draw a set that has the same number of counters as the number of cars at the beginning of the row.

www.harcourtschoolsupply.com
© Houghton Mifflin Harcourt Publishing Company
66
Core Standards for Math, Grade K

Name ____________________

Lesson 34
COMMON CORE STANDARD CC.K.CC.6
Lesson Objective: Use matching and counting strategies to compare sets when the number of objects in one set is greater than the number of objects in the other set.

Greater Than

1 2 3

2 4 5

DIRECTIONS 1. Place cubes as shown. Count and tell how many in each set. Trace the numbers. Trace the circle to show the number that is greater. **2.** Place cubes as shown. Count and tell how many in each set. Write the numbers. Circle the number that is greater.

www.harcourtschoolsupply.com
© Houghton Mifflin Harcourt Publishing Company
67
Core Standards for Math, Grade K

Name ____________________

Lesson 34
CC.K.CC.6

Accept all numbers of counters greater than 3.

DIRECTIONS 1–2. Mark beside the set that has a number of counters that is greater than the number of counters in the set at the beginning of the row. **3.** Mark under the set that has a number of counters that is greater than the number of flowers at the beginning of the row. **4.** Draw a set that has a number of counters that is greater than the number of stars at the beginning of the row.

www.harcourtschoolsupply.com
© Houghton Mifflin Harcourt Publishing Company
68
Core Standards for Math, Grade K

Answer Key

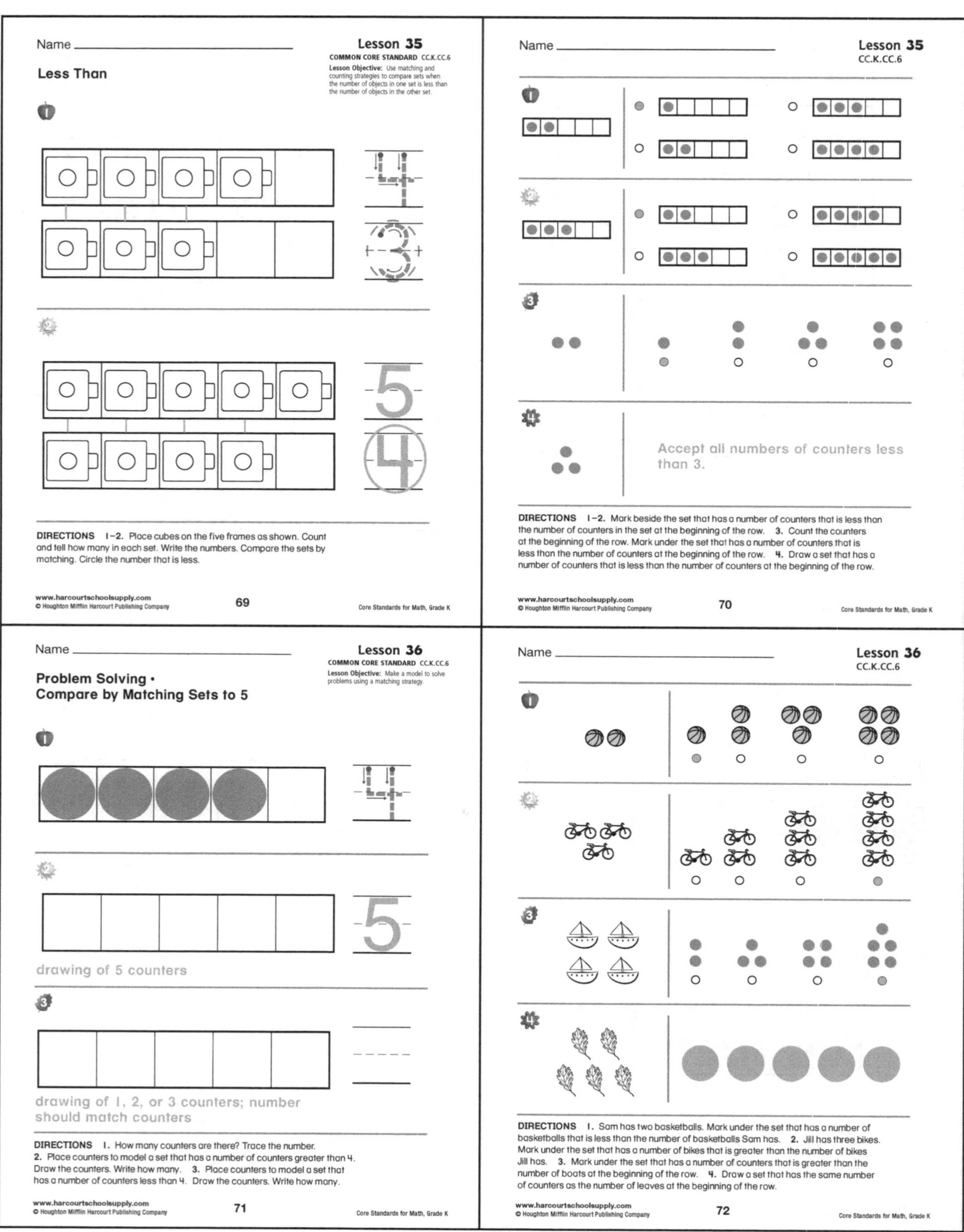

Name
Lesson 35
COMMON CORE STANDARD CC.K.CC.6
Lesson Objective: Use matching and counting strategies to compare sets when the number of objects in one set is less than the number of objects in the other set.
Less Than
4
3
5
4
DIRECTIONS 1–2. Place cubes on the five frames as shown. Count and tell how many in each set. Write the numbers. Compare the sets by matching. Circle the number that is less.
www.harcourtschoolsupply.com
© Houghton Mifflin Harcourt Publishing Company
69
Core Standards for Math, Grade K
Name
Lesson 35
CC.K.CC.6
Accept all numbers of counters less than 3.
DIRECTIONS 1–2. Mark beside the set that has a number of counters that is less than the number of counters in the set at the beginning of the row. 3. Count the counters at the beginning of the row. Mark under the set that has a number of counters that is less than the number of counters at the beginning of the row. 4. Draw a set that has a number of counters that is less than the number of counters at the beginning of the row.
www.harcourtschoolsupply.com
© Houghton Mifflin Harcourt Publishing Company
70
Core Standards for Math, Grade K
Name
Lesson 36
COMMON CORE STANDARD CC.K.CC.6
Lesson Objective: Make a model to solve problems using a matching strategy.
Problem Solving •
Compare by Matching Sets to 5
4
5
drawing of 5 counters
drawing of 1, 2, or 3 counters; number should match counters
DIRECTIONS 1. How many counters are there? Trace the number. 2. Place counters to model a set that has a number of counters greater than 4. Draw the counters. Write how many. 3. Place counters to model a set that has a number of counters less than 4. Draw the counters. Write how many.
www.harcourtschoolsupply.com
© Houghton Mifflin Harcourt Publishing Company
71
Core Standards for Math, Grade K
Name
Lesson 36
CC.K.CC.6
DIRECTIONS 1. Sam has two basketballs. Mark under the set that has a number of basketballs that is less than the number of basketballs Sam has. 2. Jill has three bikes. Mark under the set that has a number of bikes that is greater than the number of bikes Jill has. 3. Mark under the set that has a number of counters that is greater than the number of boats at the beginning of the row. 4. Draw a set that has the same number of counters as the number of leaves at the beginning of the row.
www.harcourtschoolsupply.com
© Houghton Mifflin Harcourt Publishing Company
72
Core Standards for Math, Grade K

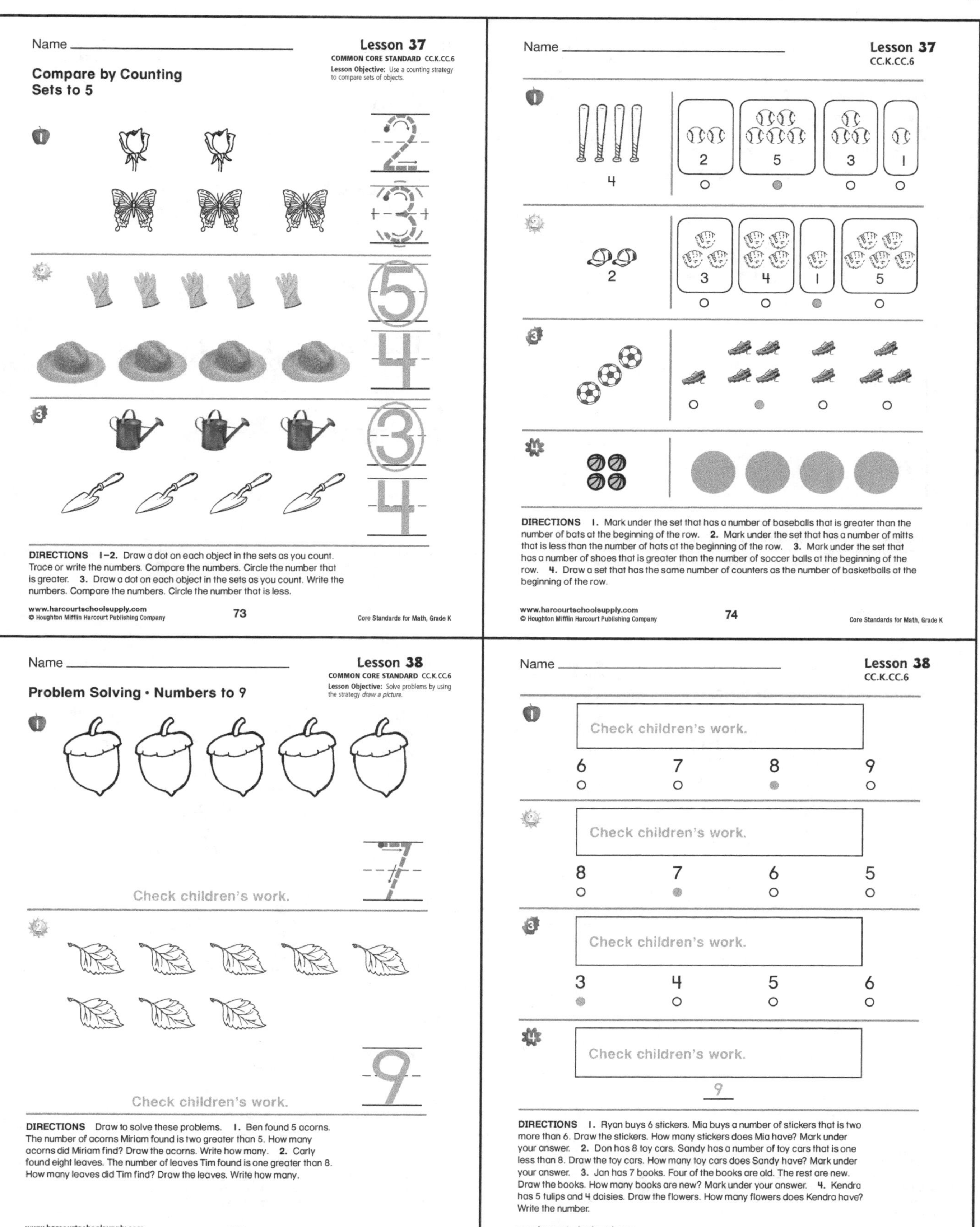
Name
Lesson 37
COMMON CORE STANDARD CC.K.CC.6
Lesson Objective: Use a counting strategy to compare sets of objects.
Compare by Counting Sets to 5
2
3
5
4
3
4
DIRECTIONS 1–2. Draw a dot on each object in the sets as you count. Trace or write the numbers. Compare the numbers. Circle the number that is greater. 3. Draw a dot on each object in the sets as you count. Write the numbers. Compare the numbers. Circle the number that is less.
www.harcourtschoolsupply.com
© Houghton Mifflin Harcourt Publishing Company
73
Core Standards for Math, Grade K
Name
Lesson 37
CC.K.CC.6
4
2
5
3
1
2
3
4
1
5
DIRECTIONS 1. Mark under the set that has a number of baseballs that is greater than the number of bats at the beginning of the row. 2. Mark under the set that has a number of mitts that is less than the number of hats at the beginning of the row. 3. Mark under the set that has a number of shoes that is greater than the number of soccer balls at the beginning of the row. 4. Draw a set that has the same number of counters as the number of basketballs at the beginning of the row.
www.harcourtschoolsupply.com
© Houghton Mifflin Harcourt Publishing Company
74
Core Standards for Math, Grade K
Name
Lesson 38
COMMON CORE STANDARD CC.K.CC.6
Lesson Objective: Solve problems by using the strategy draw a picture.
Problem Solving • Numbers to 9
Check children's work.
7
Check children's work.
9
DIRECTIONS Draw to solve these problems. 1. Ben found 5 acorns. The number of acorns Miriam found is two greater than 5. How many acorns did Miriam find? Draw the acorns. Write how many. 2. Carly found eight leaves. The number of leaves Tim found is one greater than 8. How many leaves did Tim find? Draw the leaves. Write how many.
www.harcourtschoolsupply.com
© Houghton Mifflin Harcourt Publishing Company
75
Core Standards for Math, Grade K
Name
Lesson 38
CC.K.CC.6
Check children's work.
6
7
8
9
Check children's work.
8
7
6
5
Check children's work.
3
4
5
6
Check children's work.
9
DIRECTIONS 1. Ryan buys 6 stickers. Mia buys a number of stickers that is two more than 6. Draw the stickers. How many stickers does Mia have? Mark under your answer. 2. Don has 8 toy cars. Sandy has a number of toy cars that is one less than 8. Draw the toy cars. How many toy cars does Sandy have? Mark under your answer. 3. Jan has 7 books. Four of the books are old. The rest are new. Draw the books. How many books are new? Mark under your answer. 4. Kendra has 5 tulips and 4 daisies. Draw the flowers. How many flowers does Kendra have? Write the number.
www.harcourtschoolsupply.com
© Houghton Mifflin Harcourt Publishing Company
76
Core Standards for Math, Grade K

Answer Key

Name ______________________________

Lesson 39
COMMON CORE STANDARD CC.K.CC.6
Lesson Objective: Solve problems by using the strategy *make a model.*

Problem Solving • Compare by Matching Sets to 10

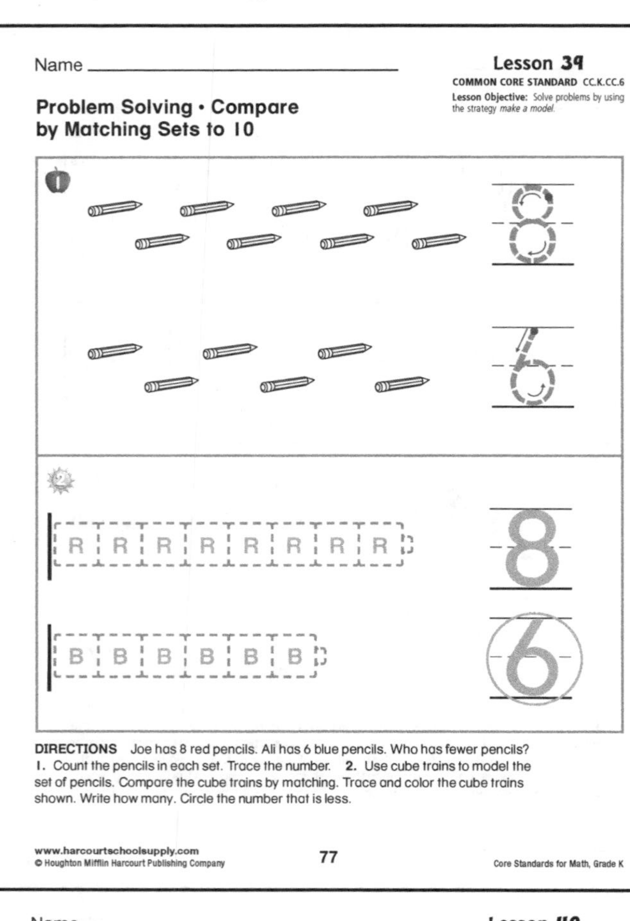

DIRECTIONS Joe has 8 red pencils. Ali has 6 blue pencils. Who has fewer pencils? **1.** Count the pencils in each set. Trace the number. **2.** Use cube trains to model the set of pencils. Compare the cube trains by matching. Trace and color the cube trains shown. Write how many. Circle the number that is less.

Name ______________________________

Lesson 39
CC.K.CC.6

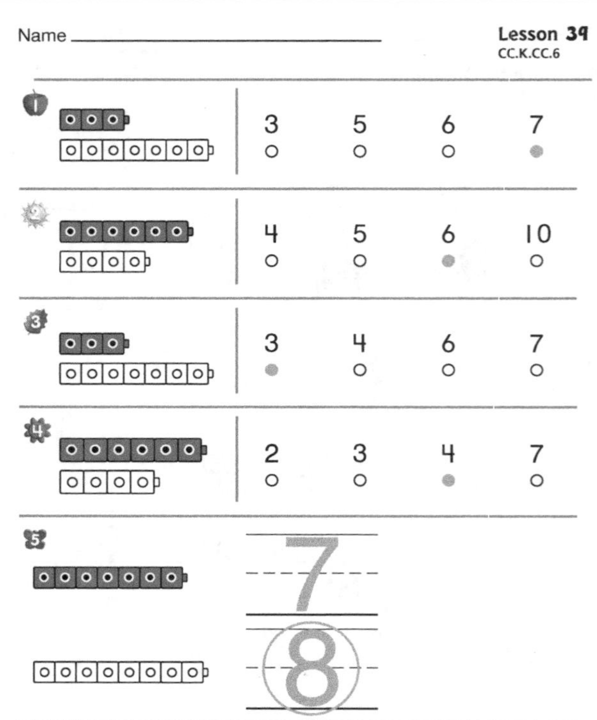

5

7

8

DIRECTIONS **1–2.** Which set has more cubes? Mark under the number that matches that set. **3–4.** Which set has fewer cubes? Mark under the number that matches that set. **5.** Compare the cube trains by matching. Write how many in each set. Which number is greater? Circle that number.

Name ______________________________

Lesson 40
COMMON CORE STANDARD CC.K.CC.6
Lesson Objective: Use counting strategies to compare sets of objects.

Compare by Counting Sets to 10

1

6

8

2

10

7

3

9

8

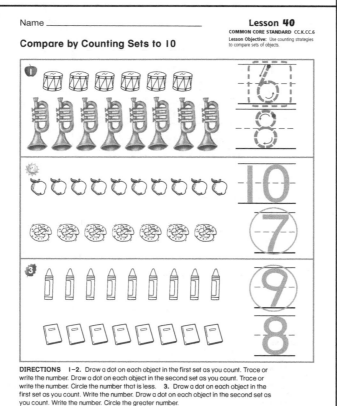

DIRECTIONS **1–2.** Draw a dot on each object in the first set as you count. Trace or write the number. Draw a dot on each object in the second set as you count. Trace or write the number. Circle the number that is less. **3.** Draw a dot on each object in the first set as you count. Write the number. Draw a dot on each object in the second set as you count. Write the number. Circle the greater number.

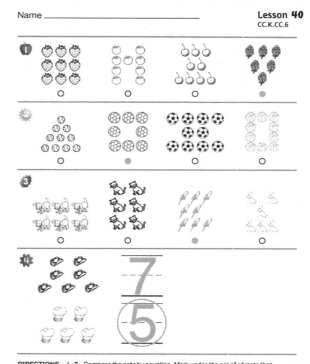

Name ______________________________

Lesson 40
CC.K.CC.6

1

2

3

4

7

5

DIRECTIONS **1–2.** Compare the sets by counting. Mark under the set of objects that has less than all the others. **3.** Compare the sets by counting. Mark under the set of objects that has more than all the others. **4.** Count how many in each set. Write the number of objects in each set. Compare the numbers. Circle the number that is less.

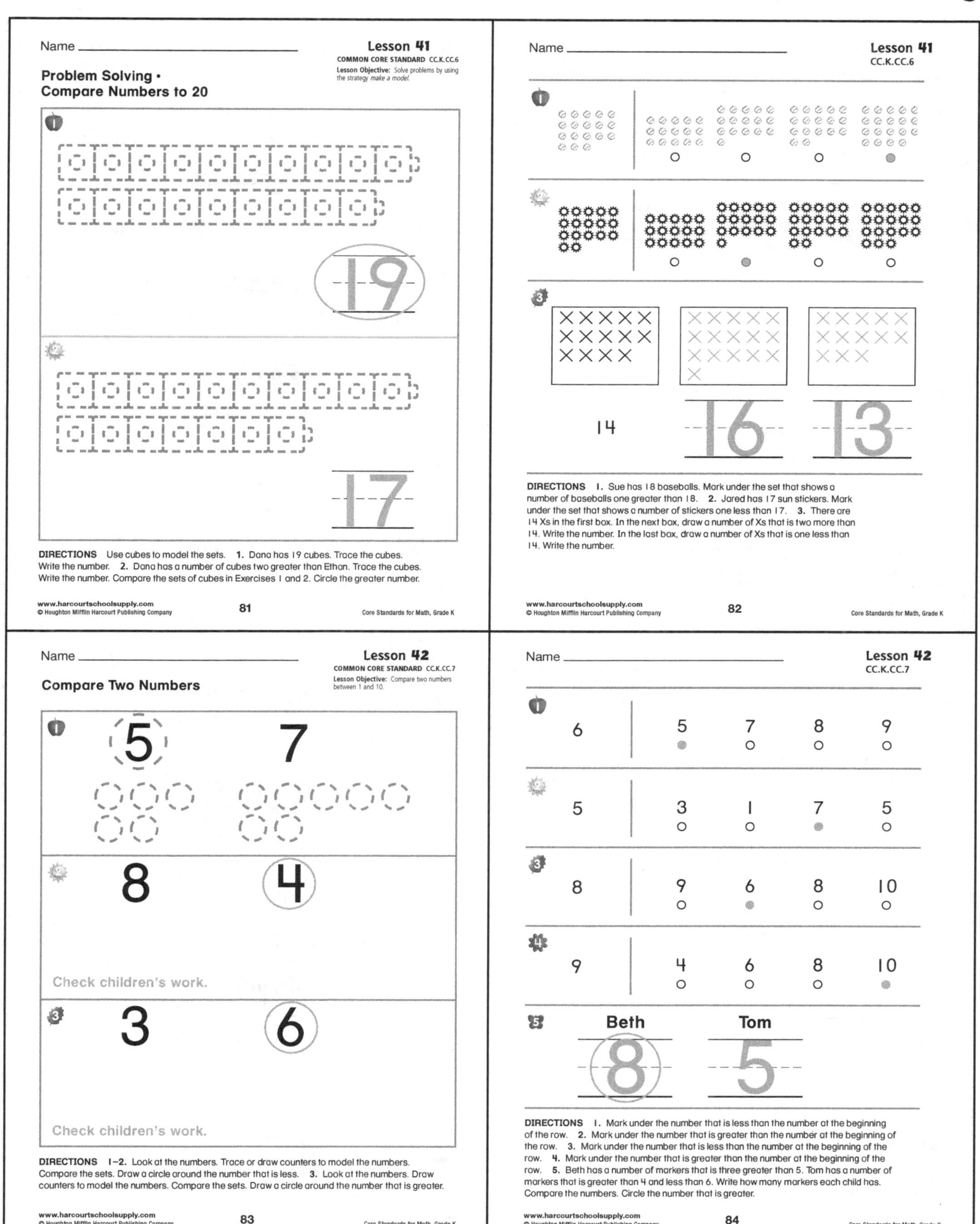

Name ______________________

Lesson 41
COMMON CORE STANDARD CC.K.CC.6
Lesson Objective: Solve problems by using the strategy *make a model.*

Problem Solving • Compare Numbers to 20

1. 19 (circled)

2. 17

DIRECTIONS Use cubes to model the sets. 1. Dana has 19 cubes. Trace the cubes. Write the number. 2. Dana has a number of cubes two greater than Ethan. Trace the cubes. Write the number. Compare the sets of cubes in Exercises 1 and 2. Circle the greater number.

Name ______________________

Lesson 41
CC.K.CC.6

3. 14 16 13

DIRECTIONS 1. Sue has 18 baseballs. Mark under the set that shows a number of baseballs one greater than 18. 2. Jared has 17 sun stickers. Mark under the set that shows a number of stickers one less than 17. 3. There are 14 Xs in the first box. In the next box, draw a number of Xs that is two more than 14. Write the number. In the last box, draw a number of Xs that is one less than 14. Write the number.

Name ______________________

Lesson 42
COMMON CORE STANDARD CC.K.CC.7
Lesson Objective: Compare two numbers between 1 and 10.

Compare Two Numbers

1. 5 (circled) 7

2. 8 4 (circled)

Check children's work.

3. 3 6 (circled)

Check children's work.

DIRECTIONS 1–2. Look at the numbers. Trace or draw counters to model the numbers. Compare the sets. Draw a circle around the number that is less. 3. Look at the numbers. Draw counters to model the numbers. Compare the sets. Draw a circle around the number that is greater.

Name ______________________

Lesson 42
CC.K.CC.7

1	6	5 ●	7 ○	8 ○	9 ○
2	5	3 ○	1 ○	7 ●	5 ○
3	8	9 ○	6 ●	8 ○	10 ○
4	9	4 ○	6 ○	8 ○	10 ●

5. Beth 8 (circled) Tom 5

DIRECTIONS 1. Mark under the number that is less than the number at the beginning of the row. 2. Mark under the number that is greater than the number at the beginning of the row. 3. Mark under the number that is less than the number at the beginning of the row. 4. Mark under the number that is greater than the number at the beginning of the row. 5. Beth has a number of markers that is three greater than 5. Tom has a number of markers that is greater than 4 and less than 6. Write how many markers each child has. Compare the numbers. Circle the number that is greater.

Answer Key

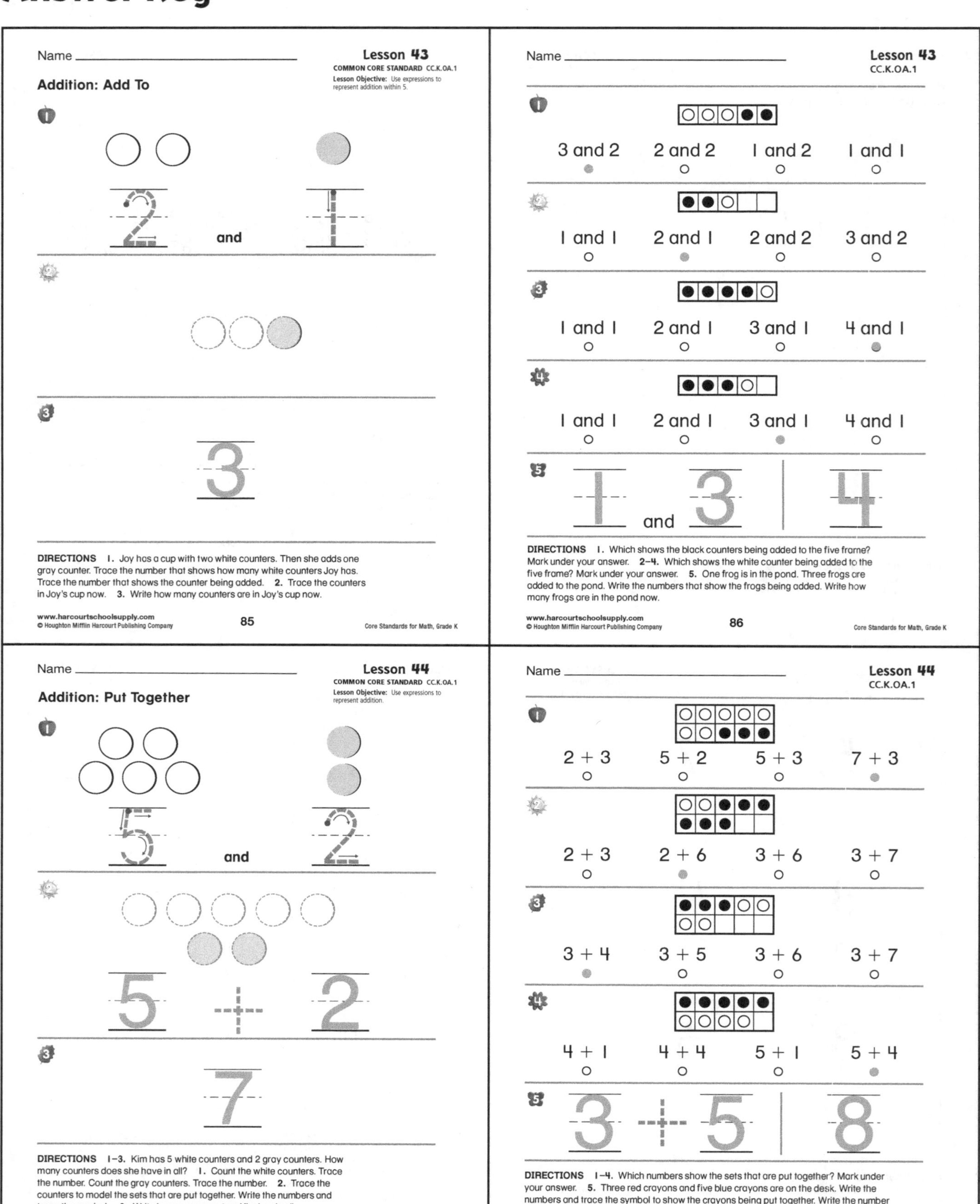

Name
Lesson 43
COMMON CORE STANDARD CC.K.OA.1
Lesson Objective: Use expressions to represent addition within 5.
Addition: Add To
2
and
1
3
DIRECTIONS 1. Joy has a cup with two white counters. Then she adds one gray counter. Trace the number that shows how many white counters Joy has. Trace the number that shows the counter being added. 2. Trace the counters in Joy's cup now. 3. Write how many counters are in Joy's cup now.
www.harcourtschoolsupply.com
© Houghton Mifflin Harcourt Publishing Company
85
Core Standards for Math, Grade K
Name
Lesson 43
CC.K.OA.1
3 and 2
2 and 2
1 and 2
1 and 1
1 and 1
2 and 1
2 and 2
3 and 2
1 and 1
2 and 1
3 and 1
4 and 1
1 and 1
2 and 1
3 and 1
4 and 1
1
and
3
4
DIRECTIONS 1. Which shows the black counters being added to the five frame? Mark under your answer. 2–4. Which shows the white counter being added to the five frame? Mark under your answer. 5. One frog is in the pond. Three frogs are added to the pond. Write the numbers that show the frogs being added. Write how many frogs are in the pond now.
www.harcourtschoolsupply.com
© Houghton Mifflin Harcourt Publishing Company
86
Core Standards for Math, Grade K
Name
Lesson 44
COMMON CORE STANDARD CC.K.OA.1
Lesson Objective: Use expressions to represent addition.
Addition: Put Together
5
and
2
5 + 2
7
DIRECTIONS 1–3. Kim has 5 white counters and 2 gray counters. How many counters does she have in all? 1. Count the white counters. Trace the number. Count the gray counters. Trace the number. 2. Trace the counters to model the sets that are put together. Write the numbers and trace the symbol. 3. Write how many counters Kim has in all.
www.harcourtschoolsupply.com
© Houghton Mifflin Harcourt Publishing Company
87
Core Standards for Math, Grade K
Name
Lesson 44
CC.K.OA.1
2 + 3
5 + 2
5 + 3
7 + 3
2 + 3
2 + 6
3 + 6
3 + 7
3 + 4
3 + 5
3 + 6
3 + 7
4 + 1
4 + 4
5 + 1
5 + 4
3 + 5
8
DIRECTIONS 1–4. Which numbers show the sets that are put together? Mark under your answer. 5. Three red crayons and five blue crayons are on the desk. Write the numbers and trace the symbol to show the crayons being put together. Write the number to show how many crayons in all.
www.harcourtschoolsupply.com
© Houghton Mifflin Harcourt Publishing Company
88
Core Standards for Math, Grade K

Answer Key

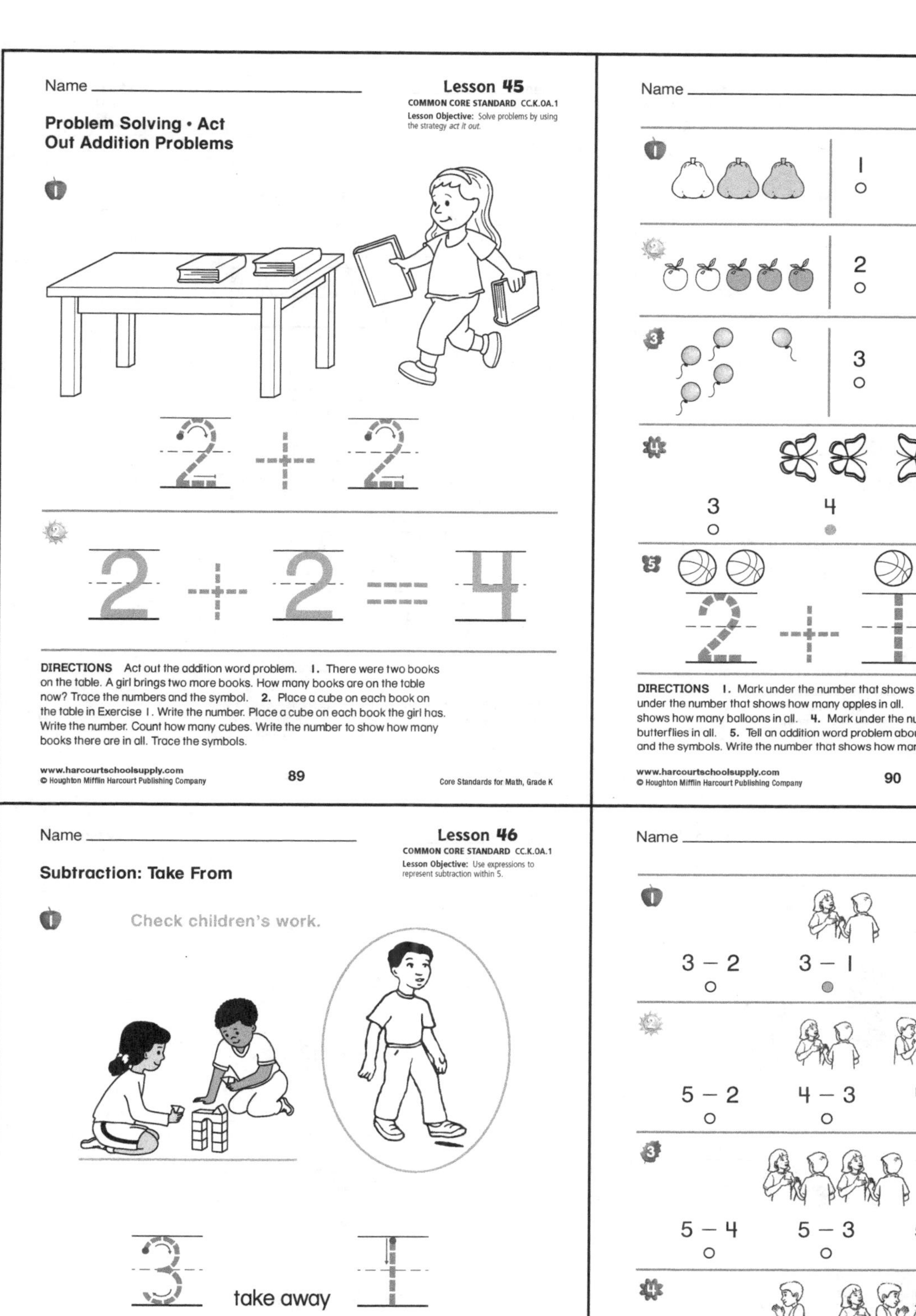

Name ______________________

Lesson 45

COMMON CORE STANDARD CC.K.OA.1

Lesson Objective: Solve problems by using the strategy *act it out.*

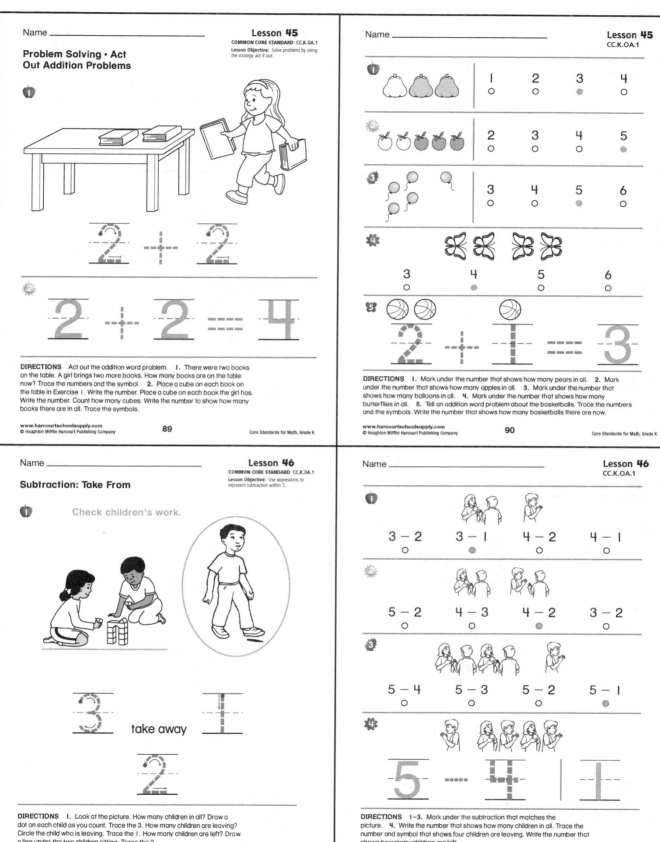

Problem Solving • Act Out Addition Problems

1

2 + 2

2

2 + 2 = 4

DIRECTIONS Act out the addition word problem. **1.** There were two books on the table. A girl brings two more books. How many books are on the table now? Trace the numbers and the symbol. **2.** Place a cube on each book on the table in Exercise 1. Write the number. Place a cube on each book the girl has. Write the number. Count how many cubes. Write the number to show how many books there are in all. Trace the symbols.

www.harcourtschoolsupply.com
© Houghton Mifflin Harcourt Publishing Company
89
Core Standards for Math, Grade K

Name ______________________

Lesson 45

CC.K.OA.1

1 — 1, 2, 3, 4

2 — 2, 3, 4, 5

3 — 3, 4, 5, 6

4 — 3, 4, 5, 6

5 — 2 + 1 = 3

DIRECTIONS **1.** Mark under the number that shows how many pears in all. **2.** Mark under the number that shows how many apples in all. **3.** Mark under the number that shows how many balloons in all. **4.** Mark under the number that shows how many butterflies in all. **5.** Tell an addition word problem about the basketballs. Trace the numbers and the symbols. Write the number that shows how many basketballs there are now.

www.harcourtschoolsupply.com
© Houghton Mifflin Harcourt Publishing Company
90
Core Standards for Math, Grade K

Name ______________________

Lesson 46

COMMON CORE STANDARD CC.K.OA.1

Lesson Objective: Use expressions to represent subtraction within 5.

Subtraction: Take From

1 Check children's work.

3 take away 1

2

DIRECTIONS **1.** Look at the picture. How many children in all? Draw a dot on each child as you count. Trace the 3. How many children are leaving? Circle the child who is leaving. Trace the 1. How many children are left? Draw a line under the two children sitting. Trace the 2.

www.harcourtschoolsupply.com
© Houghton Mifflin Harcourt Publishing Company
91
Core Standards for Math, Grade K

Name ______________________

Lesson 46

CC.K.OA.1

1 — 3 − 2, 3 − 1, 4 − 2, 4 − 1

2 — 5 − 2, 4 − 3, 4 − 2, 3 − 2

3 — 5 − 4, 5 − 3, 5 − 2, 5 − 1

4 — 5 − 4 | 1

DIRECTIONS **1–3.** Mark under the subtraction that matches the picture. **4.** Write the number that shows how many children in all. Trace the number and symbol that shows four children are leaving. Write the number that shows how many children are left.

www.harcourtschoolsupply.com
© Houghton Mifflin Harcourt Publishing Company
92
Core Standards for Math, Grade K

Answer Key

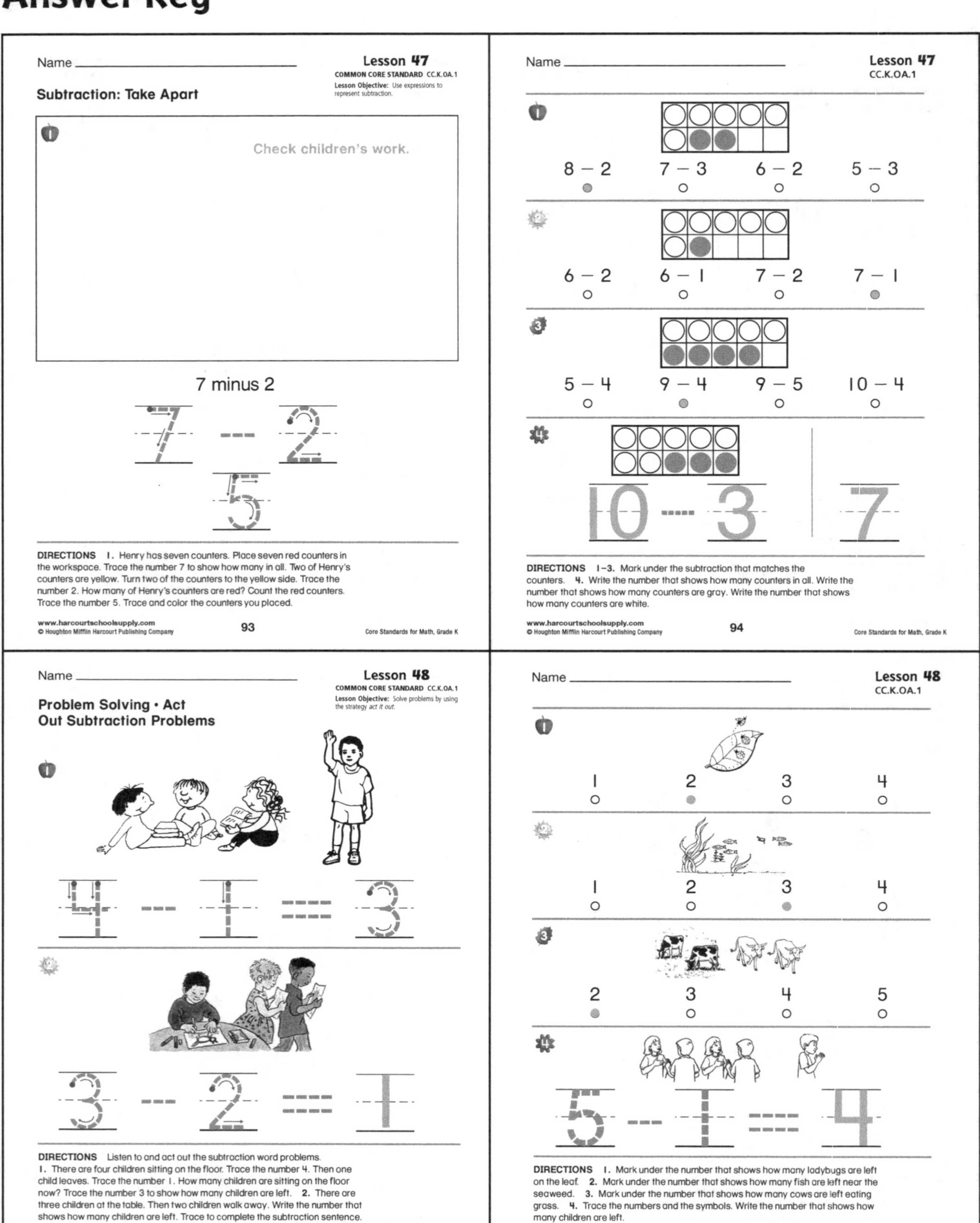

Name ______________________

Lesson 47
COMMON CORE STANDARD CC.K.OA.1
Lesson Objective: Use expressions to represent subtraction.

Subtraction: Take Apart

1 Check children's work.

7 minus 2

7 − 2

5

DIRECTIONS 1. Henry has seven counters. Place seven red counters in the workspace. Trace the number 7 to show how many in all. Two of Henry's counters are yellow. Turn two of the counters to the yellow side. Trace the number 2. How many of Henry's counters are red? Count the red counters. Trace the number 5. Trace and color the counters you placed.

www.harcourtschoolsupply.com
© Houghton Mifflin Harcourt Publishing Company 93 Core Standards for Math, Grade K

Name ______________________

Lesson 47
CC.K.OA.1

1 8 − 2 (marked) 7 − 3 6 − 2 5 − 3

2 6 − 2 6 − 1 7 − 2 7 − 1 (marked)

3 5 − 4 9 − 4 (marked) 9 − 5 10 − 4

4 10 − 3 | 7

DIRECTIONS 1–3. Mark under the subtraction that matches the counters. 4. Write the number that shows how many counters in all. Write the number that shows how many counters are gray. Write the number that shows how many counters are white.

www.harcourtschoolsupply.com
© Houghton Mifflin Harcourt Publishing Company 94 Core Standards for Math, Grade K

Name ______________________

Lesson 48
COMMON CORE STANDARD CC.K.OA.1
Lesson Objective: Solve problems by using the strategy *act it out.*

Problem Solving • Act Out Subtraction Problems

1 4 − 1 = 3

2 3 − 2 = 1

DIRECTIONS Listen to and act out the subtraction word problems. 1. There are four children sitting on the floor. Trace the number 4. Then one child leaves. Trace the number 1. How many children are sitting on the floor now? Trace the number 3 to show how many children are left. 2. There are three children at the table. Then two children walk away. Write the number that shows how many children are left. Trace to complete the subtraction sentence.

www.harcourtschoolsupply.com
© Houghton Mifflin Harcourt Publishing Company 95 Core Standards for Math, Grade K

Name ______________________

Lesson 48
CC.K.OA.1

1 1 2 (marked) 3 4

2 1 2 3 (marked) 4

3 2 (marked) 3 4 5

4 5 − 1 = 4

DIRECTIONS 1. Mark under the number that shows how many ladybugs are left on the leaf. 2. Mark under the number that shows how many fish are left near the seaweed. 3. Mark under the number that shows how many cows are left eating grass. 4. Trace the numbers and the symbols. Write the number that shows how many children are left.

www.harcourtschoolsupply.com
© Houghton Mifflin Harcourt Publishing Company 96 Core Standards for Math, Grade K

Answer Key

Name ______________________ **Lesson 49**

COMMON CORE STANDARD CC.K.OA.2
Lesson Objective: Solve addition word problems within 10 and record the equation.

Algebra • Write More Addition Sentences

2 + 5

7

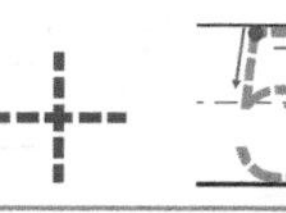

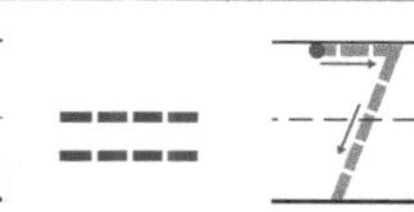

2 + 5 = 7

DIRECTIONS There were some frogs. Five more frogs come. Then there were seven frogs. How many frogs were there before? 1. Circle the frogs being added. Trace the number. How many frogs are in the set to start with? Write the number. 2. How many frogs are there now? Write the number. 3. Trace the numbers and symbols to show this as an addition sentence.

Name ______________________ **Lesson 49**

CC.K.OA.2

___ + 4 = 9

4 ○ 5 ● 6 ○ 7 ○

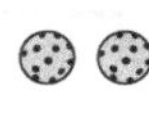

___ + 5 = 7

2 ● 3 ○ 4 ○ 6 ○

4 + 2 = 6

DIRECTIONS 1–2. Mark under the number that would complete the addition sentence. 3. Kelly had some pears. Then she got 2 more pears. Now she has 6 pears. How many pears did Kelly have to start? Complete the addition sentence.

Name ______________________ **Lesson 50**

COMMON CORE STANDARD CC.K.OA.2
Lesson Objective: Solve subtraction word problems within 10 and record the equation.

Algebra • Write More Subtraction Sentences

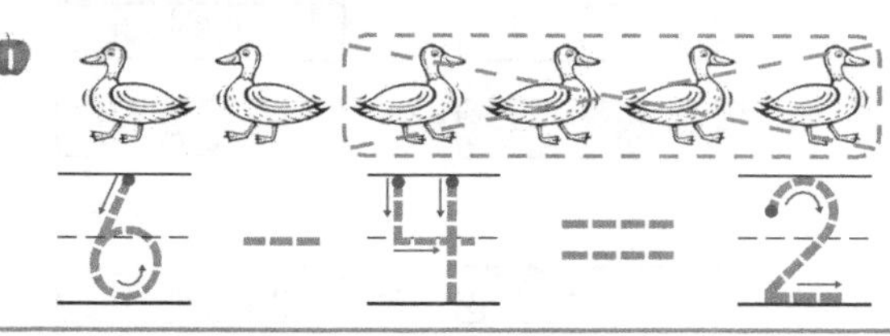

6 − 4 = 2

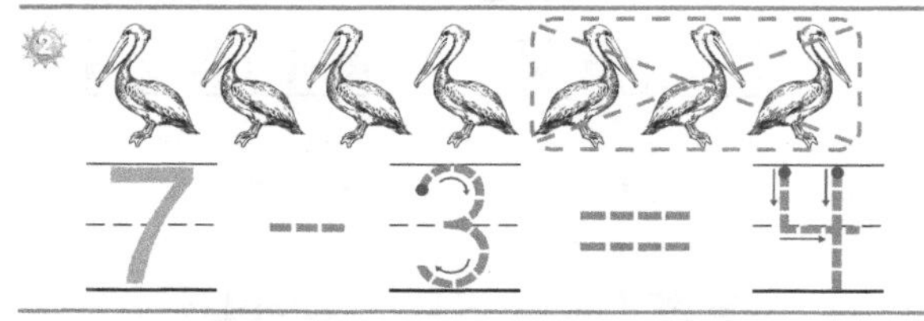

7 − 3 = 4

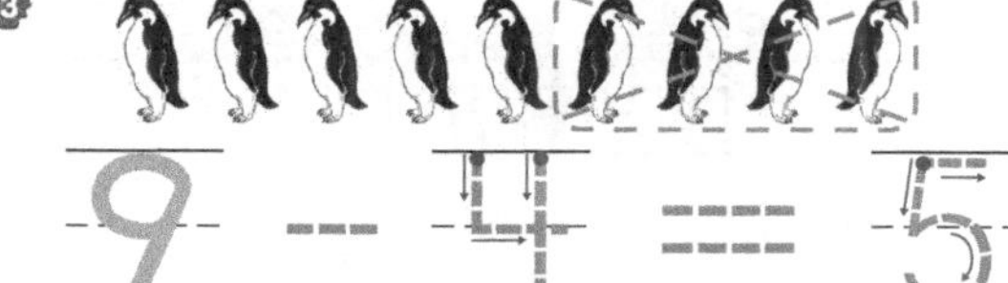

9 − 4 = 5

DIRECTIONS 1. Listen to the subtraction word problem. Some ducks are sitting. Four ducks leave. There are two ducks left. How many ducks are there to start with? Count the entire set to find how many ducks there are to start with. Trace the number. Then trace the circle and X to show how many are being taken from the set. Trace to complete the subtraction sentence. 2–3. Tell a subtraction word problem about the birds. Count the entire set to find how many there are to start with. Write and trace to complete the subtraction sentence.

Name ______________________ **Lesson 50**

CC.K.OA.2

1. ___ − 1 = 3 | 1 ○ 2 ○ 3 ○ 4 ●

2. ___ − 2 = 3 | 5 ● 6 ○ 7 ○ 8 ○

3. ___ − 3 = 4 | 2 ○ 3 ○ 7 ● 10 ○

4.

6 − 4 = 2

DIRECTIONS 1. Mark under the number that shows how many clouds you started with. 2. Mark under the number that shows how many planes you started with. 3. Mark under the number that shows how many birds you started with. 4. Count the entire set to find how many kites there are to begin with. Trace the circle and the X to show how many are being taken from the set. Write and trace to complete the subtraction sentence.

Answer Key

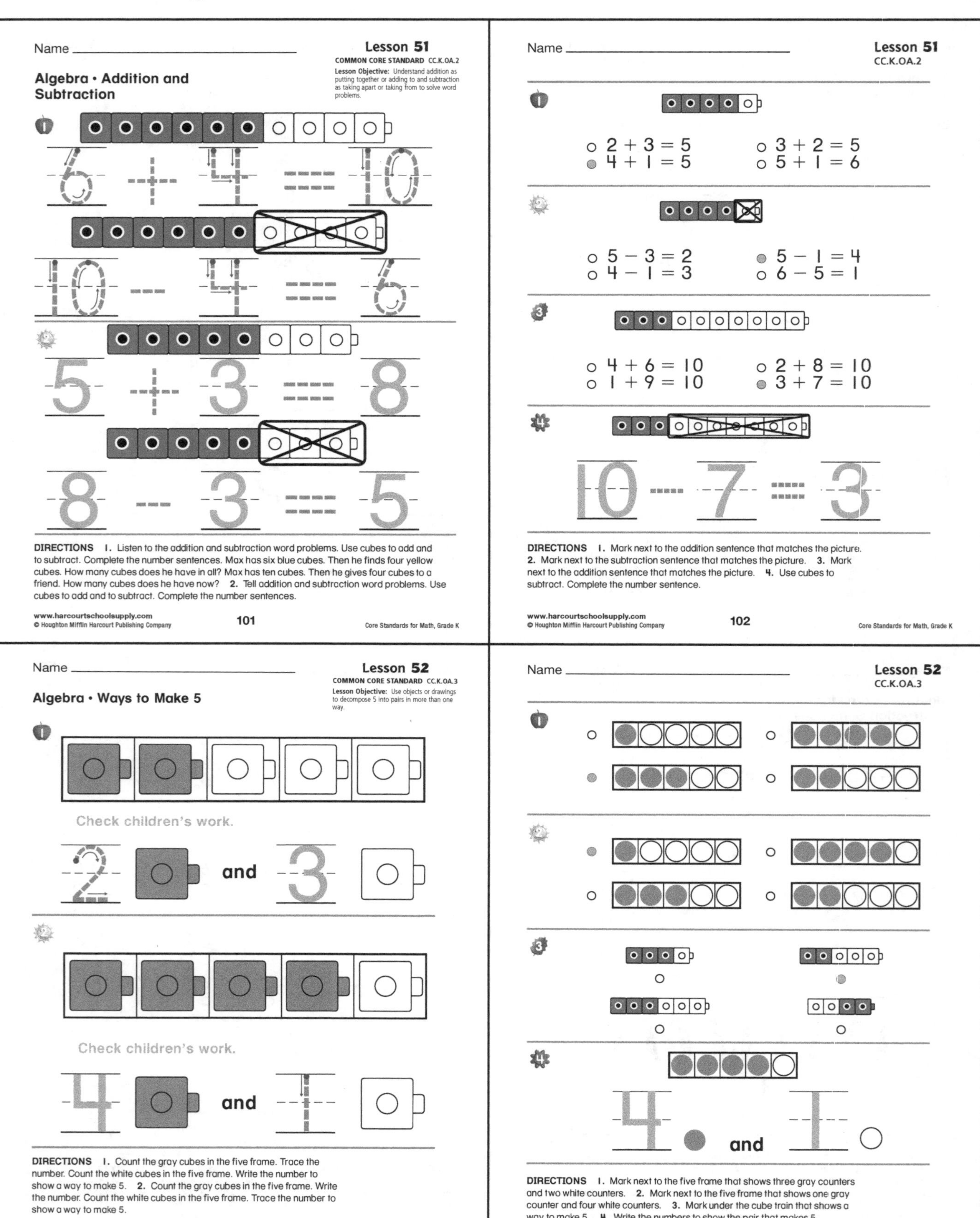

Name ______________________

Lesson 51
COMMON CORE STANDARD CC.K.OA.2
Lesson Objective: Understand addition as putting together or adding to and subtraction as taking apart or taking from to solve word problems.

Algebra • Addition and Subtraction

1. 6 + 4 = 10
   10 − 4 = 6

2. 5 + 3 = 8
   8 − 3 = 5

DIRECTIONS 1. Listen to the addition and subtraction word problems. Use cubes to add and to subtract. Complete the number sentences. Max has six blue cubes. Then he finds four yellow cubes. How many cubes does he have in all? Max has ten cubes. Then he gives four cubes to a friend. How many cubes does he have now? 2. Tell addition and subtraction word problems. Use cubes to add and to subtract. Complete the number sentences.

www.harcourtschoolsupply.com
© Houghton Mifflin Harcourt Publishing Company 101 Core Standards for Math, Grade K

Name ______________________

Lesson 51
CC.K.OA.2

1. ○ 2 + 3 = 5 ○ 3 + 2 = 5
   ● 4 + 1 = 5 ○ 5 + 1 = 6

2. ○ 5 − 3 = 2 ● 5 − 1 = 4
   ○ 4 − 1 = 3 ○ 6 − 5 = 1

3. ○ 4 + 6 = 10 ○ 2 + 8 = 10
   ○ 1 + 9 = 10 ● 3 + 7 = 10

4. 10 − 7 = 3

DIRECTIONS 1. Mark next to the addition sentence that matches the picture. 2. Mark next to the subtraction sentence that matches the picture. 3. Mark next to the addition sentence that matches the picture. 4. Use cubes to subtract. Complete the number sentence.

www.harcourtschoolsupply.com
© Houghton Mifflin Harcourt Publishing Company 102 Core Standards for Math, Grade K

Name ______________________

Lesson 52
COMMON CORE STANDARD CC.K.OA.3
Lesson Objective: Use objects or drawings to decompose 5 into pairs in more than one way.

Algebra • Ways to Make 5

1. Check children's work.
   2 and 3

2. Check children's work.
   4 and 1

DIRECTIONS 1. Count the gray cubes in the five frame. Trace the number. Count the white cubes in the five frame. Write the number to show a way to make 5. 2. Count the gray cubes in the five frame. Write the number. Count the white cubes in the five frame. Trace the number to show a way to make 5.

www.harcourtschoolsupply.com
© Houghton Mifflin Harcourt Publishing Company 103 Core Standards for Math, Grade K

Name ______________________

Lesson 52
CC.K.OA.3

4. 4 and 1

DIRECTIONS 1. Mark next to the five frame that shows three gray counters and two white counters. 2. Mark next to the five frame that shows one gray counter and four white counters. 3. Mark under the cube train that shows a way to make 5. 4. Write the numbers to show the pair that makes 5.

www.harcourtschoolsupply.com
© Houghton Mifflin Harcourt Publishing Company 104 Core Standards for Math, Grade K

Answer Key

Name ____________________

Lesson 53
COMMON CORE STANDARD CC.K.OA.3
Lesson Objective: Decompose numbers within 5 into pairs in more than one way and record each decomposition with an equation.

Algebra • Number Pairs to 5

5 = 1 + 4
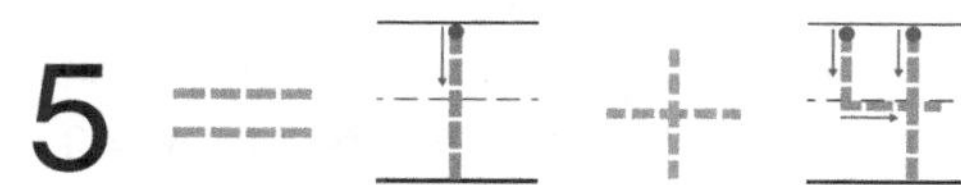

5 = 2 + 3
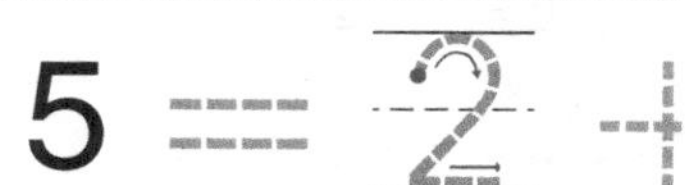

5 = 3 + 2

5 = 4 + 1

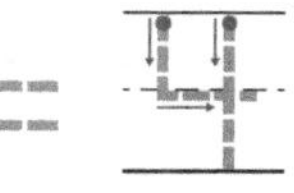
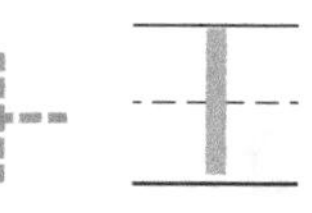

DIRECTIONS Use two-color counters. **1–4.** Place five yellow counters in a row as shown. Look at the gray number. Turn that many counters to red. How many counters are yellow? Trace or write the numbers to show a number pair that makes 5.

Name ____________________

Lesson 53
CC.K.OA.3

1. 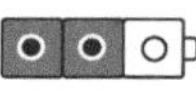
- ● 3 = 2 + 1
- ○ 4 = 3 + 1
- ○ 2 = 1 + 1
- ○ 4 = 2 + 2

2.
- ○ 3 = 1 + 2
- ○ 4 = 2 + 2
- ● 4 = 1 + 3
- ○ 5 = 2 + 3

3.
- ○ 5 = 1 + 4
- ○ 5 = 4 + 1
- ○ 4 = 2 + 2
- ● 5 = 3 + 2

4.
- ● 5 = 4 + 1
- ○ 5 = 2 + 3
- ○ 5 = 3 + 2
- ○ 4 = 3 + 1

5. 
5 = 1 + 4
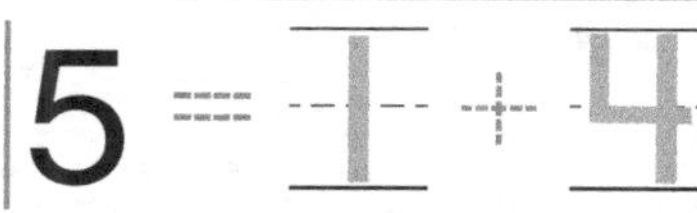

DIRECTIONS **1–4.** Mark beside the addition sentence that shows the number pair for the cube train. **5.** Complete the addition sentence that shows the number pair for the cube train.

Name ____________________

Lesson 54
COMMON CORE STANDARD CC.K.OA.3
Lesson Objective: Decompose 6 and 7 into pairs in more than one way and record each decomposition with an equation.

Algebra • Number Pairs for 6 and 7

6 = 1 + 5

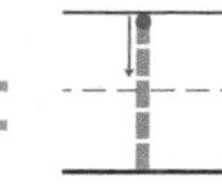
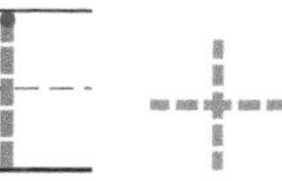

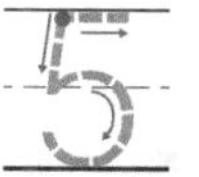

6 = 3 + 3

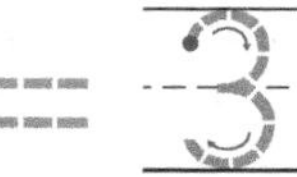

7 = 5 + 2

DIRECTIONS Use two-color counters. **1–2.** Place six yellow counters in a row as shown. Look at the gray number. Turn that many counters to red. How many counters are yellow? Trace or write the numbers to show a number pair that makes 6. **3.** Place seven yellow counters in a row as shown. Look at the gray number. Turn that many counters to red. How many counters are yellow? Trace or write the numbers to show a number pair that makes 7.

Name ____________________

Lesson 54
CC.K.OA.3

1.
- ○ 6 = 2 + 4
- ○ 6 = 5 + 1
- ○ 6 = 4 + 2
- ● 6 = 3 + 3

2.
- ● 6 = 5 + 1
- ○ 6 = 2 + 4
- ○ 6 = 4 + 2
- ○ 6 = 3 + 3

3.
- ○ 7 = 6 + 1
- ● 7 = 4 + 3
- ○ 7 = 5 + 2
- ○ 7 = 2 + 5

4.
- ○ 7 = 3 + 4
- ○ 7 = 4 + 3
- ● 7 = 2 + 5
- ○ 7 = 6 + 1

5.  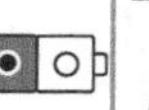
7 = 6 + 1

DIRECTIONS **1–4.** Mark beside the addition sentence that shows the number pair for the cube train. **5.** Complete the addition sentence that shows the number pair for the cube train.

Answer Key

Name ______________________

Lesson 55
COMMON CORE STANDARD CC.K.OA.3
Lesson Objective: Decompose 8 into pairs in more than one way and record each decomposition with an equation.

Algebra • Number Pairs for 8

1. 8 = 1 + 7
2. 8 = 2 + 6
3. 8 = 3 + 5
4. 8 = 4 + 4

DIRECTIONS Use two-color counters. **1–4.** Place eight yellow counters in a row as shown. Look at the gray number. Turn that many counters to red. How many counters are yellow? Trace or write the numbers to show a number pair that makes 8.

www.harcourtschoolsupply.com
© Houghton Mifflin Harcourt Publishing Company 109 Core Standards for Math, Grade K

Name ______________________

Lesson 55
CC.K.OA.3

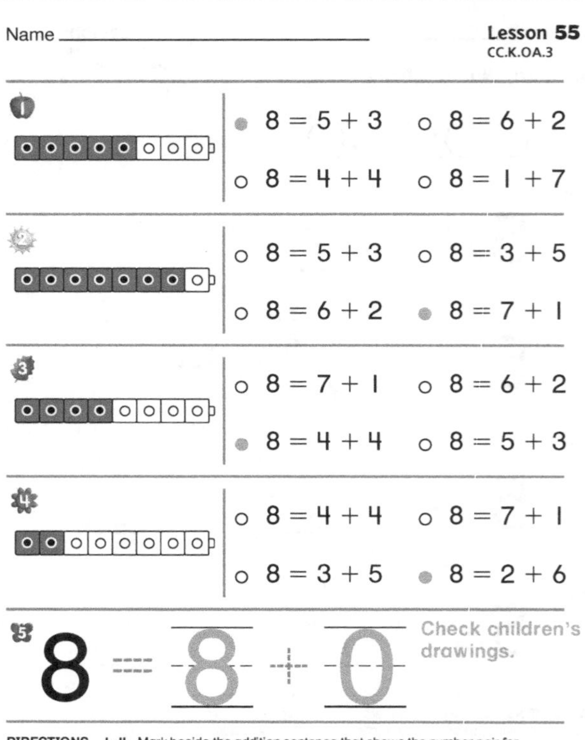

1. ● 8 = 5 + 3 ○ 8 = 6 + 2 ○ 8 = 4 + 4 ○ 8 = 1 + 7
2. ○ 8 = 5 + 3 ○ 8 = 3 + 5 ○ 8 = 6 + 2 ● 8 = 7 + 1
3. ○ 8 = 7 + 1 ○ 8 = 6 + 2 ● 8 = 4 + 4 ○ 8 = 5 + 3
4. ○ 8 = 4 + 4 ○ 8 = 7 + 1 ○ 8 = 3 + 5 ● 8 = 2 + 6
5. 8 = 8 + 0 Check children's drawings.

DIRECTIONS **1–4.** Mark beside the addition sentence that shows the number pair for the cube train. **5.** There are eight pencils in a packet. Eight of the pencils are orange. How many pencils are not orange? Draw and color to show how you solved. Complete the addition sentence to show the number pair.

www.harcourtschoolsupply.com
© Houghton Mifflin Harcourt Publishing Company 110 Core Standards for Math, Grade K

Name ______________________

Lesson 56
COMMON CORE STANDARD CC.K.OA.3
Lesson Objective: Decompose 9 into pairs in more than one way and record each decomposition with an equation.

Algebra • Number Pairs for 9

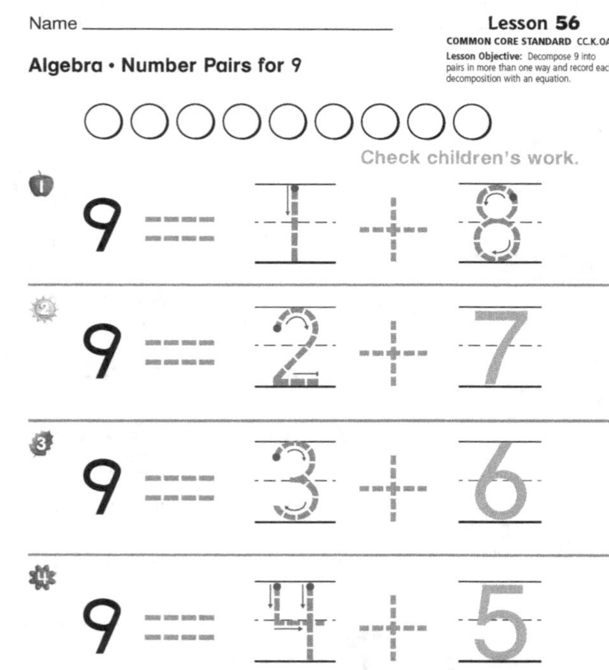

Check children's work.

1. 9 = 1 + 8
2. 9 = 2 + 7
3. 9 = 3 + 6
4. 9 = 4 + 5

DIRECTIONS Use two-color counters. **1–4.** Place nine yellow counters in a row as shown. Look at the gray number. Turn that many counters to red. How many counters are yellow? Trace or write the numbers to show a number pair that makes 9.

www.harcourtschoolsupply.com
© Houghton Mifflin Harcourt Publishing Company 111 Core Standards for Math, Grade K

Name ______________________

Lesson 56
CC.K.OA.3

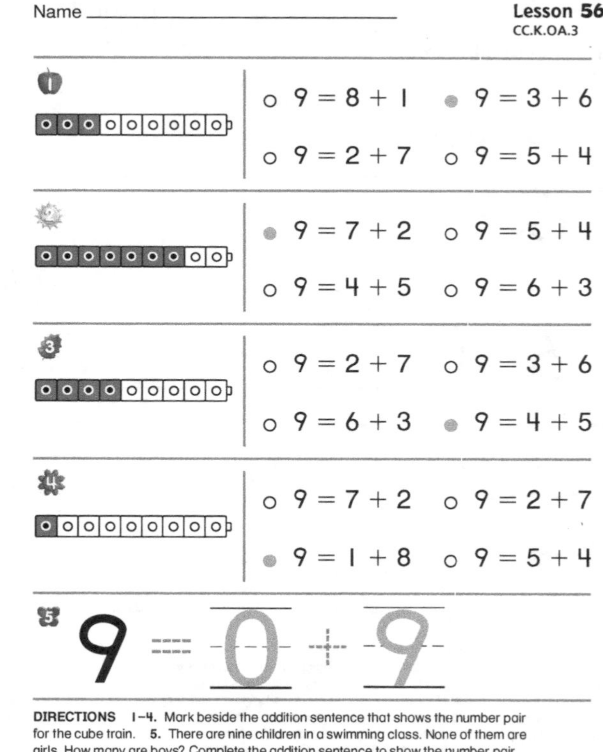

1. ○ 9 = 8 + 1 ● 9 = 3 + 6 ○ 9 = 2 + 7 ○ 9 = 5 + 4
2. ● 9 = 7 + 2 ○ 9 = 5 + 4 ○ 9 = 4 + 5 ○ 9 = 6 + 3
3. ○ 9 = 2 + 7 ○ 9 = 3 + 6 ○ 9 = 6 + 3 ● 9 = 4 + 5
4. ○ 9 = 7 + 2 ○ 9 = 2 + 7 ● 9 = 1 + 8 ○ 9 = 5 + 4
5. 9 = 0 + 9

DIRECTIONS **1–4.** Mark beside the addition sentence that shows the number pair for the cube train. **5.** There are nine children in a swimming class. None of them are girls. How many are boys? Complete the addition sentence to show the number pair.

www.harcourtschoolsupply.com
© Houghton Mifflin Harcourt Publishing Company 112 Core Standards for Math, Grade K

Answer Key

Name ______________________

Lesson 57
COMMON CORE STANDARD CC.K.OA.3
Lesson Objective: Decompose 10 into pairs in more than one way and record each decomposition with an equation.

Algebra • Number Pairs for 10

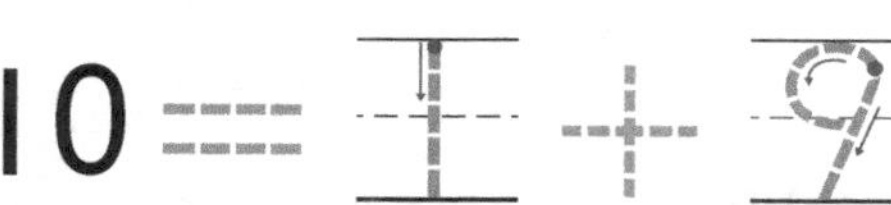

10 = 1 + 9

10 = 2 + 8

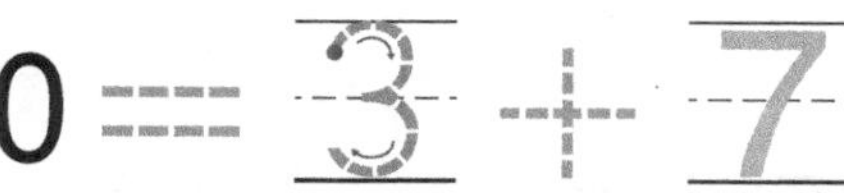

10 = 3 + 7

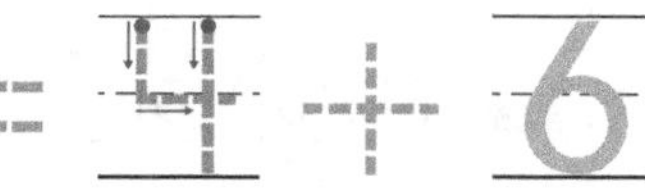

10 = 4 + 6

DIRECTIONS Use two-color counters. **1–4.** Place ten yellow counters in a row as shown. Look at the gray number. Turn that many counters to red. How many counters are yellow? Trace or write the numbers to show a number pair that makes 10.

Name ______________________

Lesson 57
CC.K.OA.3

1. ● 10 = 4 + 6 ○ 10 = 7 + 3 ○ 10 = 5 + 5 ○ 10 = 2 + 8
2. ○ 10 = 7 + 3 ● 10 = 8 + 2 ○ 10 = 9 + 1 ○ 10 = 3 + 7
3. ○ 10 = 5 + 5 ○ 10 = 6 + 4 ● 10 = 3 + 7 ○ 10 = 4 + 6
4. ○ 10 = 6 + 4 ○ 10 = 8 + 2 ○ 10 = 7 + 3 ● 10 = 9 + 1
5. 10 = 5 + 5

DIRECTIONS **1–4.** Mark beside the addition sentence that shows the number pair for the cube train. **5.** Complete the addition sentence that shows the number pair for the cube train.

Name ______________________

Lesson 58
COMMON CORE STANDARD CC.K.OA.4
Lesson Objective: Use a drawing to make 10 from a given number.

Algebra • Ways to Make 10

1. Y Y Y Y Y Y Y R R R

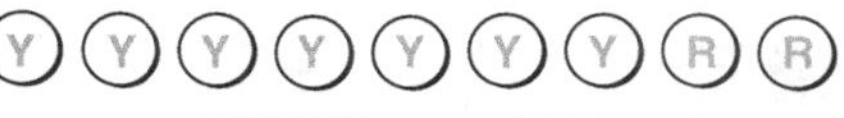

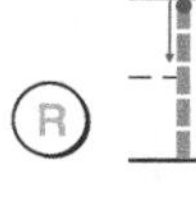

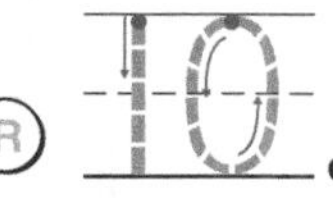

7 yellow, 3 red, 10 counters

2. Y Y Y Y Y Y R R R R

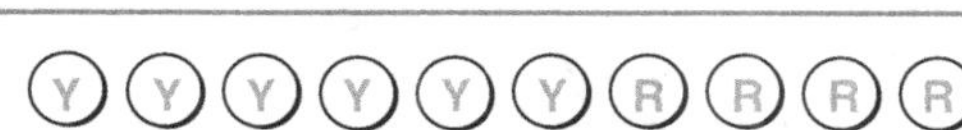

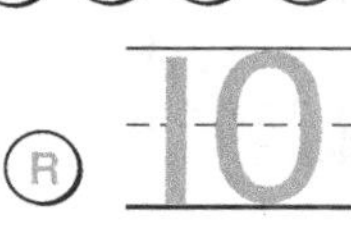

6 yellow, 4 red, 10 counters

3. Y Y Y Y Y Y Y Y R R

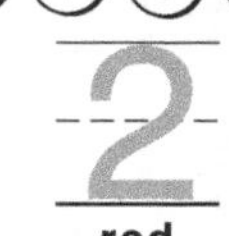

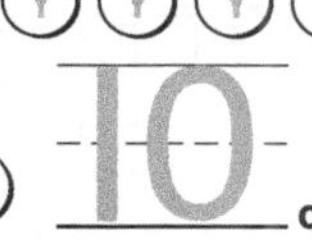

8 yellow, 2 red, 10 counters

DIRECTIONS **1.** Look at the first number. Color that many counters yellow. Color the rest of the counters red. Trace the numbers. **2–3.** Look at the first number. Color that many counters yellow. Color the rest of the counters red. Write how many red counters. Write how many counters in all.

Name ______________________

Lesson 58
CC.K.OA.4

4. 7 + 3 = 10 cubes

DIRECTIONS **1–3.** Mark next to the cube train that shows a way to make 10. **4.** Shade 7 cubes. Do not shade the other cubes. Write the number of shaded cubes. Write the number of unshaded cubes. Write how many in all.

Answer Key

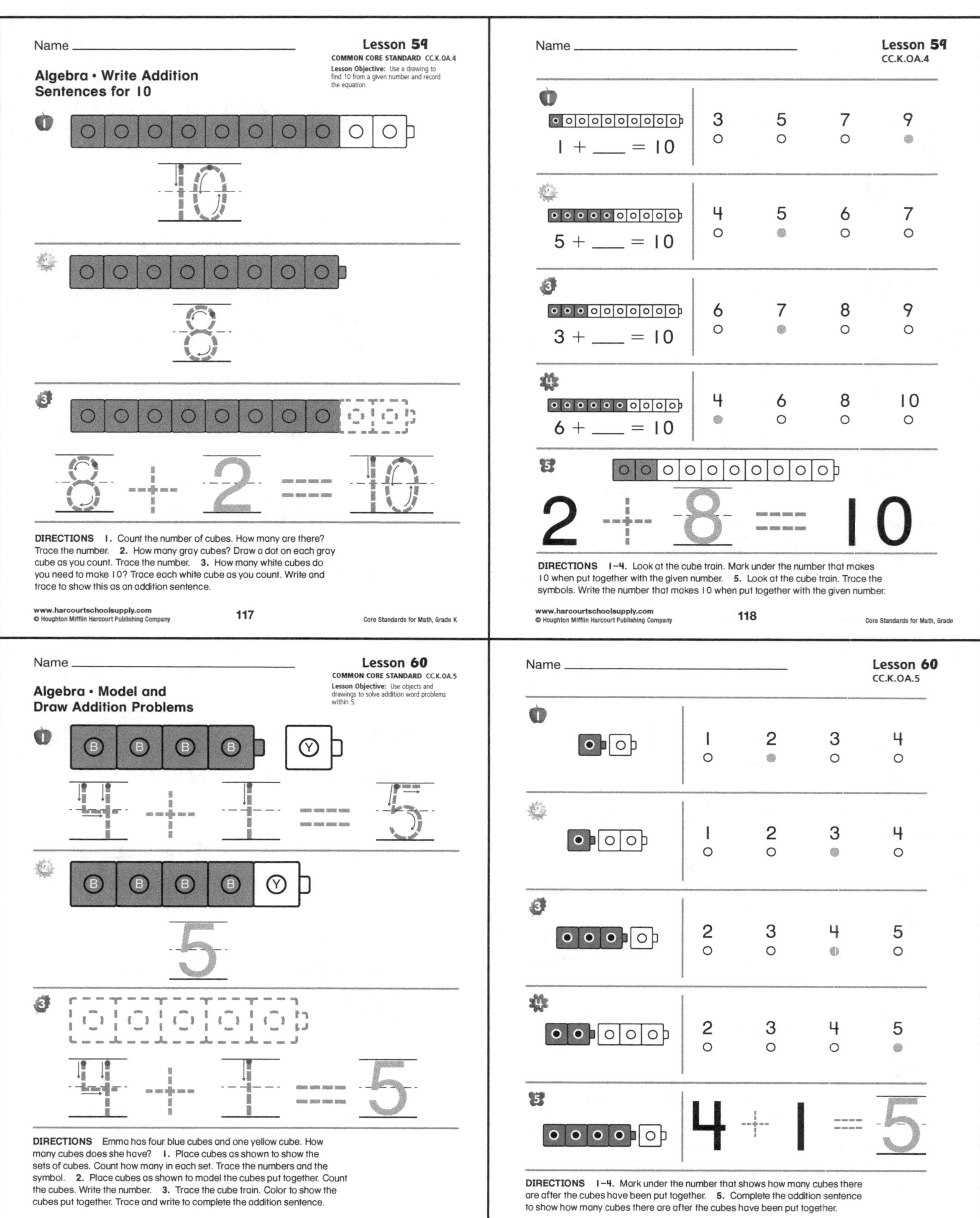

Name ______________________

Lesson 59
COMMON CORE STANDARD CC.K.OA.4
Lesson Objective: Use a drawing to find 10 from a given number and record the equation.

Algebra • Write Addition Sentences for 10

1. 10
2. 8
3. 8 + 2 = 10

DIRECTIONS 1. Count the number of cubes. How many are there? Trace the number. 2. How many gray cubes? Draw a dot on each gray cube as you count. Trace the number. 3. How many white cubes do you need to make 10? Trace each white cube as you count. Write and trace to show this as an addition sentence.

www.harcourtschoolsupply.com
© Houghton Mifflin Harcourt Publishing Company
117
Core Standards for Math, Grade K

Name ______________________

Lesson 59
CC.K.OA.4

1. 1 + ___ = 10 — 3, 5, 7, 9 (9 marked)
2. 5 + ___ = 10 — 4, 5, 6, 7 (5 marked)
3. 3 + ___ = 10 — 6, 7, 8, 9 (7 marked)
4. 6 + ___ = 10 — 4, 6, 8, 10 (4 marked)
5. 2 + 8 = 10

DIRECTIONS 1–4. Look at the cube train. Mark under the number that makes 10 when put together with the given number. 5. Look at the cube train. Trace the symbols. Write the number that makes 10 when put together with the given number.

www.harcourtschoolsupply.com
© Houghton Mifflin Harcourt Publishing Company
118
Core Standards for Math, Grade

Name ______________________

Lesson 60
COMMON CORE STANDARD CC.K.OA.5
Lesson Objective: Use objects and drawings to solve addition word problems within 5.

Algebra • Model and Draw Addition Problems

1. B B B B Y — 4 + 1 = 5
2. B B B B Y — 5
3. 4 + 1 = 5

DIRECTIONS Emma has four blue cubes and one yellow cube. How many cubes does she have? 1. Place cubes as shown to show the sets of cubes. Count how many in each set. Trace the numbers and the symbol. 2. Place cubes as shown to model the cubes put together. Count the cubes. Write the number. 3. Trace the cube train. Color to show the cubes put together. Trace and write to complete the addition sentence.

www.harcourtschoolsupply.com
© Houghton Mifflin Harcourt Publishing Company
119
Core Standards for Math, Grade K

Name ______________________

Lesson 60
CC.K.OA.5

1. 1, 2, 3, 4 (2 marked)
2. 1, 2, 3, 4 (3 marked)
3. 2, 3, 4, 5 (4 marked)
4. 2, 3, 4, 5 (5 marked)
5. 4 + 1 = 5

DIRECTIONS 1–4. Mark under the number that shows how many cubes there are after the cubes have been put together. 5. Complete the addition sentence to show how many cubes there are after the cubes have been put together.

www.harcourtschoolsupply.com
© Houghton Mifflin Harcourt Publishing Company
120
Core Standards for Math, Grade K

Name ______________________

Lesson 61
COMMON CORE STANDARD CC.K.OA.5
Lesson Objective: Solve addition word problems within 5 and record the equation.

Algebra • Write Addition Sentences

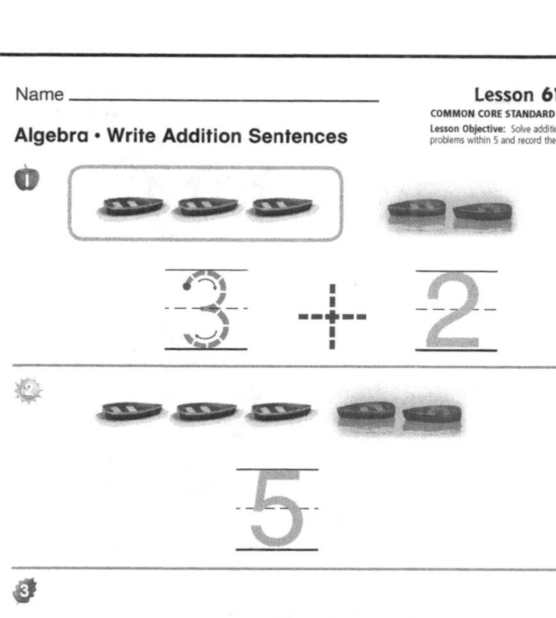

DIRECTIONS There are three boats. Some more boats come. Now there are five boats. How many more boats come? **1.** Circle the boats you start with. Trace the number. How many boats are being added to the set? Write the number. **2.** How many boats are there now? Write the number. **3.** Trace the numbers and symbols to show this as an addition sentence.

Name ______________________

Lesson 61
CC.K.OA.5

1 + ___ = 5

1 ○ 2 ○ 3 ○ 4 ●

2 + ___ = 4

1 ○ 2 ● 3 ○ 4 ○

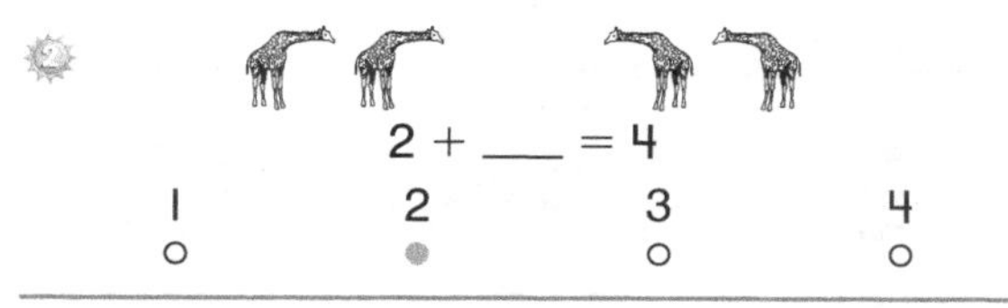

3 + ___ = 4

1 ● 2 ○ 3 ○ 4 ○

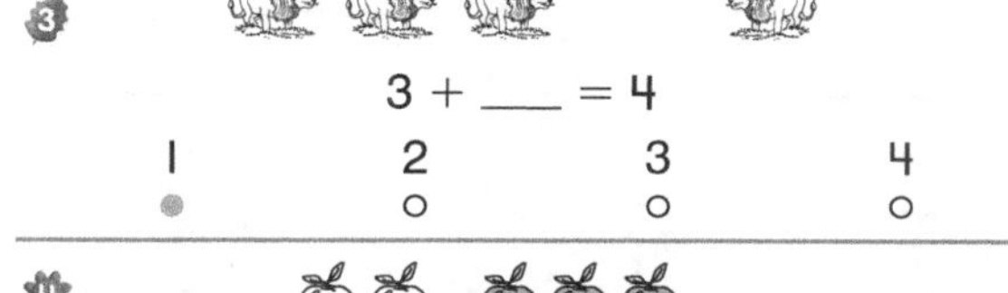

2 + 3 = 5

DIRECTIONS **1–3.** Mark under the number that would complete the addition sentence. **4.** Ian has 2 apples. Then he buys more apples. Now he has 5 apples. How many apples does Ian buy? Complete the addition sentence.

Name ______________________

Lesson 62
COMMON CORE STANDARD CC.K.OA.5
Lesson Objective: Use objects and drawings to solve subtraction word problems within 5.

Algebra • Model and Draw Subtraction Problems

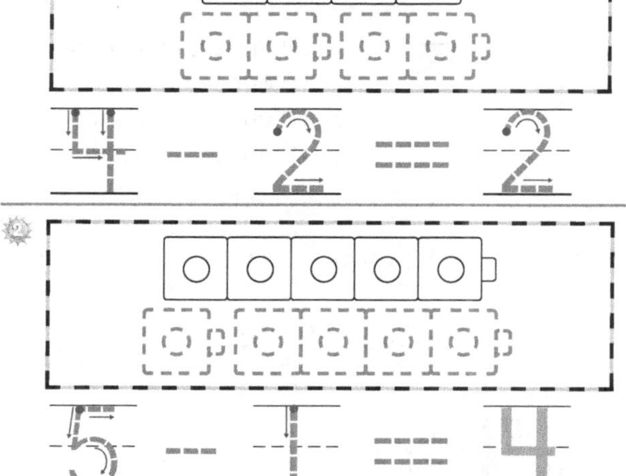

4 − 2 = 2

5 − 1 = 4

DIRECTIONS Model the subtraction word problem with cubes. **1.** There are four race cars. Two race cars are blue and the rest are green. How many race cars are green? Start with four cubes. Take apart a two-cube train. How many cubes are left? Trace the cube trains. Trace to complete the subtraction sentence. **2.** There are five rockets. One rocket is orange and the rest are red. How many rockets are red? Start with a five-cube train. Take apart one cube. How many cubes are left? Trace the cube trains. Trace and write to complete the subtraction sentence.

Name ______________________

Lesson 62
CC.K.OA.5

1. 1 ● 2 ○ 3 ○ 4 ○
2. 2 ● 3 ○ 5 ○ 7 ○
3. 2 ○ 3 ● 4 ○ 5 ○
4. 5 ○ 4 ○ 2 ○ 1 ●
5. 5 − 1 = 4

DIRECTIONS **1–4.** Mark under the number that shows how many gray cubes are left after the cubes have been taken apart. **5.** One cube is gray and the rest are white. How many cubes are white? Trace and write to complete the subtraction sentence.

Answer Key

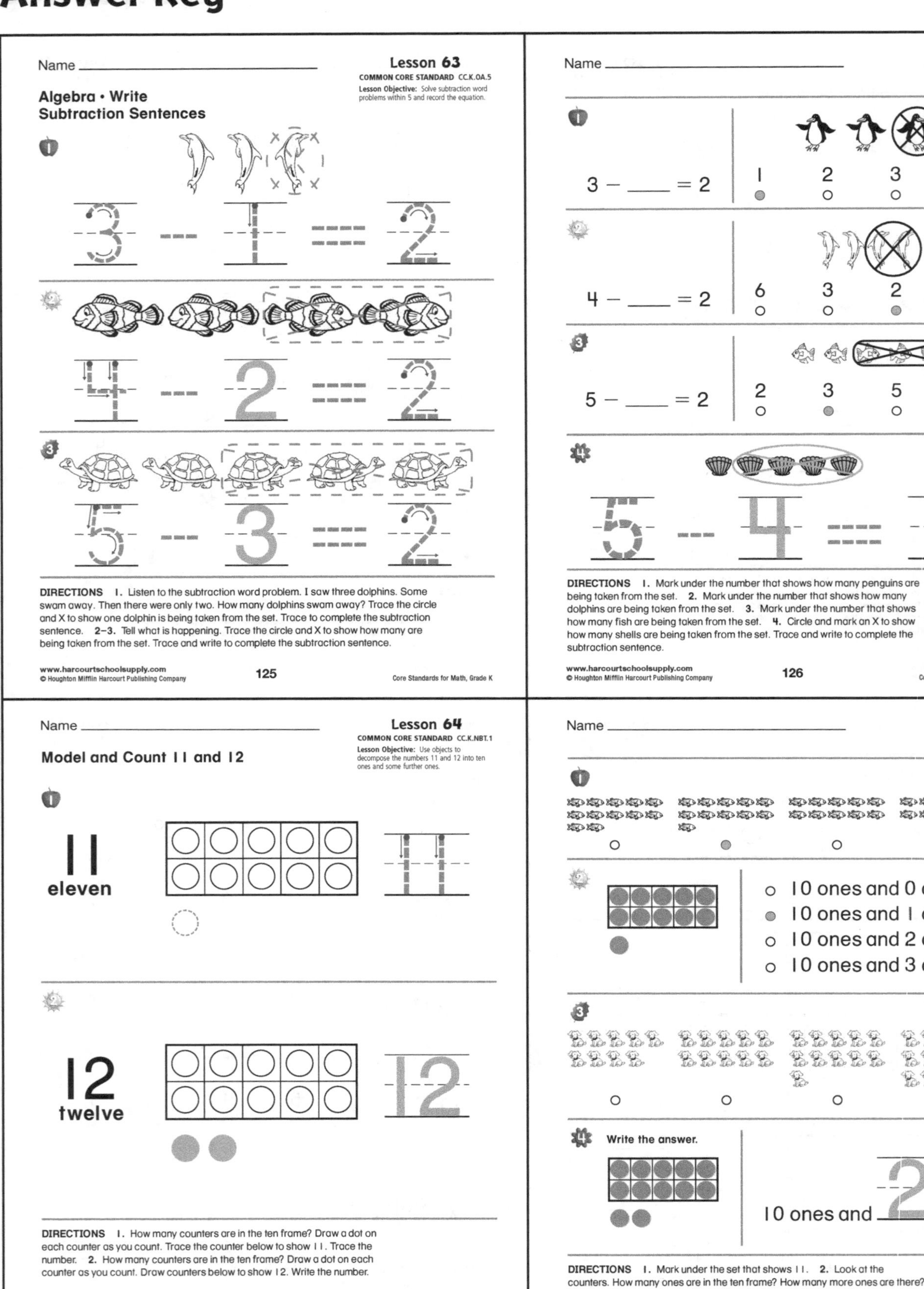

Name ______________________

Lesson 63
COMMON CORE STANDARD CC.K.OA.5
Lesson Objective: Solve subtraction word problems within 5 and record the equation.

Algebra • Write Subtraction Sentences

1. 3 − 1 = 2

2. 4 − 2 = 2

3. 5 − 3 = 2

DIRECTIONS 1. Listen to the subtraction word problem. I saw three dolphins. Some swam away. Then there were only two. How many dolphins swam away? Trace the circle and X to show one dolphin is being taken from the set. Trace to complete the subtraction sentence. 2–3. Tell what is happening. Trace the circle and X to show how many are being taken from the set. Trace and write to complete the subtraction sentence.

www.harcourtschoolsupply.com
© Houghton Mifflin Harcourt Publishing Company
125
Core Standards for Math, Grade K

Name ______________________

Lesson 63
CC.K.OA.5

1. 3 − ____ = 2 — 1 2 3 4

2. 4 − ____ = 2 — 6 3 2 1

3. 5 − ____ = 2 — 2 3 5 8

4. 5 − 4 = 1

DIRECTIONS 1. Mark under the number that shows how many penguins are being taken from the set. 2. Mark under the number that shows how many dolphins are being taken from the set. 3. Mark under the number that shows how many fish are being taken from the set. 4. Circle and mark an X to show how many shells are being taken from the set. Trace and write to complete the subtraction sentence.

www.harcourtschoolsupply.com
© Houghton Mifflin Harcourt Publishing Company
126
Core Standards for Math, Grade K

Name ______________________

Lesson 64
COMMON CORE STANDARD CC.K.NBT.1
Lesson Objective: Use objects to decompose the numbers 11 and 12 into ten ones and some further ones.

Model and Count 11 and 12

1. 11 eleven — 11

2. 12 twelve — 12

DIRECTIONS 1. How many counters are in the ten frame? Draw a dot on each counter as you count. Trace the counter below to show 11. Trace the number. 2. How many counters are in the ten frame? Draw a dot on each counter as you count. Draw counters below to show 12. Write the number.

www.harcourtschoolsupply.com
© Houghton Mifflin Harcourt Publishing Company
127
Core Standards for Math, Grade K

Name ______________________

Lesson 64
CC.K.NBT.1

1.

2.
- 10 ones and 0 ones
- 10 ones and 1 one
- 10 ones and 2 ones
- 10 ones and 3 ones

3.

4. Write the answer.

10 ones and 2 ones

DIRECTIONS 1. Mark under the set that shows 11. 2. Look at the counters. How many ones are in the ten frame? How many more ones are there? Mark next to your answer. 3. Mark under the set that shows 12. 4. Look at the counters. How many more ones than 10 ones are there? Write the number.

www.harcourtschoolsupply.com
© Houghton Mifflin Harcourt Publishing Company
128
Core Standards for Math, Grade K

Name ____________________ **Lesson 65**
COMMON CORE STANDARD CC.K.NBT.1
Lesson Objective: Use objects to decompose the numbers 13 and 14 into ten ones and some further ones.

Model and Count 13 and 14

13
thirteen

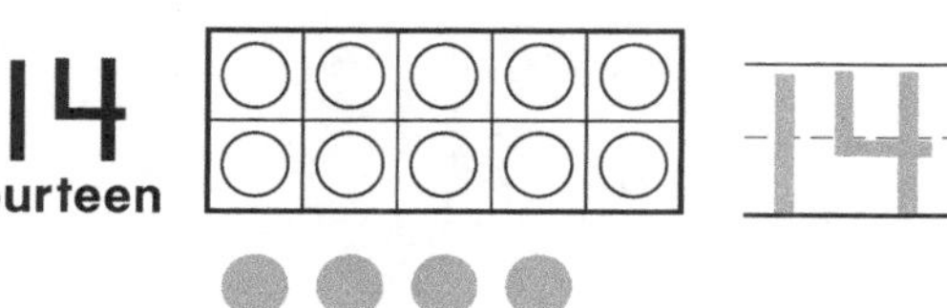

14
fourteen

DIRECTIONS 1. How many counters are in the ten frame? Draw a dot on each counter as you count. Trace the counters below to show 13. Trace the number. 2. How many counters are in the ten frame? Draw a dot on each counter as you count. Draw counters below to show 14. Write the number.

Name ____________________ **Lesson 65**
CC.K.NBT.1

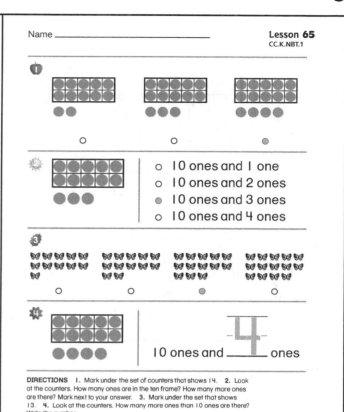

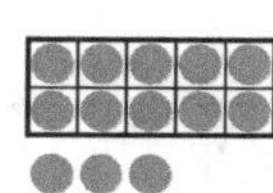

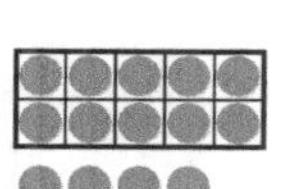

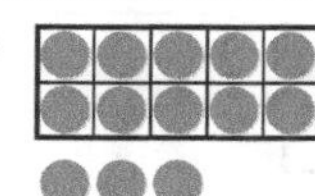

- ○ 10 ones and 1 one
- ○ 10 ones and 2 ones
- ● 10 ones and 3 ones
- ○ 10 ones and 4 ones

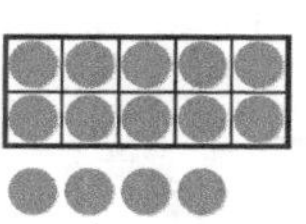

10 ones and 4 ones

DIRECTIONS 1. Mark under the set of counters that shows 14. 2. Look at the counters. How many ones are in the ten frame? How many more ones are there? Mark next to your answer. 3. Mark under the set that shows 13. 4. Look at the counters. How many more ones than 10 ones are there? Write the number.

Name ____________________ **Lesson 66**
COMMON CORE STANDARD CC.K.N
Lesson Objective: Use objects to decompose 15 into ten ones and some fur ones and represent 15 with a number nan and a written numeral.

Model, Count, and Write 15

15
fifteen

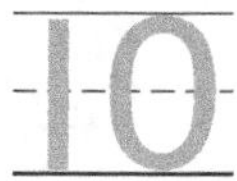

10

5

10 + 5 = 15

DIRECTIONS 1. Count and tell how many. Draw a dot on each object as you count. Trace the number. 2. Look at the objects in the ten frame in Exercise 1. Count and write the number. 3. Look at the objects below the ten frame in Exercise 1. Count and write the number. 4. Look at the ten ones and some more ones in Exercise 1. Complete the addition sentence to match.

Name ____________________ **Lesson 66**
CC.K.NBT.1

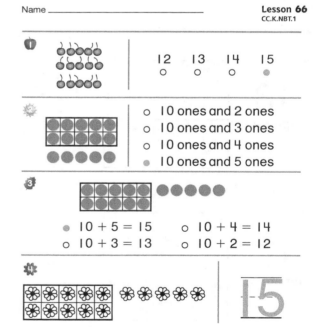

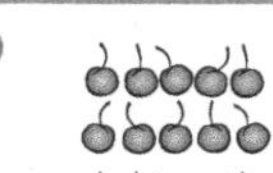

12 ○ 13 ○ 14 ○ 15 ●

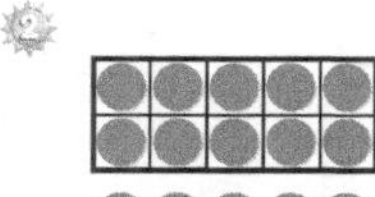

- ○ 10 ones and 2 ones
- ○ 10 ones and 3 ones
- ○ 10 ones and 4 ones
- ● 10 ones and 5 ones

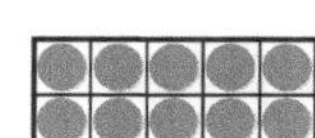

● 10 + 5 = 15 ○ 10 + 4 = 14
○ 10 + 3 = 13 ○ 10 + 2 = 12

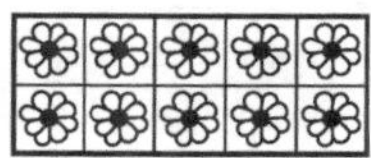

15

DIRECTIONS 1. Count. Mark under the number that tells how many. 2. Look at the counters. How many ones are in the ten frame? How many more ones are there? Mark next to your answer. 3. Look at the ten ones and some more ones. Mark next to the addition sentence that matches. 4. Count. Write the number that tells how many.

Answer Key

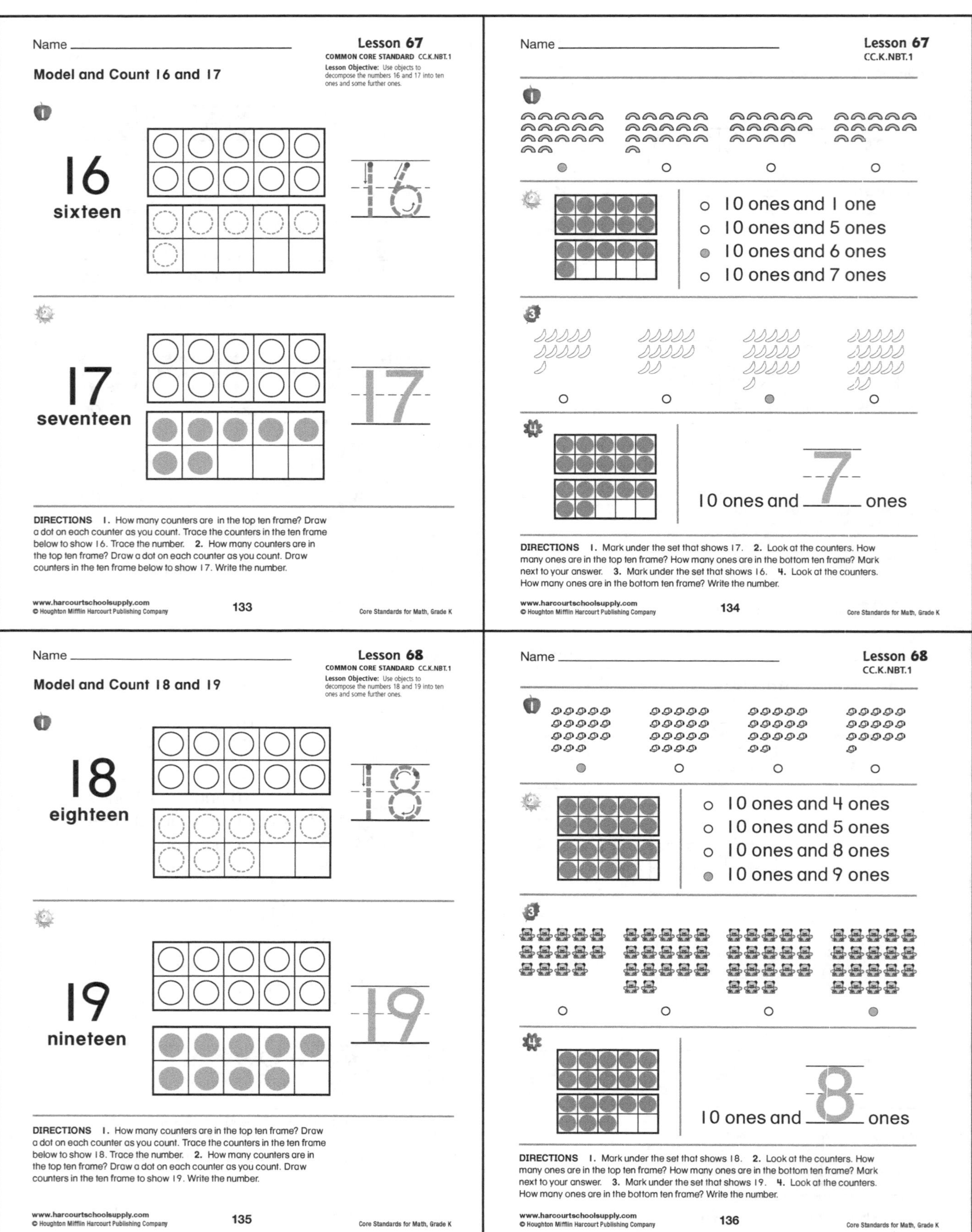

Name ______________________

Lesson 67
COMMON CORE STANDARD CC.K.NBT.1
Lesson Objective: Use objects to decompose the numbers 16 and 17 into ten ones and some further ones.

Model and Count 16 and 17

1. 16 sixteen — 16

2. 17 seventeen — 17

DIRECTIONS 1. How many counters are in the top ten frame? Draw a dot on each counter as you count. Trace the counters in the ten frame below to show 16. Trace the number. 2. How many counters are in the top ten frame? Draw a dot on each counter as you count. Draw counters in the ten frame below to show 17. Write the number.

www.harcourtschoolsupply.com
© Houghton Mifflin Harcourt Publishing Company
133
Core Standards for Math, Grade K

Name ______________________

Lesson 67
CC.K.NBT.1

1.

2.
- ○ 10 ones and 1 one
- ○ 10 ones and 5 ones
- ● 10 ones and 6 ones
- ○ 10 ones and 7 ones

3.

4. 10 ones and 7 ones

DIRECTIONS 1. Mark under the set that shows 17. 2. Look at the counters. How many ones are in the top ten frame? How many ones are in the bottom ten frame? Mark next to your answer. 3. Mark under the set that shows 16. 4. Look at the counters. How many ones are in the bottom ten frame? Write the number.

www.harcourtschoolsupply.com
© Houghton Mifflin Harcourt Publishing Company
134
Core Standards for Math, Grade K

Name ______________________

Lesson 68
COMMON CORE STANDARD CC.K.NBT.1
Lesson Objective: Use objects to decompose the numbers 18 and 19 into ten ones and some further ones.

Model and Count 18 and 19

1. 18 eighteen — 18

2. 19 nineteen — 19

DIRECTIONS 1. How many counters are in the top ten frame? Draw a dot on each counter as you count. Trace the counters in the ten frame below to show 18. Trace the number. 2. How many counters are in the top ten frame? Draw a dot on each counter as you count. Draw counters in the ten frame to show 19. Write the number.

www.harcourtschoolsupply.com
© Houghton Mifflin Harcourt Publishing Company
135
Core Standards for Math, Grade K

Name ______________________

Lesson 68
CC.K.NBT.1

1.

2.
- ○ 10 ones and 4 ones
- ○ 10 ones and 5 ones
- ○ 10 ones and 8 ones
- ● 10 ones and 9 ones

3.

4. 10 ones and 8 ones

DIRECTIONS 1. Mark under the set that shows 18. 2. Look at the counters. How many ones are in the top ten frame? How many ones are in the bottom ten frame? Mark next to your answer. 3. Mark under the set that shows 19. 4. Look at the counters. How many ones are in the bottom ten frame? Write the number.

www.harcourtschoolsupply.com
© Houghton Mifflin Harcourt Publishing Company
136
Core Standards for Math, Grade K

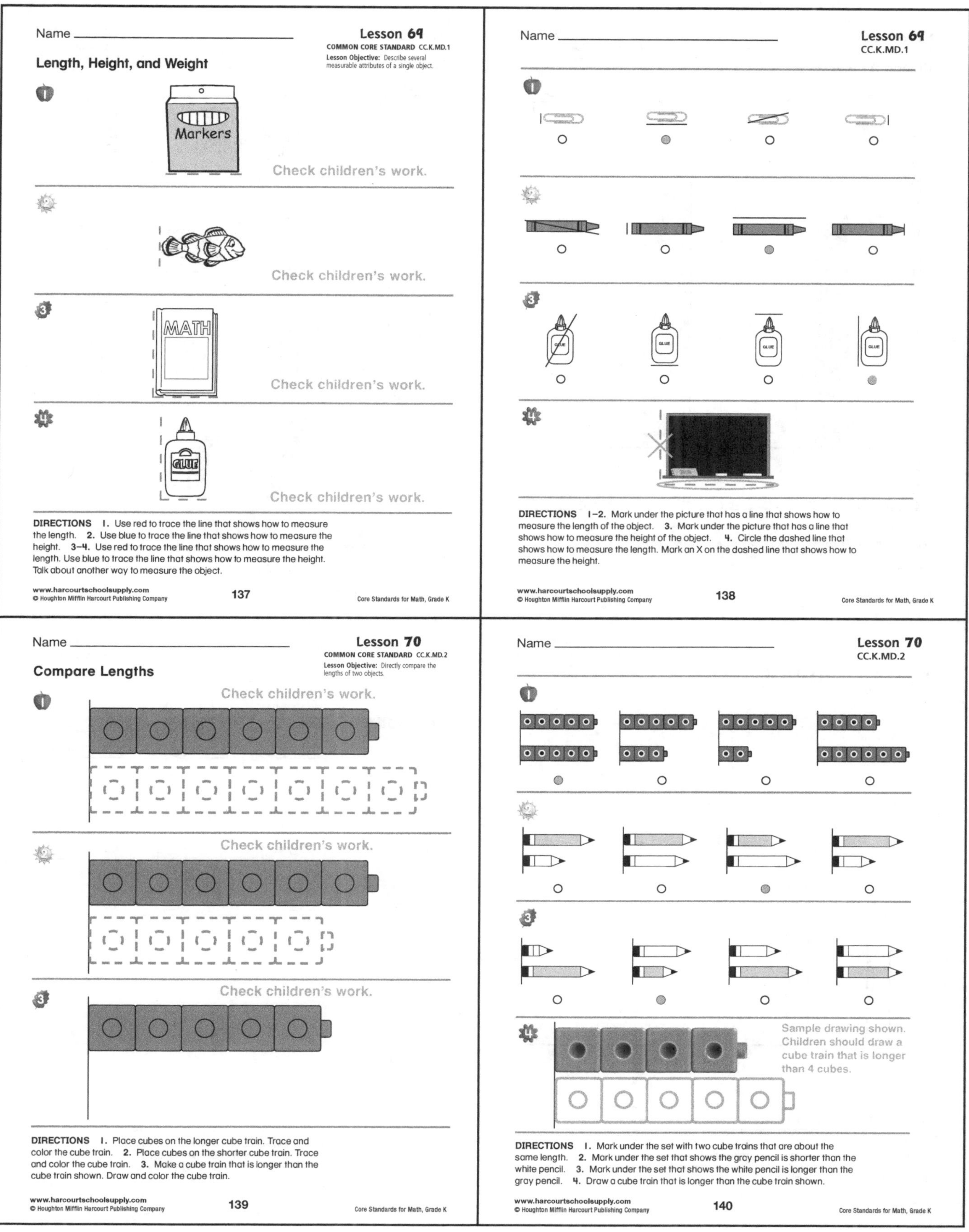

Name ____________________

Lesson 69

COMMON CORE STANDARD CC.K.MD.1

Lesson Objective: Describe several measurable attributes of a single object.

Length, Height, and Weight

1. Markers — Check children's work.

2. Check children's work.

3. MATH — Check children's work.

4. GLUE — Check children's work.

DIRECTIONS **1.** Use red to trace the line that shows how to measure the length. **2.** Use blue to trace the line that shows how to measure the height. **3–4.** Use red to trace the line that shows how to measure the length. Use blue to trace the line that shows how to measure the height. Talk about another way to measure the object.

www.harcourtschoolsupply.com
© Houghton Mifflin Harcourt Publishing Company 137 Core Standards for Math, Grade K

Name ____________________

Lesson 69

CC.K.MD.1

GLUE

DIRECTIONS **1–2.** Mark under the picture that has a line that shows how to measure the length of the object. **3.** Mark under the picture that has a line that shows how to measure the height of the object. **4.** Circle the dashed line that shows how to measure the length. Mark an X on the dashed line that shows how to measure the height.

www.harcourtschoolsupply.com
© Houghton Mifflin Harcourt Publishing Company 138 Core Standards for Math, Grade K

Name ____________________

Lesson 70

COMMON CORE STANDARD CC.K.MD.2

Lesson Objective: Directly compare the lengths of two objects.

Compare Lengths

1. Check children's work.

2. Check children's work.

3. Check children's work.

DIRECTIONS **1.** Place cubes on the longer cube train. Trace and color the cube train. **2.** Place cubes on the shorter cube train. Trace and color the cube train. **3.** Make a cube train that is longer than the cube train shown. Draw and color the cube train.

www.harcourtschoolsupply.com
© Houghton Mifflin Harcourt Publishing Company 139 Core Standards for Math, Grade K

Name ____________________

Lesson 70

CC.K.MD.2

4. Sample drawing shown. Children should draw a cube train that is longer than 4 cubes.

DIRECTIONS **1.** Mark under the set with two cube trains that are about the same length. **2.** Mark under the set that shows the gray pencil is shorter than the white pencil. **3.** Mark under the set that shows the white pencil is longer than the gray pencil. **4.** Draw a cube train that is longer than the cube train shown.

www.harcourtschoolsupply.com
© Houghton Mifflin Harcourt Publishing Company 140 Core Standards for Math, Grade K

Answer Key

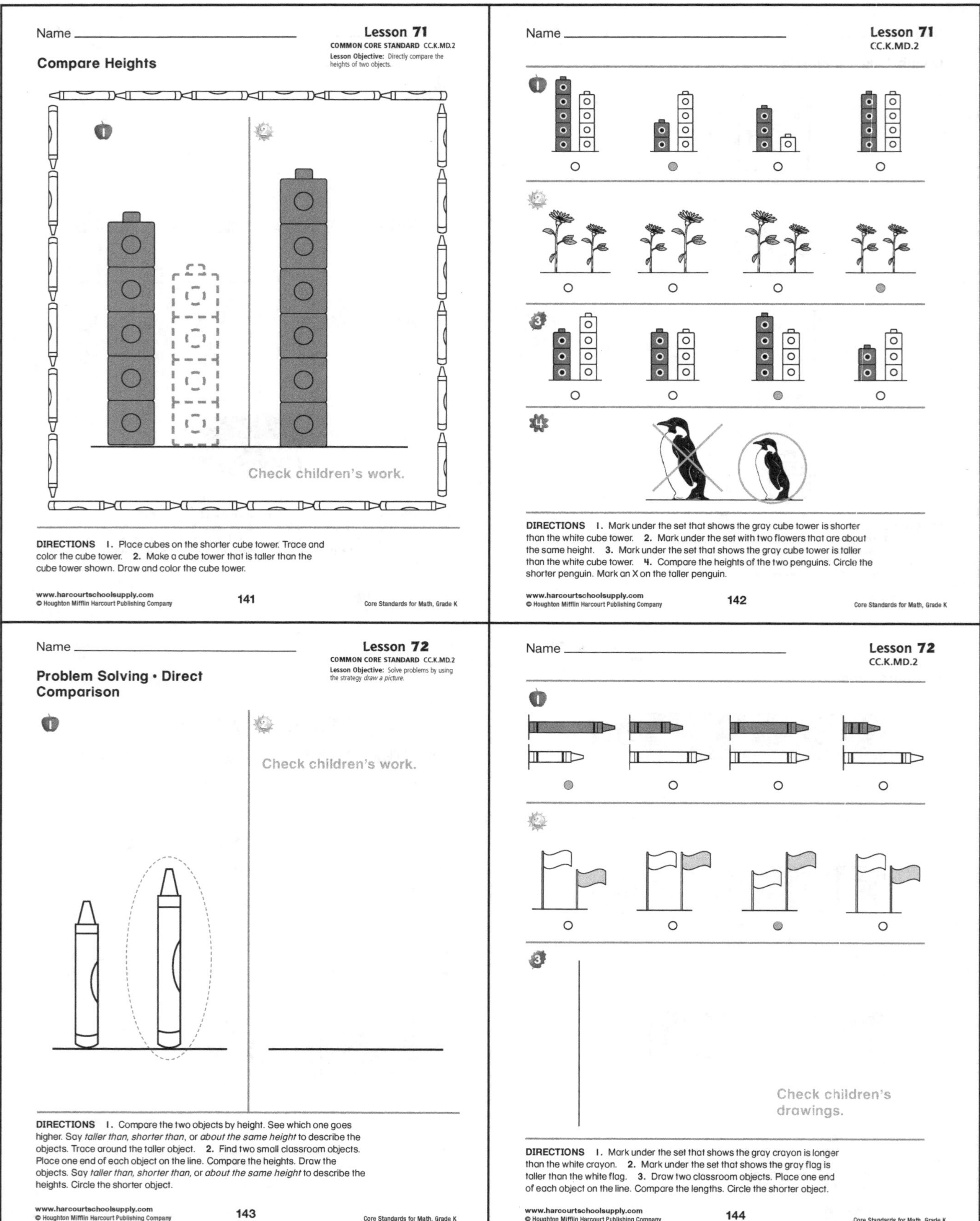

Name ______________________

Lesson 71

COMMON CORE STANDARD CC.K.MD.2

Lesson Objective: Directly compare the heights of two objects.

Compare Heights

Check children's work.

DIRECTIONS 1. Place cubes on the shorter cube tower. Trace and color the cube tower. 2. Make a cube tower that is taller than the cube tower shown. Draw and color the cube tower.

www.harcourtschoolsupply.com
© Houghton Mifflin Harcourt Publishing Company

141

Core Standards for Math, Grade K

Name ______________________

Lesson 71

CC.K.MD.2

DIRECTIONS 1. Mark under the set that shows the gray cube tower is shorter than the white cube tower. 2. Mark under the set with two flowers that are about the same height. 3. Mark under the set that shows the gray cube tower is taller than the white cube tower. 4. Compare the heights of the two penguins. Circle the shorter penguin. Mark an X on the taller penguin.

www.harcourtschoolsupply.com
© Houghton Mifflin Harcourt Publishing Company

142

Core Standards for Math, Grade K

Name ______________________

Lesson 72

COMMON CORE STANDARD CC.K.MD.2

Lesson Objective: Solve problems by using the strategy *draw a picture.*

Problem Solving • Direct Comparison

Check children's work.

DIRECTIONS 1. Compare the two objects by height. See which one goes higher. Say *taller than, shorter than,* or *about the same height* to describe the objects. Trace around the taller object. 2. Find two small classroom objects. Place one end of each object on the line. Compare the heights. Draw the objects. Say *taller than, shorter than,* or *about the same height* to describe the heights. Circle the shorter object.

www.harcourtschoolsupply.com
© Houghton Mifflin Harcourt Publishing Company

143

Core Standards for Math, Grade K

Name ______________________

Lesson 72

CC.K.MD.2

Check children's drawings.

DIRECTIONS 1. Mark under the set that shows the gray crayon is longer than the white crayon. 2. Mark under the set that shows the gray flag is taller than the white flag. 3. Draw two classroom objects. Place one end of each object on the line. Compare the lengths. Circle the shorter object.

www.harcourtschoolsupply.com
© Houghton Mifflin Harcourt Publishing Company

144

Core Standards for Math, Grade K

Answer Key

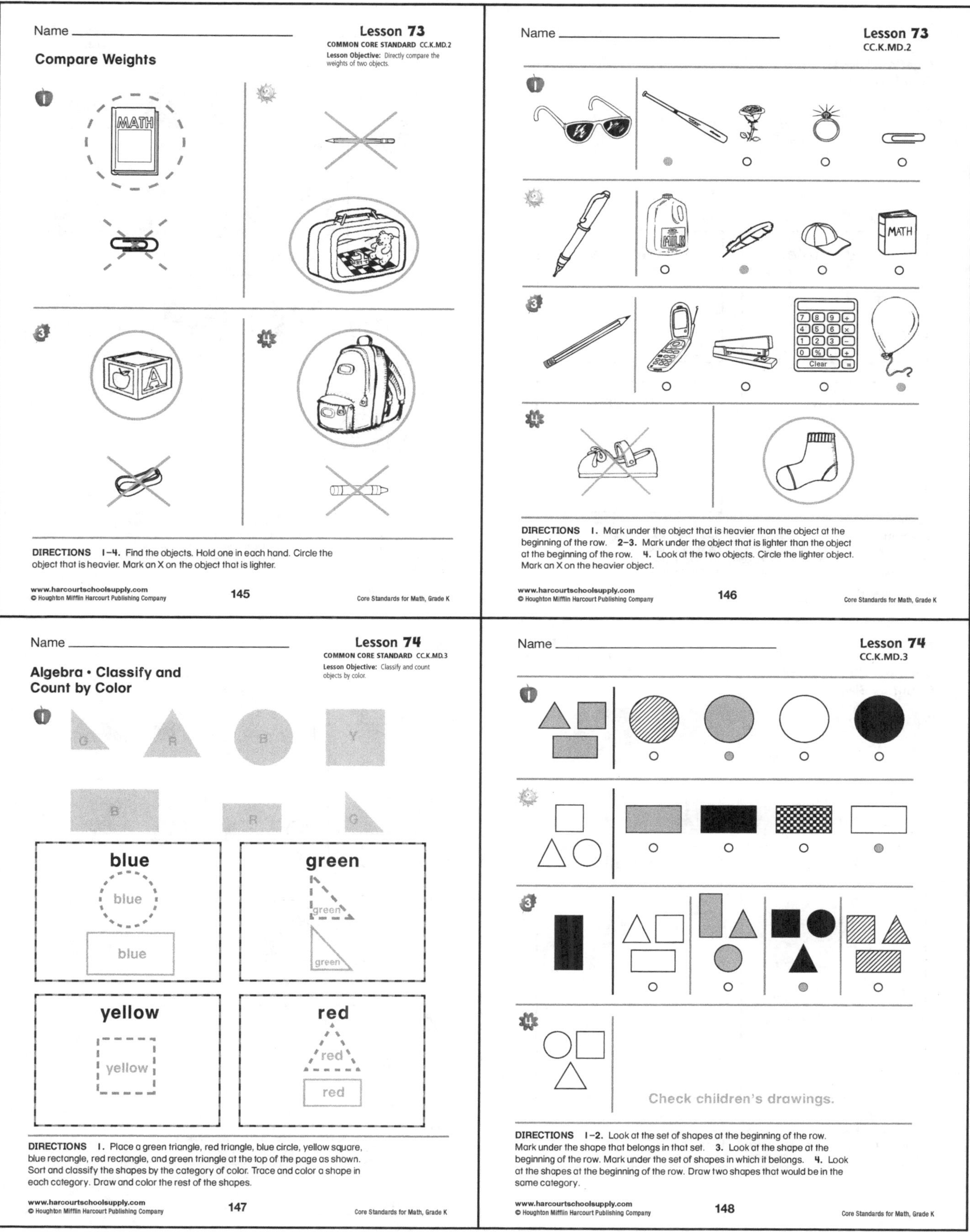
Name
Lesson 73
COMMON CORE STANDARD CC.K.MD.2
Compare Weights
Lesson Objective: Directly compare the weights of two objects.
MATH
DIRECTIONS 1–4. Find the objects. Hold one in each hand. Circle the object that is heavier. Mark an X on the object that is lighter.
www.harcourtschoolsupply.com
© Houghton Mifflin Harcourt Publishing Company
145
Core Standards for Math, Grade K
Name
Lesson 73
CC.K.MD.2
MATH
MILK
Clear
DIRECTIONS 1. Mark under the object that is heavier than the object at the beginning of the row. 2–3. Mark under the object that is lighter than the object at the beginning of the row. 4. Look at the two objects. Circle the lighter object. Mark an X on the heavier object.
www.harcourtschoolsupply.com
© Houghton Mifflin Harcourt Publishing Company
146
Core Standards for Math, Grade K
Name
Lesson 74
COMMON CORE STANDARD CC.K.MD.3
Algebra • Classify and Count by Color
Lesson Objective: Classify and count objects by color.
blue
green
yellow
red
DIRECTIONS 1. Place a green triangle, red triangle, blue circle, yellow square, blue rectangle, red rectangle, and green triangle at the top of the page as shown. Sort and classify the shapes by the category of color. Trace and color a shape in each category. Draw and color the rest of the shapes.
www.harcourtschoolsupply.com
© Houghton Mifflin Harcourt Publishing Company
147
Core Standards for Math, Grade K
Name
Lesson 74
CC.K.MD.3
Check children's drawings.
DIRECTIONS 1–2. Look at the set of shapes at the beginning of the row. Mark under the shape that belongs in that set. 3. Look at the shape at the beginning of the row. Mark under the set of shapes in which it belongs. 4. Look at the shapes at the beginning of the row. Draw two shapes that would be in the same category.
www.harcourtschoolsupply.com
© Houghton Mifflin Harcourt Publishing Company
148
Core Standards for Math, Grade K

Answer Key

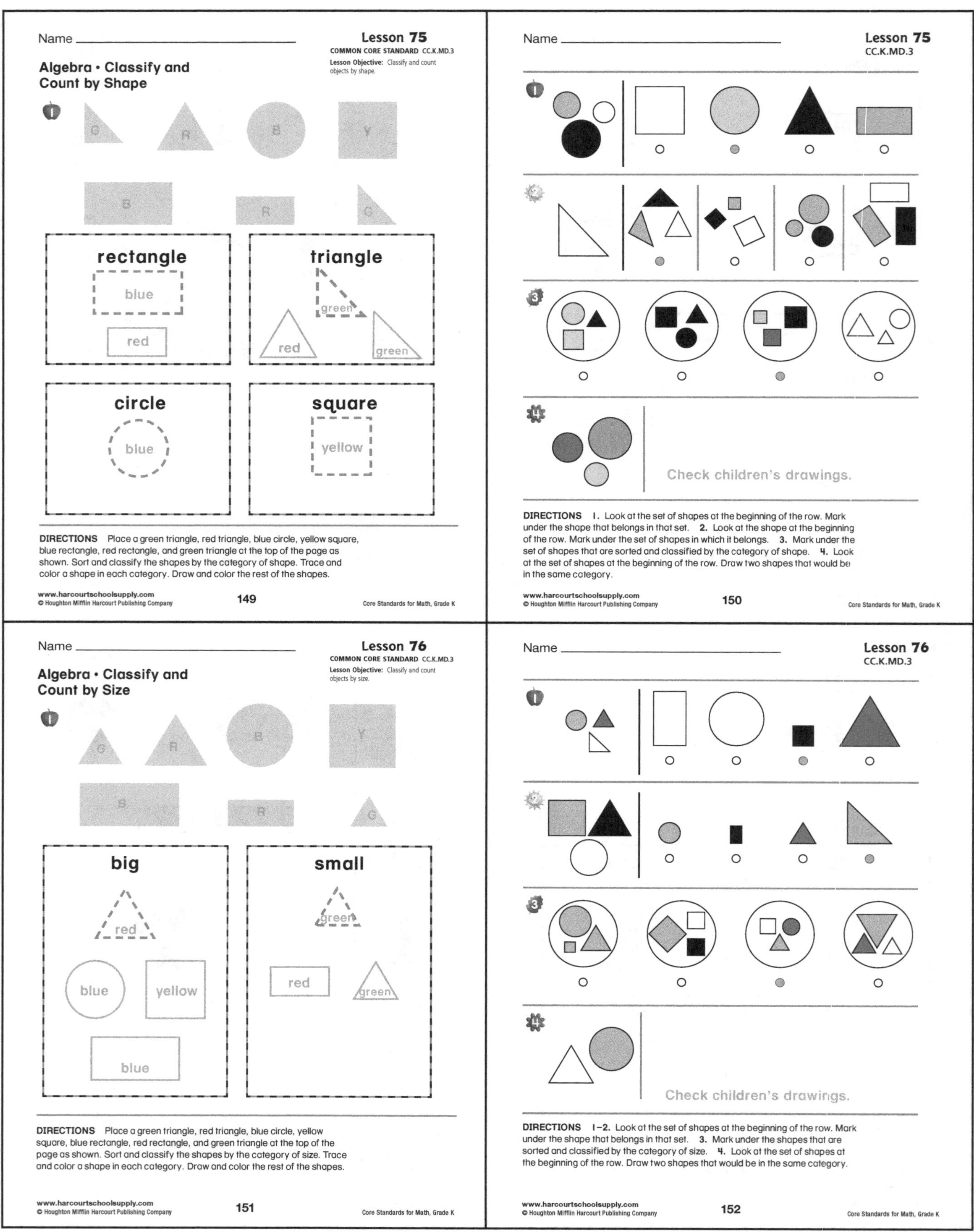

Name ______________________

Lesson 75

COMMON CORE STANDARD CC.K.MD.3

Lesson Objective: Classify and count objects by shape.

Algebra • Classify and Count by Shape

DIRECTIONS Place a green triangle, red triangle, blue circle, yellow square, blue rectangle, red rectangle, and green triangle at the top of the page as shown. Sort and classify the shapes by the category of shape. Trace and color a shape in each category. Draw and color the rest of the shapes.

www.harcourtschoolsupply.com
© Houghton Mifflin Harcourt Publishing Company 149 Core Standards for Math, Grade K

Name ______________________

Lesson 75

CC.K.MD.3

DIRECTIONS 1. Look at the set of shapes at the beginning of the row. Mark under the shape that belongs in that set. 2. Look at the shape at the beginning of the row. Mark under the set of shapes in which it belongs. 3. Mark under the set of shapes that are sorted and classified by the category of shape. 4. Look at the set of shapes at the beginning of the row. Draw two shapes that would be in the same category.

www.harcourtschoolsupply.com
© Houghton Mifflin Harcourt Publishing Company 150 Core Standards for Math, Grade K

Name ______________________

Lesson 76

COMMON CORE STANDARD CC.K.MD.3

Lesson Objective: Classify and count objects by size.

Algebra • Classify and Count by Size

DIRECTIONS Place a green triangle, red triangle, blue circle, yellow square, blue rectangle, red rectangle, and green triangle at the top of the page as shown. Sort and classify the shapes by the category of size. Trace and color a shape in each category. Draw and color the rest of the shapes.

www.harcourtschoolsupply.com
© Houghton Mifflin Harcourt Publishing Company 151 Core Standards for Math, Grade K

Name ______________________

Lesson 76

CC.K.MD.3

DIRECTIONS 1–2. Look at the set of shapes at the beginning of the row. Mark under the shape that belongs in that set. 3. Mark under the shapes that are sorted and classified by the category of size. 4. Look at the set of shapes at the beginning of the row. Draw two shapes that would be in the same category.

www.harcourtschoolsupply.com
© Houghton Mifflin Harcourt Publishing Company 152 Core Standards for Math, Grade K

Answer Key

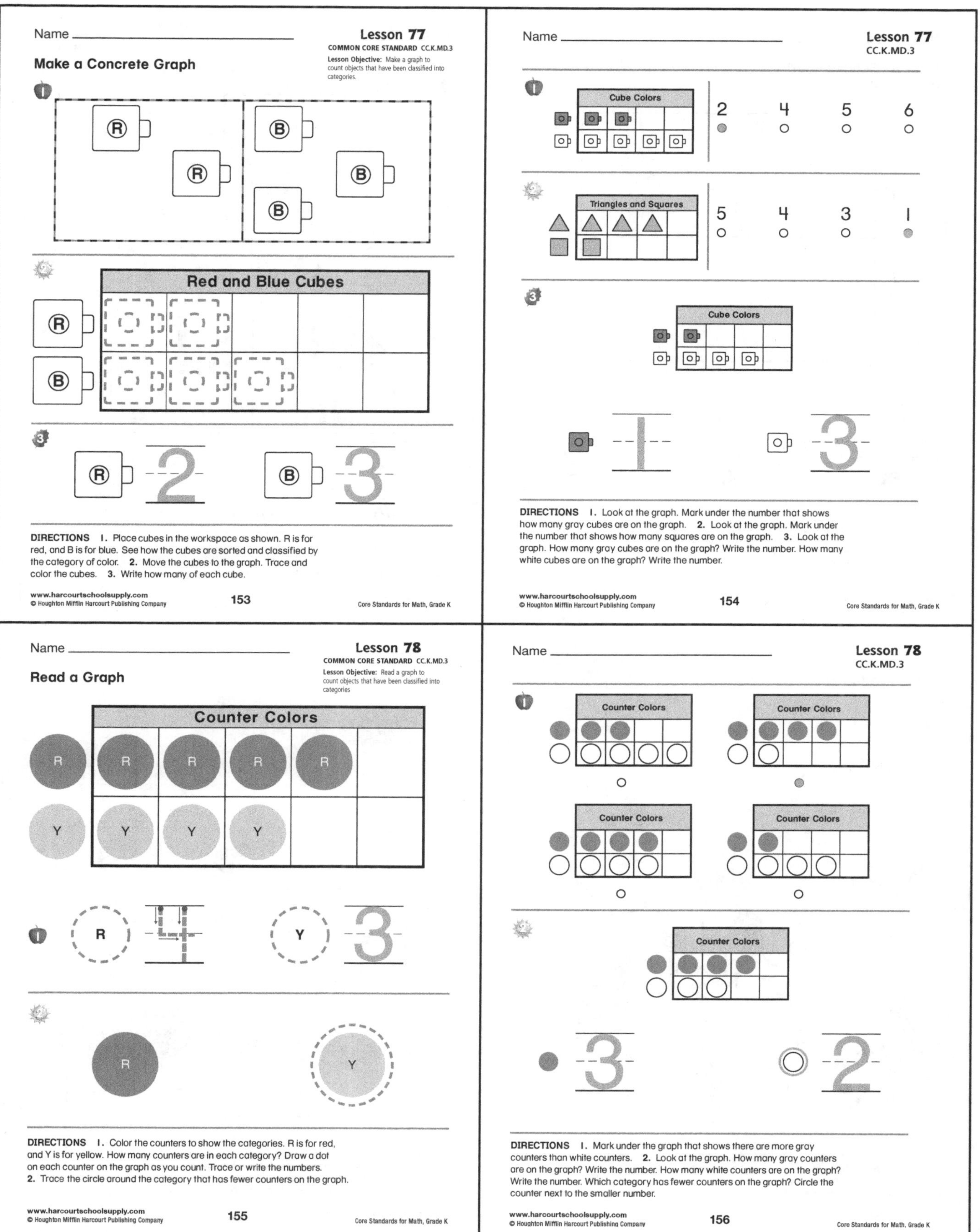

Name
Lesson 77
COMMON CORE STANDARD CC.K.MD.3
Make a Concrete Graph
Lesson Objective: Make a graph to count objects that have been classified into categories.
Red and Blue Cubes
DIRECTIONS 1. Place cubes in the workspace as shown. R is for red, and B is for blue. See how the cubes are sorted and classified by the category of color. 2. Move the cubes to the graph. Trace and color the cubes. 3. Write how many of each cube.
www.harcourtschoolsupply.com
© Houghton Mifflin Harcourt Publishing Company
153
Core Standards for Math, Grade K
Name
Lesson 77
CC.K.MD.3
Cube Colors
Triangles and Squares
DIRECTIONS 1. Look at the graph. Mark under the number that shows how many gray cubes are on the graph. 2. Look at the graph. Mark under the number that shows how many squares are on the graph. 3. Look at the graph. How many gray cubes are on the graph? Write the number. How many white cubes are on the graph? Write the number.
154
Name
Lesson 78
COMMON CORE STANDARD CC.K.MD.3
Read a Graph
Lesson Objective: Read a graph to count objects that have been classified into categories
Counter Colors
DIRECTIONS 1. Color the counters to show the categories. R is for red, and Y is for yellow. How many counters are in each category? Draw a dot on each counter on the graph as you count. Trace or write the numbers. 2. Trace the circle around the category that has fewer counters on the graph.
155
Name
Lesson 78
CC.K.MD.3
Counter Colors
DIRECTIONS 1. Mark under the graph that shows there are more gray counters than white counters. 2. Look at the graph. How many gray counters are on the graph? Write the number. How many white counters are on the graph? Write the number. Which category has fewer counters on the graph? Circle the counter next to the smaller number.
156

Answer Key

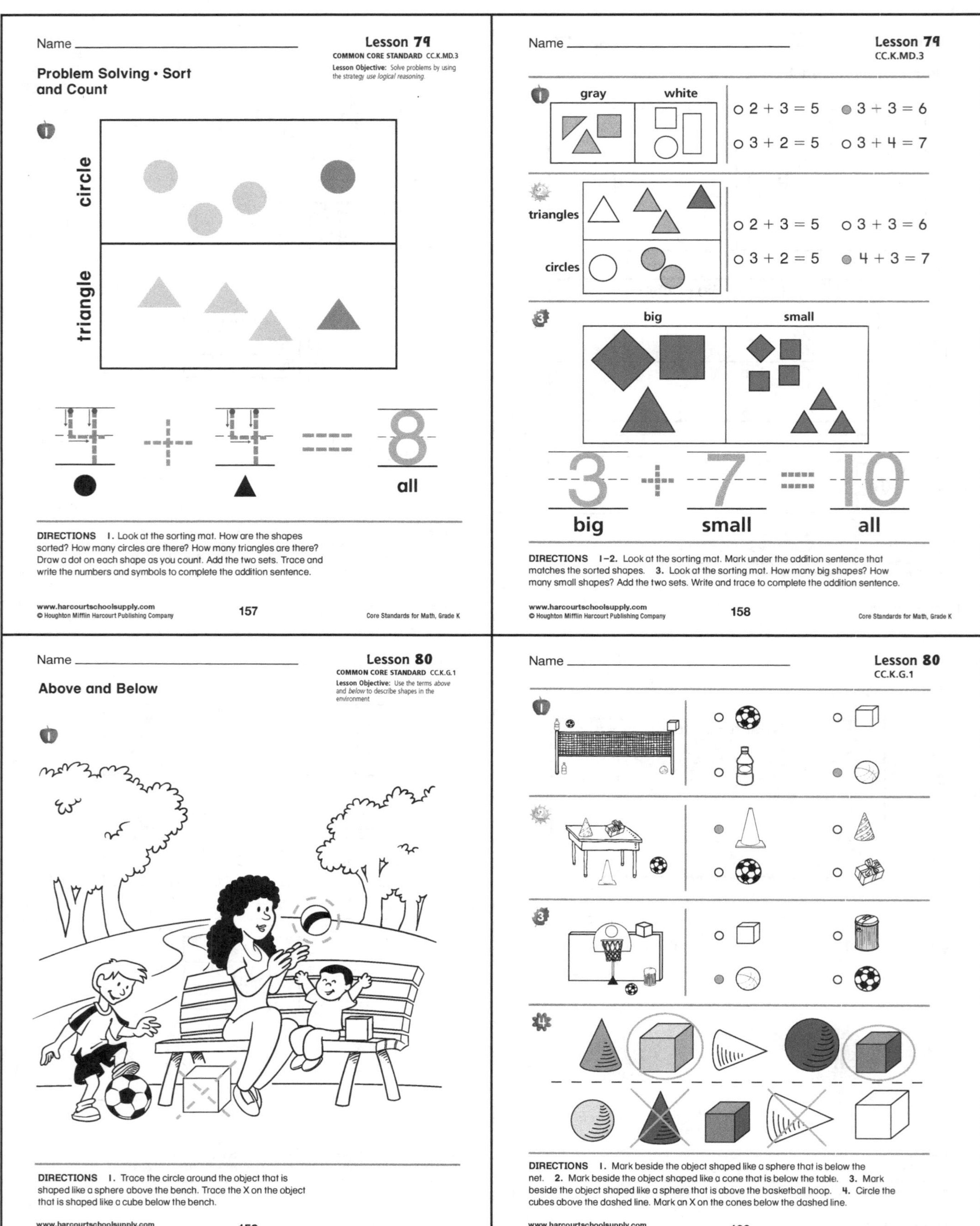
Name
Lesson 79
COMMON CORE STANDARD CC.K.MD.3
Lesson Objective: Solve problems by using the strategy use logical reasoning.
Problem Solving • Sort and Count
circle
triangle
4 + 4 = 8
all
DIRECTIONS 1. Look at the sorting mat. How are the shapes sorted? How many circles are there? How many triangles are there? Draw a dot on each shape as you count. Add the two sets. Trace and write the numbers and symbols to complete the addition sentence.
www.harcourtschoolsupply.com
© Houghton Mifflin Harcourt Publishing Company
157
Core Standards for Math, Grade K
Name
Lesson 79
CC.K.MD.3
gray
white
2 + 3 = 5
3 + 3 = 6
3 + 2 = 5
3 + 4 = 7
triangles
circles
2 + 3 = 5
3 + 3 = 6
3 + 2 = 5
4 + 3 = 7
big
small
3 + 7 = 10
big
small
all
DIRECTIONS 1–2. Look at the sorting mat. Mark under the addition sentence that matches the sorted shapes. 3. Look at the sorting mat. How many big shapes? How many small shapes? Add the two sets. Write and trace to complete the addition sentence.
www.harcourtschoolsupply.com
© Houghton Mifflin Harcourt Publishing Company
158
Core Standards for Math, Grade K
Name
Lesson 80
COMMON CORE STANDARD CC.K.G.1
Lesson Objective: Use the terms above and below to describe shapes in the environment
Above and Below
DIRECTIONS 1. Trace the circle around the object that is shaped like a sphere above the bench. Trace the X on the object that is shaped like a cube below the bench.
www.harcourtschoolsupply.com
© Houghton Mifflin Harcourt Publishing Company
159
Core Standards for Math, Grade K
Name
Lesson 80
CC.K.G.1
DIRECTIONS 1. Mark beside the object shaped like a sphere that is below the net. 2. Mark beside the object shaped like a cone that is below the table. 3. Mark beside the object shaped like a sphere that is above the basketball hoop. 4. Circle the cubes above the dashed line. Mark an X on the cones below the dashed line.
www.harcourtschoolsupply.com
© Houghton Mifflin Harcourt Publishing Company
160
Core Standards for Math, Grade K

Answer Key

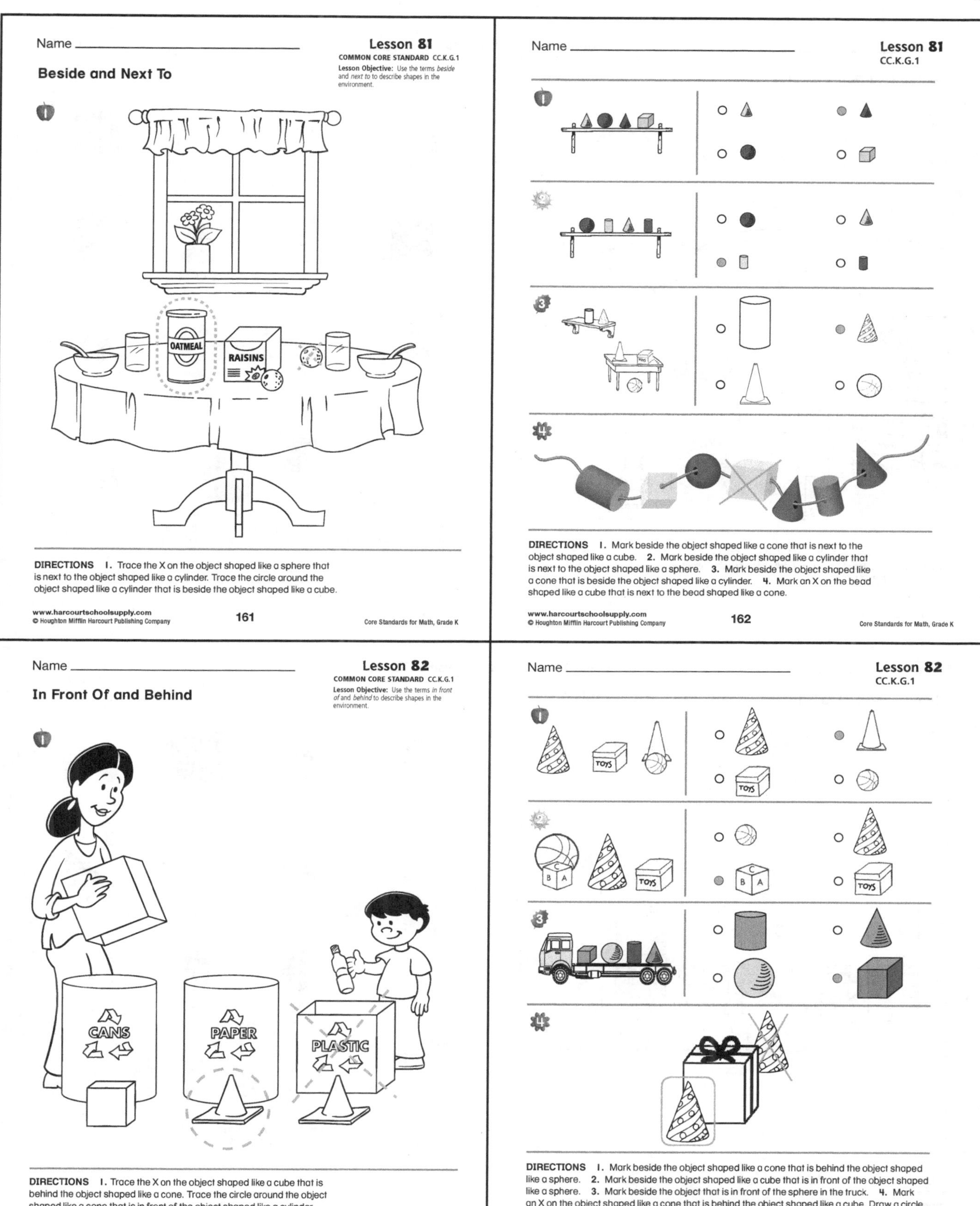

Name ______________________ **Lesson 81**

COMMON CORE STANDARD CC.K.G.1

Lesson Objective: Use the terms *beside* and *next to* to describe shapes in the environment.

Beside and Next To

DIRECTIONS 1. Trace the X on the object shaped like a sphere that is next to the object shaped like a cylinder. Trace the circle around the object shaped like a cylinder that is beside the object shaped like a cube.

www.harcourtschoolsupply.com
© Houghton Mifflin Harcourt Publishing Company 161 Core Standards for Math, Grade K

Name ______________________ **Lesson 81**

CC.K.G.1

DIRECTIONS 1. Mark beside the object shaped like a cone that is next to the object shaped like a cube. 2. Mark beside the object shaped like a cylinder that is next to the object shaped like a sphere. 3. Mark beside the object shaped like a cone that is beside the object shaped like a cylinder. 4. Mark an X on the bead shaped like a cube that is next to the bead shaped like a cone.

www.harcourtschoolsupply.com
© Houghton Mifflin Harcourt Publishing Company 162 Core Standards for Math, Grade K

Name ______________________ **Lesson 82**

COMMON CORE STANDARD CC.K.G.1

Lesson Objective: Use the terms *in front of* and *behind* to describe shapes in the environment.

In Front Of and Behind

DIRECTIONS 1. Trace the X on the object shaped like a cube that is behind the object shaped like a cone. Trace the circle around the object shaped like a cone that is in front of the object shaped like a cylinder.

www.harcourtschoolsupply.com
© Houghton Mifflin Harcourt Publishing Company 163 Core Standards for Math, Grade K

Name ______________________ **Lesson 82**

CC.K.G.1

DIRECTIONS 1. Mark beside the object shaped like a cone that is behind the object shaped like a sphere. 2. Mark beside the object shaped like a cube that is in front of the object shaped like a sphere. 3. Mark beside the object that is in front of the sphere in the truck. 4. Mark an X on the object shaped like a cone that is behind the object shaped like a cube. Draw a circle around the object shaped like a cone that is in front of the object shaped like a cube.

www.harcourtschoolsupply.com
© Houghton Mifflin Harcourt Publishing Company 164 Core Standards for Math, Grade K

Answer Key

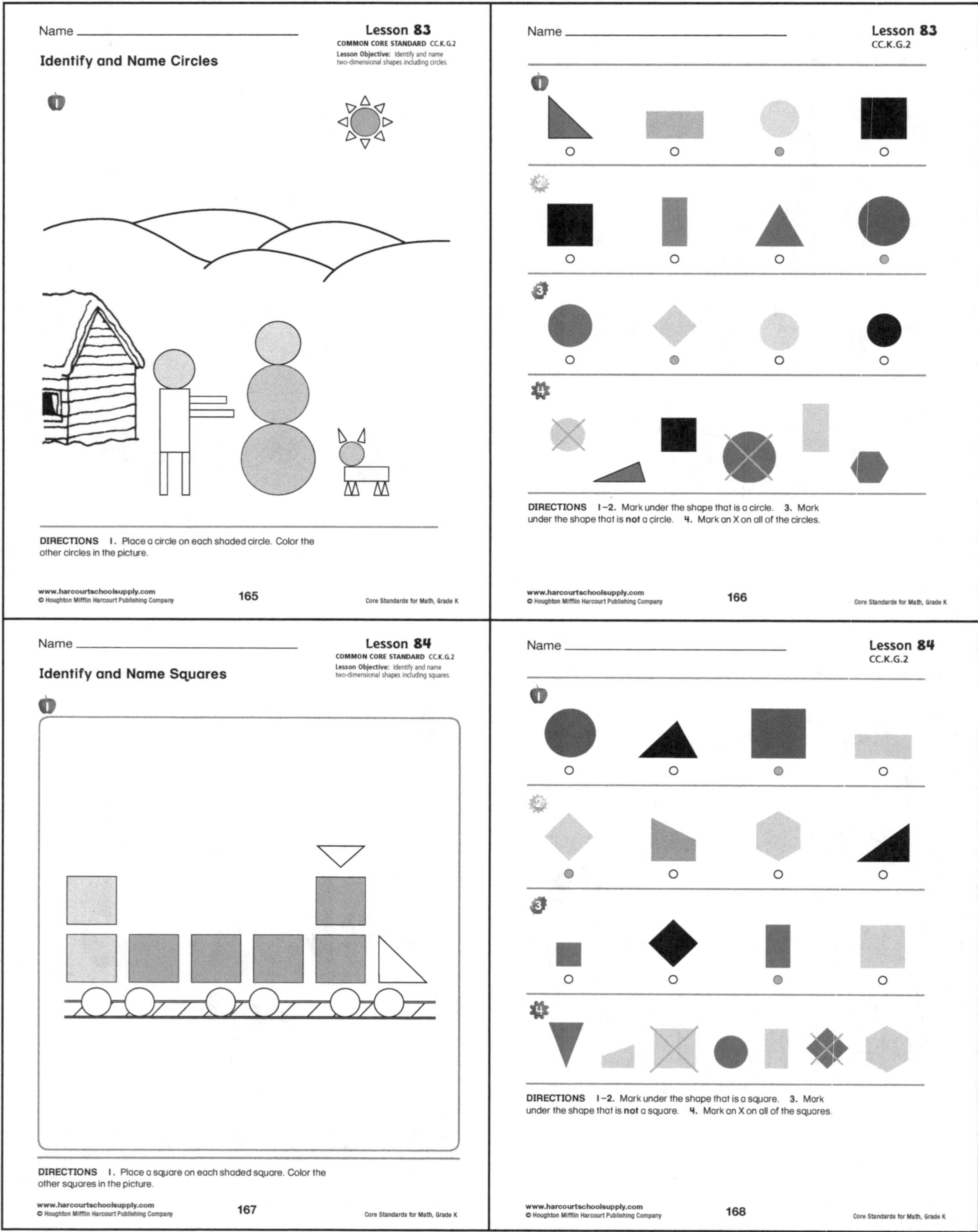

Name
Lesson 83
COMMON CORE STANDARD CC.K.G.2
Lesson Objective: Identify and name two-dimensional shapes including circles.
Identify and Name Circles
DIRECTIONS 1. Place a circle on each shaded circle. Color the other circles in the picture.
www.harcourtschoolsupply.com
© Houghton Mifflin Harcourt Publishing Company
165
Core Standards for Math, Grade K
Name
Lesson 83
CC.K.G.2
DIRECTIONS 1–2. Mark under the shape that is a circle. 3. Mark under the shape that is not a circle. 4. Mark an X on all of the circles.
www.harcourtschoolsupply.com
© Houghton Mifflin Harcourt Publishing Company
166
Core Standards for Math, Grade K
Name
Lesson 84
COMMON CORE STANDARD CC.K.G.2
Lesson Objective: Identify and name two-dimensional shapes including squares.
Identify and Name Squares
DIRECTIONS 1. Place a square on each shaded square. Color the other squares in the picture.
www.harcourtschoolsupply.com
© Houghton Mifflin Harcourt Publishing Company
167
Core Standards for Math, Grade K
Name
Lesson 84
CC.K.G.2
DIRECTIONS 1–2. Mark under the shape that is a square. 3. Mark under the shape that is not a square. 4. Mark an X on all of the squares.
www.harcourtschoolsupply.com
© Houghton Mifflin Harcourt Publishing Company
168
Core Standards for Math, Grade K

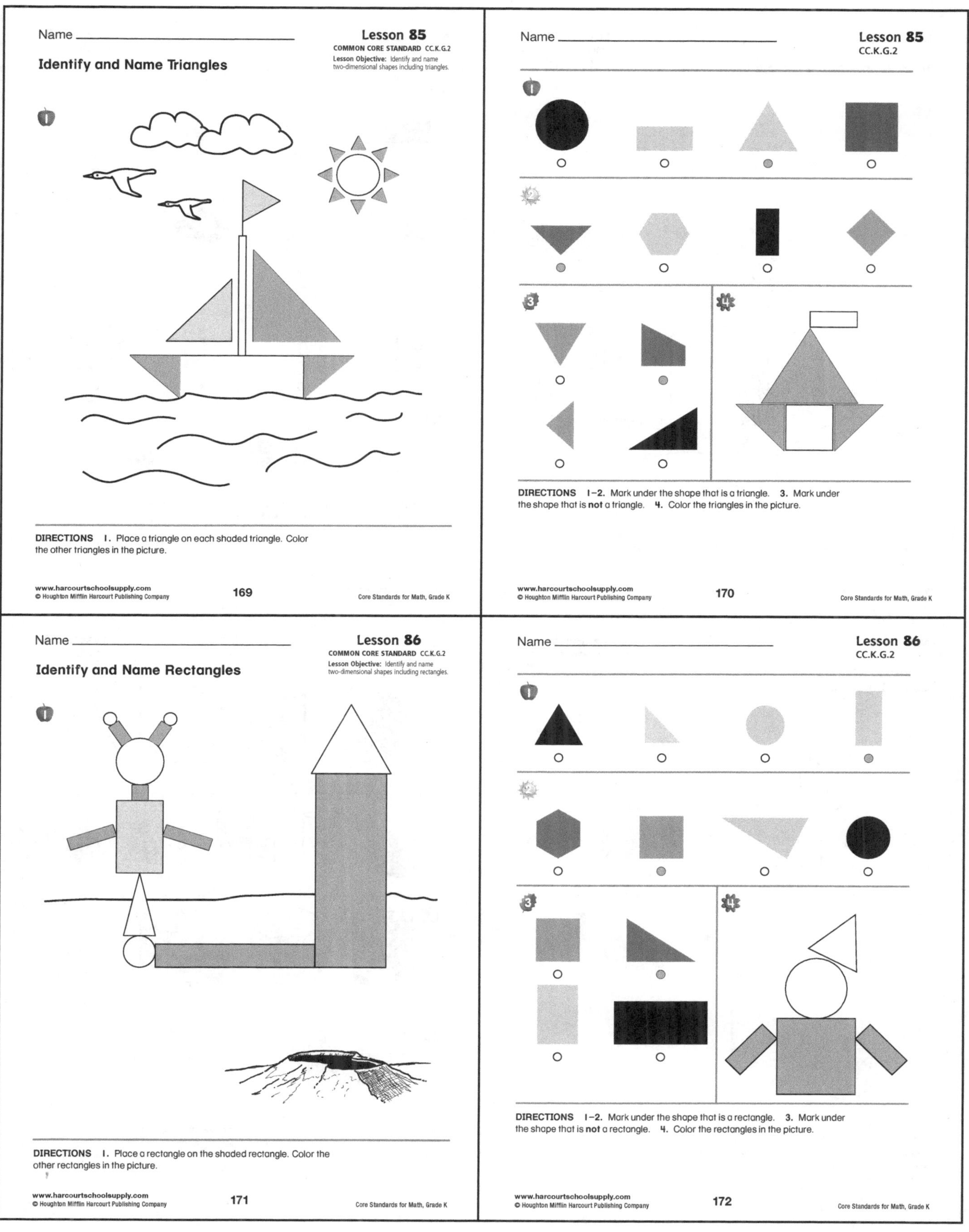
Name
Lesson 85
COMMON CORE STANDARD CC.K.G.2
Identify and Name Triangles
Lesson Objective: Identify and name two-dimensional shapes including triangles.
DIRECTIONS 1. Place a triangle on each shaded triangle. Color the other triangles in the picture.
www.harcourtschoolsupply.com
© Houghton Mifflin Harcourt Publishing Company
169
Core Standards for Math, Grade K
Name
Lesson 85
CC.K.G.2
DIRECTIONS 1–2. Mark under the shape that is a triangle. 3. Mark under the shape that is not a triangle. 4. Color the triangles in the picture.
www.harcourtschoolsupply.com
© Houghton Mifflin Harcourt Publishing Company
170
Core Standards for Math, Grade K
Name
Lesson 86
COMMON CORE STANDARD CC.K.G.2
Identify and Name Rectangles
Lesson Objective: Identify and name two-dimensional shapes including rectangles.
DIRECTIONS 1. Place a rectangle on the shaded rectangle. Color the other rectangles in the picture.
www.harcourtschoolsupply.com
© Houghton Mifflin Harcourt Publishing Company
171
Core Standards for Math, Grade K
Name
Lesson 86
CC.K.G.2
DIRECTIONS 1–2. Mark under the shape that is a rectangle. 3. Mark under the shape that is not a rectangle. 4. Color the rectangles in the picture.
www.harcourtschoolsupply.com
© Houghton Mifflin Harcourt Publishing Company
172
Core Standards for Math, Grade K

Answer Key

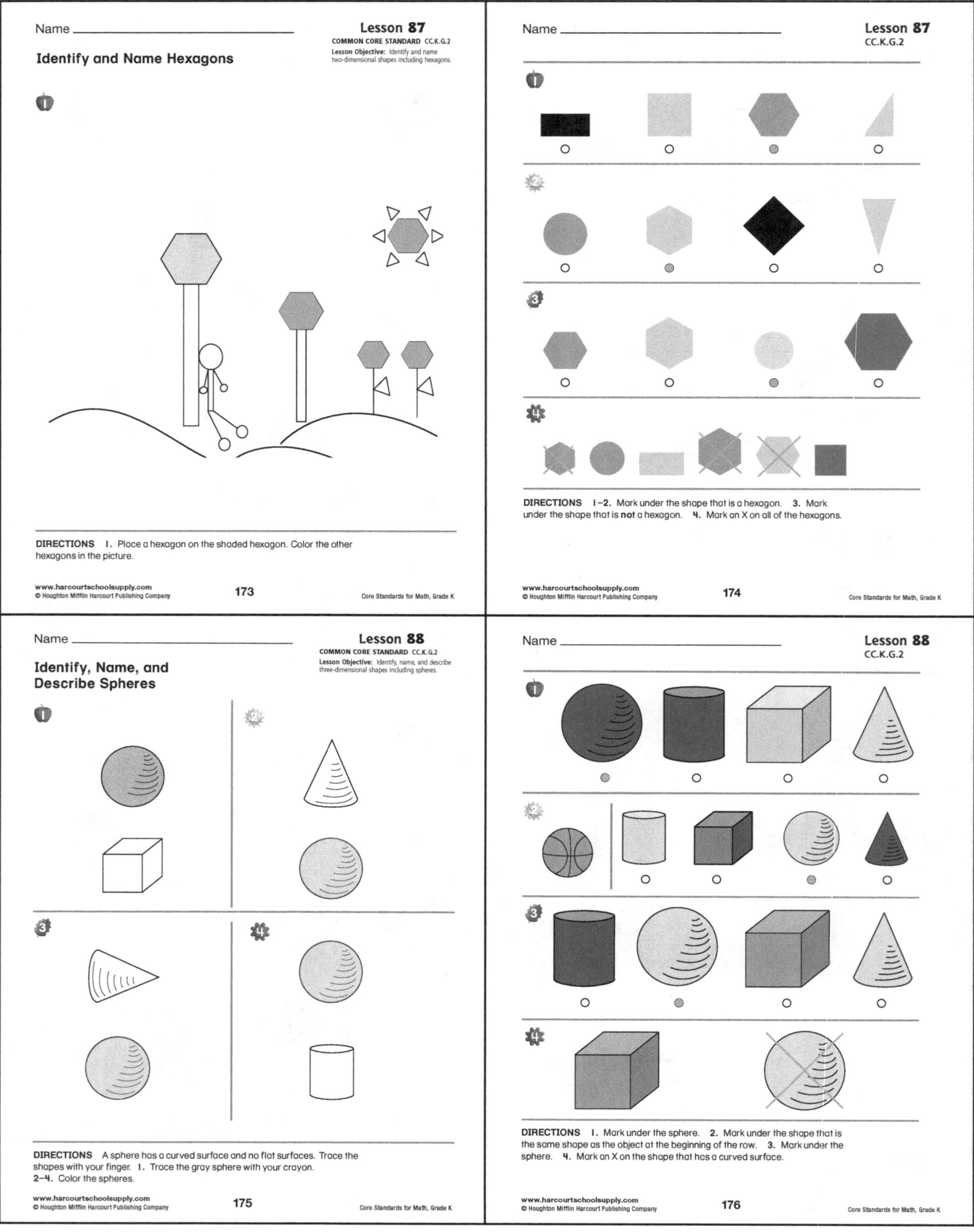

Name

Lesson 87

COMMON CORE STANDARD CC.K.G.2

Lesson Objective: Identify and name two-dimensional shapes including hexagons.

Identify and Name Hexagons

1

DIRECTIONS 1. Place a hexagon on the shaded hexagon. Color the other hexagons in the picture.

www.harcourtschoolsupply.com
© Houghton Mifflin Harcourt Publishing Company 173 Core Standards for Math, Grade K

Name

Lesson 87

CC.K.G.2

1

2

3

4

DIRECTIONS 1–2. Mark under the shape that is a hexagon. 3. Mark under the shape that is **not** a hexagon. 4. Mark an X on all of the hexagons.

www.harcourtschoolsupply.com
© Houghton Mifflin Harcourt Publishing Company 174 Core Standards for Math, Grade K

Name

Lesson 88

COMMON CORE STANDARD CC.K.G.2

Lesson Objective: Identify, name, and describe three-dimensional shapes including spheres.

Identify, Name, and Describe Spheres

1

2

3

4

DIRECTIONS A sphere has a curved surface and no flat surfaces. Trace the shapes with your finger. 1. Trace the gray sphere with your crayon. 2–4. Color the spheres.

www.harcourtschoolsupply.com
© Houghton Mifflin Harcourt Publishing Company 175 Core Standards for Math, Grade K

Name

Lesson 88

CC.K.G.2

1

2

3

4

DIRECTIONS 1. Mark under the sphere. 2. Mark under the shape that is the same shape as the object at the beginning of the row. 3. Mark under the sphere. 4. Mark an X on the shape that has a curved surface.

www.harcourtschoolsupply.com
© Houghton Mifflin Harcourt Publishing Company 176 Core Standards for Math, Grade K

Name ______________________

Lesson 89
COMMON CORE STANDARD CC.K.G.2
Lesson Objective: Identify, name, and describe three-dimensional shapes including cubes.

Identify, Name, and Describe Cubes

1

1 2 3 4 5 6

2

6 flat surfaces

DIRECTIONS 1. Look at the pictures that show all the flat surfaces on one cube. Count how many flat surfaces. Touch each number as you count. 2. Write the number that shows how many flat surfaces.

www.harcourtschoolsupply.com
© Houghton Mifflin Harcourt Publishing Company
177
Core Standards for Math, Grade K

Name ______________________

Lesson 89
CC.K.G.2

1

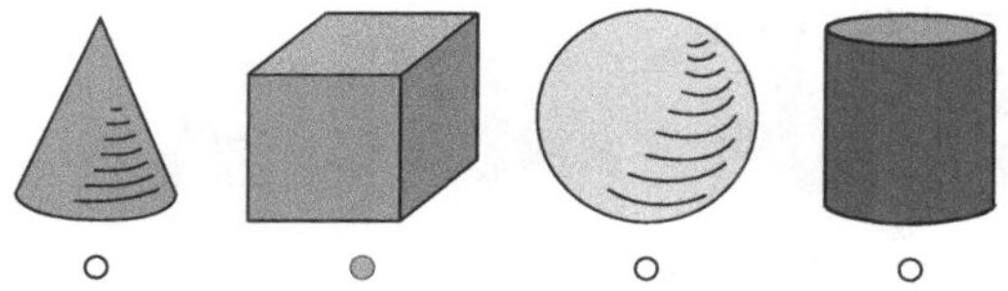

2

B A C

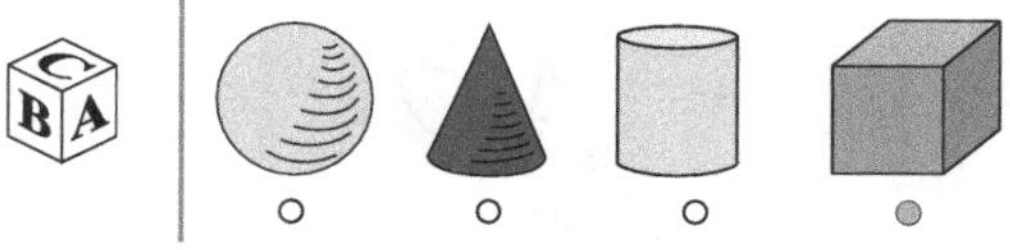

3

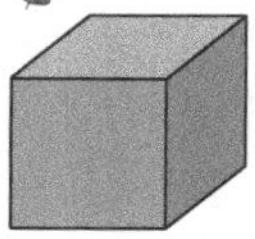

2 4 6 8

4

DIRECTIONS 1. Mark under the cube. 2. Mark under the shape that is the same shape as the object at the beginning of the row. 3. Mark under the number that shows how many flat surfaces the cube has. 4. Mark an X on the cube.

www.harcourtschoolsupply.com
© Houghton Mifflin Harcourt Publishing Company
178
Core Standards for Math, Grade K

Name ______________________

Lesson 90
COMMON CORE STANDARD CC.K.G.2
Lesson Objective: Identify, name, and describe three-dimensional shapes including cylinders.

Identify, Name, and Describe Cylinders

1

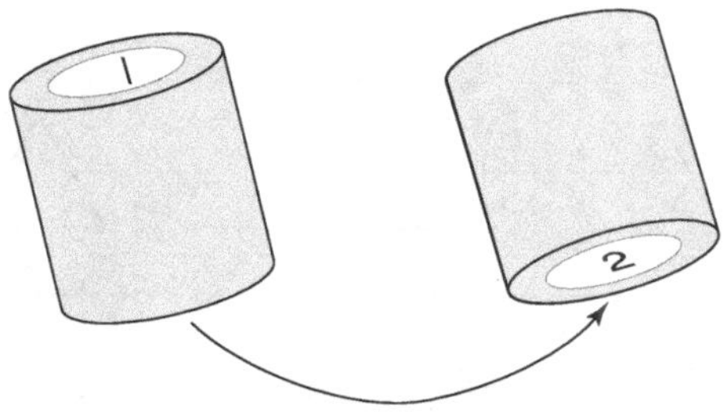

1 2

2

2 flat surfaces

DIRECTIONS 1. Look at the pictures that show the flat surfaces on one cylinder. Count how many flat surfaces. Touch each number as you count. 2. Write the number that shows how many flat surfaces.

www.harcourtschoolsupply.com
© Houghton Mifflin Harcourt Publishing Company
179
Core Standards for Math, Grade K

Name ______________________

Lesson 90
CC.K.G.2

1

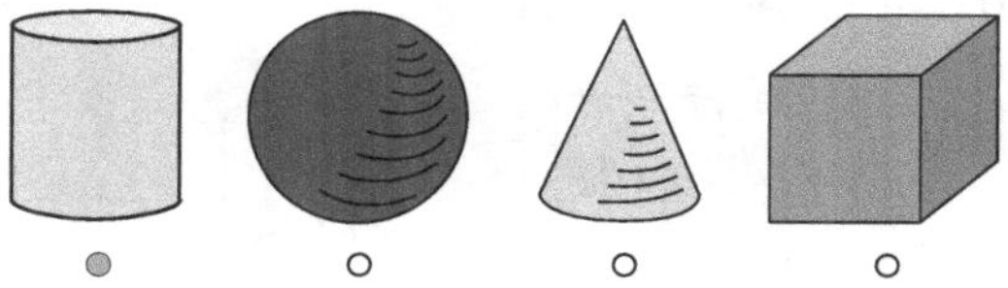

2

SOUP

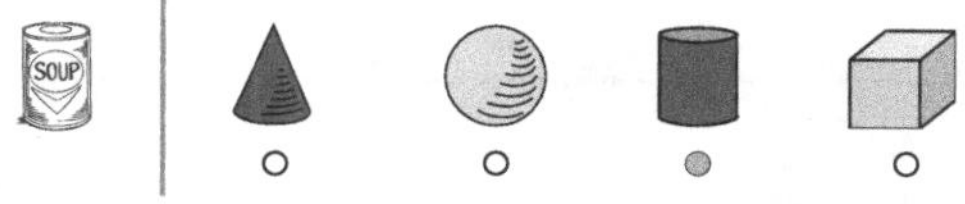

3

2 3 4 5

4

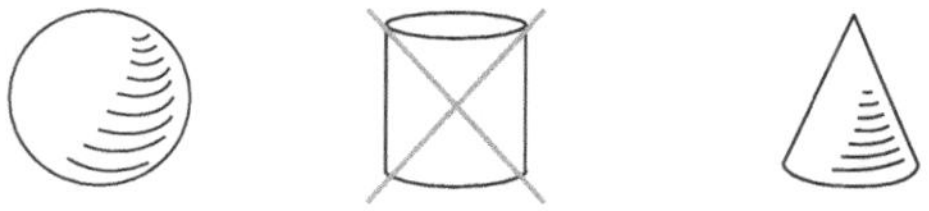

DIRECTIONS 1. Mark under the cylinder. 2. Mark under the shape that is the same shape as the object at the beginning of the row. 3. Mark under the number that shows how many flat surfaces the cylinder has. 4. Mark an X on the cylinder.

www.harcourtschoolsupply.com
© Houghton Mifflin Harcourt Publishing Company
180
Core Standards for Math, Grade K

Answer Key

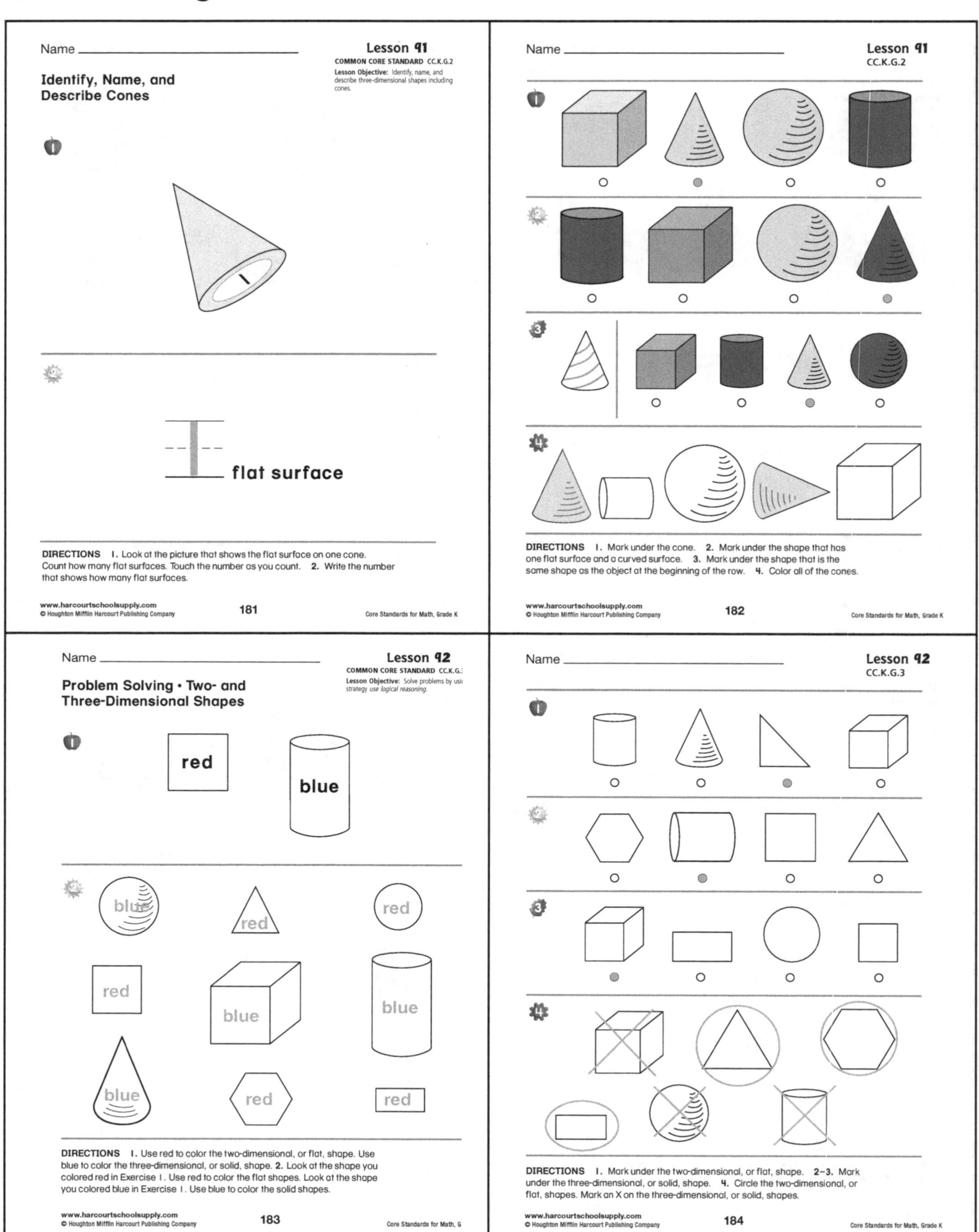
Name ____________________

Lesson 41
COMMON CORE STANDARD CC.K.G.2
Lesson Objective: Identify, name, and describe three-dimensional shapes including cones.

Identify, Name, and Describe Cones

1

1

2

1 flat surface

DIRECTIONS 1. Look at the picture that shows the flat surface on one cone. Count how many flat surfaces. Touch the number as you count. 2. Write the number that shows how many flat surfaces.

www.harcourtschoolsupply.com
© Houghton Mifflin Harcourt Publishing Company

181

Core Standards for Math, Grade K

Name ____________________

Lesson 41
CC.K.G.2

1

2

3

4

DIRECTIONS 1. Mark under the cone. 2. Mark under the shape that has one flat surface and a curved surface. 3. Mark under the shape that is the same shape as the object at the beginning of the row. 4. Color all of the cones.

www.harcourtschoolsupply.com
© Houghton Mifflin Harcourt Publishing Company

182

Core Standards for Math, Grade K

Name ____________________

Lesson 42
COMMON CORE STANDARD CC.K.G.3
Lesson Objective: Solve problems by using the strategy *use logical reasoning.*

Problem Solving • Two- and Three-Dimensional Shapes

1

red

blue

2

blue red red

red blue blue

blue red red

DIRECTIONS 1. Use red to color the two-dimensional, or flat, shape. Use blue to color the three-dimensional, or solid, shape. 2. Look at the shape you colored red in Exercise 1. Use red to color the flat shapes. Look at the shape you colored blue in Exercise 1. Use blue to color the solid shapes.

www.harcourtschoolsupply.com
© Houghton Mifflin Harcourt Publishing Company

183

Core Standards for Math, G

Name ____________________

Lesson 42
CC.K.G.3

1

2

3

4

DIRECTIONS 1. Mark under the two-dimensional, or flat, shape. 2–3. Mark under the three-dimensional, or solid, shape. 4. Circle the two-dimensional, or flat, shapes. Mark an X on the three-dimensional, or solid, shapes.

www.harcourtschoolsupply.com
© Houghton Mifflin Harcourt Publishing Company

184

Core Standards for Math, Grade K

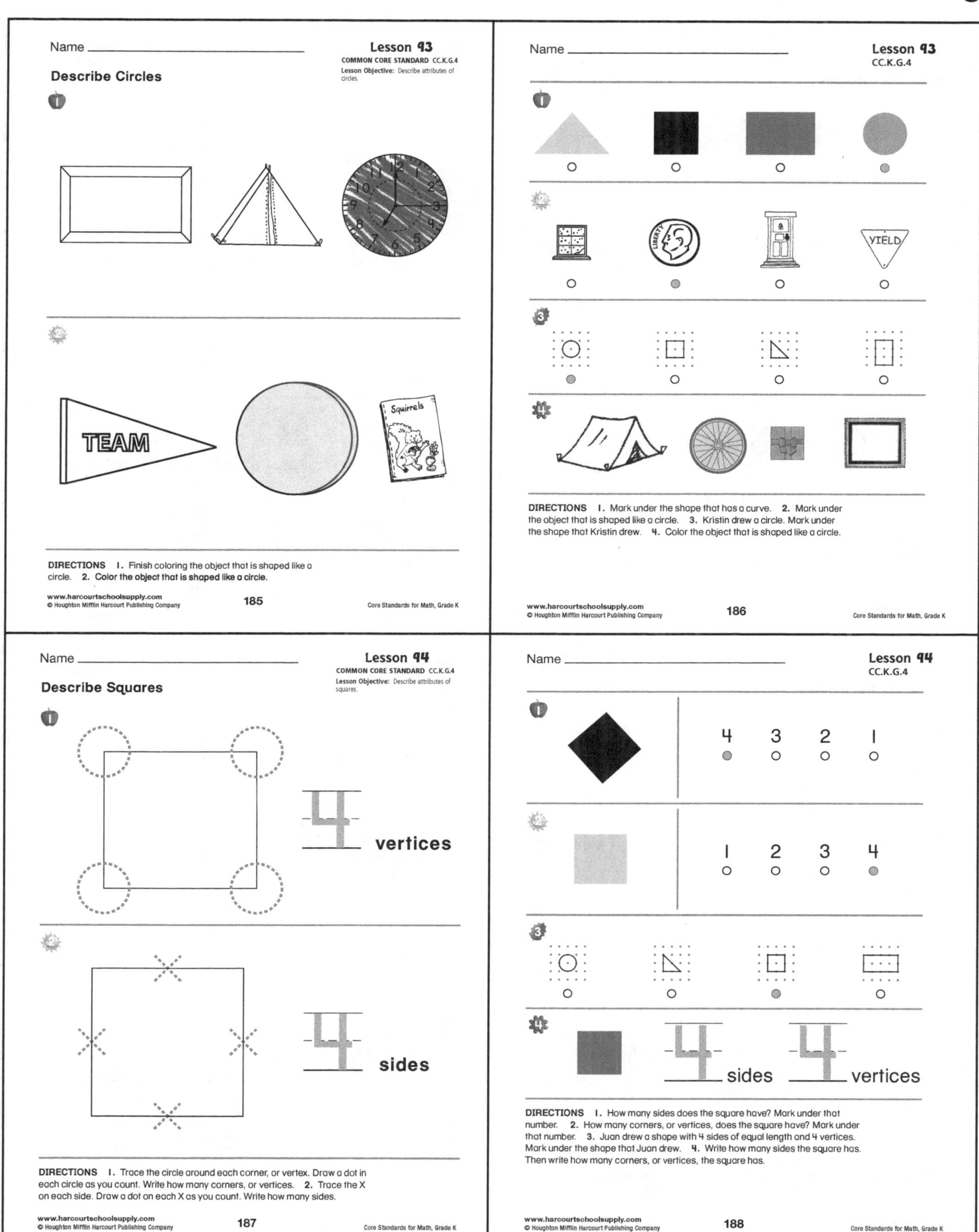

Name
Lesson 43
COMMON CORE STANDARD CC.K.G.4
Lesson Objective: Describe attributes of circles.
Describe Circles
TEAM
Squirrels
DIRECTIONS 1. Finish coloring the object that is shaped like a circle. 2. Color the object that is shaped like a circle.
www.harcourtschoolsupply.com
© Houghton Mifflin Harcourt Publishing Company
185
Core Standards for Math, Grade K
Name
Lesson 43
CC.K.G.4
YIELD
DIRECTIONS 1. Mark under the shape that has a curve. 2. Mark under the object that is shaped like a circle. 3. Kristin drew a circle. Mark under the shape that Kristin drew. 4. Color the object that is shaped like a circle.
www.harcourtschoolsupply.com
© Houghton Mifflin Harcourt Publishing Company
186
Core Standards for Math, Grade K
Name
Lesson 44
COMMON CORE STANDARD CC.K.G.4
Lesson Objective: Describe attributes of squares.
Describe Squares
4 vertices
4 sides
DIRECTIONS 1. Trace the circle around each corner, or vertex. Draw a dot in each circle as you count. Write how many corners, or vertices. 2. Trace the X on each side. Draw a dot on each X as you count. Write how many sides.
www.harcourtschoolsupply.com
© Houghton Mifflin Harcourt Publishing Company
187
Core Standards for Math, Grade K
Name
Lesson 44
CC.K.G.4
4 3 2 1
1 2 3 4
4 sides
4 vertices
DIRECTIONS 1. How many sides does the square have? Mark under that number. 2. How many corners, or vertices, does the square have? Mark under that number. 3. Juan drew a shape with 4 sides of equal length and 4 vertices. Mark under the shape that Juan drew. 4. Write how many sides the square has. Then write how many corners, or vertices, the square has.
www.harcourtschoolsupply.com
© Houghton Mifflin Harcourt Publishing Company
188
Core Standards for Math, Grade K

Answer Key

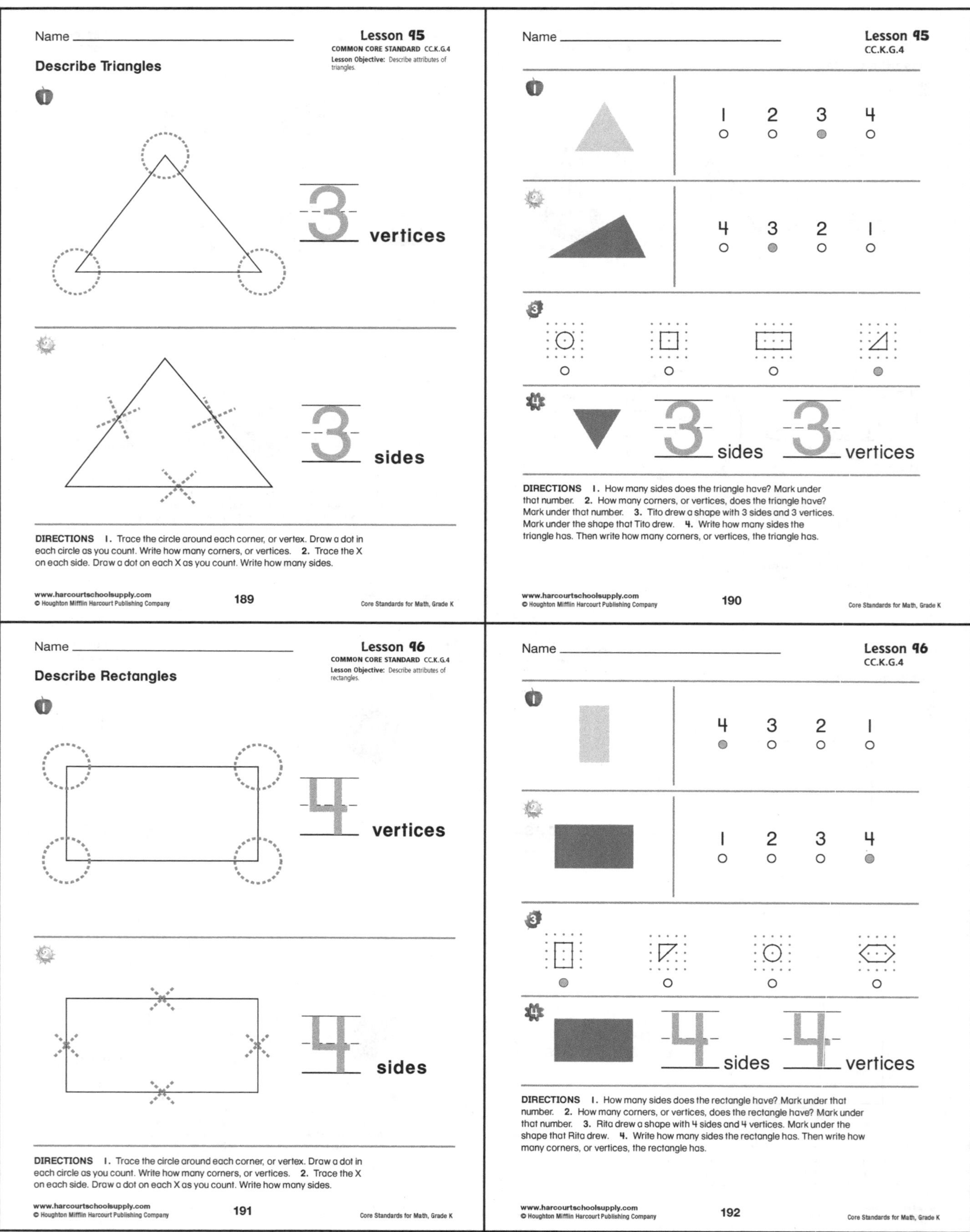

Name ______________________

Lesson 95
COMMON CORE STANDARD CC.K.G.4
Lesson Objective: Describe attributes of triangles.

Describe Triangles

1. 3 vertices

2. 3 sides

DIRECTIONS **1.** Trace the circle around each corner, or vertex. Draw a dot in each circle as you count. Write how many corners, or vertices. **2.** Trace the X on each side. Draw a dot on each X as you count. Write how many sides.

www.harcourtschoolsupply.com
© Houghton Mifflin Harcourt Publishing Company
189
Core Standards for Math, Grade K

Name ______________________

Lesson 95
CC.K.G.4

1. 1 2 3 4

2. 4 3 2 1

3.

4. 3 sides 3 vertices

DIRECTIONS **1.** How many sides does the triangle have? Mark under that number. **2.** How many corners, or vertices, does the triangle have? Mark under that number. **3.** Tito drew a shape with 3 sides and 3 vertices. Mark under the shape that Tito drew. **4.** Write how many sides the triangle has. Then write how many corners, or vertices, the triangle has.

www.harcourtschoolsupply.com
© Houghton Mifflin Harcourt Publishing Company
190
Core Standards for Math, Grade K

Name ______________________

Lesson 96
COMMON CORE STANDARD CC.K.G.4
Lesson Objective: Describe attributes of rectangles.

Describe Rectangles

1. 4 vertices

2. 4 sides

DIRECTIONS **1.** Trace the circle around each corner, or vertex. Draw a dot in each circle as you count. Write how many corners, or vertices. **2.** Trace the X on each side. Draw a dot on each X as you count. Write how many sides.

www.harcourtschoolsupply.com
© Houghton Mifflin Harcourt Publishing Company
191
Core Standards for Math, Grade K

Name ______________________

Lesson 96
CC.K.G.4

1. 4 3 2 1

2. 1 2 3 4

3.

4. 4 sides 4 vertices

DIRECTIONS **1.** How many sides does the rectangle have? Mark under that number. **2.** How many corners, or vertices, does the rectangle have? Mark under that number. **3.** Rita drew a shape with 4 sides and 4 vertices. Mark under the shape that Rita drew. **4.** Write how many sides the rectangle has. Then write how many corners, or vertices, the rectangle has.

www.harcourtschoolsupply.com
© Houghton Mifflin Harcourt Publishing Company
192
Core Standards for Math, Grade K

Answer Key

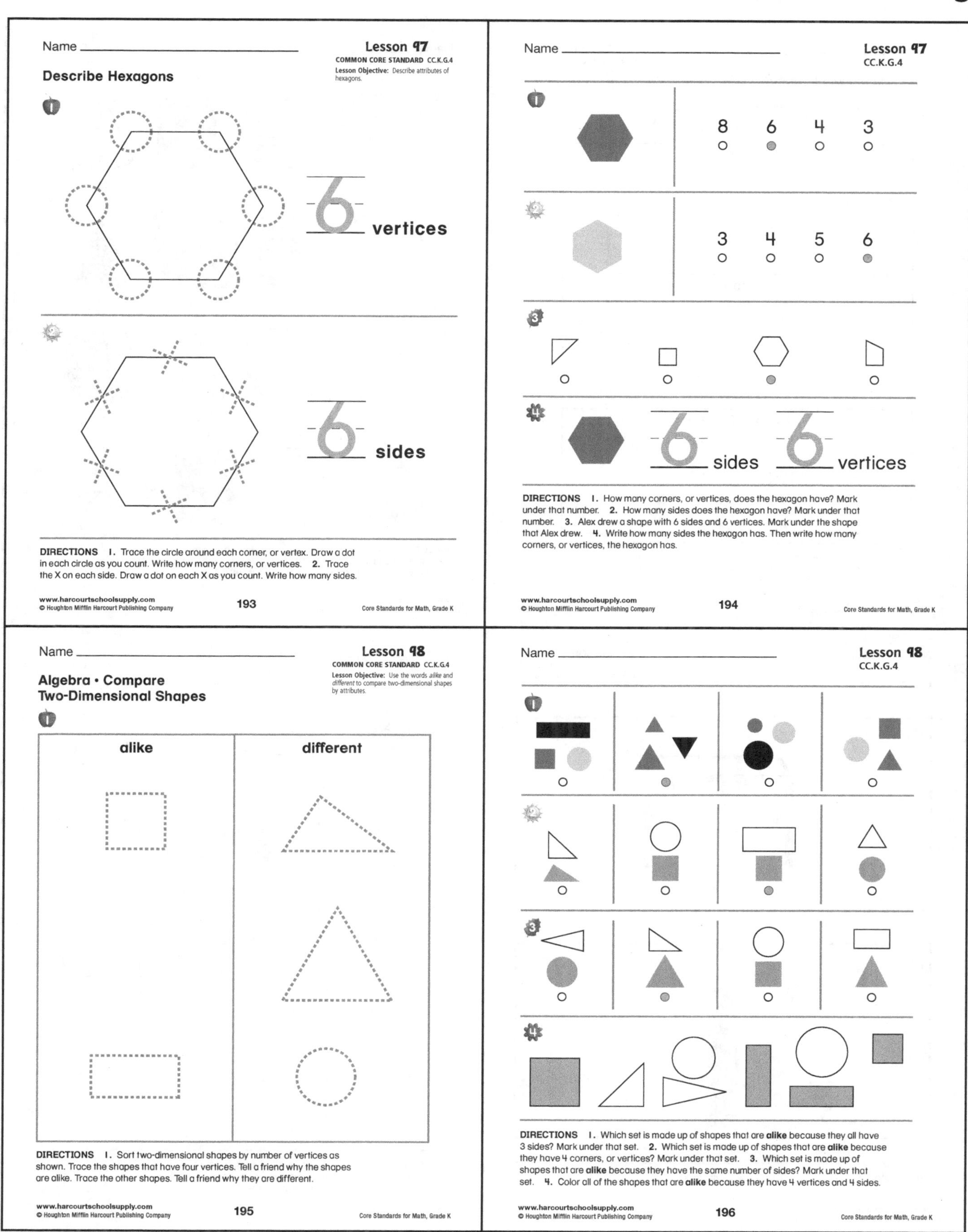

Name ____________

Lesson 97

COMMON CORE STANDARD CC.K.G.4

Lesson Objective: Describe attributes of hexagons.

Describe Hexagons

1

6 vertices

2

6 sides

DIRECTIONS **1.** Trace the circle around each corner, or vertex. Draw a dot in each circle as you count. Write how many corners, or vertices. **2.** Trace the X on each side. Draw a dot on each X as you count. Write how many sides.

www.harcourtschoolsupply.com
© Houghton Mifflin Harcourt Publishing Company
193
Core Standards for Math, Grade K

Name ____________

Lesson 97

CC.K.G.4

1

8 6 4 3

2

3 4 5 6

3

4

6 sides 6 vertices

DIRECTIONS **1.** How many corners, or vertices, does the hexagon have? Mark under that number. **2.** How many sides does the hexagon have? Mark under that number. **3.** Alex drew a shape with 6 sides and 6 vertices. Mark under the shape that Alex drew. **4.** Write how many sides the hexagon has. Then write how many corners, or vertices, the hexagon has.

www.harcourtschoolsupply.com
© Houghton Mifflin Harcourt Publishing Company
194
Core Standards for Math, Grade K

Name ____________

Lesson 98

COMMON CORE STANDARD CC.K.G.4

Lesson Objective: Use the words *alike* and *different* to compare two-dimensional shapes by attributes.

Algebra • Compare Two-Dimensional Shapes

1

alike	different

DIRECTIONS **1.** Sort two-dimensional shapes by number of vertices as shown. Trace the shapes that have four vertices. Tell a friend why the shapes are alike. Trace the other shapes. Tell a friend why they are different.

www.harcourtschoolsupply.com
© Houghton Mifflin Harcourt Publishing Company
195
Core Standards for Math, Grade K

Name ____________

Lesson 98

CC.K.G.4

1

2

3

4

DIRECTIONS **1.** Which set is made up of shapes that are **alike** because they all have 3 sides? Mark under that set. **2.** Which set is made up of shapes that are **alike** because they have 4 corners, or vertices? Mark under that set. **3.** Which set is made up of shapes that are **alike** because they have the same number of sides? Mark under that set. **4.** Color all of the shapes that are **alike** because they have 4 vertices and 4 sides.

www.harcourtschoolsupply.com
© Houghton Mifflin Harcourt Publishing Company
196
Core Standards for Math, Grade K

Answer Key

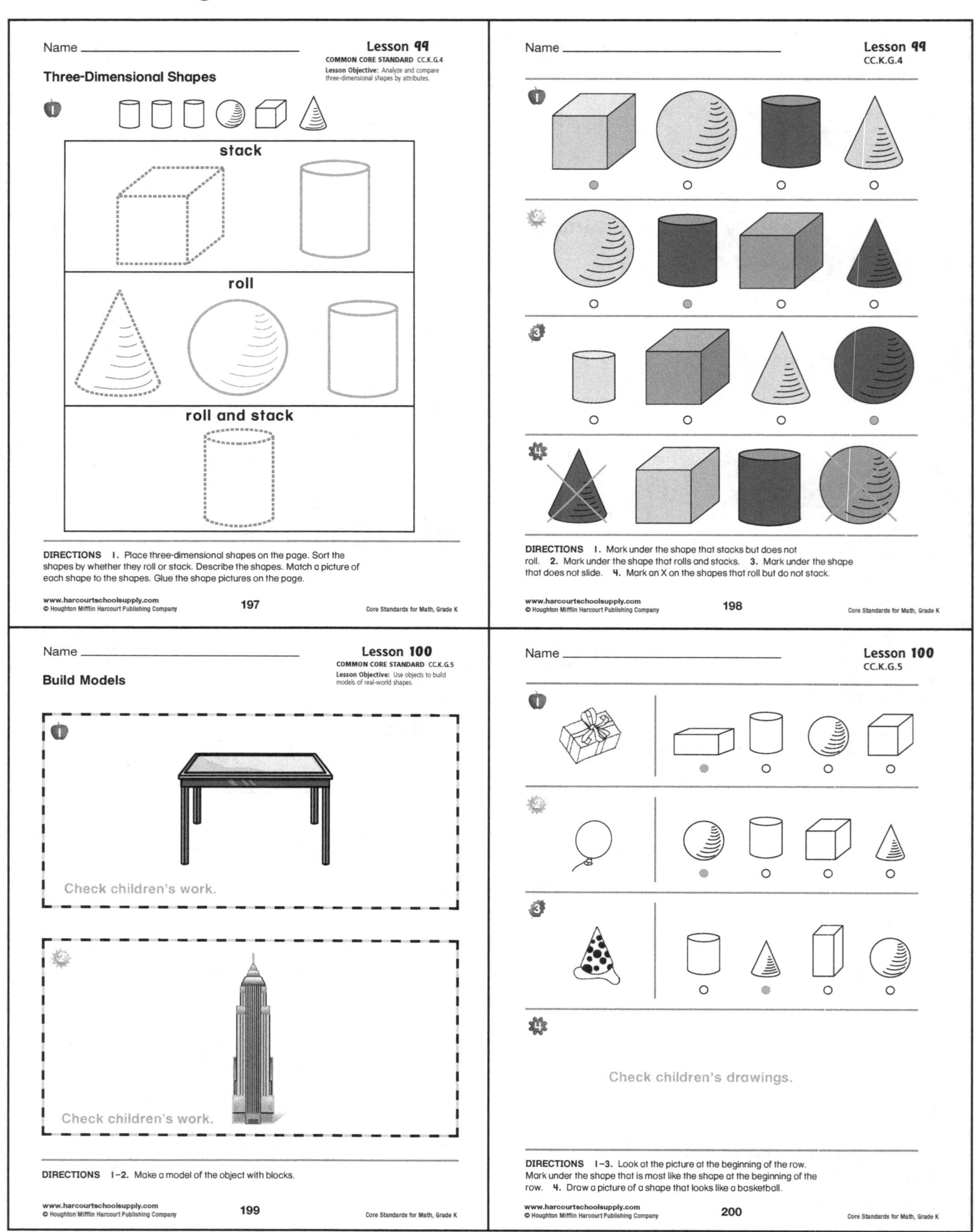

Name
Lesson 99
COMMON CORE STANDARD CC.K.G.4
Lesson Objective: Analyze and compare three-dimensional shapes by attributes.
Three-Dimensional Shapes
stack
roll
roll and stack
DIRECTIONS 1. Place three-dimensional shapes on the page. Sort the shapes by whether they roll or stack. Describe the shapes. Match a picture of each shape to the shapes. Glue the shape pictures on the page.
www.harcourtschoolsupply.com
© Houghton Mifflin Harcourt Publishing Company
197
Core Standards for Math, Grade K
Name
Lesson 99
CC.K.G.4
DIRECTIONS 1. Mark under the shape that stacks but does not roll. 2. Mark under the shape that rolls and stacks. 3. Mark under the shape that does not slide. 4. Mark an X on the shapes that roll but do not stack.
www.harcourtschoolsupply.com
© Houghton Mifflin Harcourt Publishing Company
198
Core Standards for Math, Grade K
Name
Lesson 100
COMMON CORE STANDARD CC.K.G.5
Lesson Objective: Use objects to build models of real-world shapes.
Build Models
Check children's work.
Check children's work.
DIRECTIONS 1–2. Make a model of the object with blocks.
www.harcourtschoolsupply.com
© Houghton Mifflin Harcourt Publishing Company
199
Core Standards for Math, Grade K
Name
Lesson 100
CC.K.G.5
Check children's drawings.
DIRECTIONS 1–3. Look at the picture at the beginning of the row. Mark under the shape that is most like the shape at the beginning of the row. 4. Draw a picture of a shape that looks like a basketball.
www.harcourtschoolsupply.com
© Houghton Mifflin Harcourt Publishing Company
200
Core Standards for Math, Grade K

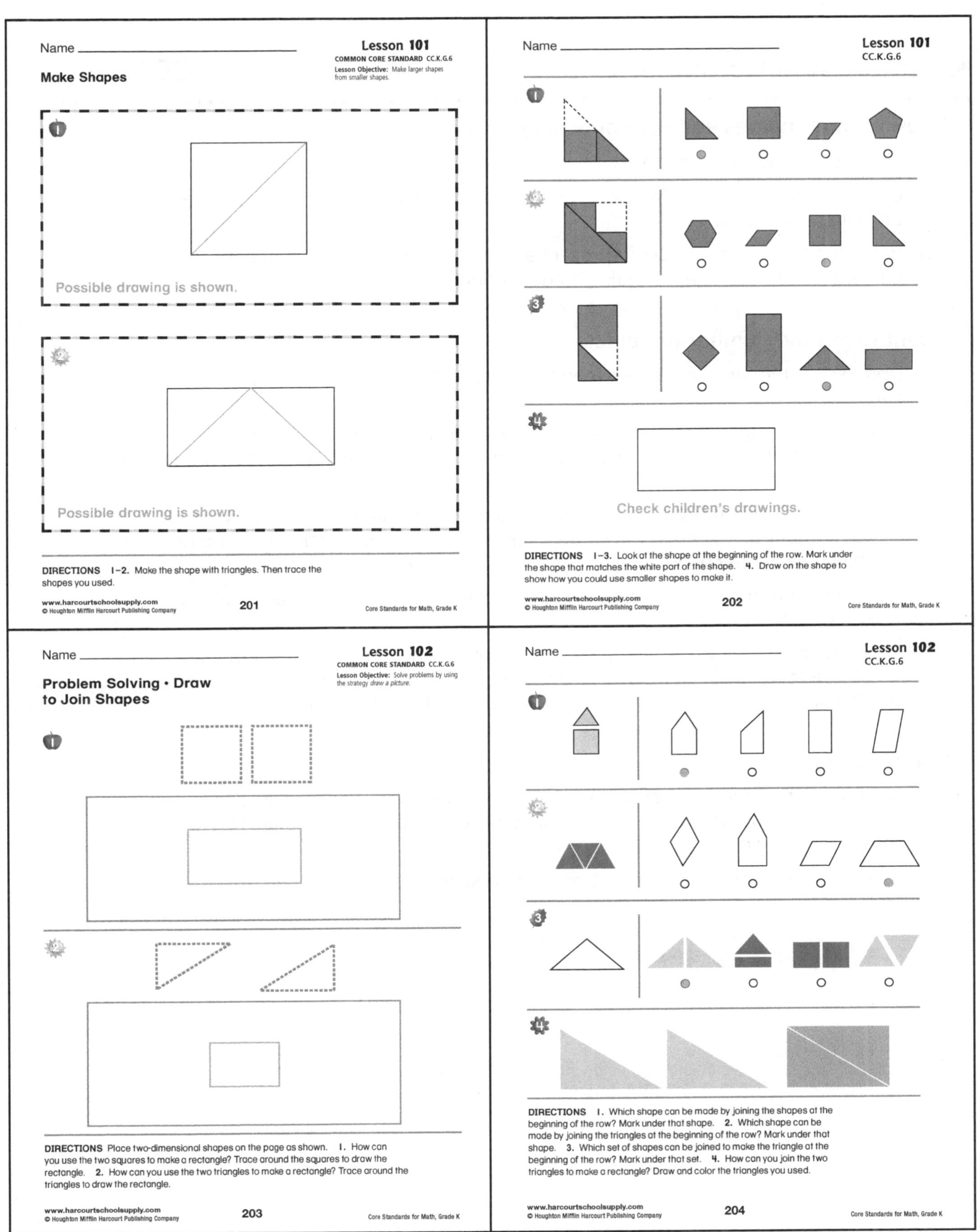
Name
Lesson 101
COMMON CORE STANDARD CC.K.G.6
Lesson Objective: Make larger shapes from smaller shapes.
Make Shapes
Possible drawing is shown.
Possible drawing is shown.
DIRECTIONS 1–2. Make the shape with triangles. Then trace the shapes you used.
www.harcourtschoolsupply.com
© Houghton Mifflin Harcourt Publishing Company
201
Core Standards for Math, Grade K
Name
Lesson 101
CC.K.G.6
Check children's drawings.
DIRECTIONS 1–3. Look at the shape at the beginning of the row. Mark under the shape that matches the white part of the shape. 4. Draw on the shape to show how you could use smaller shapes to make it.
www.harcourtschoolsupply.com
© Houghton Mifflin Harcourt Publishing Company
202
Core Standards for Math, Grade K
Name
Lesson 102
COMMON CORE STANDARD CC.K.G.6
Lesson Objective: Solve problems by using the strategy draw a picture.
Problem Solving • Draw to Join Shapes
DIRECTIONS Place two-dimensional shapes on the page as shown. 1. How can you use the two squares to make a rectangle? Trace around the squares to draw the rectangle. 2. How can you use the two triangles to make a rectangle? Trace around the triangles to draw the rectangle.
www.harcourtschoolsupply.com
© Houghton Mifflin Harcourt Publishing Company
203
Core Standards for Math, Grade K
Name
Lesson 102
CC.K.G.6
DIRECTIONS 1. Which shape can be made by joining the shapes at the beginning of the row? Mark under that shape. 2. Which shape can be made by joining the triangles at the beginning of the row? Mark under that shape. 3. Which set of shapes can be joined to make the triangle at the beginning of the row? Mark under that set. 4. How can you join the two triangles to make a rectangle? Draw and color the triangles you used.
www.harcourtschoolsupply.com
© Houghton Mifflin Harcourt Publishing Company
204
Core Standards for Math, Grade K

Common Core State Standards

Counting and Cardinality CC.K.CC

Know number names and the count sequence.

1. Count to 100 by ones and by tens.
2. Count forward beginning from a given number within the known sequence (instead of having to begin at 1).
3. Write numbers from 0 to 20. Represent a number of objects with a written numeral 0-20 (with 0 representing a count of no objects).

Count to tell the number of objects.

4. Understand the relationship between numbers and quantities; connect counting to cardinality.
   a. When counting objects, say the number names in the standard order, pairing each object with one and only one number name and each number name with one and only one object.
   b. Understand that the last number name said tells the number of objects counted. The number of objects is the same regardless of their arrangement or the order in which they were counted.
   c. Understand that each successive number name refers to a quantity that is one larger.
5. Count to answer "how many?" questions about as many as 20 things arranged in a line, a rectangular array, or a circle, or as many as 10 things in a scattered configuration; given a number from 1–20, count out that many objects.

Compare numbers.

6. Identify whether the number of objects in one group is greater than, less than, or equal to the number of objects in another group, e.g., by using matching and counting strategies.
7. Compare two numbers between 1 and 10 presented as written numerals.

Operations and Algebraic Thinking CC.K.OA

Understand addition as putting together and adding to, and understand subtraction as taking apart and taking from.

1. Represent addition and subtraction with objects, fingers, mental images, drawings, sounds (e.g., claps), acting out situations, verbal explanations, expressions, or equations.
2. Solve addition and subtraction word problems, and add and subtract within 10, e.g., by using objects or drawings to represent the problem.
3. Decompose numbers less than or equal to 10 into pairs in more than one way, e.g., by using objects or drawings, and record each decomposition by a drawing or equation (e.g., $5 = 2 + 3$ and $5 = 4 + 1$).
4. For any number from 1 to 9, find the number that makes 10 when added to the given number, e.g., by using objects or drawings, and record the answer with a drawing or equation.
5. Fluently add and subtract within 5.

Common Core State Standards

Number and Operations in Base Ten CC.K.NBT

Work with numbers 11–19 to gain foundations for place value.

1. Compose and decompose numbers from 11 to 19 into ten ones and some further ones, e.g., by using objects or drawings, and record each composition or decomposition by a drawing or equation (e.g., $18 = 10 + 8$); understand that these numbers are composed of ten ones and one, two, three, four, five, six, seven, eight, or nine ones.

Measurement and Data CC.K.MD

Describe and compare measurable attributes.

1. Describe measurable attributes of objects, such as length or weight. Describe several measurable attributes of a single object.
2. Directly compare two objects with a measurable attribute in common, to see which object has "more of"/"less of" the attribute, and describe the difference.

Classify objects and count the number of objects in each category.

3. Classify objects into given categories; count the numbers of objects in each category and sort the categories by count.

Common Core State Standards

Geometry CC.K.G

Identify and describe shapes (squares, circles, triangles, rectangles, hexagons, cubes, cones, cylinders, and spheres).

1. Describe objects in the environment using names of shapes, and describe the relative positions of these objects using terms such as *above, below, beside, in front of, behind,* and *next to*.
2. Correctly name shapes regardless of their orientations or overall size.
3. Identify shapes as two-dimensional (lying in a plane, "flat") or three-dimensional ("solid").

Analyze, compare, create, and compose shapes.

4. Analyze and compare two- and three-dimensional shapes, in different sizes and orientations, using informal language to describe their similarities, differences, parts (e.g., number of sides and vertices/"corners") and other attributes (e.g., having sides of equal length).
5. Model shapes in the world by building shapes from components (e.g., sticks and clay balls) and drawing shapes.
6. Compose simple shapes to form larger shapes.